THE
dEMOCRATIC
eXPERIENCE

THE
democraTic
eXperience

A SHORT AMERICAN HISTORY

VOLUME I
THIRD EDITION

Carl N. Degler   Stanford University
Thomas C. Cochran   University of Pennsylvania
Vincent P. De Santis   University of Notre Dame
Holman Hamilton   University of Kentucky
William H. Harbaugh   University of Virginia
Arthur S. Link   Princeton University
Russel B. Nye   Michigan State University
David M. Potter
Clarence L. Ver Steeg   Northwestern University

With the editorial cooperation of James M. McPherson,
Princeton University, for Part 4

Scott, Foresman and Company
Glenview, Illinois   Brighton, England

Library of Congress Catalog Card Number: 72–189444
ISBN 0–673–07915–5

Regional offices of Scott, Foresman and Company are located in Dallas, Texas; Glenview, Illinois; Oakland, New Jersey; Palo Alto, California; Tucker, Georgia; and Brighton, England.

preFace

The reception accorded the original and second editions of THE DEMOCRATIC EXPERIENCE has justified the continued belief that there is an increasing need in colleges and universities for a concise yet scholarly textbook of American history. The number of short introductory courses continues to multiply, while many instructors of more extensive courses have come to prefer a brief text that leaves room for the instructor to introduce source materials, add to the variety of the reading, and develop emphases of his own choice. The third edition is now available in two volumes, furthermore, to provide greater flexibility in course scheduling and to accommodate the needs of those students who elect only one semester of the traditional two-semester American history course.

In this newly revised edition of THE DEMOCRATIC EXPERIENCE, the text has been reworked, and new material has been added, to reflect a growing interest in the histories of American minority groups and women. While the Part Introductions continue to indicate the thrust of central issues of their respective periods, they include a new emphasis on changing historical interpretations which seeks to show how, to successive generations of historians, the historical significance of a period changes over time. In addition, the Part Introductions each conclude with a series of questions designed to stimulate judgment and interpretation rather than mere factual recall; the reader is invited to draw out for himself the significance of earlier periods to his own experience and to exercise his intelligence on the historical materials presented in each of the Parts. Numerous changes have been made elsewhere, including a new book design, a new illustration program which presents eight photo-essay variations on themes from the Preamble to the Constitution, and the updating of bibliographies, charts, and tables.

The Publishers wish to express their appreciation to the following: to Louis B. Wright of the National Geographic Society for his contribution to a previous edition; to James M. McPherson of Princeton University for assistance in the revision of Part 4 of Volume I; and to David Hall of Boston University for special help in the preparation of this edition.

THE PUBLISHERS

CONTENTS

APPENDICES

PHOTO ESSAYS

The photo essays which appear in these volumes are intended as pictorial variations on eight themes embodied in the Preamble to the United States Constitution. In contemporary visual terms, the picture essays suggest our conflicting feelings of fulfillment vs. frustration of the ideals set forth by the Constitution.

MAPS AND CHARTS

PHOTO CREDITS

tHE
dEMOCRATic
eXpERiENCE

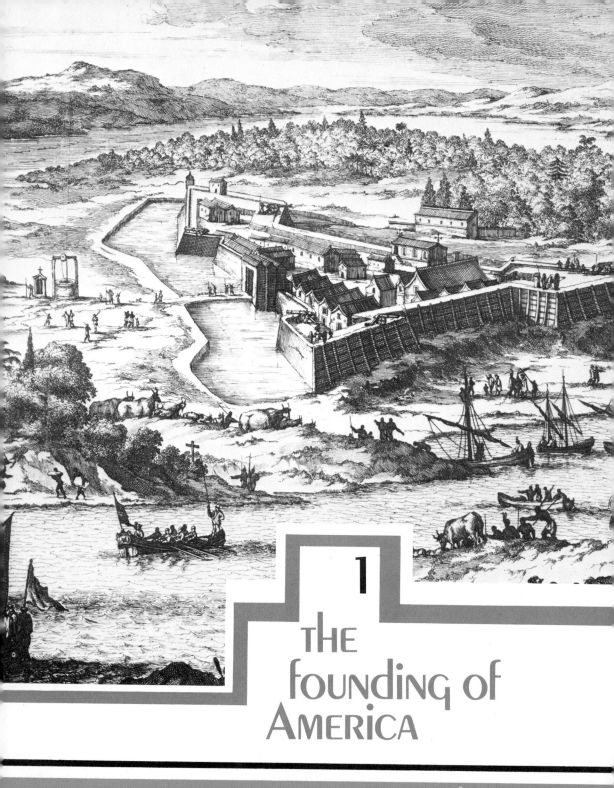

1

THE
founding of
AMERICA

THE FOUNDING OF AMERICA BROUGHT INTO CONTACT, AND CONFLICT, the Indians (whose early ancestors had come from Asia), blacks from Africa, and whites from Europe. Indians occupied both American continents, and in some areas—Peru, Central America, Mexico—developed remarkable civilizations. The major "nations" along the eastern shoreline of the present-day United States—the Algonquins, the Iroquois, Cherokees, and Creeks—never reached the cultural heights of these Indian people, but they, too, created sophisticated social organizations, strong political alignments, and thriving economies.

Millions of Africans came to the Americas in bondage. Of this number, at least 400,000 reached the English colonies by 1770—the great majority after 1700. Even though most came as slaves, these blacks brought with them skills and talents equal or superior to those of the contemporary European peasant and the ordinary Indian. For centuries the effects of this extraordinary migration were overlooked by historians, but there can no longer be any question that the culture of the Africans survived in the New World.

But it was Europe that put its stamp on the colonies that would create the United States of America. At the end of the fifteenth century Europe was stirring with new interests and fresh vitality. A spirit of secularism focused attention upon the goodness of the world that man had inherited. No longer could the priest insist that this vale of tears was but a brief abiding place where one seasoned his soul for bliss in the world to come. Men wanted comforts and pleasures here below in a greater quantity and variety than they had known before. The Venetians and the Genoese, enterprising Italian traders that they were, had long brought luxury goods from the Near East and the Orient to please the wealthy of Europe. Now the demand was greater. More money was available. Silver mines in the Tyrol and elsewhere in eastern Europe were producing more precious metal, and the circulation of money was increasing. With more money in more hands than earlier generations had known, the demand for goods and commodities multiplied, especially for those goods that came from the East.

Bartholomew Diaz in 1486 rounded the Cape of Good Hope and came back to suggest the possibility of a passage to India. A few years later, a Genoese in the service of Spain, one Christopher Columbus, persuaded Queen Isabella of Castile to help finance a western voyage that he promised would lead to Asia and riches. When Columbus sailed from Palos on August 3, 1492, he believed that he could open a new trade route that would enable Spain to tap the wealth of Asia. When on October 12 he made a landfall in the Caribbean (perhaps Watling Island), he thought he had reached the outskirts of China; and a bit later, when he landed on Cuba, he sent messengers in search of the Great Khan. After four voyages across the Atlantic, Columbus died, still believing that he had discovered a sea route to Asia.

Within a generation after Columbus' discovery of America, Europe witnessed other events that would in time profoundly influence not only the Old World but the development of the New. On October 31, 1517, Martin Luther nailed to the door of the castle church in Wittenberg his famous ninety-five theses challenging debate on alleged corruptions in the Catholic Church, then the only recognized church in western and central Europe. No one in Wittenberg could have foreseen that this gesture would begin a cataclysmic movement known to history as the Protestant Revolt, which gave birth to the various Protestant sects and split Christendom into rival, often warring, Protestant and Catholic nations. Nor was it foreseen that this movement would determine the nature of many of the settlements in North America. In England a few years later King Henry VIII renounced the pope of Rome and in a "Protestant" move had himself declared supreme head of the Church of England. The causes of Henry's action were not religious, nor did religious belief lead his daughter, Elizabeth I, to maintain the Protestant position in England; but the effects of England's change to Protestantism on the history of Europe and of the New World were enormous. Under Elizabeth, Englishmen began a long contest with Catholic Spain, the great colonial power in the New World. Out of that contest came the determination to establish English colonies in America. Under Elizabeth's Protestant successor, James I, Englishmen in 1607 finally gained a permanent foothold on the Atlantic seaboard at Jamestown.

The majority of the English colonists in North America were middle-class Protestants who farmed and engaged in a smattering of trade when they were able to produce surplus goods. The institutions of self-government that set the English colonies apart from colonies of other nations eventually led to a conflict with the mother country that ended in successful revolt and creation of a new republic. By then, the colonies had developed a culture dramatically different from that of England, with a broad variance of subcultures representing not only immigrants from the Continent but also the native Indians and the imported Africans. By 1776 almost every element that was to determine the future of the United States had been implanted: an economic system based on private ownership, a social system based on a middle-class majority, a great diversity of religions, a variety of ethnic groups, racial conflict, and social attitudes that penetrated far deeper than class distinctions.

In their interpretations of the past, historians are influenced by the interest and attitudes of their own times. Thus students of the colonial period in the Progressive Era—from around the turn of the century until 1917 (see Part VI)—saw the Revolution as not only a rebellion against British rule but also as an internal rebellion against control by an upper-class minority. Themselves in revolt against the power of big business and political bosses, they looked on colonial America as an undemocratic society in which the few suppressed the many until the political and social upheaval of the Revolution.

Around mid-century, after surviving the Great Depression and World War II, Americans looked at their society, present and past, much less critically. They were struck by the differences between themselves and Europeans; and colonialists found that these differences had developed very early. Research indicated that older historians had been wrong: instead of being suppressed and disfranchised, a great many ordinary Americans in the eighteenth century had been qualified to vote. The

Revolution, then, had not been in part an internal revolt but instead the unified effort of Americans to break with an Old World that had become foreign to them.

More recently, with the turning away from nationalism and the questioning of our success in practicing democracy, some historians have called attention to the fact that the breadth of the franchise in the colonial period did not mean significant participation and that, broad as it was, it still denied participation to blacks and to seamen and others at the bottom of the white social hierarchy. These scholars emphasize the stability of colonial society, rather than the fluidity the somewhat older generation of historians underscores. They see the Revolution not as the culmination of a coherent political progression but as a bombshell that disrupted the established political structure and opened the way to change.

FOR THOUGHT AND DISCUSSION

As you read Part I, think about the following questions. In reaching conclusions about them, you may have to draw on what you know of history from other sources and on your own intelligence and imagination.

1. What manner of men were the colonists—otherworldly saints? bourgeois profiteers? beggars and thieves?

2. Given their social, political, and religious backgrounds, how was it possible for the colonists to participate in enslavement of blacks and expulsion and extermination of Indians?

3. What would have happened in the colonies if there had been no slaves? How might an absence of slaves have affected colonial history? the history of the United States?

4. How serious a barrier to our understanding the colonists is the difference between religious attitudes in the seventeenth and eighteenth centuries and religious attitudes in the 1970s? Is there any way to overcome it? (Can parallels be drawn between the enthusiasts of the Great Awakening and today's "Jesus freaks"?)

5. Did the various acts passed by Parliament cause serious hardship to the colonists generally? Which class of colonists was most inconvenienced by them?

6. Was the "liberty" the colonists sought a matter of ideals or of dollars and cents? Was the American Revolution a revolution of "the people"? of the monied, propertied class? of radical troublemakers?

We the
People
of the
United
States

CHAPTER 1

EVOLUTION OF THE AMERICAN COLONIES

BACKGROUND TO COLONIZATION

The Beginnings of European Expansion.   America had been discovered as early as A.D. 1000, when the Vikings dominated northern Europe and the northern Atlantic, yet their adventures did not stimulate European expansion into the New World. Obviously, a significant change had taken place in Western Europe by the time of Columbus' voyage in 1492, not only making overseas expansion possible but also instilling an adventurous spirit among Europeans so that they were eager to explore new lands and new opportunities.

Essentially, it was a change from medieval agrarianism and the feudal mind to economic developments characteristic of early modern Europe and the inquiring mind. In the Middle Ages, western Europe had been dominated by the feudal and manorial system in which each man's place in society—ranging from the peasantry to the nobility—was determined by his relationship to the land. The commodities produced were consumed by the inhabitants of the manor. But the rise of early modern capitalism brought a revival of trade, the rise of the city, the emergence of a merchant class, production for an outside market, and the growth of banking; and as a result men were no longer dependent exclusively upon their relationship to the land. Business transactions brought an accumulation of money, and money could be employed to finance new enterprises.

The mind of Europe also was awakened. The Crusades, beginning in the eleventh century, introduced western Europe to the ways of the Near East and to such exotic commodities as spices and silks. Italian merchants—most notably, Marco Polo—journeyed all the way to China and Japan. The fear of the unknown and of new experiences which gripped many people in the Middle Ages gave way to the spirit of innovators, men whose minds were stimulated by a curiosity about the unknown, men who wished to exploit the riches of the East.

Portugal was the first nation bordering the Atlantic to engage in wide-scale exploration, especially along the western coast of Africa. This primacy was not accidental. Portugal was the first of the Atlantic nations to be unified, giving its leaders an opportunity to look outward rather than to be preoccupied with internal disorder. Among the most forward looking was Prince Henry the Navigator (1394–1460), who established a center for the study of cartography and astronomy and for the improvement of ships and seamanship. Portugal was eventually rewarded when Bartholomew Diaz rounded Africa's southernmost Cape of Good Hope in 1486 and when Vasco da Gama reached India by way of the Cape of Good Hope in 1498.

The significance of national unity was underscored when Columbus' voyage in 1492 coincided with the expulsion of the Moors from Spain by the capture of Granada. Columbus' voyage, sailing west to reach the fabulous riches of the East, marked the great historical divide which eventually made the Atlantic rather than the Mediterranean the principal artery of trade and communication.

The efforts of Portugal and Spain to find new routes to the East were prompted in large part by their desire to challenge the commercial monopoly of the Italian cities, which, because of their geographical position, dominated trade with the East by way of the Mediterranean and the Levant. By sailing around the world in 1519–22 and showing a substantial profit despite the loss of all but one ship, as well as the commander and most of the men, the expedition of Ferdinand Magellan proved that the Mediterranean could be bypassed and the Italian monopoly broken.

Spain followed up the voyage of Columbus by establishing an American empire, thereby setting an example which the other nations of western Europe attempted to imitate. The Spaniards constructed a tightly knit, closely supervised colonial system whose object was to make its American colonies a source of wealth for the mother country and to prevent any encroachment by other nations. In 1574, long before the English had established a successful colony in the New World, the Spanish population in Mexico City alone exceeded 15,000; throughout the New World it exceeded 160,000. More than two hundred Spanish cities and towns had been founded, and Mexico City boasted a university. The principal agency used by Spain to transplant the culture of the Old World to the New was the Catholic Church, the only church in existence in the Western world at the time the Spanish colonial system was founded. The Spanish colonial policy, unlike that followed later by the English, considered native peoples as subjects of the sovereign; the result was a fusion of cultures, still characteristic of Latin America today.

Factors in English Expansion.   Although John Cabot, representing the English crown, explored the eastern coast of North America within a decade of Columbus' voyage, successful English settlement was delayed for a century. As a consequence, economic, religious, and political factors affecting the English colonies were entirely different from those that had influenced the Spanish colonies.

The two outstanding economic changes were in trade and agriculture. Whereas no trading companies flourished in 1500, over two hundred English trading companies operated aggressively by 1600, including the Muscovy Company (1553), the Levant Company (1592), and the famous East India Company (1600). In 1500 German and Italian merchants dominated English trade; by 1600 this domination had been eliminated and a strong group of English merchants had emerged. In 1500 most of the raw wool raised in England was shipped to Flanders to be made into cloth; by 1600 an indigenous English textile industry absorbed much of the wool produced in England.

These economic changes had a direct effect upon the development of the English colonies. The first three successful English colonies in America—Plymouth, Virginia, and Massachusetts Bay—were planted by cooperatively owned joint-stock companies, precursors of modern corporations, in which a number of investors pooled their capital. Many of the men engaged in the American enterprises had gained their experience in trading companies elsewhere, and they continued to participate in trading enterprises throughout the world. As Charles M. Andrews, a prominent historian of the colonial period, has written: "English America would hardly have been settled at this time had not the period of occupation coincided with the era of capitalism in the first flush of its power."

The experience in trade influenced mercantilist thought in England. Mercantilism embodied a set of economic ideas held throughout western Europe from 1500 to 1800, though the precise measures taken differed from country to country. The mercantilist advocated that the economic affairs of the nation should be regulated to encourage the development of a strong state. In addition to this broad policy, he customarily subscribed to a number of propositions: a nation could become stronger by exporting more than it imported, resulting in a "favorable balance of trade"; national self-sufficiency should be encouraged by subsidizing domestic manufactures; a nation's wealth was to be measured by the amount of precious metals it could obtain (thus the emphasis on the accumulation of bullion); labor should be regulated for the well-being and benefit of the state; and colonies should be established to provide the nation with raw materials that it was unable to produce.

Although this does not exhaust the list of arguments put forward by mercantilist thinkers, it does show that trade was considered one of the most important measures of a nation's wealth and that colonies were valued because they contributed to that wealth. In England the mercantile emphasis between 1500 and 1600 was upon internal regulation; after 1600 the emphasis was on external regulation, particularly the commercial relationship of England to its colonies. The phenomenal increase in English mercantile activity not only provided an agency—the joint-stock company—to plant colonies but also provided a national purpose for doing so.

A second significant economic change took place in agriculture. Between 1500 and 1600 an enclosure movement gained strength in Britain. Essentially, "enclosure" meant that smaller landholdings in certain areas of England were incorporated into larger holdings, forcing some Englishmen off the land. The result was a dislocation of population which caused many political thinkers to conclude that England was overpopulated and that therefore almost anyone should be permitted to go to the New World to reduce "overpopulation." Spain, by contrast, had restricted immigration to selected individuals favored by the crown.

In the sixteenth century the Protestant Reformation swept through Europe and profoundly affected the religious and political development of England, which in turn placed an enduring stamp upon its colonies in America. In 1500 England (and the Continent) was within the fold of the Catholic Church. By 1600 not only had England broken away and established the national Anglican Church, but the religious rupture had also encouraged the rise of religious splinter groups. This diversity of faiths was carried directly to the New World: of the first four settlements, Virginia was Anglican, Plymouth was Separatist, Massachusetts Bay was Puritan, and Maryland was Catholic.

The story of this religious rupture in England is too involved for extended treatment in this text, but what is particularly important is that in the process of waging his contest with the Roman Catholic Church, King Henry VIII enlisted the aid of Parliament. Parliament passed a series of enactments creating a national church, culminating in the Act of Supremacy (1534), which made Henry, instead of the pope, the ecclesiastical sovereign of England. Eventually, by means of parliamentary acts, lands in England belonging to the Roman Catholic Church were taken over by the king, greatly enhancing his wealth.

The ramifications of these actions invaded almost every sphere of English life, but two had most effect on the colonies: (1) the king, by utilizing the support of Parliament, demonstrated that in practice the authority of the crown was limited—a concept carried to the English colonies in America and a concept in direct contrast to Spanish doctrine, which held the power of the sovereign to be without restriction; (2) the break with the Catholic Church produced a wide diversity of religious groups.

Some Englishmen, believing that separation from the Catholic Church should never have taken place, remained Roman Catholics. Others felt that Henry VIII and, later, Elizabeth I had not gone far enough. The Puritans, an impassioned and vocal minority, believed that the Reformation in England had stopped short of its goal, that ritual should be further simplified, and that the authority of crown-appointed bishops should be lessened; however, they resolved to stay within the Church of England and attempt to achieve their goals—that is, "purify" the church—without a division. The Separatists, a small minority, believed that each congregation should become its own judge of religious orthodoxy. They were no more willing to give allegiance to the crown than they had been to the pope. This religious fractionalism was transferred to the American colonies.

Early in the seventeenth century, a number of English "dissenters"—men and women who were dissatisfied with political, economic, or religious conditions in England—were ready to migrate to the New World; English trading companies provided an agency for settlement.

THE ENGLISH SETTLEMENTS

One hundred and fifteen years after the discovery of America, the English had not established a single permanent foothold in the Western Hemisphere. Although they had made several voyages and two attempts at settlement, as late as 1600 they had not one colony to show for their efforts. By 1700 some twenty colonies, with 350,000 inhabitants stretched all the way from Newfoundland on the North Atlantic to the island of Barbados in the southern Caribbean. Heavy losses originally deterred growth, but promoters and settlers learned to adjust to the new environment. By the end of the century their settlements had taken root, had attained prosperity, and had entered upon a stage of steady growth. The English dream of expansion overseas had become a reality, and Britain looked with pride upon its American empire.

Founding Virginia. The first permanent English colony in America was Virginia. In the year 1606 King James I granted a group of London merchants the privilege of establishing colonies in "the part of America commonly called Virginia." Securing a charter, this Virginia Company of London raised sufficient funds by the sale of shares to outfit three ships and send them to Virginia, where on May 24, 1607, 120 men established a settlement, Jamestown, on the banks of the James River.

The early Jamestown settlers had no experience in colonization; many of them had come for adventure rather than from any desire to become permanent residents in the wilderness. They knew nothing of subsistence farming and displayed little ingenuity. Although the James River teemed with fish, they nearly perished for want of food. Of the first five thousand people who migrated to Virginia, fewer than a thousand survived.

Gradually, however, the Jamestown colonists devised ways of making a livelihood. Some traded with the Indians and began a traffic that would grow in importance with the years. Others planted foodstuffs and learned to raise Indian corn. John Rolfe, who married the Indian princess Pocahontas, developed the skill of growing tobacco profitably. Rolfe's contribution ensured Virginia's prosperity, for tobacco was a commodity much in demand in Europe.

In governing the colony, the Virginia Company at first adopted a policy of having severe laws administered by a strong-armed governor, but after this failed, it made the momentous decision to let the settlers share in their own government. When Governor George Yeardley arrived in Virginia in 1619, he carried instructions to call annually an assembly to consist of two members, or burgesses, from the various local units in the colony, these burgesses to be elected by residents on a basis of almost complete manhood suffrage. This assembly, which met in the church at Jamestown in the summer of 1619, was the first representative law-making body in English America and as such was the forerunner of representative government in the United States. Even when the Virginia Company at last succumbed to bankruptcy in 1624 and lost its charter, with the result that Virginia became a royal colony, the company's greatest contribution was preserved intact: the Virginia House of Burgesses continued to meet. It was ironical that this transfer took place under King James i, for it meant that the very monarch who was the most severe enemy of Parliament in England was also, unwittingly, the one who permitted representative government in America to become a regular part of the system of colonial government under the crown.

The Coming of Africans. The first Africans came to Virginia in 1619. The records do not reveal whether they were brought as servants or slaves, but it is known that by 1650 Virginia had both black freemen and black slaves. African immigration grew slowly during the seventeenth century. In 1680 Africans, mostly slaves, comprised only 4 percent of the total population, widely scattered throughout the eastern seaboard.

Late in the seventeenth century the pace of importation of African slaves quickened. Most were brought to the Southern colonies of Maryland, Virginia, North Carolina, South Carolina, and eventually Georgia. By the beginning of the American Revolution blacks comprised 20 percent of the population; the number of blacks—400,000—was equal to the total population of New England. Given the size of this single ethnic group, it is hardly surprising that the unwilling immigrants from Africa had an enduring impact on life in what was to become the United States of America.

The Pilgrims in Plymouth. The first permanent settlement in New England was made by colonists who arrived off Cape Cod in the *Mayflower* in December of 1620. They had been granted permission to settle farther south, but their ship had been blown off course. The core of the group of about a hundred settlers was a small, devoted band of Separatists, part of a larger number of religious dissenters who had left England for Holland in 1608. Unsuccessful there, thirty members of the congregation had decided to emigrate to the New World. The expedition, which put out from Plymouth, England, was financed by a joint-stock company in which the Separatists, their fellow passengers, and outside investors participated.

The story of these Separatists, who now called themselves Pilgrims, has become a part of the American legend: the hardships of the first winter, the friendship of the Indians Samoset and Squanto, who taught the settlers to plant corn, and the first harvest and thanksgiving festival. The little colony at Plymouth achieved a significant place in the American imagination.

The "Great Migration" to Massachusetts Bay. Although the character and heroism of the Pilgrims bequeathed a poetic heritage to the American people, the larger colony of Massachusetts Bay contributed more to New England's civilization. The main body of settlers, under the leadership of John Winthrop, arrived in the summer of 1630 in the *Arbella.* This was one of four ships that carried the first wave of the "Great Migration" which between 1630 and 1640 brought some 20,000 people into Massachusetts.

The Winthrop group—most of them Puritans—had managed to obtain a royal charter for the Massachusetts Bay Company. Unlike other colonial enterprises, this company vested control, not in a board of governors in England, but in the members of the company who themselves were emigrating. They came bringing their charter with them and were self-governing, subject only to the English crown. Voting privileges were granted to those who were members of the Congregational Puritan Church of the colony, and during the early years of settlement a close relationship between church and state was the key to authority and life-style. But in all cases the civil magistrates, not the clergy, held preeminence.

During the ten years after the landing of the *Arbella,* Massachusetts Bay became the most populous English colony in the New World. From towns established at Boston, Cambridge, Dorchester, Salem, and elsewhere, groups from time to time broke away and moved into fresh territory. In the summer of 1636, for example, the Reverend Thomas Hooker, with about one hundred of his followers, set out on foot from Cambridge and settled a new township at Hartford, in what became Connecticut. Other towns proliferated in similar fashion.

The Spreading Colonies of New England. Occasionally colonists left Massachusetts Bay because they had offended the ruling authorities or because they were discontented with a thoroughgoing Puritan commonwealth that punished nonconformists severely and tried to impose its religious tenets upon all comers. Freedom of conscience or religion was not a virtue of Massachusetts Bay. Roger Williams, pastor of the church at Salem, was banished from the colony in 1635 because he had complained publicly that interference of the clergy in politics threatened the freedom of individual congregations, and because he questioned the right of the settlers to take land from the Indians. Williams fled in the dead of winter to the Narragansett Indians, and in January 1636 he arranged to purchase land from the Indians for a little settlement which he called Providence. Before long, other fugitives from the persecution of the Puritan clergy in Massachusetts Bay found their way to Williams' colony, including a group led by the religious rebel, Anne Hutchinson.

The Providence settlers made a compact which guaranteed liberty of conscience to all men regardless of faith and which provided for the separation of church and state. Other groups came to the area and settled at Portsmouth, Newport, and Warwick, and in 1644 Parliament granted Williams a charter which united the various groups in what is now Rhode Island into one civil government. A royal charter in 1663 once more reiterated the liberties established earlier; this charter remained the basis of Rhode Island's laws until 1842. Rhode Island was far ahead of its time in its legal provisions: as early as 1647, for example, it outlawed trials for witchcraft and imprisonment for debt.

Massachusetts Bay emigrants settled a colony at New Haven under conservative Puritan leadership. As in Massachusetts, only church members were permitted to vote, a policy which in effect gave the church political control over the affairs of the colony. Since the Scriptures made no mention of jury trials, New Haven—in contrast to other New England colonies—forbade such trials and left the dispensation of justice in the hands of the magistrates. In 1662 Connecticut received a royal charter which confirmed the rights of self-government and provided for the Fundamental Orders, a platform of government extending the franchise to nonchurch members. To the distress of New Haven, that colony was absorbed into Connecticut and the guarantees of Connecticut's charter extended to its citizens.

Other Massachusetts Bay residents moved into New Hampshire and Maine, where settlers had already established themselves in small fishing villages. Massachusetts laid claim to both regions; after many disputes, New Hampshire in 1679 gained a royal charter and freed itself from the domination of Massachusetts, but Maine was not separated until 1820.

Catholic Maryland.   While Virginia was gradually gaining vitality, a neighboring colony developed on its northern flank. In 1632 Sir George Calvert, First Lord Baltimore, received from Charles i a charter for the tract of land extending from the fortieth degree of north latitude to the south bank of the Potomac River. Calvert, a Roman Catholic, intended to make Maryland a refuge for oppressed Catholics. He died before he could settle his grant, but his son Cecilius became lord proprietor and sent his brother Leonard to take possession of Maryland, where the first group of Catholic settlers landed on March 25, 1634.

A "proprietary colony" such as the Calverts obtained was a return to a feudal and baronial system which in the seventeenth century was becoming outmoded. The manorial system of land tenure, which made the inhabitants of Maryland tenants of the Calverts instead of landowners, was the source of much unrest and would never have lasted at all had the Calverts not made tenancy approximate ownership.

In order to attract settlers and make the colony pay, the Calverts from the outset encouraged Protestants as well as Catholics to go to Maryland, and though most of the manorial families were Catholic, Catholics never constituted a majority of the population. Catholics and Anglicans held separate worship, and Lord Baltimore would not allow the Jesuits in the colony to place any restrictions upon Protestants. In 1649 he sponsored the famous Maryland Toleration Act, which guaranteed freedom of worship to all Christians. This was not yet full liberty of conscience, for there was a death penalty for non-Christians, but the act marked an advance in the direction of ultimate religious freedom.

Proprietary Colonies. Except for Maryland, the original colonies were established by joint-stock companies, but after 1660 almost all the newly founded colonies were proprietaries. Joint-stock companies as a whole did not make a profit, and business enterprisers became less interested in investing in colonial establishments. After 1660 King Charles II began to grant large segments of American land to those who had supported the Stuart claim to the throne during the period of Puritan control in England (1642–60). Proprietors had been unsuccessful in the late sixteenth century because they could neither command sufficient capital nor sustain a colonizing effort over an extended period of time, but with the successful founding of Virginia, Maryland, Plymouth, and Massachusetts Bay, the risk of founding proprietary colonies was greatly reduced. As a result, the territory of the Carolinas was given to a number of proprietors in 1663, and Pennsylvania was founded in 1682. New Jersey began as a proprietorship but eventually was made a crown or royal colony, in which affairs were directed by crown officials. New York also began as a proprietary colony, under the Duke of York, after its capture from the Dutch; it became a crown colony when York ascended the throne as James II.

The Capture of New York. In 1609 Henry Hudson, an Englishman in the employ of the Dutch East India Company, sailed the Hudson River as far as the present town of Albany, and in 1623, after the monopoly of a private Dutch company in the area had run out, the Dutch West India Company was formed to develop trade in the region along the river that Hudson had discovered. Since the citizens of Holland were largely content, the new company had trouble finding colonists. Included among the early settlers were French Protestant refugees and non-Dutch emigrants from Holland. From the earliest times, New Netherland (later New York) was a polyglot region. Despite incompetent governors, quarreling inhabitants, and frequent wars with the Indians, the colony made progress, and New Amsterdam (New York City) became an important shipping point for furs and farm products. With a population of 2500, it was second only to Boston as a trading port. The colony as a whole had about eight thousand settlers, some of them English.

The English had never admitted the right of the Dutch to the territory they had occupied. In 1664 Charles II named his brother James, Duke of York, proprietor over lands occupied by the Dutch in the New World. York sent out an expedition to take over New Netherland, the English claiming that this was not an act of war but merely an action to regain from the Dutch West India Company territory that was rightfully English. With an English fleet in the harbor of New Amsterdam, the Dutch governor, Peter Stuyvesant, surrendered on September 8, 1664. The town and territory were both rechristened New York in honor of the royal proprietor.

The Dutch occupation of the Hudson valley had benefited the English far more than the new overlords cared to admit. Had the Dutch not been in possession in the first half of the seventeenth century, when English settlements on the Atlantic seaboard were too sparse and weak to prevent the French from moving down the Hudson from Canada, the thin line of English colonies along the coast might have been divided by England's traditional enemy, France.

The Jerseys. Soon after the Duke of York took over New Netherland in 1664, he granted the land between the Hudson and the Delaware to John Lord Berkeley and Sir George Carteret, royalists who had defended the island of Jersey against the Parliamentarians during the Puritan Revolution in England. Berkeley sold his proprietary right to two Quakers, and in 1676 the province was divided into East Jersey (belonging to Carteret) and West Jersey (which became a Quaker colony). The later division of the two portions of New Jersey among many heirs of the proprietors bequeathed a land problem so complex that it vexes holders of real estate in that state to the present day.

Penn's Experiment. In 1681 King Charles II granted to William Penn, a Quaker, a charter to the land between New Jersey and Maryland, naming him and his heirs forever owners of the soil of Pennsylvania, as the domain was called. Penn set about establishing a colony that would serve as a refuge for persecuted Christians from all lands. He drew up his celebrated first Frame of Government and made various concessions and laws to govern the colony, which already had a conglomerate group of English, Dutch, Swedish, and Finnish settlers scattered here and there. After his own arrival in Pennsylvania, he provided for the calling of a popular assembly on December 4, 1682, which passed the "Great Law," guaranteeing, among other things, the rights of all Christians to liberty of conscience.

Penn determined to keep peace with the Indians and was careful to purchase the land which his settlers occupied. The tradition of a single "Great Treaty" signed under an ancient elm at Kensington is probably a myth, but Penn held many powwows with the Indians and negotiated treaties of peace and amity after purchasing needed land. To the credit of Penn and the Quakers, these agreements with the Indians were, for the most part, conscientiously kept.

Pennsylvania's growth from the first was phenomenal. Penn's success was largely due to his own skill as a promoter, for he wrote enticing tracts and on preaching journeys described the opportunities offered by his colony. Mennonites from Switzerland and Germany—especially Pietists from the Rhineland, which had so often been overrun by invading armies—soon were coming to Pennsylvania in large numbers. Dutch sectarians, French Huguenots, Presbyterian Scots from Ulster, Baptists from Wales, and distressed English Quakers also came. Somewhat after the Mennonites, Lutheran emigrants from Germany swarmed into Pennsylvania's back country, where they cleared the forests and developed fertile farms. From the beginning Pennsylvania was prosperous.

Settlement of the Carolinas. Among the later colonies to be settled was Carolina, which also began as a proprietorship: eight courtiers received from Charles II on March 23, 1663, a grant of the territory between the southern border of Virginia and

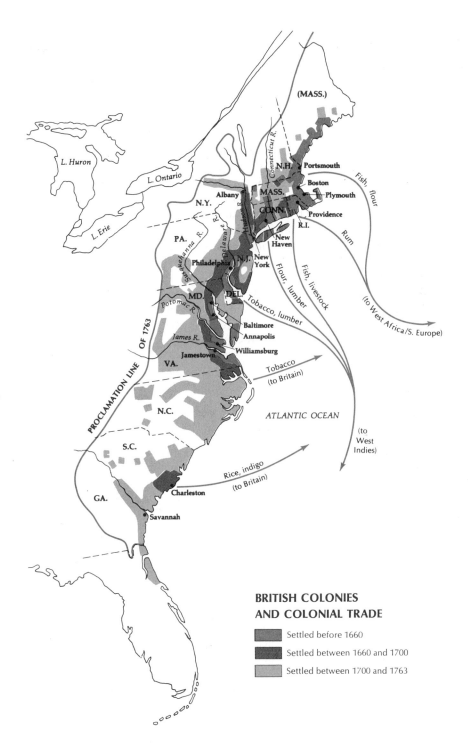

L. Huron

L. Ontario

L. Erie

(MASS.)

N.H. Portsmouth

Boston

Albany MASS. Plymouth

N.Y. CONN.

Providence

R.I.

New Haven

PA.

N.J. New York

Philadelphia

MD. DEL. Tobacco, lumber

Baltimore

Annapolis

Williamsburg

Jamestown

VA.

N.C.

S.C.

GA.

Charleston

Savannah

Connecticut R.

Susquehanna R.

Delaware R.

Hudson R.

Potomac R.

James R.

PROCLAMATION LINE OF 1763

Fish, flour

Rum

Flour, lumber

Fish, livestock

(to West Africa/S. Europe)

Tobacco (to Britain)

ATLANTIC OCEAN

(to West Indies)

Rice, indigo (to Britain)

BRITISH COLONIES AND COLONIAL TRADE

Settled before 1660

Settled between 1660 and 1700

Settled between 1700 and 1763

Spanish Florida. The proprietors drew up an instrument of government called the Fundamental Constitutions (probably the handiwork of the English political philosopher John Locke), which provided for a hierarchy of colonial nobility and set up a platform of government with a curious mixture of feudal and liberal elements. The Fundamental Constitutions eventually had to be abandoned in favor of a more workable plan of government.

The division of Carolina into two distinct colonies came about gradually. English settlers were already occupying land around Albemarle Sound when the proprietors received their charter, and Albemarle continued to attract a scattering of settlers. It was geographically remote from the other settlement on the Ashley and Cooper rivers to the south. As the two separate sections gained population, they set up separate legislative assemblies, approved by the proprietors. In 1710 the proprietors appointed a governor of North Carolina, "independent of the governor of Carolina," thus recognizing the separation of North from South Carolina. In 1721 South Carolina was declared a royal province, and eight years later North Carolina also became a crown colony.

Georgia.   Georgia, founded in 1733, was administered for two decades by twenty trustees in England. Georgia was established to serve many purposes: as an extension of the southern provincial frontier; as a buffer or a first line of defense between the Spanish colony of Florida and the English settlements; as a planned Utopia where the trustees hoped to establish a model society; as a refuge for persecuted Protestants from Europe; as a new opportunity for men who had been released from debtor's prisons in England; and as a model "colony" that would produce commodities that England wanted, notably silk and citrus fruits. Because of these multiple objectives, no single one was carried out with success. In fact, by 1740 many of its colonists had left, and there were few new immigrants. Not until the crown took over the colony in the 1750s was Georgia rescued, and even then it did not flourish until after the American Revolution.

COLONIAL ADMINISTRATION AND POLITICS

Administration of the English Colonies.   In London, administrative agencies to govern the colonies were slow in evolving. Originally, a committee of the King's Privy Council, the Lord Commissioners for Plantations, directly supervised the colonies. Variations of this committee operated until 1675, when the Lords of Trade was created—an agency whose vigorous actions set a new standard in colonial policy. It opposed the disposition on the part of the crown to issue proprietary grants and advocated revoking them, bringing such colonies under direct royal control.

The most important effort of the Lords of Trade was made in 1686, when it established the Dominion of New England. The charter of Massachusetts Bay had been annulled in 1684, and the Dominion represented an attempt to centralize the authority of the crown by creating a super-colony, including Massachusetts, New Hampshire, Connecticut, Rhode Island, New York, and New Jersey. It was expected that eventually Pennsylvania would also be incorporated within the framework of the Dominion. The crown, acting upon the recommendation of the Lords of Trade, appointed Edmond Andros as governor, to reside in Boston, with his deputy to reside in New York. No provision was made for an assembly, although there was to be a council of advisers. Andros, unfortunately, was of limited mind and petty spirit; he was scarcely the man to carry out such a dramatic, far-reaching colonial experiment. Resentment among the colonies included within the Dominion was intense, not only because their original charters had been arbitrarily set aside, not only because the crown had appointed the arbitrary Andros, but because they lacked a representative assembly.

A twist of fate—England's Glorious Revolution of 1688, which deposed the despotic James II and firmly championed Parliament, and thus representative government, in England—provided an opportunity for the colonials to overthrow the Dominion. Acting on the premise that Governor Andros now represented a discarded royal regime, the colonials imprisoned him as a signal of their allegiance to the new government in England set up under William and Mary. Each colony that had been included within the Dominion hastily returned to its previous path of colonial self-government. Thus the Glorious Revolution marked the end of an experiment to consolidate the colonies within a larger framework to be administered more directly by home authorities.

In many respects, the experiment of the Dominion of New England was a turning point in colonial political affairs. At this time the colonials were not yet strong enough to defeat the royal will. If the experiment had been a success, individual self-government within the colonies would have been eliminated and the entire course of American history might have been changed. With the fall of the Dominion, the individual colonies received a new lease on life, and they used it to gain strength politically and economically.

In 1696 the Lords of Trade were replaced by the Board of Trade, an administrative agency which survived into the period of the American Revolution. During the eighteenth century Parliament was overwhelmed with its own problems—namely, the internal political transition to parliamentary supremacy in England and the turmoil of foreign policy—and could not spare the time to formulate new policies for the empire. As a result, the general policies formulated very early in the century were followed throughout the period regardless of changing circumstances. An instruction issued to a governor in 1750 was little changed from instructions given in 1700. The American provinces were changing, England was changing, the world was changing, but British imperial policy remained, for the most part, unchanged.

The Political Structure. English colonies in America experienced a vigorous political life, in contrast to the colonies of other western European countries. The concept of self-government was transferred to the English colonies almost from the outset in most settlements, but the political structure generally took more definitive shape early in the eighteenth century.

The political structures that evolved in royal, proprietary, and charter colonies were remarkably similar. Each colony had a governor who executed colonial laws, served as commander in chief of the militia, presided over the colony's highest court of appeals, and enforced relevant British enactments. In a proprietary colony like Pennsylvania the governor looked after the interests of the proprietor, most notably in the disposition of land, but he was also expected to enforce the imperial policies laid down by the home authorities. Usually the governor was appointed by the crown, although in proprietary colonies the proprietor held this prerogative and in Rhode Island and Connecticut the governor was elected by the legislature.

Most colonies had a council whose members served as advisers to the governor, comprised the upper house of the legislature, and sat as the highest court of appeal in the colony. Generally these council members were appointed by the crown upon the recommendation of the governor, but exceptions were made. Members of the council were customarily the more affluent colonials, many of whom had powerful friends in England. In a number of colonies the council, although acting in self-interest, was the spokesman for the people against the prerogative of the governor. The council wished to control office patronage, the distribution of lands, and the like.

A colonial assembly, which served as the lower house of the legislature, was elected by the freemen. By the eighteenth century every colony had instituted property requirements as a requisite for freemanship, but recent research has demonstrated that these requirements did not seriously restrict the number of eligible voters. Property requirements for officeholding, however, were frequently much higher than the requirements for suffrage, so that a member of the assembly had to be a person of some means. "Professional politicians" who had no other means of a livelihood were rare in the American provinces.

During the eighteenth century the assemblies of every colony gained power. Among the specific powers obtained by most assemblies were the rights to initiate legislation, to judge the qualifications of their own members, and to elect their speakers. The assemblies were somewhat less successful in determining when elections should be held and in extending the membership of the assembly.

Whereas the basic constitutional position of the home authorities was that the power of the assemblies and the grant of self-government itself were merely an extension of "the royal grace and favor," to be offered, modified, or even eliminated as the crown determined, the constitutional position held by the assemblies was that their power and authority derived from the consent of the governed. The assemblies conceived of themselves as replicas of the British House of Commons, and they attempted to imitate it in waging their contest for power against the prerogative of the governor, representing the crown or the proprietor.

Conflicts were inevitable between constitutional positions that differed so markedly. The principal expression of this conflict arose between the assemblies and the governor. The assemblies attempted to restrict the scope of the governor's operations by controlling the disbursement of funds appropriated by the legislature, by failing to appropriate monies for projects asked for by the governor, and occasionally by refusing to pay the governor's salary until he accepted the legislation passed by the assembly.

Local Government. The structure of English local government at the time the colonies were founded was transplanted, for the most part, to the New World. Among the more important officials were the county sheriffs and the justices of the peace. Although other positions that were important in England, such as lord lieutenant, did not flourish in the New World, local government in the United States today descends directly from the colonial period.

Local disputes over land titles and other matters were settled by the county courts. Colonial legislation was enforced by the justices of the peace in cooperation with the sheriff, and taxes were collected by the sheriff. In practice, therefore, local government served as a major link between the colonial government and the people of the New World colonies.

Politics in Operation. In every colony, at some time or another, domestic disputes developed which were fought out in the political arena. The issues of land, currency, proportionate representation, defense, and the Indian trade were among those that arose most frequently. In a colony such as Virginia, where tobacco was the principal staple, tobacco inspection acts aroused lively political disputes. Seldom did political parties develop. Generally, a coalition of forces, drawn in most cases from various parts of a province, united to support or defeat a measure. Once the issue was decided, the coalition disintegrated. Whereas a political split between the eastern and western parts of a province was characteristic of a colony like Pennsylvania, which was growing at a swifter pace than most of its sister colonies, the major political division in New York was between influential families whose wealth was based on land and influential families whose wealth was based on commerce. These political issues and the conflicts they aroused were evidence not of internal disorder but of political maturity—of vigorous, healthy self-government in action.

COLONIAL ECONOMY

New England. The rise of capitalism throughout western Europe, which coincided with the founding of the English colonies, determined that the American provincial economy would be capitalistic in orientation, with an emphasis on trade, production for market, and eventual regional specialization. Each colony's economy at the outset was rather primitive—merely an appendage of the economy of the mother country— but shortly after the mid-eighteenth century an indigenous, well-developed capitalism emerged.

The economic development of New England was strongly influenced by the systems of land distribution and of trade. In the seventeenth century land was granted by the legislature to groups—usually church congregations—which in turn distributed the land among their members. The result was the encouragement of the famous New England township system, whose principal aim was to maintain an effective social-religious community. Each family was customarily granted a town lot, after provision for the church, sometimes a school, and a village green had been made. Plots of land outside the town were then distributed among members of the group, with common land retained for grazing purposes and a specified number of acres reserved for latecomers. Distributing the land in this fashion meant that all members of the group would be in close proximity to the church, the heart of the Puritan community; that sending youngsters to school would raise no serious problems; that towns would become the basis for representative government; and that town meetings would provide the political structure to resolve local issues.

In the eighteenth century the New England land system changed. With the central purpose of a concerted social-religious community declining in importance, settlement along western frontier lands seldom was made by church groups. Instead, men of influence and means began to purchase large blocs of land for speculative purposes, selling off smaller parcels to the individual farmer or prospective farmer. Even in the older towns conditions changed. Original settlers or descendants of original settlers moved out, often selling their land to a third party. Absentee ownership of town lots and township lands was common. Whereas in the seventeenth century town proprietors were nearly always residents of the town, in the eighteenth century this was not so.

Although farming was the predominant occupation in New England up to 1640, trade gained increasing importance thereafter. From 1640 to 1660 the English were preoccupied with civil war and political upheaval at home, and colonials began to replace the English merchant as the trading enterpriser. It was at this time that the developing resources of New England fisheries helped open up trade between the Puritans of New England and Puritans who had settled in the West Indies.

New England merchants gradually gained a position of economic and political primacy. By the end of the seventeenth century they had already begun to replace the Puritan magistrates as the source of economic and political power, and by the 1760s they constituted the single strongest voice in New England. It is important to remember that merchants were not alone in their dependence on trade for prosperity. The artisans who repaired canvas and built vessels, the farmers who exported meat products—in fact, the entire population in one way or another—were partly dependent upon prosperous commercial relations. Meat, fish, and lumber, the principal articles of export, found their major market in the West Indies. New England was also dependent on its role as a carrier of exports from other provinces and of imports from England.

For labor, New Englanders depended largely on members of their own families, though they sometimes hired local servants and imported indentured servants—that is, adult whites who bound themselves to labor for a definite period, usually three to five years, in exchange for passage to America. New England, in contrast to some of the other regions, was attractive to skilled workers because they could find a ready market for their talent in an area dominated by a town system. Each town needed a carpenter and a blacksmith.

The Southern Colonies.   Three significant factors affected the economic development of the Southern colonies: the distribution of land, the evolution of the plantation system, and the tremendous production of staples for market. In the seventeenth-century Chesapeake colonies (Virginia and Maryland) land was distributed directly to individuals, in contrast to the practice in early New England.

Moreover, the colonials, instead of settling in groups, scattered up and down the rivers of the Chesapeake area. Each planter tried to have his own landing where an ocean-going vessel could readily load the tobacco he produced and unload the goods he had ordered from England. This method of settlement made the county the basis of local government, discouraged the establishment of a school system because of the distances involved, and markedly influenced the transplantation of the Anglican Church (see Chapter 3).

In the seventeenth century the average landholding was relatively small, since manpower to cultivate extensive landholdings was lacking. The headright system, whereby a planter could obtain fifty acres of land for each dependent or servant he brought to the colonies, allowed the first accumulations of land to occur; but it was not until the eighteenth century, when American colonists obtained control of the machinery to distribute land, that large grants became fairly common.

Though slaves were imported into the Chesapeake colonies and into South Carolina in the seventeenth century, the principal labor force was composed of indentured servants, including convicts and paupers who were sentenced to labor in America. Over 1500 indentures were imported annually into Virginia alone in the 1670s and the 1680s. But as the plantation system became larger, as the black slave became a relatively less expensive source of labor, as the Middle colonies—New York, the Jerseys, Pennsylvania, Delaware—expanded to attract the indentured servant, and as the supply of English indentures decreased because the demand for labor in England increased, the institution of slavery became fastened upon the eighteenth-century Southern colonies. A society that had been made up largely of yeomen now became dominated by a planter elite and a caste system of black slaves.

Tobacco continued to be the main staple in the Chesapeake colonies, but rice and indigo became prominent in South Carolina. (The widow Elizabeth Pinckney introduced indigo as a crop.) Naval stores became a major export of North Carolina. Deer skins were the most important goods obtained through trade with the Indians.

In the seventeenth century no merchant group developed in the Southern colonies because planters corresponded directly with English merchants, but in the eighteenth century an important merchant group developed in strategically located Charleston, South Carolina, entrepôt for a vast hinterland. Its emergence affected the social structure in the Southern colonies, where the large planter was unchallenged by a mercantile interest centered in cities.

The Middle Colonies. During the eighteenth century English migration decreased because demand for laborers and opportunities for advancement greatly increased at home as Britain expanded its trade and manufactures. However, a tremendous influx of non-English peoples—Germans, Scotch-Irish, Irish, Swiss, and French Huguenots—into the Middle colonies resulted in expansion of that region at a rate exceeding that of New England or the Southern colonies.

The reasons for the migration of non-English peoples were fundamentally economic, although religious intolerance and fear of destructive wars at home sometimes played a part. Opportunities for the Scotch-Irish in Ireland were limited, whereas opportunities in the New World appeared much more attractive. German

Pietists came to Pennsylvania in large numbers because that colony offered an attractive land policy as well as religious toleration.

Land policies in Pennsylvania, the Jerseys, and New York varied greatly. In New York land was granted to royal favorites, who established extensive manors; an ordinary settler was often forced to accept a leasehold and become a renter instead of obtaining clear title to the land. The distribution of lands in Pennsylvania was much more favorable. Small grants could be obtained by outright purchase; in fact, Scotch-Irish settlers on the frontier of Pennsylvania frequently assumed title to the land by right of settlement and refused to pay the proprietors.

New York and Philadelphia developed into major ports in the eighteenth century; Philadelphia, in fact, became the second largest city within the British empire. Both cities developed a strong mercantile class and attracted skilled artisans—cabinetmakers, silversmiths, gunsmiths, and the like. Both exported grain, the principal commodity of the Middle colonies, which became the "breadbasket" of colonial America.

Pennsylvania's rapid growth and early economic maturity reflected the astonishing general growth of the colonies. The handful of English settlers had become 250,000 strong by 1700; by 1760 the colonies provided a good livelihood for a population of approximately two million—almost half the population of England. No wonder, then, that trade quadrupled, that banking and currency became important issues, that tradesmen and merchants carried on sophisticated economic practices, that a stable society was formed, and finally, that the American economic system was sufficiently developed to sustain the shock of political separation from the mother country and to finance a war for independence. All the ingredients of a well-developed commercial capitalism were present.

English Regulatory Acts.   As the economy of the American provinces matured, imperial regulations were enlarged to prevent foreign commercial competition and the competition of colonial manufactures with those of the mother country. Although restrictions were placed on the tobacco trade as early as the 1620s, a series of enactments passed from 1651 to 1700 laid the actual framework for the English imperial system.

The Navigation Act of 1651 was designed primarily to reduce competition from foreign shipping. It provided that non-European goods brought to England or its possessions could be transported only in English (including colonial) ships and that goods from the Continent could be brought into England or its possessions only in vessels belonging to the country that had produced the goods. A second Navigation Act (often called the Enumeration Act) passed in 1660 closed the loophole which had permitted colonials to import directly from Europe. It provided that all goods, regardless of origin, could be imported into or exported from any English colony only in English ships. "Enumerated" goods—including sugar, cotton, indigo, dye goods, and tobacco—of colonial origin were to be shipped only to England or its colonies; they could not be exported directly to other European countries.

The Enumeration Act was particularly hard on Virginia and Maryland, for it meant that colonial tobacco—which the English market could not absorb—had to be shipped to England and then reexported to Continental markets. Reexportation costs—including handling charges, storage charges, and the costs of frequent loss of tobacco stored in English warehouses—were extremely high. Historians have suggested that the enumeration of tobacco produced an economic depression in Virginia and Maryland in the late seventeenth century and led eventually to the concentration of land ownership, since only the large-scale producer could meet the disadvantages of the market.

In 1663 a third Navigation Act—the Staple Act—required that most commodities (excluding salt, servants, and wine) imported into the colonies from Europe had to be shipped from England in English-built ships. A fourth Navigation Act in 1673 was passed to close a loophole colonials exploited when they shipped enumerated commodities from one colony to another without unloading the cargo at the point of destination and then transported the cargo directly to the European market. The Act of 1673 provided that whenever the vessel carried enumerated commodities, a plantation duty—that is, a bond—had to be paid before a ship could clear a colonial port. A final enactment in 1696 provided for the creation of vice-admiralty courts in America, to place the enforcement of the navigation laws in the hands of men appointed directly by the crown.

The research of historian Lawrence Harper indicates that the burden of the Navigation Acts was greater at the end of the seventeenth century than at any other time during the colonial period and that the acts were seldom evaded. Evasion was to come later with the Molasses Act of 1733.

Whereas in the seventeenth century the English regulations were principally directed at commerce, in the eighteenth century, with the maturing of the American economy, the regulations were principally directed at manufactures. The Woolen Act of 1699, which forbade colonial export of wool products, had little impact upon the American colonies because their exportation of textiles was limited; but the Hat Act of 1732—which prohibited exportation of hats from one colony to another and severely restricted the colonial hat industry—adversely affected New York and New England, which had exploited a vital European market. The act eliminated this colonial enterprise, greatly benefiting London hatters, who had exerted pressure in Parliament to pass the bill.

The Molasses Act of 1733—which showed that Britain in the eighteenth century was not unconcerned with commercial regulation—placed a heavy duty upon sugar, rum, molasses, and other commodities imported from the non-British West Indies. This enactment seriously hampered the trade of the American colonies, which had imported these commodities—molasses in particular—in quantity from Spanish and French colonies at a price cheaper than could be obtained in the British West Indies. Because the act seriously encroached upon this customary channel of trade, the Molasses Act was evaded by extensive smuggling.

The Iron Act of 1750 encouraged the colonial production of pig and bar iron for use by the English iron and steel industry but prohibited the building of slitting mills, forges, and other iron-finishing equipment. Certain colonies, notably Pennsylvania, defied the prohibition, and when war broke out between France and England in 1752, the home authorities were unable to enforce the act with vigor. After 1763, of course, the continual crises between the mother country and the colonies prevented effective enforcement.

BRITAIN WINS SUPREMACY IN NORTH AMERICA

Early Conflicts with the French. The shifting balance of power in eighteenth-century Europe, brought about in part by the emergence of France and Britain as the major nations of the Western world, produced a ceaseless contest for position in both the Old World and the New. To the English colonials, the strength of New France was a particular danger: French fur traders in the wilderness were capable of stirring up the Indians to hostility against English traders and settlers who began to penetrate the transmontane region, and French control over the interior threatened to curb the westward expansion of the English colonies in America.

The War of the Spanish Succession (1702–13), or Queen Anne's War, as it is known in America, saw a conflict of the colonists with both Spanish and French forces. In 1739 Great Britain attacked Spain in a conflict which soon merged into the War of the Austrian Succession, or King George's War (1740–48). Believing that the time was ripe to neutralize French power in Canada, the governor of Massachusetts organized a force of militia, and on June 17, 1745, the Americans, in one of the most audacious—and lucky—episodes in the colonial wars, captured Louisbourg, a fort on Cape Breton Island. In 1748, however, the British returned the fortress to the French in exchange for Madras in India.

Preliminaries to the Great War for Empire. The French now showed a greater determination than ever to hold Canada and the Ohio and Mississippi valleys. In 1755 they erected blockhouses to fortify the Ohio and Allegheny river valleys against the British.

In the meantime, planters from Virginia and Maryland had organized the Ohio Company to exploit virgin lands as far west as the present site of Louisville, Kentucky. To prevent these western lands from falling into possession of the French, the governor of Virginia in 1753 sent George Washington, a young surveyor, into the Ohio valley to remonstrate with the French commander. The mission accomplished nothing, and when Washington was sent back the next year with a force of men, his little army was surrounded, captured, and sent home. Thus began the conflict that was to develop into the French and Indian War and explode in Europe as the Seven Years' War (1756–63), allying England and Prussia against France, Austria, and Spain.

With the danger of an Indian war threatening the whole frontier, the colonies were particularly concerned with counterbalancing the Indian allies of the French. To conciliate the powerful Iroquois, who had given invaluable support to the English in the past, the British government called a conference in Albany of commissioners from seven Northern and Middle colonies. This "Albany Congress" was more important for its political proposals than for its few accomplishments in dealing with the disaffected Iroquois. Because the delegates realized that a closer union of the colonies was needed to provide better collective defense and control of Indian affairs, they listened attentively to the "Plan of Union" put forward by one of Pennsylvania's leading citizens, Benjamin Franklin. Franklin's proposal would have brought all of the colonies under "one general government" with an executive and legislature, but with each colony retaining its separate existence and government. No colony gave the plan serious consideration, however, and the British government disregarded it altogether.

To protect the colonies, the British government sent two regiments of regulars and a British fleet. In an attempt to dislodge the French from Fort Duquesne, a strategic position that controlled the upper Ohio valley, a detachment of regulars and colonial militia under British General Edward Braddock marched toward the fort but was ambushed and routed by French and Indian forces. After Braddock's defeat, George Washington was given the responsibility of protecting more than three hundred miles of the Virginia frontier against incursions of Indians and French marauders.

The year 1755 was a period of almost unrelieved misfortune for the British, and for the next two or three years the war raged intermittently and disastrously along the whole frontier, with the French under the Marquis de Montcalm winning a succession of victories in the north.

A New Policy Brings British Victory. William Pitt, who had become Secretary of State for War in 1757, realized that part of the trouble in America lay in the incompetence of Britain's officers. To remedy this, he ordered to America fresh troops under a new command. He also won more wholehearted cooperation from the American provincials by promising that Britain would reimburse the individual colonies for their war expenditures.

The campaign against the French soon began to show favorable results. The victory that finally decided the issue in Canada came on September 13, 1759, when General Wolfe led a successful attack on Quebec, which had been under siege since late June. The capture of Quebec sealed the fate of France in North America. Elsewhere—in Europe and India—British arms were also victorious, and France could do nothing but capitulate. In 1762 France ceded Louisiana to Spain in recompense for aid in the war and a year later, by the Treaty of Paris, ceded to Great Britain all of Canada except the tiny islands of St. Pierre and Miquelon. The very magnitude of the British victory paved the way for the disintegration of the British Empire in America.

CHAPTER 2

REVOLUTION AND INDEPENDENCE 1763–83

BACKGROUND OF THE REVOLUTION

The Character of the Revolution.   The American Revolution was one of the great epochs in human history, not only because it brought a separation between Great Britain and its colonies in America but also because it was the first revolution of modern times founded on the principles of self-government and the protection of individual liberty. In this context, the American Revolution became a beacon to light the way for peoples the world over.

The American Revolution was, in fact, many-sided. It was a War for Independence in which the colonies fought to be separated from the strongest nation in the world, Great Britain; it was a civil war in which Englishmen fought Englishmen and occasionally colonials fought colonials; it was part of a world war; it involved a struggle for power within each colony; and it was a nationalist movement in which the colonies, after separating from Britain, formed a lasting union—an important decision that Americans today take for granted but that was not necessarily predestined. Although the purpose of the Revolution was not to establish democracy any more than it was to establish a union, one of the results of the struggle within certain states was to give the average American a greater voice in government.

Finally, it should be remembered that the first revolt by colonials against the homeland in modern times—the American colonies against Britain—occurred under the most enlightened and least burdensome imperial system of contemporary Europe. The whites who lived in the English colonies enjoyed far more privileges in every sphere of life than did their counterparts in the French and Spanish colonial systems. Why were the least restricted colonials the first to revolt? The American colonials had enjoyed what they conceived of as their liberties for a century or more, and they had no intention of seeing these liberties restricted, even if, comparatively, they were better off than colonials elsewhere. Although the Revolution was not inevitable, any action to limit existing privileges automatically produced friction. How deep the friction was to become depended upon the course of events and the response to these events by American colonials and by the authorities in Britain.

The Need for Adjustment in the British Imperial System.   The crises within the empire from 1763 to 1776 were provoked by a series of specific enactments, but to review the prelude to revolution in such narrow terms is to misconstrue the essential issues that were in dispute. An adjustment in the relationship between Britain and its colonies was made inevitable by the sweeping changes that occurred during the eighteenth century. The colonial and commercial systems of Britain had been established in the seventeenth century; the theory which underlay the system was several centuries old. When the system was inaugurated, England possessed only a few colonies. After the Peace of 1763, Britain had more than thirty colonies, scattered throughout the world, each with its individual characteristics. Did the policies initiated in the 1660s suit conditions as they existed in the colonies in the 1760s? Should the same system apply to India and Massachusetts?

Even without the specific crises that occurred between 1763 and 1776, the British-colonial relationships required adjustment to meet the realities of the times. Three major changes were clearly evident: the American colonies had matured; the political transition in England by which Parliament had steadily gained power at the expense of the crown required a redefinition of relationships within the empire; and the colonies in the New World had become a critical factor in the European balance of power.

By 1760 the British colonies in America were no longer infants dependent solely upon the protection of the mother country. From limited self-government to mature self-government, from inexperience with authority to experience, from a primitive to a complex, well-developed indigenous economy—this had been the course of the American colonies. Any imperial system that failed to recognize these realities was doomed. As it existed, the imperial system had become, in some of its parts, an anachronism. The American provinces had become an insatiable market for British goods; the British system failed to adjust to this fact. The American colonies required a more enlightened money and banking policy; the British system tried to apply outworn theories. The American colonies produced statesmen, and even geniuses, but most American talent was unacknowledged.

The political transition in England required a rethinking of the constitutional structure of the empire. The colonies had been established under the auspices of royal charters; they had been administered through the king, the executive authority. As Parliament assumed greater authority, fundamental questions arose: Did Parliament have unlimited legislative supremacy over the colonies? Did Parliament gain the executive power previously exercised by the crown? The home authorities said yes; American colonials said no. Moreover, the Industrial Revolution of the eighteenth century in England introduced new problems with regard to mercantile theories, notably the importance of colonies as markets, which were never resolved.

During the eighteenth century the Spanish, French, and British colonies in the New World had become increasingly critical factors in the European balance of power. Beginning particularly with the Peace of Utrecht in 1713, the European powers attempted to establish an equilibrium in that balance. It was clearly tipped in England's favor by the Peace of Paris in 1763, when Britain acquired New France in North America as well as French possessions elsewhere in the world. These British acquisitions created uneasiness and uncertainty throughout western Europe. France began to explore avenues to redress the balance of power. Soon after 1763 the French recognized the possibility of doing so, not by recapturing its lost colonies nor by capturing British colonies, but by encouraging a separation between Britain and its colonies in America. This reasoning was responsible for French intervention in 1778 on behalf of the Americans.

Any one of these major changes in the eighteenth century—the maturation of the colonies, the political and economic transition in Britain, and the diplomatic evolution—was destined to produce problems. Together, they helped to produce a revolution.

The Constitutional Issue.   As mentioned in the previous chapter, the British and the American colonials had differing concepts of the constitutional structure of the empire. The British assumed that the self-government practiced by the separate colonies was a favor granted by the mother country—a favor that could be enlarged, curtailed, or even eliminated. The ultimate authority rested in Britain; the colonies possessed no power except that granted by the home authorities. The colonials, on the other hand, construed self-government to rest upon the consent of the governed (the colonial electorate), not upon the royal grace and favor. The Americans believed they possessed rights (at first called the Rights of Englishmen, later called American Rights) which Britain could in no way curtail. Each colonial assembly viewed itself as struggling against a royal governor (and thus against the king) in much the same fashion as the House of Commons was gaining power at the king's expense.

The rising power of Parliament posed an additional question: What were the limits to the legislative power of Parliament as it applied to the colonies? Conflict on this point was inevitable, and it became a critical issue in the revolutionary crisis that developed.

Constitutional Confrontations.   During the French and Indian War certain British policies annoyed the American provincials. In 1759 the Privy Council instructed the governor of Virginia to refuse to sign any bill which failed to include a "suspending clause"—that is, a clause which prevented the act from becoming effective until it had been approved by the home authorities. In 1761 general writs of assistance, empowering officers of the British customs service to break into and search homes and stores for smuggled goods, provoked strong opposition from the provincials, who claimed that the writs were contrary to law and to the natural rights of men. In that same year the Privy Council prohibited the issuance in New York and New Jersey of judicial commissions with unlimited tenure, specifying that such commissions must always be subject to revocation by the king, even though in England judges no longer held their posts at the king's pleasure. In 1764 the Currency Act extended to all colonies the restrictions upon the issuance of paper money which previously had applied only to Massachusetts.

Problems of Defense and Western Lands.   The Peace of Paris of 1763 eliminated the French threat to English expansion on the North American continent and made available to English colonials opportunities in the West that had been denied them for a quarter of a century. However, the Peace of Paris raised problems with regard to the administration and distribution of this land. It also raised the issue of revenue to pay the costs of administering the empire. Most important, the Peace of Paris, by eliminating the French threat, made the American provincials bolder in stating their views and, once they had adopted a position, more tenacious in clinging to it.

Among the principal problems faced by the British was the settlement of the territory west of the Alleghenies. The issue was complicated by the revolt in 1763 of the western Indians under the leadership of Pontiac, chief of the Ottawa tribe. Farms and villages along the whole of the colonial frontier from Canada to Virginia were laid waste. The uprising was put down largely by British troops, but the problem of future defense assumed great importance. This incident, together with a previous policy of appointing a commander in chief for America, produced a major decision on the part of the British: to quarter ten thousand British regulars on the American mainland and in the West Indies.

However well-intentioned, this action met with stern provincial opposition. Americans who had faced the French competition at close quarters for a century could not understand why British troops were needed now that the French menace had been eliminated. Ill will between the British redcoats and the colonials increased the tension, especially in New York (after 1765) and in Boston (after 1768), where the troops were stationed. Moreover, the colonials were not accustomed to the accepted British practice of expecting the people who were being "defended" to quarter the troops. The Quartering Act of 1765, which required New York colonials to house the soldiers and to make available supplies, was bitterly resented.

The solution to the problem of western lands beyond the Appalachians was equally irritating. If the colonies in immediate proximity to the western lands, like Pennsylvania, New York, Virginia, and the Carolinas, were permitted to extend their boundaries westward, colonies without a hinterland—Connecticut, Rhode Island, New Jersey, and Maryland, to name the most obvious—would be placed at a disadvantage. Should new colonies, therefore, be formed in the territory beyond the Appalachians?

The solution formulated by the British government was the Royal Proclamation Line of 1763, which established a line along the crest of the Alleghenies west of which colonials could not take up land. This policy of delay seemed sensible in London, but the colonials were impatient to take advantage of the new territory. Virginians had fought in the French and Indian War specifically to open this area to settlement. Not only were frontiersmen eager to exploit these opportunities, but land companies in Pennsylvania, Virginia, and New England, whose membership included affluent colonials and Englishmen, wished to act. For these men the Proclamation Line was a disappointment—an unexpected barrier to enterprise and opportunity.

The Proclamation Line, intended originally as a temporary measure to gain time for a permanent policy, was not revoked before the Revolution. Meanwhile, the Quebec Act of 1774 further annoyed the provincials by annexing the western lands north of the Ohio River to the Province of Quebec. The former French colony, viewed by the colonials as the enemy, was to be rewarded, while the faithful colonists who had fought to free that territory from French control were denied the fruits of their sacrifices.

The problems of western lands and defense did not bring on the Revolution, but they were a grievance which, when added to other irritations, decreased the probability of compromise and increased the chances of hostility.

Constitutional Issue of the Stamp Act. George Grenville, who became Prime Minister in 1763, was neither an imaginative nor a clever man, but he was a determined one. Coming into office just at the close of the French and Indian War and feeling, as most of his countrymen did, that the American colonists were the greatest beneficiaries of the vast territory bordering the Ohio and Mississippi rivers that had been won from the French, he was determined that the colonists should pay at least part of the costs of defending and pacifying this territory. Currently no revenue was coming from the colonists to aid in imperial defense; duties imposed by the Molasses Act of 1733 were being evaded by smugglers, and, in fact, the American customs service was costing more to operate than it was collecting in fees. Thus, in 1764 Grenville led Parliament to adopt the Sugar Act, an act intended to produce revenue—a purpose clearly stated in its preface—by enforcing the payment of customs duties on sugar, wine, coffee, silk, and other goods. Although it reduced the duty on molasses bought from non-British sources from 6 pence to 4 pence per gallon—on the surface, an attractive reduction—provincials actually had been smuggling in molasses for no more than a pence and a half per gallon as a bribe to customs officials. Now Grenville intended to enforce the trade laws by stricter administrative procedures. The crux of the issue, however, was the British intention to tax the colonists for purposes of revenue. Before this, duties had been imposed merely as a means of regulating the trade of the empire.

The issue of taxation, raised by the Sugar Act, was brought to a crisis in the Stamp Act of 1765, which provoked spontaneous opposition throughout the colonies. The Stamp Act placed a stamp fee on all legal documents, deeds and diplomas, custom papers, and newspapers, to name the most obvious articles. It directly affected every articulate element in the community, including lawyers, merchants, preachers, and printers. Moreover, the act raised not only the question of who had the right to tax but also the more significant questions: Who had what power? Could Parliament legislate for the colonials in all matters? Was Parliament's authority without limit or were there bounds beyond which it could not reach—bounds based upon certain rights inherent in all Englishmen?

The conflict was contested on two levels, that of specific action and that of constitutional debate. In every colony the men appointed as Stamp Act collectors were forced to resign, sometimes under the threat of force. Sons of Liberty were organized in key colonies to enforce the colonially imposed prohibition on the use of stamps; occasionally mob spirit carried opposition to extremes, as it did in Massachusetts when a band of provincials ransacked the home of the lieutenant governor. The courts and the ports which could not, in a strictly legal sense, operate without using the stamps continued after a momentary lull to carry out their regular functions in defiance of the act.

Each colonial legislature met to decide on a course of action, the most famous incident occurring in the Virginia House of Burgesses, where Patrick Henry introduced resolutions declaring that the "General Assembly of this Colony have the only and *sole exclusive* Right and Power to lay Taxes and Impositions upon the Inhabitants of This Colony." Any other course, said Henry, would tend "to destroy British as well as American Freedom." At the invitation of Massachusetts, nine colonies sent delegates to New York in October 1765 to form the Stamp Act Congress, in which a set of resolutions was adopted denying the authority of Parliament to tax the colonials. A boycott of British goods—the use of economic coercion to achieve political ends—was introduced on the theory that the colonial market was so necessary to Britain that it would abandon the act to regain the market.

On the second level, that of defining constitutional theory, the respective arguments of the colonials and the authorities in England developed differently. Colonials argued that they could not be free without being secure in their property and that they could not be secure in their property if, without their consent, others could take it away by taxes. This argument revealed the close tie between property and liberty in the mind of the eighteenth-century Anglo-Americans.

The British responded by saying that the Americans were not being taxed without their consent because they were "virtually," if not directly, represented in Parliament. British exponents argued that many areas in Britain—notably Manchester and other substantial communities—were not directly represented in Parliament, but that no one denied that an act of Parliament had authority over those communities. The same concept of "virtual representation," so asserted British leaders, applied to the colonies.

The colonies vigorously opposed this interpretation of representation. Most of the colonial legislatures echoed Maryland's argument "that it cannot, with any Truth or Propriety, be said, That the Freemen of this Province of Maryland are Represented in the British Parliament." Daniel Dulany, a Maryland attorney, in his *Considerations on the Propriety of Imposing Taxes in the British Colonies,* argued that even those people in Britain who did not have the right to vote were allied in interest with their contemporaries. "But who," he asked, "are the Representatives of the Colonies?" Who could speak for them?

> The Right of Exemption from all Taxes without their Consent, the Colonies claim as *British* Subjects. They derive this Right from the Common Law, which their Charters have declared and confirmed. . . . A Right to impose an internal Tax on the Colonies, without their Consent *for the single Purpose of Revenue,* is denied; a Right to regulate their Trade without their Consent is admitted.

In brief, the colonists argued, Parliament had power, but not unlimited power. It could *legislate* and thus impose external duties to regulate trade, but it could not levy a *tax* for revenue. In time, as the revolutionary crisis deepened, the colonial position was modified to deny Parliament's authority to legislate for or tax the colonists for any purpose whatsoever.

A view much closer to the eventual stand taken by the colonists was expressed by George Mason of Virginia, who implicitly denied the infinite subordination of the colonies. "We rarely see anything from your [the English] side of the water free from the authoritative style of a master to a school boy: 'We have with infinite difficulty and fatigue got you excused this one time; pray be a good boy for the future, do what your papa and mama bid you.'" He warned the British that "such another experiment as the stamp-act would produce a general revolt in America."

Parliament backed down—not on the principle at issue, but on the act itself. The Stamp Act was repealed in 1766. At the same time, however, the Declaratory Act was passed, stating that Parliament possessed the authority to make laws binding the American colonists. The Americans mistakenly believed not only that their arguments were persuasive but that the economic pressure brought on by the boycott of English goods had been effective. The boycott, in fact, delayed action rather than hastened it, but the Americans, unaware of its failure, were to employ the boycott as a standard weapon against the British at each time of crisis.

The Townshend Duties. The next major crisis arose in 1767. Misled by Benjamin Franklin, who in February 1766 had told the House of Commons that the provincials objected only to internal taxes, not to taxes on trade, the British Parliament in 1767 enacted the Townshend Duties on glass, lead, paper, paints, and tea. These import or "external" taxes were designed to exploit the distinction between internal taxes and external duties which Parliament mistakenly supposed the Americans were making. At the same time, Parliament reorganized the customs service by appointing a Board of Customs Commissioners to be located at Boston. The following year, 1768, troops were sent to Boston, in part at least because of the urging of the Customs Commissioners. The Townshend Duties failed to awaken the spontaneous reaction of the Stamp Act, but they tested once again the colonial versus British theory of the empire and posed anew the question: What were the limits to the power of Parliament?

Again the American colonists resorted to a boycott, although no intercolonial congress was called. John Dickinson, in his *Letters from a Farmer in Pennsylvania,* reaffirmed the position of the colonials that duties, even "external" duties, could not be levied primarily to obtain revenue, though measures enacted to regulate trade were admitted as a proper prerogative of Parliament. Dickinson's essays were not revolutionary in tone or in spirit; neither, however, did they back away from the fundamental position taken by the colonists, that they alone could levy a tax upon themselves.

As for the British, the Board of Customs Commissioners that came to enforce the Navigation Acts, the Sugar Act of 1764, and the Townshend Duties carried out its responsibility in such a perfidious way that the commissioners were properly accused of customs racketeering. But the real significance of the Board was the breadth of opposition it aroused. Not merely those colonists most vulnerable to its activity— particularly New England merchants—were disposed to stand against the British, but a consensus of opposition pervaded all the colonies, many of which experienced no serious problem with customs officials. This consensus was made possible because of a more profound issue: Where did the regulatory power of Parliament end and that of the colonials begin?

The Townshend Duties disappointed their advocates, for they did not produce the revenue expected. In 1770, therefore, the British repealed the Townshend Duties (except the duty on tea, which was retained as a symbol of Parliament's right to tax);

the Americans relaxed their opposition and reopened their ports to British goods, though they condemned tea drinking as unpatriotic.

On March 5, 1770, by coincidence the same day the Townshend Duties were repealed, the "Boston Massacre" took place. A small group of townspeople, described by the Boston lawyer John Adams as a "motley rabble of saucy boys, negroes, and mulattoes, Irish teagues and outlandish Jack Tars," shouted catcalls and insults and hurled snowballs and rocks at British troops on duty. After a scuffle erupted, the redcoats opened fire, killing three persons and wounding eight. Among the slain was Crispus Attucks, an escaped slave, who, according to one witness, led the charge against the redcoats.

'TIS TIME TO PART

The Boston Tea Party and the Coercive Acts. Beginning in 1772, provoked by a British decision to pay the salary of the lieutenant governor out of customs revenues and thus free him from dependence on the colonial assembly, a Committee of Correspondence was established in Massachusetts at the urging of Sam Adams, John Adams' radical cousin. Many other colonies followed the Massachusetts pattern and formed such committees in order to keep one another informed of possible British action. In 1772 the *Gaspee,* a customs vessel that had gone aground while in pursuit of colonial shipping, was boarded and burned off Providence, Rhode Island, by a group that included prominent citizens. These isolated incidents indicated that Americans had not abandoned their position but that, unless new provocations occurred, the situation probably would remain static. In 1773 and 1774, with the Boston Tea Party and the passage of the Coercive Acts, the conflict between Great Britain and its colonies entered a new and conclusive phase.

By the Tea Act of May 1773 the British government permitted the British East India Company, which had built up an excess stock of tea in England, to market— "dump" would perhaps be a more accurate term—it in America. The company was also authorized to employ its own agents in this transaction, and thus, in effect, to seize monopolistic control of the American market. With this act the British reawakened the latent hostility of the American colonists. When the ships carrying the tea arrived, they were met with unbroken opposition. In some ports, the ships were forced to return to England without unloading; in other cases the tea was placed in a warehouse to prevent its distribution; in Boston a band of men, haphazardly disguised as Indians, dumped the tea into the harbor.

The reaction in England upon hearing the news was prompt and decisive: punitive legislation must be passed to teach those property-destroying Massachusetts provincials a lesson. This position was endorsed by members of Parliament previously well disposed to the Americans. In quick succession, three Coercive or "Intolerable" Acts were passed: the Boston Port Act (March 31, 1774), which closed that port to commerce; the Massachusetts Government Act (May 30, 1774), which altered the manner of choosing the Governor's Council and, more significantly, indicated to the

Americans that parliamentary power knew no limits; and, finally, the Administration of Justice Act (May 30, 1774), which removed certain cases involving crown officials from the jurisdiction of Massachusetts. The other colonies immediately rallied to the support of Massachusetts in opposing these "Intolerable Acts"—much to the surprise of the British authorities, who had expected the support rather than the condemnation of the colonies outside Massachusetts. After all, had not property been destroyed? No action on the part of the Americans revealed the basic issue so clearly. Essentially, the issue was not customs racketeering, or the presence of redcoats, or the problem of western lands, or even taxes. The issue was: Who had what power?

The Coercive Acts set in motion a series of actions and counteractions which led directly to separation. If there was any one point at which the Revolution seemed to become inevitable it was in 1774, with the passage of the Coercive Acts and the colonial response to those acts. What would Parliament do next, the colonists asked themselves. Change the administration of justice in Virginia? Eliminate self-government in New York? Close the port of Philadelphia? Once the supremacy of Parliament in all areas was conceded, self-government would live merely on sufferance.

The colonials at this stage were not calling for independence; such a step was too frightening. The Americans had lived within the British Empire for more than a century; it was the most enlightened government of its time, where liberty was a word that meant something. Separating from Britain in the 1770s was somewhat similar to abruptly changing today the form of government under which we have lived since 1789. It was not a step to be taken, as the revolutionary fathers later declared in the Declaration of Independence, for light and transient causes.

The Provincials Act.   Events proceeded once again on two levels—that of action and that of theory. The First Continental Congress was called to meet in Philadelphia in September 1774. A number of important decisions made early in the deliberations set the tone of the meeting. Carpenters Hall, instead of the legislative chambers of Pennsylvania, was selected as the meeting hall, a victory for Sam Adams of Massachusetts and those who wished to take firm action against Britain. A more important show of strength came when resolutions proposing a union of colonies and regarded as conciliatory were offered. They were tabled by a close vote, and the Suffolk Resolves were adopted, asserting that the colonies should make no concessions until Britain first repealed the Coercive Acts, thus placing the burden of conciliation upon the home authorities. In addition, the First Continental Congress adopted a series of resolutions embodying its position and sent them off to the king. At the same time a Continental Association was established to cut off trade with the British. Although Congress avowed its "allegiance to his majesty" and its "affection for our fellow subjects" in Great Britain, the stand it took placed Britain on notice.

When the First Continental Congress adjourned, its members agreed to meet again in the spring of 1775 if no action was forthcoming from Britain. Conditions failed to improve; in fact, they became worse. In Massachusetts "minutemen" were training to guard against possible actions by British redcoats stationed in Boston; guns, powder, and other military stores were being collected at Concord. When on April 18,

1775, the British military governor sent out from Boston about seven hundred British regulars to destroy the stores at Concord, they were met by minutemen companies in Lexington and Concord. At Lexington eight Americans were killed. With minutemen swarming in from the countryside, the redcoats faced unexpected hazards on their return to Boston. Before the day was spent, they suffered nearly three hundred casualties and escaped total destruction only because reinforcements came from Boston. Dogging the regulars all the way, the minutemen encamped on the land approaches to Boston and began a siege. Meanwhile, on May 10, New England forces led by Benedict Arnold and Ethan Allen captured Fort Ticonderoga on Lake Champlain and subsequently moved northward to seize points along the Canadian border.

When the Second Continental Congress met in May 1775, the thin line between peace and war was in danger of vanishing. Congress appointed a Virginian, George Washington, commander in chief of the provincial forces surrounding Boston. His nomination by John Adams, a Massachusetts man, revealed the determined effort of the Americans to present a united front. Congress tried to win Canada to its cause but failed. On July 6, 1775, Congress adopted the "Declaration of the Causes and Necessity of taking up Arms" in an attempt to assure fellow Britons that dissolution of the union was not intended but neither would Americans back away from their convictions. "Our cause is just. Our union is perfect. Our internal resources are great, and, if necessary, foreign assistance is undoubtedly attainable." In August 1775 the king declared that his subjects were in rebellion and began to recruit foreign mercenaries and prepare the British regulars.

During the remainder of 1775 the Americans attempted the conquest of Canada, chiefly in order to deprive Britain of a base of attack. After capturing Montreal and being repulsed at Quebec, the Americans withdrew.

Beginning in January 1776 the movement for independence gained ground. Thomas Paine published his *Common Sense,* asserting "'tis time to part." Appreciatively read by thousands upon thousands, *Common Sense* helped to crystallize opinion. By late spring a number of colonies instructed their delegates to advocate independence. On June 7, 1776, Richard Henry Lee of Virginia, once again reflecting the unity of the colonials regardless of region, introduced a resolution calling for independence. It was adopted on July 2 by such a close vote that the deliberate absence of several Pennsylvania delegates who were not convinced that independence was the best policy provided the winning margin.

The Declaration of Independence.   Action and theory were moving together. In 1774 James Wilson, later a Supreme Court justice, had published *Considerations on the Authority of Parliament,* which posed a series of questions: "And have those, whom we have hitherto been accustomed to consider as our fellow-subjects, an absolute and unlimited power over us? Have they a natural right to make laws, by which we may be deprived of our properties, of our liberties, of our lives? By what title do they claim to be our masters? . . . Do those, who embark freemen in Great Britain, disembark slaves in America?" Wilson answered by affirming, without qualification, that Parliament had no authority over the colonies. Their dependence upon Britain was exclusively through the crown; the colonies were "different members of the British

Empire . . . , independent of each other, but connected together under the same sovereign."

Wilson's assumption underlay the philosophy of the Declaration of Independence. The colonists directed the entire document against the king; nowhere is Parliament mentioned.

The Continental Congress could have separated from Britain by means of a simple declarative resolution; an elaborate document to explain the reason for revolution was unnecessary. That such a document was written is in itself an insight into the nature of the Revolution, for it was not of tattered flags, of starved and desperate people, or of lawlessness. Its leadership included some of the most substantial and prominent men in America. Because of their influential position and their regard for law, these men and their associates felt a deep need to explain to a "candid world" why they took such a drastic step.

Five delegates of the Continental Congress, among them John Adams and Benjamin Franklin, were assigned the task of writing the Declaration, but the draft was composed by Thomas Jefferson of Virginia. Modest changes were made by the members of the committee, and the document was then debated in Congress, where additional alterations were made.

The philosophy upon which the Declaration was based was that which underlay treatises written by John Locke on the occasion of the English Glorious Revolution of 1688; the similarity in ideas and even in phraseology is striking. The Declaration appealed to the highest authority within the intellectual structure of the eighteenth century, "the Laws of Nature and Nature's God." It asserted that all men are created equal, that each person is endowed with certain rights that cannot be set aside, that included among these rights are "life, liberty, and the pursuit of happiness." What this felicitous phrase meant was to be defined more carefully later in state and national constitutions. But the Declaration reaffirmed what Americans in their experience had long practiced: that governments, based upon the consent of the governed, are established to secure these rights. The king, the symbol of the British government, failed to honor his obligation; the Declaration included a list of specific charges that add up to a devastating indictment, too often treated by historians as an excuse or a rationalization for an act already taken. With the acceptance of the Declaration by the Continental Congress, the British view that the rights of the colonies depended on the sufferance of the royal grace and favor was forever demolished.

The Declaration operated as a divisive as well as a unifying force. Colonials were finally required to choose the side they wished to support—to remain loyal to Britain or to select the path of Revolution. It was not an easy choice by any means. A number of men who had firmly supported the colonial position throughout the crises, became Loyalists. In fact, more people proportionately left the colonies because of the consequences of the Declaration than were to flee France at the time of the French Revolution.

With the Declaration, the character of the conflict changed. Whereas the colonials had been secretly soliciting aid from France since 1775, the Continental Congress, representing an independent people, now established ministries throughout Europe to obtain recognition and help for the United States. Washington, who had been leading a militia force to obtain recognition of the rights of colonials, now headed an army fighting for American independence. Thirteen colonies became thirteen states with the problem of working out appropriate constitutions. Facing the experience of union, the Americans also had to work out an acceptable constitutional structure for the national government. With the Declaration, the Continental Congress was no longer an extralegal body of rebels but the symbol of a sovereign nation.

The Internal Revolution. Emphasis has been placed on the principal issue— what were the limits of the power of Parliament?—but historians have investigated a second question: Within each colony, who was to possess authority? Their point of view has ranged widely on this question. Some have insisted that the issue of who was going to rule at home was preeminent, that the break with Britain was brought about by radical dissenters within each colony who were so anxious to overthrow the power structure in their colony that they worked for revolution to accomplish this purpose. Other historians contend that those who held power in the late colonial period wished to preserve it and that they were willing to fight to maintain it.

The present consensus among historians is perhaps best expressed as follows: Conflicts within individual colonies contributed to the coming of the Revolution because men hoped to correct grievances under a new regime. However, this internal struggle for control was not the decisive or preeminent force. The principal issue was the conflict over the constitutional framework of the empire. Even without an internal struggle, the Revolution would have occurred. The internal grievances are related, however, to later developments in the revolutionary and post-revolutionary periods as Americans set about to resolve their own problems.

PROSECUTING THE WAR

Continental Congress. To make independence a reality, the war had to be won. Though the Continental Congress had neither a specific grant of authority nor a fixed constitutional basis until 1781, it resolved financial, military, diplomatic, and constitutional questions during this critical period. Occasionally, action lagged and arguments centered upon trivialities, but Congress should be remembered for its major achievements rather than for its minor failures. It unified the American war effort and fashioned an instrument of national government without violating individual liberty and without producing dissension so divisive as to splinter the Revolution. Most of America's greatest leaders served at one time or another in the Congress, gaining their first political experience at the national rather than at the colony-state level.

Revolutionary Finance. One of the early problems facing Congress was how to finance the war. Four major methods were used: Loan Office Certificates, the equivalent of present-day government bonds; requisitions, that is, requests for money and later supplies from individual states; foreign loans, which were insignificant until 1781; and paper currency.

The first issues of paper money were made by Congress before the Declaration of Independence. This avenue of revenue was one that had been used by many colonies during the colonial period. At first the paper money circulated at its face value, but as more money was issued, its value declined (although intermittently the value of the currency increased when successful military operations revived hopes for a quick victory). By the spring of 1781 the value had declined so precipitously that paper currency cost more to print than it was worth once it was printed. Up to that point, however, paper money paid for no less than 75 percent of the cost of the war. After 1781 foreign loans became especially important, because these loans provided capital for the establishment of a national bank, the Bank of North America, from which the government borrowed money in excess of the bank's capitalization. After 1781, Morris Notes—a form of paper currency backed by the word of Robert Morris, the Super-intendent of Finance—helped to restore the public credit. At the conclusion of the war the national government as well as the various states had incurred a substantial debt that was to figure in the movement to write the federal Constitution of 1787.

Military Strategy.   The British did not take advantage of their most promising military strategy until 1782, when, too late, they managed to blockade all the American ports. An intensive blockade, if it had been coordinated with swift, devastating land campaigns to lay waste the resources of the Americans, might have brought success, for the British, in order to win, had to demand unconditional surrender. The Americans, to be successful, needed an army in the field as a symbol of resistance. Any negotiations automatically recognized the United States as an independent nation because a sovereign power does not negotiate with rebels.

The first military operations of the British were concentrated in the Middle states, with an eye to dividing the United States physically, crippling its unity, and exploiting the possibility of support from American Loyalists. When this failed, the emphasis shifted to the Southern theater of operations beginning in 1780.

Slavery and the Revolution.   The policy of enlisting blacks in the Continental forces changed throughout the course of the war. At the beginning of the fighting the Continental army and most state militias accepted black enlistments, both slaves and freemen. Prince Estabrook, a black, fought at Lexington, for example, and Peter Salem fought at Lexington, Concord, and Bunker Hill. One Rhode Island regiment included 125 blacks, of whom 30 were freemen.

Early attitudes changed. A Council of War convened by General Washington in Massachusetts in October 1775 decided not to accept further enlistment of blacks because other troops, especially those from the South, refused to accept them as equals. Free blacks protested to Washington, and in December 1775 he ordered the reopening of enlistments to free blacks. Meanwhile, he requested the Continental Congress to review the issue. In January 1776 Congress ruled that free blacks who had already served could reenlist, but other blacks, whether slave or free, were excluded. The pattern set by the Continental army was followed by state militias.

The British attitude fluctuated as much as that of the American provincials. The British recognized that recruiting slaves would cripple the planter colonies, so they promised freedom in exchange for service. They offered indentured servants the same promise. When planters found their slaves leaving to answer the British call, they became alarmed and angry. In Virginia slave patrols were doubled to catch runaways. Each planter in the Southern colonies tended to keep a sharper eye on the men and women in bondage.

Toward the end of 1776 and early in 1777, Continental policy changed once again. Blacks were recruited for the Continental and state navies. The state of Maryland enlisted blacks in its militia, and even the Virginia militia was willing to accept blacks. By 1779 the Continental Congress recommended that South Carolina and Georgia raise a military force of five thousand black soldiers. Owners of slaves who enlisted were to be compensated, and the slaves in return would receive freedom and $50 in cash. The two states rejected the recommendation, but enlistment of blacks did grow in the North. In 1781 Baron Von Closen found that one fourth of the encampment of soldiers at White Plains was composed of blacks.

A few faltering steps were taken toward emancipation during the war years. In 1780 Pennsylvania provided for the gradual abolition of slavery. In 1784 Connecticut and Rhode Island followed Pennsylvania's lead, and soon thereafter New York and New Jersey followed suit. In 1783 the Supreme Court of Massachusetts ruled that the phrase "men are created free and equal" meant what it said, thereby freeing slaves in that state. In contrast, a proposal in the Maryland legislature to free slaves lost by a vote of 32 to 22. Significantly, no grand plan of emancipation was adopted anywhere in the new nation.

The reason was largely the attitude of the white man toward the black man. Jefferson, in a public statement called *The Summary View,* acknowledged that slaves should be freed, but he also declared that blacks were inferior human beings. He could never bring himself to free his own slaves, even though Washington eventually did. The fear of living with blacks as equals, the loss of property, and the social consequences paralyzed the movement to free the slaves. So the possibility faded, to be taken up again by a later generation that resolved the issue on the battlefield.

The War in the North. Washington forced the British under General Sir William Howe to abandon Boston by capturing Dorchester Heights in March 1776. Howe loaded his troops on transports and sailed to Nova Scotia to prepare for an attack on New York. He took with him more than a thousand Loyalists who preferred residence in Canada to independence from Great Britain. In an effort to prevent Howe's taking New York, Washington moved south and occupied Brooklyn Heights on Long Island. There on August 27, 1776, Howe with an army of thirty-three thousand attacked and defeated Washington, who withdrew to Manhattan Island. After the British had occupied New York, Washington retreated to New Jersey. British troops continued to occupy the city for the duration of the Revolution.

With an army that seemed destined to disappear entirely at times—it once dwindled to three thousand men—Washington could not hope to recapture New York or prevent the British from making further advances. Only the stupidity or laziness of General Howe prevented the annihilation of the American forces. But Washington managed to keep the semblance of an army together and on two occasions won startling victories over British units. On Christmas night, 1776, he crossed the

Delaware, fell on a garrison of Hessian troops at Trenton, and captured or killed most of them. Again, on January 3, he won a small battle at Princeton and marched with his army to Morristown, where he established winter quarters.

In 1777 Howe bestirred himself sufficiently to send an army by sea against Philadelphia. Washington proceeded overland south of Philadelphia and met units of Howe's army at Brandywine Creek on September 11, 1777, suffering defeat after being badly outmaneuvered. Howe entered Philadelphia with ease, but British units were severely tested when Washington launched an unexpected counterattack at Germantown on October 4. Though the American army was defeated, its offensive spirit aided the cause of independence at home and in France.

In the meantime the British had planned a three-pronged attack to capture the Hudson valley and thus isolate New England from the colonies to the south. From Canada, General Sir John Burgoyne was to push southward down Lake Champlain and the upper Hudson with the expectation of joining Howe moving up the Hudson from New York City; Burgoyne would then join Howe in an attack on Philadelphia and the occupation of other rebel territory to the south. But Howe received conflicting orders and decided that the immediate capture of Philadelphia was more urgent than cooperating with Burgoyne. Burgoyne had also expected to converge with a third British force (mostly Loyalists and Indians) moving eastward from Lake Ontario along the Mohawk valley, but this force was beaten back by American troops at the Battle of Oriskany. Nevertheless, throughout the summer of 1777 Burgoyne pressed southward toward Albany. At last, failing to receive aid from either Howe or the force from Lake Ontario, he suffered complete defeat in two battles fought near Saratoga; and on October 17, 1777, he surrendered his entire army of 5800 men to American General Horatio Gates. Thus ended the British hope of isolating New England by occupying the Hudson valley.

European Aid to the Americans.   The victory over Burgoyne and the Battle of Germantown had significant political results. They indicated to European politicians that the Americans could win independence and that British power could be crippled by the loss. France, of course, was anxious for revenge upon its ancient enemy, and the efforts of American diplomats in Paris now began to bear fruit. Benjamin Franklin proved a most effective ambassador to France. Wearing a fur cap as the symbol of republican and frontier simplicity, he soon became the toast of Paris and made friends with those politicians best able to help the American cause. On February 6, 1778, he consummated an alliance with France. Since Spain was at this time closely allied with France, America expected aid from Spain, but these hopes were never fulfilled. Eager to gain the access to American markets which Great Britain had long prevented, Holland also provided aid, largely in the form of loans underwritten by the French. France immediately supplied limited funds to aid the American cause and in 1780 dispatched troops and ships. French ports were now opened to such war vessels as the Americans had, and privateers could attack British vessels and stand a better chance of getting away to a safe haven. The French navy provided sea power that the colonies had previously lacked. European aid, prompted by self-interest, contributed to the American victory.

MAJOR REVOLUTIONARY CAMPAIGNS

New Campaigns in the North. The winter of 1778 was a bitter one for Washington. His army went into winter quarters at Valley Forge, not far from Philadelphia, where Howe and the British were quartered. Because the British could pay in gold, farmers kept them supplied with everything they could want, while Washington's troops nearly starved and went barefoot in the snow, not because supplies were unavailable but because their distribution was badly administered.

Howe, notorious for his dilatoriness, was relieved by Sir Henry Clinton, who evacuated Philadelphia and returned to New York for a new campaign in the North.

Washington, without the power to inflict defeat, could only hang on the flanks of the British army. He established a base at White Plains, New York, and saw to it that West Point on the Hudson was fortified. The arrival off New York of a French naval force under Count d'Estaing did little to help the American cause, for D'Estaing showed little audacity and soon sailed away to the West Indies. Only from the western frontier was the news encouraging. George Rogers Clark, leading a group of frontiersmen, helped to hold the West against the British.

The War in the South.   In the southern theater of operations the British captured Savannah (1778) and Charleston (1780) and hoped to collaborate with the Loyalists in the interior and gain control of Georgia and the Carolinas. Despite the efforts of American guerrilla bands the fate of the South remained in doubt. In August 1780 the British under Cornwallis inflicted a disastrous defeat upon American forces at Camden, South Carolina, but this defeat was redeemed in October by the destruction of a Loyalist force at the Battle of King's Mountain near the North Carolina border and the brilliant victory of Daniel Morgan and his farmer-cavalrymen at the Battle of Cowpens, South Carolina, in January 1781. These successes turned the tide in the Carolinas. Through the winter, spring, and summer of 1781, General Nathanael Greene, commander of the American army in the South, skillfully threw militia, cavalry, and guerrilla forces against the British armies. By autumn those British that had not moved north to Virginia with Cornwallis were pocketed in a small area about Charleston, South Carolina.

Battle of Yorktown.   Meanwhile, in 1780 the French dispatched an army of 5500 men under an able soldier, the Count de Rochambeau, to aid Washington. These troops encamped at Newport, while Rochambeau and Washington waited to see what success collaborative effort would bring. The Count de Grasse, a brilliant French naval commander with a well-equipped squadron, had arrived in the West Indies. After an exchange of correspondence, de Grasse decided that his squadron could attack more successfully in the Chesapeake than in the harbor of New York, so a decision was made for a coordinated land and sea attack in Virginia, where Cornwallis' army, supplemented by troops under the turncoat Benedict Arnold, was being engaged by forces led by French general Lafayette. Washington and Rochambeau began to move their armies southward, a maneuver which the British believed was a feint to catch them off guard in New York, where they expected the main attack to take place. With de Grasse controlling the Chesapeake Bay area and with a French and American force of fifteen thousand men surrounding Cornwallis' camp on the York peninsula, Cornwallis was doomed. He surrendered on October 19, 1781. As his men marched out to lay down their arms, a band played "The World Turned Upside Down." When the news of Yorktown reached Britain, the king's ministers agreed that peace must be made with the rebellious colonies.

The War in Retrospect.   The war had been a strange and at times a hopeless one for the Americans. But Washington had emerged as a persistent, determined leader. He may have lacked brilliance as a military tactician, but he had the courage, integrity, and character essential to successful command. Despite the demoralization of his forces by lack of supplies, by desertions, and occasionally by mutinies, he held on until the Americans, with French help, achieved victory.

British incompetence played a part in the eventual outcome of the war. Without the assistance that British commanders—Howe and Clinton, particularly—unwittingly gave the patriots, the end might have been different. It was the good fortune of America that Great Britain had been engaged in a world war, and that some of its best troops and more competent commanders were in India, Africa, the West Indies, and elsewhere.

Although a few young Frenchmen like Lafayette came to America to fight for the patriots out of sheer idealism, the alliance of the Bourbon powers, France and Spain, against Great Britain was not motivated by love of liberty or of the republican principles so nobly stated in the Declaration of Independence. By a trick of fate, these very principles of liberty would exercise an enormous influence in France within a few years and would overturn the French monarchy. But in the conflict between the colonies and Great Britain, France was merely playing the game of power politics. It hoped to wreak revenge on an ancient enemy and perhaps to regain some of the American territory it had lost.

Spain also had an interest in territory west of the British possessions in North America. To weaken Great Britain's strength in the New World would provide possible opportunities for later aggrandizement there for France and Spain. A weak and struggling republic without money and friends would be easy to dominate and perhaps to devour.

France had promised its satellite, Spain, that it would help wrest Gibraltar from the British, but they had attacked Gibraltar in vain. Now France proposed to appease Spain with territory west of the Appalachians. In the peace negotiations, which had begun even before Yorktown, the disposition of western territories was a critical consideration.

The Peace of Paris, 1783. To negotiate a peace with England, Congress appointed five commissioners: Benjamin Franklin, envoy in France; John Jay, American agent in Spain; John Adams, envoy in Holland; Henry Laurens; and Thomas Jefferson. Only the first three, assembled at Paris, took an active part in the discussions. At the outset, Jay was suspicious of the motives of the Count de Vergennes, the French foreign minister, and of the British agent, Richard Oswald. Oswald came with instructions to treat with the commissioners as if they represented rebellious colonies. Jay insisted that Oswald go back and obtain new instructions to treat with the representatives of the "Thirteen United States," which would be tantamount to recognizing at the outset the independence of the new republic. This Oswald did.

Although the commissioners had received from Congress full power to negotiate the best treaty possible, Congress had specifically instructed them to take no steps that France would not approve. Since Jay was convinced that France was determined to sacrifice American interests to satisfy Spain, he persuaded Adams and Franklin to deal secretly with England and to make a preliminary treaty that promised favorable terms. The news leaked out and Vergennes was incensed, but Franklin, a great favorite of the French, managed to placate him by admitting that their action was merely an "indiscretion." Nevertheless, the preliminary treaty had established the pattern for the final treaty, which was signed on September 3, 1783.

Great Britain, partly to sow dissension between the Bourbon allies and partly to win the friendship of the late colonies and to keep them from becoming satellites of France, offered such favorable terms that Vergennes in anger declared that the English were ready to "buy peace rather than make it." Instead of letting Spain have the trans-Appalachian region, Great Britain agreed that the Mississippi should be the western boundary of the United States. Although Franklin had tried to obtain all of Canada "to insure peace," it was agreed that the Great Lakes should determine the northern border. In the end, Great Britain gave the Floridas back to Spain, and, in accordance with the treaty, the southern border of the United States was set at 31° north latitude. The provisions of the treaty seemed clear, but in some areas the boundary lines were not definitely stated. In Maine the border remained in dispute for years.

The treaty also provided that American citizens were to enjoy the same fishing rights in Canadian waters as British subjects. The two countries agreed that the Mississippi River would be forever open to navigation by both American and British shipping. The British demanded restitution of Loyalist property confiscated during the war, but all Congress could do was to recommend that this be done. Since Congress had no authority over the states, it was agreed that suits might be brought by British subjects in the state courts for the recovery of debts. The Treaty of Paris was ratified by Congress on January 14, 1784.

EFFECTS OF THE WAR

Unrestricted Trade.　Wars traditionally result in social and financial upheavals, and the American Revolution was no exception. Within the twenty years of controversy and war, old and settled traditions were altered, and the patterns of a new society emerged.

No longer were the American colonies the source of raw materials supplied exclusively to Great Britain, as had been the case in colonial times. Dutch, French, Spanish, and Portuguese ships could slip into American ports and load tobacco, wheat, corn, meat, rice, and other products needed in Europe. Despite the war—even as a result of it—some American merchants made more money than ever before, and some European commodities, received in exchange for produce, were more abundant during the war than previously.

A few fortunes were made by war profiteers, but, more important, a network of colonial merchants experienced the challenges and problems of unrestricted trade on an international scale. Patriotism did not keep dealers from making 200 or 300 percent profit on clothing and supplies needed by the Continental soldiers. New industries, particularly war industries, developed. Iron foundries multiplied. Gunsmiths flourished, and factories for the manufacture of muskets, gunpowder, and cannon were built, particularly in New England and in Pennsylvania. Since the usual trade in English woolens and other fabrics was cut off, cloth making was encouraged.

The Westward Movement.　With the elimination of the prohibition against

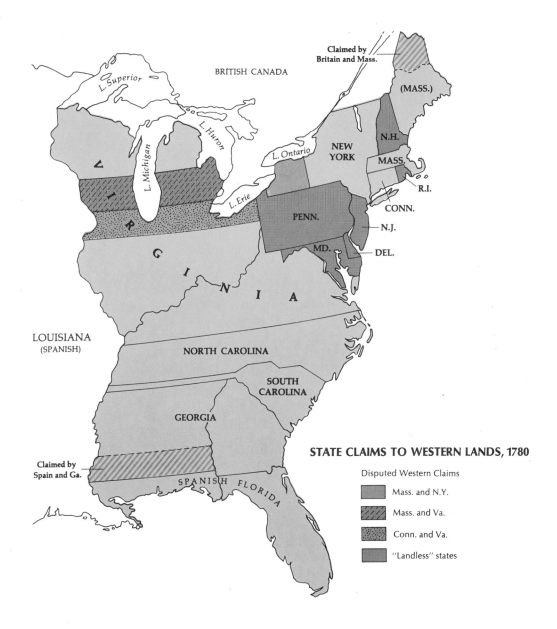

BRITISH CANADA

L. Superior

L. Michigan

L. Huron

L. Ontario

L. Erie

V I R G I N I A

LOUISIANA
(SPANISH)

Claimed by
Spain and Ga.

SPANISH FLORIDA

Claimed by
Britain and Mass.

(MASS.)

N.H.

NEW
YORK

MASS.

R.I.

CONN.

PENN.

N.J.

MD.

DEL.

NORTH CAROLINA

SOUTH
CAROLINA

GEORGIA

STATE CLAIMS TO WESTERN LANDS, 1780

Disputed Western Claims

- Mass. and N.Y.
- Mass. and Va.
- Conn. and Va.
- "Landless" states

movement into the trans-Appalachian region that the British had tried to enforce after 1763, fresh migrations began. Frontiersmen were soon filtering into valleys and clearings beyond the mountains. In 1776 Virginia had organized into a county a portion of what later became the state of Kentucky. Before the Revolution, frontiersmen from Virginia had settled on the Watauga River in what became Tennessee. After the Revolution, uprooted citizens and restless souls all along the frontier began a trek west that would continue until one day the whole of the American continent would be occupied. Land companies were organized, and within a few years speculation in western lands became an obsession.

Modifications of American Society.   Socially, the Revolution brought changes. The most immediate result was the elimination of royal governors, other British officials, and the cliques of socially elite that gathered about them. Even in colonies having no royal officials, those who were subservient to the mother country were swept out and new men took their places.

Yet as important as these changes were, the United States nowhere experienced the kind of social revolution that swept France a few years later. The structure of American society was modified rather than radically altered. In Virginia, for example, the influence of the tidewater aristocrats diminished somewhat, and back-country politicians of the type represented by Patrick Henry gained power; but the families that had produced leaders before the Revolution still continued to supply many of the leaders in the new nation.

One reason the new republic moved with relative ease from the status of a colony to that of a self-governing nation was the tradition of local responsibility established in all of the colonies early in the development of the British settlements. This inheritance from the British tradition of local self-government ensured a reservoir of leadership from which individuals could be drawn for any level of responsibility required.

Soon after the Declaration of Independence, a committee was appointed to draw up Articles of Confederation to bind the thirteen states together into a union. It took more than a year to draft the Articles, and they then had to be submitted to the states for ratification. This took until the spring of 1781. Among the most important contributions of the Articles were their preservation of the union and their definition of powers to be granted to the central government as opposed to the state governments. The operation of the Articles, together with the formation and operation of state governments, is more properly the subject of Chapter 4 on the postwar period.

During almost the entire war—that is, until 1781—the rebel colonies operated under the authority of the extralegal Continental Congress; the delay in ratifying the Articles of Confederation was due chiefly to a conflict of economic interests. Massachusetts, Connecticut, New York, Virginia, Georgia, and the Carolinas—under the terms of colonial charters, royal grants, Indian treaties, or proprietary claims— asserted ownership of tremendous grants of lands in the West. To be able to retain these western lands would be a great economic boon; sale of the back regions would provide the state governments with a steady income and make it unnecessary for them to tax their citizens at all. Naturally the advantage that would come to states with western land claims was resented by the states with fixed boundaries. They protested that the War for Independence was being fought for the benefit of all and that every state should share in the rewards to be found in western territory. Thus these landless states were reluctant to sign the Articles of Confederation until the westward limits of the existing states were set and until Congress, the central government, was given authority to grant lands and to create new states beyond these limits.

The debate was not motivated entirely by the question of the equality of the states. Land speculators had formed companies in Maryland and Pennsylvania, for example, and had made purchases from the Indians in the Ohio valley. Now they wished governmental validation of their titles, but how could they secure clear title to land claimed by Virginia and New York when such states were inclined not to recognize the Indian purchases made by out-of-state residents?

Eventually, after considerable political maneuvering and propagandizing, both sides gave in. Between 1777 and 1781 the land companies vacated their claims to western territory purchased from the Indians, and upon recommendation of a congressional committee in 1780, the landed states, led by Virginia, New York, and Connecticut, gave up claim to most of the trans-Appalachian country, thus making the western lands the territory of the nation. In February 1781 the last of the landless states, Maryland, ratified the Articles, and on March 1 the Confederation was formally proclaimed. The problem of western lands was now placed squarely before the new central government (see Chapter 4 for a discussion of western lands and Indian policy during the early years of the Republic).

When the war was over, many thoughtful citizens throughout the country feared that the loose provisions of the Articles of Confederation would not permit the evolution of a nation strong enough to survive. For example, in foreign policy much depended upon the power of a centralized authority. Furthermore, a central authority was required to establish the financial stability of the nation and to deal with problems of credit, the issuance of money, and the maintenance of national defense—functions beyond the capacity of individual states. These problems and their solution would form an important chapter in constitution making.

A final word should be said about the American Revolution not only as a symbol in the history of the United States but as a guiding light for generations of people the world over. As the first anti-imperialist, anti-monarchial revolution of modern times, the American Revolution inspired imitators in Europe and Latin America in the nineteenth century and in Africa and Asia in the twentieth. The principles of revolution—government by consent of the governed, the inviolate rights of mankind that no government can invade—spoke to the hearts and minds of people in other nations and other lands.

The fact was and the fact is that the American Revolution is not exportable. Other people and other nations are the products of their own particular circumstances and experience. But the language, the idealism, the ideas—these take on a life of their own.

CHAPTER 3

PATTERNS OF COLONIAL CULTURE

COLONIAL SOCIAL STRUCTURE

Influences on Cultural Development. In intellectual and social life, as in political and economic life, the first English settlers shared the attitudes, ambitions, and habits of thought of their peers in the home country. During the colonial period, however, these characteristics were modified—in part because of the changing intellectual life of England, which affected the colonies in a variety of ways, and in part because the men and women born and educated in America knew at first hand only the ways of their colonial countrymen. They experienced English culture and English intellectual currents second-hand. Furthermore, the immigration of non-English peoples brought added diversity and dimension to the provincial social and intellectual scene. An evaluation of the degree of distinctiveness of American culture depends on the relative weight placed upon those elements—English, American, and non-English. Because individual historians have placed different emphasis upon these factors, their judgments have differed; but all agree that conditions in the New World influenced social and intellectual development.

English Society. In Elizabethan England, the top level of society consisted of noble families, whose position depended upon extensive land holdings and the favors which accrued to a privileged segment of society. The nobility was not quite a closed circle: younger sons who did not inherit a substantial estate or title generally sought their fortunes through the life of the gentry, through commerical connections, or through the professions; and it was possible for a highly successful entrepreneur to penetrate the nobility, though full-fledged acceptance was often delayed for several generations.

Below the nobility ranked the gentry, the country gentlemen. The life of the gentry centered around the land; the country gentleman knew his tenants and their problems, and he experienced at first hand the vicissitudes, as well as the blessings, of farming. The gentry served as the backbone of governing authority, in part because the sovereign encouraged their participation as a shield against ambitious nobles. The gentry formed the largest group in Parliament, and they held those local offices which were mainly responsible for enforcing the statutes of the state. Marriage alliances between gentry and commerical families were fairly frequent, and gentry families contributed younger sons to trade, to adventure, to the military, to the church, and sometimes to the universities.

Below the gentry ranked the yeomen, who could be leaseholders, renters, or owners of small estates. A yeoman was the dirt farmer of Elizabethan days, a man attached to the soil who lived a simple life and farmed with frugality. The laborers and servant classes of Elizabethan England ranked below the yeomen. A laborer might be an apprentice who in time would enter a trade and make a good living, or he might be a man who worked for daily wages and whose chances of rising to a better social and economic position were remote. In the same fashion, to be a servant could mean to serve with a gentry family in the expectation that by means of a good marriage or hard work an elevation of status could be secured, or it could involve the meanest kind of position, from which no escalation of status seemed possible.

The Transplanted Social Structure.   The English social structure was not transplanted intact to America. Members of the English aristocracy did not come to America; because they were relatively content and well off at home, they had no incentive to migrate to a primitive New World wilderness. Occasionally, younger sons of noble families came to America to try their fortune, but even this element was rare.

For the other end of the social structure—day laborers and servants—migration to the New World was restricted, since the impoverished were unable to pay transportation costs. But servants were transported by the gentry class, and as the system of indentured servitude became widespread after the mid-seventeenth century, laborers sometimes took advantage of the system and migrated.

The first settlers, then, were principally drawn from the yeomanry and the gentry, the latter bringing servants with them. At the outset, these class divisions were scrupulously maintained. In early Massachusetts, to cite an illustration, a laborer's wife who appeared at church wearing a frock or hat of a quality that, in the eyes of the elders, exceeded the social station of laborer was severely admonished. (For the role of women in early America, see pp. 131–33.)

Influence of the American Environment.   Modifications in this structure during the colonial period gave rise to a social structure indigenous to English America. The gradual growth of a system of indentured servitude enabled people without money to emigrate to America, where they usually became yeoman farmers or free laborers. Men who arrived as hired servants or as yeomen sometimes acquired substantial estates through industry or good fortune. Ships' captains who brought immigrants to certain colonies claimed headrights—an allotment of fifty acres of land for each person transported—and these grants formed the nucleus around which some landed estates were formed. Labor was so scarce that a skilled workman not only could make a good living but also could become an employer. Men of modest means who engaged in trade built up strong mercantile firms, and wealth brought an elevation of social status and often political power.

Among the most important determinants of social position in America was the possession of land, and its very abundance helped to encourage a more mobile society. Nowhere was this more clearly demonstrated than in the Chesapeake colonies. In the first century of settlement the vast majority of the settlers in Virginia and Maryland were yeomen or indentured servants who were able to rise to the status of yeomen after completing their term of servitude. During various crises of the seventeenth century, especially during the Puritan ascendency in England of the 1640s and 1650s and immediately after the restoration of the Stuart monarchy in 1660, members of gentry families or, more rarely, younger sons of noble families migrated to Virginia, but they acted as no more than leaven to the loaf. The Virginia gentry class that gradually emerged was made up primarily of men who had risen to this status in America. It was not a gentry group transplanted to America.

By the late seventeenth and early eighteenth centuries, the Virginia gentry were imitating their English counterparts by participating in gaming, riding, and sports; by encouraging leisurely learning, an indulgence in books, and an amateur interest in science and writing; by serving as the leading political group; by opening their doors to travelers, in part because the stranger brought news and thus was welcome, and in part because offering such hospitality was the mark of a gentleman; and by belonging to the established Anglican church and serving as vestrymen.

The colonial elite which evolved in each colony was composed of families who had, over several generations, gained wealth in America—through the acquisition of land, through trade, or through business operations. The pinnacle of Virginia society—except for the governor and a limited number of crown appointees—was made up of the gentry.

In summary, the structure of colonial society differed from that of English society in three important respects. First, the top level of English society—the nobility—was shorn off by the process of transplantation. Second, although some of the structure of American society had its counterpart in England—the gentry and the yeomanry, for example—the composition of American classes was not the result of direct transplants from England. Third, the structure of society in America reflected somewhat different contours from that in England. In America there were more slaves who were condemned to perpetual servitude and who had little if any mobility; but there were fewer servants, because the opportunities to acquire land and other forms of wealth were so abundant. American society ranged, therefore, from the colonial elite—the important merchants in Massachusetts and Rhode Island, the planters along the Chesapeake and in the Carolinas, and the large landholders in New York and Pennsylvania—to the small farmers and skilled workmen, to the unskilled workmen and servants, and finally, at the base, to the slaves.

The special contours of American society also reflected a modification of professional opportunities. A man in England could always advance professionally through the church, the military, or the law. In America, the church in New England offered an avenue for advancement for a time, but by the eighteenth century a man looking for advancement generally sought out land and commerce, not the church. Moreover, Americans, accustomed to their special militia forces, could not advance professionally through the naval or military service. In America, a man who had already achieved status as a merchant or landholder was placed in command of a colonial expedition.

Not until the 1730s and 1740s did the practice of law gain sufficient status to become an avenue for advancement. In earlier periods, merchants and landholders frequently served as their own lawyers. Only as colonial society became more sophisticated did the practice of law become a profession. A number of colonials, some of whom were already in a substantial social position—James Otis and John Adams in New England, John Dickinson in the Middle colonies, and Patrick Henry and Charles Pinckney in the Southern colonies—improved their status by becoming expert in the practice of law.

The seed of American society was English, but the American environment dramatically affected its growth. Its evolution, as a result, was distinctive, not a replica.

THE SOCIAL CONSEQUENCES OF SLAVERY

Slavery was introduced into the American colonies early in the seventeenth century, with the arrival in Virginia of a ship carrying blacks from Africa in 1619, but the fateful, enduring consequences of slavery did not take shape until late in the century. The episode of 1619 represented the further enlargement of the slave trade which had operated in Africa for three or four centuries and which had entered the experience of the New World when the Spanish imported African slaves to work in the mines and fields of New Spain.

Throughout English America, however, the white indentured servant dominated the lower reaches of the social system during the seventeenth century. In 1671, for example, Governor Berkeley of Virginia estimated that the colony's population was 82 percent free white, 13 percent indentured servants, and 5 percent slaves. In proportion to their population, Rhode Island and New York imported slaves at a rate equal to that of Virginia.

Between 1690 and 1730 the slave population in the Southern colonies escalated at an astonishing rate. The slave population of Virginia was reported to be 2000 in 1670; 6000 in 1700; and 12,000 in 1708. By 1750 the slave population in South Carolina was estimated to be 39,000, the white population only 25,000.

Several factors help explain this sudden change. Fertile land, a generous land policy, and freedom of religion in the Middle colonies, especially Pennsylvania, early in the eighteenth century encouraged white indentured servants to settle there rather than in the Southern colonies. Meanwhile, the Southern colonies were undergoing a westward movement of their own. To cultivate the newly opened land, the Southern planters needed an inexpensive labor force and solved their problem by increasing the importation of slaves. England assisted in this by vigorously pushing the slave trade.

Immediate Consequences.   The social consequences, then and in the years ahead, were devastating. Elaborate codes for the conduct of slaves were officially enacted. Slaves were declared property by colonial statute. The slaves, who brought with them an African culture of which the planters were only slightly aware, clashed with the white population. The period was marked by slave revolts, some of which, like the Stono Rebellion in South Carolina, stunned the white population. Fear of slave revolts caused the political leaders to take defensive measures. Laws were passed restricting slave importation and encouraging the importation of white indentured servants, and white settlements on the frontier were promoted as protection for the older slave-centered communities.

Long-term Consequences. The most enduring result of slavery was to set blacks to one side in the social strata and, with minor exceptions, to condemn them to perpetual bondage. The black was deprived of those particular benefits that are often listed as peculiarly American—the chance to improve one's position, the opportunity to provide a better life for one's children, the dictum that hard work is rewarded by success. Slavery excluded the black from the American tradition.

The eighteenth century, therefore, witnessed a strange spectacle: there was a developing consciousness with respect to the definition of political liberty, consummated by the American Revolution, while at the same time perpetual bondage was being inflicted upon a vast number of men and women, the black Americans, who came to the colonies under compulsion. This duality has not yet been fully resolved.

THE AGE OF FAITH

In America's intellectual and religious life, as in its social structure, English ideas and practices transplanted to the New World were modified by the unique American environment.

The late sixteenth and early seventeenth centuries in England were an Age of Faith, and the characteristics of this age were indelibly stamped upon the English colonies in America. The Protestant Reformation in Europe had unleashed a flood of ideas concerning the role of the church, qualifications for church membership, and man's relationship to God—particularly the degree of man's freedom of will. Were individual men elected by God and thus saved from eternal damnation? Or could men win salvation through individual faith and the exercise of free will? The Englishman of the early seventeenth century was endlessly concerned with points of doctrine like these.

Puritanism in England. When Henry viii broke with the Roman Catholic Church and established the Church of England, of which he, as king, served as the head, specific church practice and doctrine were little altered. But within the Anglican Church, opposition groups that became known as Puritans gradually emerged. In varying degrees, they protested against practices of the Church of England. All Puritans agreed that to become a member of God's elect an individual must undergo a "conversion experience," in which he sensed a spiritual rebirth; and most agreed that certain rituals within the church service should be changed (for example, inspired, extemporaneous prayers should replace the traditional formal prayers). Puritans definitely disagreed, however, on the question of church government.

One group, the Presbyterian Puritans, followed the precepts of John Calvin. They believed in a close church-state relationship in which policies would be established by the ruling hierarchy and, once adopted, would be enforced among the individual congregations. In addition, the Presbyterian Puritans believed that the church should include the nonelect as well as the elect, since mortal man was not capable of knowing with certainty whom God had elected for salvation.

A second group of Puritans were the Non-Conforming Congregationalists. They believed, first of all, that a church should be composed only of the elect and that such men and women could be identified. In their view the invisible church, God's elect, and the visible church, the church in daily operation, were one. The Non-Conforming Congregational Puritans held that individual congregations should rule themselves and that church doctrine and practice should be enforced by the individual congregation, not by a superior church hierarchy. Both these groups of Puritans—the Presbyterians and the Congregationalists—were willing to remain within the Church of England and to carry out their reforms, their "religious revolution," within the structure of the established church.

It would be a mistake to assume that in England Puritans and conforming Anglicans were directly opposed. Actually, they shared many of the same convictions: that man was sinful, to be liberated only by God's grace and saved by faith rather than by deeds; that a learned ministry was required to find Biblical truth; and that God conversed with man through His revealed word, the Bible.

A group closely related to the Puritans—though less influential—were the Non-Conforming Congregational Separatists. As their name indicates, these people held many of the same views as the Non-Conforming Congregational Puritans; they agreed that the invisible and visible church were one and that individual congregations should enforce church doctrine and practice. But they differed on one vital matter. The Separatists believed that reforming the Church of England was an impossible task, so they wished to separate from the church. In the eyes of the king, their views were particularly dangerous, because by following their religious inclinations they were in effect repudiating the king as head of the church; their religious-intellectual position, therefore, carried with it strong political implications.

Puritanism in America. The people who settled in New England were the Non-Conforming Separatists, a small, uninfluential group who founded Plymouth, and the Non-Conforming Congregational Puritans, who founded Massachusetts Bay and spread throughout New England. That the Puritans settling New England were of the nonconforming sect is an important factor, because these New England Puritans for more than a half century fought savagely against any evidence of Puritan Presbyterianism. Unlike the Presbyterians, the New England Puritans were convinced that the church should not include the unregenerate as well as the regenerate, the nonelect as well as the elect.

Although Puritanism was to have a dramatic career in England, where the Presbyterian Puritans, at least for a time, gained strength, in America Puritan ideas were transformed into a distinct social organization only in New England. The Puritans there conceived of themselves as a covenanted people. In essence, the "covenant theology" held that God made a contract with man setting down the terms of salvation. God pledged himself to abide by these terms. This covenant in no way changed the doctrine that God elected the saints, but it explained why certain people were elected and others were not. How did a person know that he was numbered among the elect? By experiencing God's grace and reflecting this regeneration before his peers.

Because the terms of the covenant were to be found in the Bible, the Bible became the rule of conduct and was constantly searched for meaning and interpretation. Because of the covenant, each law, each act, each policy demanded literal Biblical support.

Believing in the vigorous use of reason, the Puritans supported the idea of a highly trained clergy and a literate laity. Although several leaders conceded that laymen might find subtle theological points difficult to follow, they agreed that all churchmen should attempt to master the contours of theological inquiry. The Puritans firmly opposed all religious enthusiasms or any evidence of self-revelation (the doctrine that God revealed himself directly to an individual). For this reason, both the Puritans and the Anglicans abhorred the Quakers. The "inner light" which, the Quakers claimed, involved a mystical force and a direct communication between God and man was, to the New England Puritans, offensive, as they demonstrated when they hanged several Quakers who refused to leave Massachusetts Bay.

The New England Puritans turned to congregationalism as a form of church government, but they attempted informally to retain close ties among the individual congregations by means of synods, or assemblies of delegates, which discussed and decided ecclesiastical affairs. Theoretically, each congregation could select its own course of action, but in practice a consensus of the Puritan leaders usually determined the course. It would be a mistake to think that the Puritan clergy were all-powerful; indeed, conformity to Puritan beliefs was enforced by civil authority. Lay leaders like John Winthrop, not the leading ministers, were primarily responsible for the banishment of colonials who protested against the Puritan doctrines.

The premises of New England Puritanism affected every sphere of life—political, economic, cultural, social, and intellectual. For example, land was distributed to church congregations so that a social-religious community could be created and sustained. Settlement by towns enabled the Puritans to center their lives and activities around the church, and designated practice could easily be enforced. With the Puritans in political control and thus able to determine those groups who were to receive land grants, the objective of creating a Bible Commonwealth could be achieved.

Equally important was the impact of Puritanism upon education and literature. Because the Puritans firmly believed in a rational religion, they soon began to think about establishing a center of higher learning to continue the tradition of a learned ministry untainted by divergent strains of theology. The upshot was the founding of Harvard College in 1636. At first a Harvard education consisted of two years of relatively rigorous training. Harvard's principal aim was to produce a trained ministry, but because its curriculum was based upon a broad training in the humanities, with emphasis on the classics, it served in addition to light the lamp of learning in the New World. There were no other institutions of higher learning in the colonies until the College of William and Mary was founded in 1693, and this college failed to provide an active program until the eighteenth century.

The premise of a reasoned religion also called for a literate laity, and the New England Puritans responded by enacting legislation for the establishment of a school system. Town settlements made schools practical; in 1642 an act was passed which required every town of fifty or more householders to establish an "elementary school" to teach the fundamentals of reading and writing. An enactment of 1647 required each community of one hundred householders or more to provide a "grammar school," a school to prepare students for college by means of vigorous instruction in the Greek and Latin classics. Historians have debated the nature of these schools, some asserting that they marked the beginning of a public school system in America, and others arguing with equal vigor that the schools were, in fact, no more than appendages of the established church. The source of funds for the schools was public, but the schools reflected the consensus of the religious community.

New England Puritans expressed themselves in prose and poetry; sometimes their tone was harsh, but it was always unmistakably clear. Sermons were cultivated as an art form and were published by the press founded in Massachusetts Bay in 1639. This press became the voice of Puritanism in America. Its productivity was fabulous; its output exceeded that of the presses of Cambridge and Oxford in England.

In addition to sermons, the press published prose and poetry. The best seller was Michael Wigglesworth's *Day of Doom,* a 224-verse epic describing the Day of Judgment. It has been estimated that *Day of Doom,* with its harsh, unrelieved cadences, was read by half the New England population.

A more attractive and enduring contribution to literature was made by Anne Bradstreet, whose sensitive verse was published in England and New England, and by the metaphysical poet Edward Taylor, whose work went unpublished until the twentieth century. The joys expressed in Taylor's religious poems and the passionate love for her husband that Mrs. Bradstreet wrote of in verses not published in her lifetime are healthy reminders that Puritans were not necessarily either grim or cold.

Books were constant companions of the Puritan fathers; most were on religious subjects, although a smattering of Latin grammars, a few histories, and some English literature were in evidence. Some of the best works of New England colonials in the seventeenth century—William Bradford's *Of Plymouth Plantation* and John Winthrop's *Journals*—were not published until modern times.

Influence of the New World Environment. During the seventeenth century, Puritanism in America was gradually modified by New World conditions. This modification took numerous forms: in theology, in church practice, and in the everyday life in shops, ships, and farms. The course of this change has been brilliantly analyzed in exacting detail by historian Perry Miller, but for purposes of this text a single example—the adoption of the Half-Way Covenant in 1662—will suffice.

The church, you will recall, was presumably made up exclusively of the elect, the covenanted people. Children of the elect, however, sometimes failed to evidence "conversion" and thereby to demonstrate the election which would qualify them for full membership within the church. As the body of church members became smaller in proportion to the total population, the clergy feared that the influence of the church in the community at large would be seriously undermined. By the terms of the Half-Way Covenant, therefore, the children of the elect who had not entered full membership in the church were nevertheless permitted to have their children baptized. Baptism enabled the children to participate in some, though not all, of the sacraments of the church. This opening wedge, which made an association with the church possible without proof of "election," was gradually widened until a number of prominent ministers advocated opening the church to those who tried to live according to the precepts of the church even though they could not prove regeneration.

The New World environment affected other areas of Puritan intellectual life as well. The intellectual vigor of Harvard College declined; its historian, Samuel Eliot Morison, marks the low point as the 1670s. Its intellectual direction became, at least to old-line Puritans, "radical," which meant that it diverted from early Puritan precepts and intellectual rigor. The enforcement of the school acts lagged, and few intellectuals of late seventeenth-century New England could match the intellectual creativity of the first-line Puritans.

Making the terms of church membership easier was also important outside intellectual life. During most of the seventeenth century only church members could vote in the colony-wide elections of Massachusetts Bay, and therefore a substantial majority of the population failed to qualify for the franchise. Thus, broadened church membership had direct political effects. In 1691 when a new charter made property ownership the basis for franchise, the Puritans lost outright control of Massachusetts, but the church as a social-religious institution was a powerful influence in New England well into the nineteenth century.

The Transplanted Anglicans.   In the Age of Faith, the Anglican Church was transplanted to Virginia; it later expanded into the Carolinas and Maryland, and in the eighteenth century to the Middle colonies and New England. In contrast to Puritanism in America, Anglicanism did not center around theological disquisitions and dogmas. The theological structure of Anglicanism was exclusively the product and concern of the clerical hierarchy within England. A highly learned Anglican ministry did not migrate to America.

As a result, the influence of the New World environment cannot be measured in terms of its modification of doctrine but in terms of its modifications of church practice and of church ceremonials. For example, the Anglican Church in England was highly centralized and carefully supervised by its hierarchy, but in America it became a decentralized church ruled by laymen. In America the Anglican vestries became so powerful that for all intents and purposes church government in practice resembled congregationalism. The clergy who migrated to America were almost impotent before the vestry, a dramatic departure from conditions in England.

The Anglican parishes in seventeenth-century America were much too large, and this, too, affected church practices. A clergyman could not readily serve his congregation when its membership was widely scattered. Laymen, therefore, began to read the services on the Sabbath, and laymen soon exercised a role in religious functions which violated the canons of the church. Because people found it difficult to travel ten or twelve miles to church on horseback or by boat, they did not appear at services. Moreover, because of the distances, weddings took place on a plantation rather than in church, and the dead were buried on the plantation in an unconsecrated family plot rather than in consecrated church ground—again a violation of church ordinances.

The absence of a guiding intellectual premise in the Chesapeake colonies dramatically affected education and literature. The scattered nature of the settlement made a community school impractical: by the time the children arrived at the schoolhouse by horseback or boat, it would be time for them to return home. Consequently, responsibility for education was placed upon the family, not upon the community, and the finances and intellectual values of an individual family determined its response.

Obviously, in comparison with the lesser folk, the Virginia gentry had a decided advantage in a plantation system which made public schools well-nigh impossible. Occasionally, when a sufficient number of plantations were proximate, Old Field Schools were founded in which the children were taught by a clergyman or by the wife of a planter. More often a family or a group of families hired an indentured servant to teach the children. With no way of obtaining an advanced education in the colony, those planters who wished their children to receive a college education sent them to England. William Byrd II, born in 1674, was educated at a grammar school in England and was later associated with mercantile firms in Holland and in London before being trained in law at the English Inns of Court. He returned to America to take his place as one of the most prominent Virginians of the seventeenth and early eighteenth centuries.

The literature read in the Chesapeake colonies was more like than unlike that read in New England, but the literary productivity was different in quantity and character. In the Chesapeake colonies, as in New England, religious books and the Bible occupied a prominent place on the reading tables. In addition, the classics, Homer's *Iliad,* Roman historians, and books on law and on medical treatment were included in many libraries. Whereas the published writings of New Englanders were profuse and almost exclusively religious in character, those of the Chesapeake region were limited and nonreligious. Robert Beverley's *History and Present State of Virginia,* originally published in 1705, consummated the literary output of the Chesapeake colonies in the seventeenth century. The direct style and illuminating observation of the *History* make it an important source for historians today.

THE EIGHTEENTH-CENTURY MIND

The Enlightenment in England.   During the seventeenth century, English intellectual life underwent a transformation triggered by the momentous advance of science and the application of the theoretical framework of science to all phases of human experience. The writings of the father of scientific reasoning, Francis Bacon, marked the beginning of a movement called the Enlightenment, which was consummated by the great scientific discoveries of Sir Isaac Newton, whose *Mathematical Principles of Natural Philosophy* (published in 1697) set forth, by precise demonstration, the laws of motion and gravitation. Newton was to the eighteenth century what Einstein is to the twentieth.

As Newton had discovered laws in the physical universe, reasoned many men, so laws must operate in the relationship between man and the universe. In summary, eighteenth-century Enlightenment thought held that God as the Prime Mover had created the universe with a perfectly operating, harmonious system of immutable laws—the laws of nature. Once the universe was created, God was inconsequential; only the immutable laws of nature were important, and they were the highest authority to which man could appeal. Belief in God as merely the Prime Mover was called deism. The laws of nature could be discovered only by reason, and therefore a premium was placed on learning and on books. Once a law was discovered, men should adjust their lives and the institutions they had created—for example, their political and educational systems—to conform with these laws. The closer the alignment between man and the laws of nature, the closer human institutions would be to perfection. In this view, man was perfectible and progress was inevitable.

It should be emphasized that the ideas of the Enlightenment affected only a small minority of Englishmen and far fewer colonials; most people went about their daily lives unaware of intellectual trends. Enlightenment ideas did not gain strong advocates in America until the mid-eighteenth century, and even then their influence was sharply restricted. In England, for example, Enlightenment ideas permeated literature as well as political thought; in America, Enlightenment ideas found expression in political thought but not in literature. The Declaration of Independence, you will recall, appeals to the "laws of nature and nature's God."

Although the Enlightenment dominated intellectual life in England, it constituted only one current in the mainstream of intellectual life in eighteenth-century America. The widespread immigration of non-English groups brought a diversity of cultures. Coming as they did from the rank and file, the non-English immigrants were usually much more interested in opportunities than in ideas. Moreover, the large migration of German Pietists reinforced the influence of an evangelical religious faith which was reflected in the Great Awakening of the 1720s to 1750s (see p. 62). Whereas the impetus of the Age of Faith in the late sixteenth and much of the seventeenth century dominated seventeenth-century colonial America, in the eighteenth century the colonies reflected what was to become a characteristic of the American mind—a wide diversity of intellectual streams. To understand this multiple mind, this discussion will center upon the growth of toleration and the emergence of secularization, the religious awakening of the eighteenth century, and the Enlightenment in America.

The Growth of Toleration. The basis for the rise of religious toleration in England and America was laid in the political-religious upheaval of the mid-seventeenth century and the subsequent restoration of the Stuart monarchy. After the Glorious Revolution of 1688 had won for Parliament a more balanced role in relationship to the authority of the crown, the Toleration Act of 1689 gave sufferance to all Protestant sects in England. The act was made necessary not only by the recent turmoil but also by the new science, which encouraged a thorough reexamination of religious doctrine and beliefs.

In America, the background for toleration had been laid as early as 1636, when Roger Williams founded Rhode Island. In a sense, Williams backed into the principle of religious toleration. He had found the Puritans of Massachusetts Bay imperfect in their religious fervor, and he consequently vowed to pray only with those he knew to be regenerate. Because he was unsure of other men, he finally was forced to pray only with his wife. From this restricted, impractical position, Williams took the long step to religious toleration on the premise that since he could not determine precisely which persons were regenerate, he had no alternative but to extend toleration to everyone with religious convictions. Williams' ultimate attitude of toleration was well in advance of the mainstream in England and in America.

The Maryland Toleration Act of 1649 lent impetus to the growth of toleration, though it arose not from broad humanitarian principles but from immediate circumstances. Maryland, established originally as a Catholic refuge, was being heavily populated by Protestants. Not only were the Catholics in a minority, but because of the Puritan domination in England, they were seriously threatened by persecution. The Toleration Act, advocated by Lord Baltimore, was intended to protect the Catholic minority and to forestall action against Baltimore's proprietorship.

Toleration flourished in the eighteenth century, in part because of seventeenth-century precedents but, more important, because the realities of the eighteenth century made intolerance an anachronism. The migration of dissenter sects from Germany, the emergence of an intercolonial Presbyterian church increasingly fortified by newly arrived Scots and Scotch-Irish, the spread of Anglicanism throughout the colonies, the intercolonial migrations from Pennsylvania south to Georgia, the application of the English Toleration Act in America—these developments made toleration a necessity. The diversity of religious faiths made any other course impossible.

Toleration for provincial America did not mean disruption of church-state establishments. Men of all faiths were taxed, for example, to maintain the Anglican church in Virginia and the Congregational church in Massachusetts, although in each colony men of differing faith could practice it without undue molestation. The separation of church and state became a question of principle during and after the American Revolution, when it was apparent that no single church was sufficiently strong to be elevated to the status of a national church.

The Rise of Secularism. The emergence of secularism is related to the growth of toleration, for restraint is seldom achieved when religious zeal is white hot. The people who migrated to America in the eighteenth century were primarily seeking opportunity, not religious toleration. If toleration had been their principal desire, the German Pietists could easily have migrated to Rhode Island—and at an earlier date. But choice Pennsylvania land in combination with religious toleration proved to be a superior attraction. Moreover, the new generations of Americans who were native born turned with avidity to enrichment and advancement; they were less concerned than their seventeenth-century forebears with the saving of souls.

Perhaps the best index of the rise of secularism is the production of the provincial press. In the eighteenth century, newspapers flourished. The first was published in Boston in 1704; by the 1750s almost every colony had one newspaper and a number had several. In contrast to Michael Wigglesworth's *Day of Doom* of the seventeenth century, almanacs became the best sellers of the eighteenth century. *Poor Richard's Almanac,* which Benjamin Franklin edited in Philadelphia from 1732 to 1758, sold ten thousand copies a year and became the most popular reading matter—except for the Bible—in the colonies. The emergence of secularism can also be detected in the appearance of touring companies of English actors. Williamsburg had a theater in 1716. In the 1770s satirical patriotic plays by Mercy Otis Warren were published, as were the verses of Phillis Wheatley, who had been brought from Africa as a slave.

The Great Awakening. The growth of toleration and the emergence of secularism should not obscure a third significant and persistent theme of eighteenth-century intellectual and social life, the Great Awakening, an evangelical religious movement—a series of revivals preached by stirring evangelists and causing the greatest emotional excitement—that swept through colonial America. The Great Awakening began in the Middle colonies, in part because the German migration carried with it the Pietist movement from Europe; in part because the rapid expansion characteristic of the Middle colonies tended to overtax traditional religious institutions and thus to encourage the creation of new organizations and new forms for religious expression; and in part because a church-state relationship did not exist to thwart an evangelical movement. In the 1730s the Great Awakening extended into New England, where its fire-and-brimstone preachers drew large revivalist crowds in cities and towns. In the 1740s and 1750s the movement reached into the Southern colonies, carried along in part by the migration of the Scotch-Irish and Germans southward along the eastern edge of the Appalachians. The absence of towns and the presence of the Anglican establishment in the Southern colonies had precluded early manifestations of the Awakening in that section of the country.

Among the noted preachers associated with the Great Awakening was Jonathan Edwards of the Northampton Church in Massachusetts. Because of his remarkable intellectual and philosophical gifts, Edwards is often called the greatest theologian America has produced. Edwards used Enlightenment reasoning to construct a theological paradox to Enlightenment ideas. Beginning in the 1720s, many New England ministers were influenced by a theology basing salvation on human moral effort as well as divine grace. Edwards opposed this tendency and reasserted the absolute justice of God's power to elect or to condemn as He chose. Conversion and redemption Edwards further described as a supernatural illumination of the soul, an effusion of God's beauty in the mind, an intuitive vision of the holiness that is in God and Christ; thus Edwards' test of conversion was in some respects more rigorous than formerly. Overall, he defended with exceptional skill the basic Calvinistic position that God was omnipotent and that, before God, man was impotent. Edwards was scarcely representative of most Awakening preachers, whose intellectual gifts were limited and who appealed to the emotions rather than to the mind.

The Great Awakening caused divisions within existing church organizations. Those church members attracted to the evangelical group were called "new lights"; they attempted to wrest control of the church from the conservative members who held power, the "old lights." The Awakening fervor also was responsible for the founding of four colleges by separate religious denominations: Dartmouth (Congregationalist), Princeton (Presbyterian), Brown (Baptist), and Rutgers (Dutch Reformed). The premise in each case was that the existing institutions of higher learning—Yale, for instance, which had been founded in 1701—were unsuitable for training acceptable "new light" ministers.

The Awakening, because it was an intercolonial movement, strengthened intercolonial ties. Many historians have advanced the idea that, by emphasizing the individual and his relationship to God, it aroused a democratic spirit which influenced the revolutionary generation. This generalization cannot be proved or disproved, but it seems fair to suggest that in reviewing traditional institutions—which in this case happened to be ecclesiastical institutions—the Awakening encouraged a climate of freedom.

The Enlightenment in America. The greatest influence of the Enlightenment in America was the encouragement it gave to scientific inquiry. Cotton Mather, the most prominent New England clergyman in the late seventeenth and early eighteenth centuries, was attracted to scientific investigation; he was an advocate of smallpox inoculations when others greeted this medical advance with uncertainty or fear. William Byrd II of Virginia, along with other colonials, belonged to England's Royal Society and frequently sent observations of New World phenomena to his friends in England.

The contribution of most colonials was to that aspect of science called "natural history." Almost every botanical specimen collected in America constituted a contribution to knowledge because it added to the storehouse of scientific information. John Bartram, who collected specimens throughout the provinces and cultivated rare species in his garden at Philadelphia, was called the finest contemporary "natural botanist" by Carolus Linnaeus of Sweden, the foremost botanist in Europe. Another celebrated work was Mark Catesby's extraordinary *Natural History of Carolina.*

Only Benjamin Franklin contributed to theoretical science, although many of his provincial contemporaries pursued allied investigations with vigor and persistence. Fortunately for Franklin, he entered a field of physics in which relatively little work had been done, and thus he was not handicapped by his lack of background, particularly his limited knowledge of mathematics. His identification of lightning as electricity and his observations with regard to the flow of electricity and the equalization that took place between highly charged particles and those less highly charged were contributions which won him a reputation throughout Europe.

Although science became increasingly important within the curricula of the colleges, it was pursued most fervently by men outside the institutions of learning who, like proper eighteenth-century generalists, were interested in politics, science, writing, and other broad-gauged, stimulating activities. Representative of this group was the American Philosophical Society, founded in 1744. Its membership included Dr. John Mitchell of Virginia, a fellow of the Royal Society, whose major interest was botany; Cadwallader Colden, whose intellectual interest ranged from electricity to a history of the Iroquois Indians; and David Rittenhouse of Pennsylvania, an astronomer and mathematician. As the impact of science in colonial America makes clear, the Enlightenment, unlike Puritanism, was peculiarly the possession of the educated and social elite.

Yet in several ways Enlightenment ideas encompassed the whole people. First of all, provincial America, because it represented a new, formative society, appeared in the eyes of some European and American observers to be the laboratory of the Enlightenment. American society, free from the incrustations of the centuries, could presumably adjust to the immutable laws of nature more readily than could that of Europe. Indeed, American intellectuals were confident that a perfect society was already being created. For this reason, the French found in Franklin a living inspiration, an image of a new society. In political thought and practice, provincial Americans, regardless of status or location, embraced many Enlightenment ideas. The right of men to challenge a governmental system when it stood athwart the immutable laws of nature, and the right of men to replace such a government with one which conformed with nature's laws, were two assumptions of the Enlightenment which deeply penetrated the American mind.

Cultural Maturity. Colonial America made no great progress in the arts; nor could such manifestations of cultural life be expected of a people whose principal energies were devoted to creating a new civilization. Yet Philadelphia stood as a cosmopolitan city, second in population only to London within the British empire. The American cities in the aggregate, as well as the American countryside, comprised a stimulating atmosphere which bred men of intelligence, indeed of genius, as well as men whose contributions to statesmanship would endure beyond those of most of their cultivated counterparts in England.

The standard criteria for evaluating the level of intellectual life, therefore, do not apply to provincial America. What were important were its zest for learning, its new modes of society, its mobility, its ability to prosper and to set examples that in time would be imitated. The promise of the American "minds" fashioned from the experience of the seventeenth and eighteenth centuries formed the foundation upon which American nationhood and an American culture were to be built.

BIBLIOGRAPHY

The most comprehensive studies of the settlement of the English colonies in America are Charles M. Andrews, *The Colonial Period of American History,* 4 vols. (New Haven: Yale University Press, 1934–38 [vol. I is also available in paperback from the same publisher]); Herbert Levi Osgood, *The American Colonies in the Seventeenth Century,* 3 vols. (Gloucester, Mass.: Peter Smith); and Herbert Levi Osgood, *The American Colonies in the Eighteenth Century,* 4 vols. (Gloucester, Mass.: Peter Smith). Andrews gives a judicial appraisal of controversial questions; Osgood, despite his lack of interpretation, provides important material found nowhere else. An account of the colonies within the framework of the whole empire will be found in Lawrence Henry Gipson, *The British Empire Before the American Revolution,* 15 vols., rev. ed. (New York: Alfred A. Knopf, 1958–65).

Useful single-volume treatments of the colonial development are Curtis P. Nettels, *The Roots of American Civilization,* 2nd ed. (New York: Appleton-Century-Crofts, 1963); Louis B. Wright, *The Atlantic Frontier** (Ithaca: Cornell University Press, 1963); Clarence L. Ver Steeg, *The Formative Years* (New York: Hill and Wang, 1964); and David Hawke, *The Colonial Experience* (Indianapolis: Bobbs-Merrill, 1966).

A succinct account of the establishment of all the southern colonies except Georgia is to be found in Wesley Frank Craven, *The Southern Colonies in the Seventeenth Century** (Baton Rouge: Louisiana State University Press, 1949). The most recent and most detailed history of Virginia in this period is Richard L. Morton, *Colonial Virginia,* 2 vols. (Charlottesville: University of Virginia, 1960). A discussion of the transit of English social ideas to Virginia will be found in Louis B. Wright, *The First Gentlemen of Virginia** (Charlottesville: University of Virginia, 1964). The history of South Carolina as a colony is treated in detail in Edward McCrady, *The History of South Carolina Under the Proprietary Government, 1670–1720* (New York: Russell, 1969, reprint of 1899 edition). Samuel A. Ashe, *History of North Carolina,* 2 vols. (Greensboro, N.C.: C. L. Van Noppen, 1971, reprint of 1925 edition) gives considerable space to the colonial period. More recent is Hugh T. Lefter and Albert R. Newsome, *North Carolina; the History of a Southern State,* rev. ed. (Chapel Hill: University of North Carolina Press, 1963). E. Merton Coulter, *Georgia,* 2nd ed. (Chapel Hill: University of North Carolina Press, 1960) gives a good brief account of the colonial period.

Excellent biographical material is to be found in Samuel E. Morison, *Builders of the Bay Colony** (Boston: Houghton Mifflin, 1963). Important studies of New England communities are Richard Bushman, *From Puritan to Yankee* (Cambridge, Mass.: Harvard University Press, 1967), Sumner C. Powell, *Puritan Village** (Middletown, Conn.: Wesleyan University Press, 1970), and Kenneth A. Lockridge, *A New England Town** (New York: W. W. Norton, 1970). Perry Miller, *Orthodoxy in Massachusetts, 1630–1650** (New York: Harper & Row, 1970) is a valuable introduction to the religious history of the Puritans. In *The New England Mind: The Seventeenth Century** (Boston: Beacon Press, 1961) and *The New England Mind: From Colony to Province** (Boston: Beacon Press, 1961) the late Perry Miller gives a minute account of Puritan theology. A revised account is in Robert Middlekauff, *The Mathers* (New York: Oxford University Press, 1971).

A synthesis of material on the early history of New York will be found in Alexander C. Flick, ed., *History of the State of New York,* 10 vols. in 5 (Albany: State University of New York Press, 1933–37). For material on Pennsylvania see Gary B. Nash, *Quakers and Politics* (Princeton: Princeton University Press, 1968).

Information about the social history of the colonies is supplied by two studies of family structure and demography, John Demos, *A Little Commonwealth** (New York: Oxford University Press, 1971) and Philip Greven, *Four Generations* (Ithaca: Cornell University Press, 1969). The attitudes of white colonists concerning blacks are described in Winthrop Jordan, *White over Black** (Baltimore: Penguin Books, 1969). Indian-white relations may be traced in Verner W. Crane, *The Southern Frontier** (Ann Arbor: University of Michigan Press, 1956), George T. Hunt, *The Wars of the Iroquois** (Madison: The University of Wisconsin Press, 1960), and Alden Vaughan, *New England Frontier: Indians and Puritans, 1620–1675** (Boston: Little, Brown, 1965).

For the structure of eighteenth-century colonial politics see Patricia Bonomi, *A Factious People: Politics and Society in Colonial New York* (New York: Columbia University Press, 1971), Charles Sydnor, *American Revolutionaries in the Making** (New York: Free Press, 1965), and Bernard Bailyn, *The Origins of American Politics** (New York: Vintage Books, 1968).

For a discussion of ideas leading up to independence see Carl L. Becker, *The Declaration of Independence* (New York: Alfred A. Knopf, 1942) and Bernard Bailyn, *The Ideological Origins of the American Revolution** (Cambridge, Mass.: Harvard University Press, 1967). For political aspects of the years of controversy see Lawrence H. Gipson, *The Coming of the American Revolution, 1763–1775** (New York: Harper & Row, 1954); Edmund S. and Helen M. Morgan, *The Stamp Act Crisis** (New York: Macmillan, 1963); Edmund S. Morgan, *The Birth of the Republic, 1763–1789** (Chicago: University of Chicago Press, 1956); and Allan Nevins, *The American States During and After the Revolution, 1775–1789* (New York: Augustus M. Kelley, 1924). A useful survey of this period is Evarts B. Greene, *The Revolutionary Generation, 1763–1790** (Chicago: Quadrangle, 1971). A succinct account of the campaigns of the Revolution may be found in Piers Mackesy, *The War for America* (Cambridge, Mass.: Harvard University Press, 1964).

* Denotes a paperback.

2

THE
YOUNG
REPUBLIC

THE FIRST FOUR DECADES OF AMERICAN LIFE AFTER THE REVOLUTION were important decades—years in which the work of independence was completed, the Republic shaped, the national character determined, a foreign policy developed, the federal system established. This was a period of important events and crucial decisions, yet we have no good name for it. It was dominated by no single great figure, but by several; it exhibits no internal consistency, for during these years everything that was done was being done for the first time. If it could be characterized at all, it might be called a period of precedents.

The problems faced by the postrevolutionary generation were considerable and urgent; solutions to them had to be found or compromises made swiftly, if the Republic was to survive. Its leaders had first of all to create a new and viable political system. Everything the Old World had learned to depend on for safety and stability—an established church, a monarch, an army, a strong legal tradition, and, in fact, a history—the United States abandoned in favor of a somewhat dubious trust in the ability and integrity of the average man.

Visitors to the new nation in the years after the war found this trust difficult to understand. The United States was defiantly *not* like England or the Continent (which made it puzzling enough), and its principles and aims, in terms of the old order, simply did not seem to make sense. In the light of contemporary judgments, there was not much reason to believe that the United States *would* succeed.

The majority of American leaders, however, faced the future with vigor and confidence. They began with certain advantages, as the astute French traveler Tocqueville observed, in "that the American arrived at a state of democracy without having to endure a democratic revolution, and that he is free without having to become so." Americans did not have to destroy a feudal society in order to evolve a new one; the country began its existence without hereditary royalty, a standing army, or an entrenched aristocracy.

Postwar leaders could join forces, then, "to make liberty," as William Miller phrased it at the time, "a *practical* principle, and to *prove* it." However much these men may have disagreed about the *means* of realizing the principles of the Revolution, there were none who wished to undo it. The present necessity, they agreed, was to strike the proper balance between ideal and reality which the Constitution came to represent. Problems posed by foreign policy were equally urgent. The War of 1812 raised for the first time the question of the United States' position vis-à-vis other nations' wars. Should the country be neutral? Could it be, when the outcome might irrevocably affect America's future? Did the Monroe Doctrine represent the beginnings of the nation's long search for security, independence, and equality in its international relations?

In domestic policy there were other turning points. During the 1790s the Supreme Court considered itself a quasi-governmental economic force, whose aim, Justice Samuel Chase said, was to protect the rights of property, "for the protection whereof the government was established." But John Marshall and after him Roger Taney made the Court an instrument for expanding business and assisting economic enterprise, thus shaping for the next century the structure and direction of American capitalism. Not until late in that century did the Court begin to establish some control of the economic sector; not until our own century did it move toward the expansion of personal and civil rights.

Given the precarious state of the Republic, its self-confidence was remarkable. The postrevolutionary generation felt that its example might provide the spark to activate an age of revolutions, toppling all other existing forms of government in the Western world. Jefferson found it "impossible not to be sensible that we are acting for all mankind." If this "bold and sublime" American experiment worked, Thomas Paine said in *Common Sense,* "the birthday of a new world is at hand." The future, said Joel Barlow, belonged to these "new men in a new world."

No period in American history, perhaps, exhibited more ebullience and confidence—yet these men were realistic, too. Beneath their sunny confidence one may detect shadows of doubt and uncertainty. They hoped to create a free, just, and equal society, but they knew the frailties of human nature (their own included) and were well aware of the limitations of human will and knowledge. Those who sought to make a society that guaranteed the rights of life, liberty, and property also followed an implacable policy of conquest against the Indian and protected a system of slavery (in common with other nations) that refused those rights to a sizable segment of the population. While the new American society was more fluid, diverse, and open than that of any other of its time, it also had effective ways of dispossessing and oppressing some of its own elements.

Not surprisingly, historians have made, and continue to make, differing assessments of the men and events of these years. The nationalist historians of the early nineteenth century, to whom the concept of class conflict was unknown, drew the Founding Fathers in primary colors as statesmen of more than mortal wisdom. Some nineteenth-century historians saw the Constitution as a temporary victory of nationalism over sectionalism; others as the climax of the Revolution; still others as the attempt of a counterrevolutionary minority to curb the powers of the majority. In the twentieth century some have seen it as motivated primarily by economic self-interest, others as the product of consensus among men whose differences were not so great as they had formerly seemed.

In the same way, views of the War of 1812 have shifted over the years. Nineteenth-century interpreters tended to accept Madison's claim that it was fought to preserve the national honor and guarantee America's maritime rights. Later historians saw it, in part at least, as an imperialist push toward acquisition of Canada and Spanish America or as a means for the new Western states to protect and extend their frontiers—by defeating both the Indians and England.

From the vantage point of two hundred years of subsequent experience, one can easily find flaws in what the postrevolutionary generation planned and failures in what it did. But it is only just to recognize that these men did not have the tools and concepts of modern anthropology and psychology to deal with their social problems and that the techniques of modern political and social research were not available to them. That is to say, in effect, that the Founding Fathers were men of their times—possessed of the same biases and virtues, the same blindnesses and perceptions that characterize all men everywhere at any time. Yet the goal they set for their new nation still remains one of dazzling promise; and if their reach exceeded their grasp, what they accomplished should not be disparaged just as it should not be overpraised. They *did* make a nation, against great odds and out of great principles, which they hoped would be, as Jefferson called it, "the last best hope of mankind."

FOR THOUGHT AND DISCUSSION

1. Given his background and the climate of opinion in his times, can the pioneer farmer justly be condemned as a ravager and despoiler of the land?

2. Taking into account contemporary anthropological theory and the press of population westward to new lands, can you suggest workable alternative policies toward the Indian tribes that Congress might have followed?

3. Do you see any parallels between "Mr. Madison's War" and other wars in our history, like "Mr. Wilson's War" and "Mr. Johnson's War"? Has the President's power as commander in chief been a dangerous factor in our international relations?

4. What is the significance of a *written* constitution?

5. Why would Congress find it possible to compromise the issue of slave states versus free states in 1819 but not in 1860?

6. What has been the significance for the United States of the two-party political system that developed in the early Republic? Would a multi-party system be better? Could such a system have developed? Why didn't it?

in ordeR
to form a
more perfect
UnioN

CHAPTER 4

ESTABLISHING THE REPUBLIC
1781–1800

THE SEARCH FOR STABILITY

The Articles of Confederation. Of prime importance in the political life of the United States throughout its history has been the problem of federalism—the division of power between the states and the federal government—or, more simply, the issue of local control or "states' rights" versus central authority. The origins of this problem are to be found in the British imperial system of the mid-eighteenth century. At the center of this system had stood Great Britain, whose government had directed foreign affairs and intercolonial relations with the view of keeping the machinery and policies of the empire working in harmony. At the extremities of this system had been the colonies themselves, each of which had attained the right to govern its internal affairs.

In practice, however, the dividing line between imperial and local affairs was variously interpreted, and out of the conflict of interpretations arose the American Revolution. With the Declaration of Independence, the American colonies rejected the government in London altogether and, under the pressures of war, united sufficiently to set up a central authority of their own making—the Confederation.

When Richard Henry Lee on June 7, 1776, offered a resolution to the Continental Congress declaring American independence, he also proposed that "a plan of confederation be prepared and transmitted to the respective colonies for their consideration and approbation." A committee headed by John Dickinson of Pennsylvania presented such a plan to the Continental Congress on July 12, and on November 15, 1777, after more than a year of debate, the Articles of Confederation were approved and sent to the states for ratification.

Because the loyalty of individual Americans was strongly attached to their states, it was readily agreed that the states should hold the sovereign powers of government. The Articles were designed to create an assembly of equal states, each of which retained its "sovereignty, freedom, and independence, and every Power, Jurisdiction, and right." The Articles of Confederation therefore created a quasi-federal system with a new Congress almost exactly like the wartime Continental Congress which then existed, in which each state—regardless of size, population, or wealth—had an equal vote. The Articles delegated to Congress the power to declare war, make peace, conclude treaties, raise and maintain armies, maintain a navy, establish a postal system, regulate Indian affairs, borrow money, issue bills of credit, and regulate the value of coin of the United States and the several states. However, nine of the thirteen states had to give their consent before any legislation of importance could be enacted, and enforcement of the decisions of Congress depended upon the cooperation of all the states. For example, Congress could make treaties but could not force the states to live up to their stipulations; it could authorize an army but could not fill its ranks without the cooperation of each state; it could borrow money but had to depend on requisitions from the states to repay its debts. The Articles provided no standing agencies of enforcement: Congress could pass laws, but there was no formal executive or judicial branch to execute and adjudicate them. The day-to-day operations of government were handled rather precariously by officials or committees appointed by Congress.

Because of their recent quarrels with Parliament over questions of taxation and commercial regulation, the states also withheld two key powers from their new central government: the power to levy taxes (Congress could merely request contributions from the state legislatures) and the power to regulate commerce. Without these powers the Confederation government could not depend upon a regular and adequate supply of revenue to sustain its own functions, nor could it attempt to foster a national economy, a factor essential to the political unity of America.

The central government, therefore, was what the Articles called it—nothing more than "a firm league of friendship." Sharing a common cause or facing common danger, its members could work together with some measure of effectiveness; any suspicion that Congress would infringe upon their own right of independent action, however, would throw the states on their guard.

The State Governments. The Declaration of Independence in 1776 made necessary the creation of two kinds of government: central and local. While only tentative motions were made toward centralization, the people were quick to make the transition from colonial government to state government. Actually the process was one of revision and adaptation, since each of the former colonies already possessed a government with its own methods of operation. Indeed, two states (Connecticut and Rhode Island) continued to operate under their colonial charters, simply by deleting all references to the British crown. Ten other states completed new constitutions within a year after the Declaration of Independence, and the last (Massachusetts) by 1780. The state constitutions, though varying in detail, reflected both the colonial experience and the current revolutionary controversy.

The framers of the constitution placed the center of political authority in the legislative branch, where it would be especially responsive to popular and local control. As a Massachusetts town meeting bluntly resolved in 1778, "The oftener power Returns to the hands of the people, the Better . . . Where can the power be lodged so Safe as in the Hands of the people?" Members of the legislature, if they wished to be reelected, had to keep in mind the feelings of their people "back home." Legislators were held constantly accountable by being restricted to brief terms: in ten states the lower house, which originated tax legislation, was newly elected every year; in Connecticut and Rhode Island every six months; and in South Carolina every two years.

Framers of the constitutions, remembering their recent troubles with royal governors and magistrates, restricted the powers of governors and justices almost to the vanishing point. The average governor, contemporary jokesters claimed, had just about enough authority to collect his salary.

The imbalance of power among the branches of government often severely hampered the states' abilities to meet and solve the political and economic problems which faced them during and after the war. Yet whatever their shortcomings, these constitutions were the first attempts to translate the generalities of the Declaration into usable instruments of government. They were constructed on the premise, novel to the eighteenth century, that a government should be formed under a *written* document, thus recognizing for the first time in modern political life the difference between fundamental and statute law. The introduction of such precisely formed instruments of governmental law, on such a grand scale, was a major contribution to the science of government.

The state constitutions reaffirmed the powerful colonial tradition of individual freedom in their bills of rights, which guaranteed each citizen freedom of religion, speech, and assembly, trial by jury, the right of habeas corpus, and other natural and civil rights. In general, they extended the voting franchise to the majority of white male citizens. In all states, a man had to own some property to vote; in many, he had to own a more substantial amount to hold office. Since property formed the basis for voting qualifications, and since the states quickly enlarged opportunities to own land, most white males could probably meet the requirements. (New Jersey gave the vote to women, only to withdraw it later.) Over the years, gradual abolition of property qualifications further widened the suffrage.

The popular fear of governmental power tended to render the state governments politically and financially impotent. Afraid to antagonize the voters who could quickly run them out of office, legislators had difficulty, for example, in passing effective measures of taxation; and, even when they did, revenue men were hard put in forcing collections from the people.

THE CONFEDERATION PERIOD

Such was the political framework within which the new nation entered the "critical period," 1783–89, from the close of the Revolutionary War to the inauguration of the federal government under the Constitution. Long after the label of "critical period" was first introduced by historian John Fiske in 1889, historians came to acknowledge that the years of the Confederation were more creative and constructive than once was supposed. During these years a peace was won on terms highly favorable to the United States; an orderly policy for western territorial expansion was established; a postwar recession was overcome and replaced by economic prosperity; the population increased; and the Constitution was born. Nevertheless, except in regard to western lands, the achievements of the period were largely due to the efforts of individuals and groups and to some of the more foresighted state governments. The central govern-

NORTHWEST TERRITORY

L. Superior

WISCONSIN
Admitted
1848

L. Michigan

Mississippi R.

L. Huron

MICHIGAN
Admitted
1837

L. Erie

ILLINOIS
Admitted
1818

INDIANA
Admitted
1816

OHIO
Admitted
1803

SEVEN
RANGES
First area surveyed
under Ordinance of 1785

ment was much too dependent on the conflicting whims of the several states to be consistently effective.

Establishing a Western Policy.   Ratification of the Articles of Confederation was slow: it was not until late in 1779 that twelve states gave their approval, and Maryland, the last to ratify, did not do so until 1781. During almost the entire war, therefore, the country operated under the authority of the Continental Congress without a formal central government.

The solution of the western land problem (see Chapter 2), which kept Maryland from ratifying the Articles, was of paramount importance to the new government. It represented a first step toward nationalization, and made certain that the nation, as it moved west, would gradually evolve as a unit rather than as thirteen colonies with a set of permanently dependent territories. It also meant that since Congress now controlled all the western lands, it could determine a central policy for the development of its vast unpopulated territory.

During and after the Revolution a stream of settlers poured west, creating an urgent need for a systematic plan of land sale and territorial government. A Land Ordinance passed by Congress in 1785 provided for a government survey to divide the land of the Northwest Territory (north of the Ohio River, west of Pennsylvania, and east of the Mississippi River) into townships of thirty-six square miles, each township to be split into thirty-six sections of one square mile (640 acres) each and each section into quarter sections. Four sections in every township were reserved as bounties for soldiers of the Continental army, and another section was set aside for the use of public schools. The remainder of the land was to be sold at public auction for at least one dollar an acre, in minimum lots of 640 acres.

The Ordinance of 1785 proved advantageous to wealthy land speculators, who bought up whole townships and resold them at handsome profits. Sensing even greater returns, a group of speculators (including some congressmen and government officials) pressed for further legislation to provide a form of government for the Northwest; the result was the Northwest Ordinance of 1787, based largely on a similar ordinance drafted by Jefferson in 1784 but never put into effect.

Though it favored the wealthy land speculator over the indigent farmer, the Northwest Ordinance did provide a model for translating the unsettled Northwest, by orderly political procedures, from frontier to statehood. It provided that Congress should appoint from among the landholders of the region a governor, a secretary, and three judges. When the territory reached a population of five thousand free adult males, a bicameral legislature was to be established. When there were sixty thousand free inhabitants (the population of the smallest state at that time), the voters might adopt a constitution, elect their own officers, and enter the Union on equal terms with the original thirteen states. From three to five states were to be formed from the territory. Slavery was forbidden in the area, and freedom of worship and trial by jury were guaranteed.

So successfully did the Northwest Ordinance accomplish its political aims that it set the pattern for the absorption of the entire West (as well as Alaska and Hawaii) into the Union. Settlers flooded into the Northwest Territory as soon as the ordinance went into effect; the great drive westward had begun, not to cease for another hundred years.

Relations with Europe. Perhaps the most serious problems facing Congress under the Articles arose from its lack of a unified, coherent foreign policy and its lack of authority to evolve one. The core of diplomatic power lay equally among the states, each of which possessed the right to arrange its own foreign affairs, with the national government virtually helpless to operate independently. The United States was in a most delicate position in regard to England, France, and Spain. There was no reason to suppose that Britain intended to allow America to remain independent without interference if Britain's interests dictated otherwise. The United States, for its part, desperately needed trade agreements with Europe and especially with England, its largest market. It was also involved in a border dispute with Spain over Florida, and when the Spanish, who controlled the lower Mississippi and New Orleans, closed them to American trade in 1784, the nation was in trouble. If Congress could not open the Mississippi to trade, a number of Western leaders favored either taking New Orleans by force or joining a British protectorate which might help them do so. Washington felt that the West in 1784 was so near to secession that "the touch of a feather" might divide it from the country. The Spanish, who needed American trade, seemed willing to negotiate, and in 1785 the Spanish minister Diego de Gardoqui discussed terms with Secretary of Foreign Affairs John Jay. Both diplomats were bound by specific instructions which led to a stalemate; eventually Jay in 1786 agreed to a commercial treaty which allowed the United States to trade with Spain, but not with its colonies, if the Americans would "forbear" navigation of the Mississippi River though not the *right* to use it. Such a roar of protest went up from the West that Jay let the negotiations lapse. The Spanish helped matters in 1788 by opening the river under restrictions with which the West could live, though not happily, until the issue was settled by the Pinckney Treaty of 1795. These negotiations with Spain not only pointed up the impotence of the Articles in foreign affairs but left behind in the West a lingering suspicion of the East.

The Difficulties of Trade. When the colonies left the imperial system, thus giving up their favored economic position, American merchants and shippers found themselves in cutthroat competition with the British, Dutch, and French for world markets. John Adams tried unsuccessfully for three years to make some kind of trade agreement with England, but as Lord Sheffield commented, putting his finger squarely on the commercial weaknesses of the Articles of Confederation, "America cannot retaliate. It will not be an easy matter to bring the Americans to act as a nation. They are not to be feared by such as us."

Sheffield proved to be correct, for when Congress asked the states in 1784 for exclusive authority to regulate foreign trade over a fifteen-year period, the states immediately refused. Under the Articles of Confederation, Congress was powerless to do more than protest.

Domestic commerce as well as foreign trade suffered from interstate rivalries. The states used their power to levy tariffs, creating barriers that seriously hampered domestic commerce and caused further dissatisfaction with the central government. At the same time, American industry was struggling to survive. The war and blockade stimulated American manufacturing by cutting off imports from Britain and the Continent; some of the states, in fact, offered premiums and subsidies for the production of manufactured goods. But with the return of peace much of the artificial stimulation which had encouraged American industry was withdrawn, and the inevitable postwar slump set in. Capital was short, the currency disordered, transportation deficient, and investments risky.

Frenzied Finances. The Articles of Confederation gave the national government no power to tax; if the states refused to pay their levies in full or on time, Congress simply was forced to accumulate ever larger foreign and domestic debts. The states responded erratically to Congress' requests for taxes, so that while Congress occasionally had money, it never had enough at the right time. Although Congress repudiated most of its war debts by simply cancelling out millions of dollars in the currency issued under the Continental Congress, the country in 1785 still owed about $35 million in domestic debts and a growing foreign debt. The states, meanwhile, had war debts of their own, which they increased after the war by assuming that part of the congressional debt owed their citizens.

In addition to these debts, both national and state governments lacked a uniform, stable, sound currency. There was no trustworthy federal currency, and the states were loaded with badly inflated wartime paper money. The postwar slump which hit the country in 1783, sinking to its lowest point in mid-1786, affected the farmer and the small debtor most of all. In states where they controlled the legislatures, the solution seemed easy: seven state legislatures simply approved the issue of paper money in larger quantities; in addition, to help distressed farmers, they passed "stay laws" to prevent creditors from foreclosing mortgages.

Crisis and Rebellion. At the depth of the depression in 1786 there was a severe hard-money shortage; farmers, especially, were in difficulty. Protest meetings in several states won some concessions from the legislatures, but in Massachusetts, when mobs of unruly men closed the courts at Northampton, Worcester, and Springfield, thereby preventing farm foreclosures and prosecutions for debt, Governor James Bowdoin sent militia to scatter them.

In reply to Bowdoin, Daniel Shays, a veteran of the Revolution, organized a band of farmers in 1786 for an attack on the Springfield Arsenal, from which he hoped to get arms. The governor sent a force of militia (paid for by contributions from Boston businessmen) to protect the arsenal, and Shays' poorly mounted attack in February 1787 failed miserably. In a few weeks the leaders of the rebellion had been captured and convicted, and a few sentenced to death. The legislature pardoned them all, however—even Shays, who was released in 1788.

Shays' Rebellion had swift effects in Massachusetts: Governor Bowdoin was defeated in the next election by John Hancock, and the legislature prudently decided to grant the farmers some measure of relief. The effect on the country at large was equally swift, and much greater. As Abigail Adams wrote Thomas Jefferson, when "ignorant, restless desperadoes, without conscience or principles" could persuade "a deluded multitude to follow their standards . . ." who could be safe, anywhere in the land? "There are combustibles," wrote Washington, "in every state which a spark might set fire to."

The Drift Toward a New Government. Even the most earnest states' rights advocates were willing to admit the existence of imperfections in the Articles of Confederation, and proposals for conventions to discuss their amendment had already appeared in the New York legislature in 1782 and Massachusetts in 1785. In 1786, under the cloud of Shays' Rebellion, Congress agreed that the Articles needed revision, though as James Monroe told Jefferson, "Some gentlemen have inveterate prejudices against all attempts to increase the powers of Congress, others see the necessity but fear the consequences."

It remained for Alexander Hamilton of New York to seize the initiative. When Virginia invited representatives from the states to meet at Annapolis in 1786 for a discussion of problems of interstate commerce, Hamilton called upon the states to appoint delegates to a meeting to be held in May 1787 at Philadelphia, to discuss ways "to render the Constitution of the Federal Government adequate to the exigencies of the Union." Since at almost the same time Daniel Shays' men, pursued by Boston militia, were providing an example of the kind of "exigency" Hamilton referred to, his call found receptive audiences in the states. Congress adopted his suggestion and authorized a convention "for the sole and express purpose of revising the Articles of Confederation and reporting to Congress and the several legislatures such alterations and provisions therein."

While there were those who believed that the Articles could be amended and reworked into an effective and efficient government, a number of determined political leaders—among them Hamilton, Madison, John Jay, and Henry Knox—were convinced that the country's interests demanded a much stronger central government; they believed in executive and judicial control rather than legislative and did not fully trust the decentralized, mass-dominated state governments. There was a general belief among the mercantile and financial classes that, as Madison wrote, the United States needed the kind of government which would "support a due supremacy of the national authority, and leave in force the local authorities so far as they can be subordinately useful."

FRAMING A NEW CONSTITUTION

The Question of Federalism.   The meetings at Philadelphia began on May 25, 1787. Conspicuously absent were many of the popular leaders of the prerevolutionary era. These "antifederalists," men like Samuel Adams and Patrick Henry, had involved themselves in the Revolution when it still comprised a scattering of colonial protests and then state revolts, rather loosely guided by the Continental Congress. Deeply devoted to winning independence for their own states, most of these men continued to believe that the states should be governed without the interference of a strong central government. Some antifederalists, like George Clinton of New York, had a vital stake in local state politics, which the enlargement of the powers of a continental government might endanger. Others saw the need to strengthen the Confederation but insisted that the supremacy of the states should not be basically altered. All of the antifederalists were passionately convinced that a republican system could survive only on the local level, under their watchful eyes. A republic on a continental scale was beyond their imagination.

The fifty-five delegates who made their appearance in the Philadelphia State House were men of generally broader views. George Washington (chosen presiding officer of the convention) and Benjamin Franklin were distinguished representatives of an older generation, long experienced in guiding the military and diplomatic affairs of the colonies as a whole. Most of the delegates, however, were men in their thirties or forties whose careers had only begun when the Revolution broke out and whose public reputations had been achieved as a result of their identification with the continental war effort. With the coming of peace, these "nationalists" were disquieted by the ease with which the states slid back into their old provincial ways. In vainly advocating revenue and commerical powers for the Confederation Congress, Robert Morris, James Wilson, Gouverneur Morris, James Madison, Alexander Hamilton, Charles Pinckney, and others began to see the futility of trying to govern a large country with thirteen states following diverse policies.

These federalists distrusted unchecked power in government as much as their opponents did; however, they believed that under the current system power *was* being exercised in one quarter without effective restraints. Jefferson branded it the "legislative tyranny" of the states. There was no way to appeal the decisions of the legislators;

the executive and judicial branches, and even the central Confederation, were powerless to overrule the legislative branch. In addition, nations abroad were beginning to look with contempt upon the disunited states, and there were even dangerous signs of territorial encroachments—by Britain in the Northwest and by Spain in the South and Southwest. National survival and prestige, the federalists insisted, demanded that a stronger central government be created.

The Philosophy of the Constitution. The feeling of urgency which permeated the minds of the delegates goes far toward explaining their eagerness to reach compromises on matters in dispute. Whenever the debates became deadlocked, speakers would arise and warn of the consequences should the Convention fail. Said Elbridge Gerry at mid-session: "Something must be done or we shall disappoint not only America, but the whole world. . . . We must make concessions on both sides." And Caleb Strong warned, "It is agreed, on all hands, that Congress are nearly at an end. If no accommodation takes place, the Union itself must soon be dissolved."

Such warnings climaxed a series of heated arguments during the meetings; while differences of opinion continued to arise, they were mostly over matters of detail and method. The Founding Fathers were in essential agreement in regard to the broad outlines of the new government and in regard to political principles, learned through years of experience in dealing with a "tyrannous" Parliament and serving in state legislatures and in Congress.

First, they believed that the central government must be empowered to act without the mediation of the states and to exercise its will directly upon individual citizens. It must have its own administrative agencies, with the ability to enforce its own laws and treaties, to collect its own revenues, and to regulate commerce and other matters of welfare affecting the states generally.

Secondly, they believed that power in government, though imperative, must somehow be held in check. Like most enlightened men of the eighteenth century, they recognized that human nature was not perfect. "Men are ambitious, vindictive, and rapacious," said Alexander Hamilton, and while his language was strong, his appraisal of human nature was generally shared by his colleagues. They agreed with the French political philosopher Montesquieu that "men entrusted with power tend to abuse it." The system advocated by Montesquieu to prevent this evil was to distribute the functions of government among three coequal branches of government, each of which would hold a veto or check on the power of the others. This doctrine of "separation of powers" had earlier been outlined by John Adams:

> A legislative, an executive, and a judicial power comprehend the whole of what is meant and understood by government. It is by balancing each of these powers against the other two, that the efforts in human nature toward tyranny can alone be checked and restrained, and any degree of freedom preserved in the constitution.

That such a system had failed in the state governments did not shake the delegates' faith in the *principle* of separation of powers. The states had only gone through the motions of creating three branches; in actuality they had not given the executive and judicial branches sufficient checks on the legislatures, which in some states were running riot in control of government.

Finally, most of the delegates were committed to some form of federalism, the political system which would unite the states under an independently operating central government while permitting them to retain some portion of their former power and identity. Few agreed with George Read of Delaware that the states "must be done away." Even Alexander Hamilton, who formally introduced such a scheme, acknowledged that the Convention might "shock the public opinion by proposing such a measure." It was generally agreed that the states must remain; the argument arose over how, in operating terms, power could be properly distributed between the states and the national government.

The Convention at Work. Four days after the Convention opened, Edmund Randolph of Virginia proposed fifteen resolutions, drafted by his colleague James Madison, which demonstrated immediately that the general intent was to proceed beyond mere revision of the Articles of Confederation in favor of forming a new national government. This "Virginia Plan" proposed a national executive, a national judiciary, and a national legislature consisting of two houses, both representing the states proportionally according to either population or tax contributions, with the lower house popularly elected and the upper house chosen by members of the lower. Although William Paterson proposed a rival "New Jersey Plan," which in substance would merely have enlarged the taxation and commerce powers of the Confederation Congress, it was never seriously considered. The Virginia Plan, after four months of debate, amendment, and considerable enlargement, became the United States Constitution.

Although the delegates agreed upon the main features of the new government, discord over the details almost broke up the Convention. That a breakup was avoided is attributable in part to the delegates' recognition of the urgent need for compromise and concession. They were pressed to balance special interest against special interest, the large states against the small, section against section, in order to realize a constitution that the majority could accept. No individual could be perfectly satisfied with the result, but each could feel that the half loaf he garnered for his interest was far better than none.

Major opposition to the original Virginia Plan came from the small states; in the existing Congress each of their votes was equal to that of any large state, but under the proposed system of proportional representation in the national legislature they would be consistently outvoted by the larger, more populous states. The large states retorted that government should represent people, not geography. "Is [a government] for *men*," asked James Wilson, "or for the imaginary beings called *States?*" The issue came down to the question of how federal the federal government should be. In acknowledging the permanence of the states, were the delegates obligated to go further and introduce the concept of the states into the very structure and representation of the new central government?

The final answer to this question was yes. In the end, the large states gave in. After the New Jersey Plan was rejected and the principle of a bicameral legislature established, the small states, while hesitating to object to proportional representation in the lower house, persisted in claiming the right of equal representation for states in the Senate, or upper house. And by threatening to walk out of the Convention, they won. In essence, this "Great Compromise," as it came to be called, was hardly a compromise at all. The major issue concerned representation in the Senate, and when the large states conceded on this point, they received no concession in return. However, the major crisis of the Convention had been resolved.

In the process of accepting a two-house legislature, the delegates acknowledged not only a balance between large and small states but also a balance between the common people and propertied, supposedly conservative interests. Many delegates had argued against giving the people a direct voice in government; "The people," said Roger Sherman, "should have as little to do as may be about the government. They want information, and are constantly liable to be misled." Elbridge Gerry pointed to the "evils" that "flow from the excess of democracy." Other delegates agreed, however, with James Madison, who stated "that the great fabric to be raised would be more stable and durable, if it should rest on the solid foundation of the people themselves." Thus the basis of representation in the lower house was set at one representative for every forty thousand persons—each representative to be elected by voters eligible to elect "the most numerous branch of [their] State legislature." On the other hand, the senators of the upper house—two from each state—were to be chosen by the state legislatures, putting them at a second remove from popular control. As a result, the Senate was expected to represent the more conservative interests, "to consist," as John Dickinson noted, "of the most distinguished characters, distinguished for their rank in life and their weight of property." In sum, the two houses of Congress were to balance the rights of the lower and higher ranks of society, but with the edge given to the higher.

Another issue arose over the manner of choosing the President, the head of the executive branch of the new government. To have the national legislature appoint him, as the original Virginia Plan proposed, might mean, it was argued, that a candidate to that high office would be "a mere creature of the legislature." A second plan, championed by James Wilson, called for popular election of the President; but the delegates had too great a distrust of unchecked democracy to find this plan fully acceptable. Other proposals sought to bring the states into the elective process by having either the state legislatures or the governors combine to elect the nation's chief executive.

The final compromise embodied elements from all these plans. Each state legislature was to appoint a number of presidential "electors" equal to the total number of senators and representatives to which the state was entitled in Congress. The electors would meet in their own states and vote for two presidential candidates, and the candidate receiving the majority of votes from all the states would become President. It should be noted that the method of choosing the electors was left to the decision of the state legislatures. Thus, the legislatures might decide to keep the power of appointment in their own hands, as most of them did, or they could submit the appointment to popular vote, a method which became widespread only much later. In either case, the electoral system was intended to minimize popular influence in the choice of the President.

Few of the delegates, however, believed that the election would end in the electoral college. It was believed that each state would try to advance a native son, and thus no candidate would receive a majority vote. In that event, the election would be referred to the House of Representatives, where votes would be taken by state delegations, each state having one vote. In effect, this presidential compromise echoed the earlier issue over proportional representation. In the first phase of the election, votes would be drawn on the basis of population; in the second phase, on the basis of statehood.

The conflict between North and South was not so serious in the Convention as it was later to become, but the differing sectional economies did arouse specific issues of governmental structure and powers. Because the South was an agricultural region dependent on a world market for its staple exports like tobacco and rice, it wanted commercial regulation—tariffs and export duties—eliminated or minimized. South-erners were also committed to slavery, not necessarily through moral conviction of its justice but because of their inescapably large investment in slave labor. Finally, the Southern states, six in number and comparatively less populous than the Northern states, were aware that in Congress they would be outnumbered by the North. They thus felt compelled to secure constitutional guarantees for their sectional interests before launching a new government in which they could be consistently outvoted.

In the North, on the other hand, agricultural products like grain and livestock had for the most part a ready domestic market. Many Northerners were more interested in having the government promote shipping and foster manufacturing by means of protective tariffs. Many also roundly condemned slavery and demanded an end to the "nefarious" slave trade. Their attitude, however, was not entirely without self-interest. The Convention had already agreed that direct taxes were to be assessed on the basis of population. The North was quite willing to have slaves counted as part of the population in apportioning such taxes, thus upping the South's assessments, but objected to counting slaves in apportioning representation in the House of Representatives, a plan which would enlarge the Southern delegations.

The Convention resolved these differences by negotiating compromises. In regard to commerce, the South won a ban on export taxes and a provision requiring a two-thirds vote in the Senate for ratification of treaties; in return, the North secured a provision that a simple congressional majority was sufficient to pass all other acts of commercial regulation. The slave trade was not to be prohibited before the year 1808, but a tax of ten dollars might be imposed on each slave imported. The so-called three-fifths compromise specified that five slaves would equal three free men for purposes of both taxation and representation.

The influence of the states in the framework of the new constitution was greater than some nationalists would have liked. But one of the most important factors shaping the delegates' decisions was their practical recognition that they had to offer a constitution which the people would approve, and popular loyalty to the respective states was too strong to be ignored.

Referral to the States. By the close of the summer the Constitution was slowly taking shape, and on September 17, 1787, twelve state delegations voted approval of the final draft. Edmund Randolph and George Mason of Virginia, along with Elbridge Gerry of Massachusetts, refused to sign it, feeling that it went too far toward consolidation and lacked a bill of rights. (Randolph, however, later decided to support it.) The remaining thirty-nine delegates affixed their signatures and sent the document to Congress with two recommendations: that it be submitted to state ratifying conventions especially called for the purpose, rather than directly to the voters; and that it be declared officially operative when nine (not thirteen) states accepted it, since there was real doubt that any document so evolved could ever get unanimous approval. Some of the delegates feared that they had far exceeded their instructions to *revise* the Articles, for the document they sent to Congress certainly represented much more than revision.

Federalists and Antifederalists. The new Constitution met with great favor and equally great opposition in the states. Its strongest proponents, who adopted the name "Federalists," were drawn from the ranks of bankers, lawyers, businessmen, merchants, planters, and men of property in the urban areas. Hamilton and Jay favored it in New York; Madison, Randolph, and John Marshall argued for it in Virginia; and the fact that Washington and Franklin, the two most honored Americans, supported it was much in its favor. Opposition to its ratification came from the small farmers, laborers, and the debtor, agrarian classes. However, it is misleading to arrange the argument over ratification on lines of economic interest alone, however convenient. Obviously there were businessmen and merchants who voted for the document because they felt it would mean expanded markets, better regulation of commerce, greater credit stability, and less control of economic affairs by the states. Just as obviously there were farmers and debtors who voted against it for equally self-interested reasons. But the lines of demarcation between rich and poor, or mercantile and agrarian interests, were by no means so clear in the voting as one might expect. Claiming that the nation could obtain progress and prosperity under the Articles if they were revised, the Antifederalists accused the Convention of creating a government that eventually, as George Mason of Virginia thought, might "produce either a monarchy or a corrupt aristocracy"; there was "apprehension," Rufus King of New York told Madison, "that the liberties of the people are in danger."

On the other hand, the Federalists, who might more accurately have been called "nationalists," possessed a group of leaders of great drive and organizing skill; it was not easy to outargue or outmaneuver men such as Hamilton, Jay, Madison, James Wilson, or Henry Knox. Furthermore, they had the initiative and kept it, giving their opposition little time to temporize or organize. The Federalists immediately began an energetic campaign for ratification in their own states. In New York, where opposition was strong, the Constitution was brilliantly defended in a series of eighty-five newspaper articles written by Hamilton, Madison, and Jay. The essays later were collected in a single volume called *The Federalist.*

The Antifederalists had only a few such talented leaders; George Clinton, Patrick Henry, Elbridge Gerry, Luther Martin, and James Warren were able men, but none, for example, was capable of producing the brilliant *Federalist* papers or of handling the New York campaigns as Hamilton did. The Antifederalists tried to fight the battle piecemeal, without a positive program, and showed a curious reluctance to match the aggressive, shrewd campaigning of the Federalists.

It has long been fashionable among historians, particularly in the earlier twentieth century, to consider the struggle over ratification as a contest between "conservatives" and "liberals." If the Declaration of Independence represented "radical" or revolutionary thought, the Constitution, it was assumed, therefore represented a conservative counterrevolution which undid some of the Revolution's work. On reexamination, however, it becomes less clear which side deserves which label. It was the Federalists, after all, who proposed the bold, decisive change to carry out to completion the powerful nationalism engendered by the revolutionary effort. This was a daring step—to create a single, unified nation from a bundle of disparate states bound together by common consent and national pride. The Antifederalists, fearful of any power not under their direct restraint, preferred the status quo; to them, apparently, the great experiment in federalism suggested by the Constitution seemed too new, too dangerous. They could not conceive of a nationalized government which did not threaten republican principles.

The Constitution Ratified.　The ratification of the document proceeded smoothly in most of the smaller states, which were generally satisfied with the compromises set up to protect them. By January 1788 five states (Delaware, New Jersey, Georgia, Connecticut, and Pennsylvania) had accepted it, with strong opposition to it recorded only in Pennsylvania. The Massachusetts state convention ratified the Constitution by a vote of 187 to 168 after a long dispute, and then only after attaching a strong recommendation for a bill of rights. Maryland and South Carolina ratified, while New Hampshire, the ninth state, took two conventions (the second by a margin of nine votes) to accept it in June 1788. Legally the Constitution could go into effect, yet most people understood that without New York and Virginia it could not function successfully.

In Virginia, the Federalists won a narrow victory, 89 to 79, on June 25. Like Massachusetts, Virginia attached proposals for twenty changes and a recommendation for a specific bill of rights. In New York, Hamilton and the Federalists pulled the document through on July 26 by the breathtakingly small margin of 30 to 27. North Carolina refused to ratify until a bill of rights was actually attached to the Constitution, and finally approved it in late 1789. Rhode Island held out until 1790.

The debates over the ratification indicated that the chief issue was the Constitution's lack of a bill of rights, so in 1789 the First Congress proposed ten amendments (ratified in 1791) to guarantee popular government and individual freedom. Of the ten, the First prohibited Congress from interfering with freedom of speech, press, religion, and assembly; initially pertaining only to the federal courts, the Fifth placed the citizen under "due process" of law, and the Sixth and Seventh guaranteed trial by jury. The Tenth reserved to the people and to the states all powers not delegated to the federal government, thereby providing a guarantee of decentralized political power.

The ideas expressed in the Constitution were themselves implicit in the Articles,

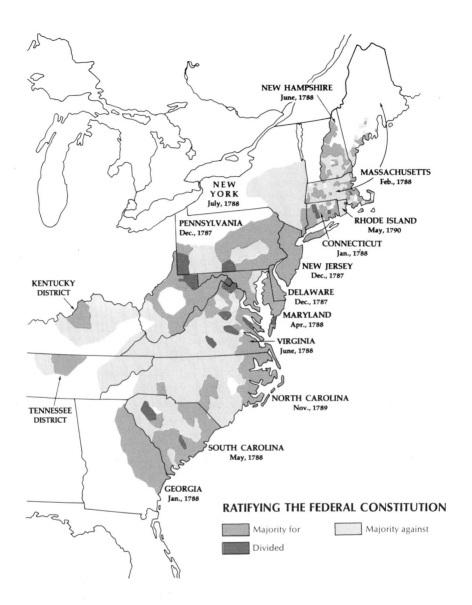

NEW HAMPSHIRE
June, 1788

MASSACHUSETTS
Feb., 1788

NEW YORK
July, 1788

RHODE ISLAND
May, 1790

PENNSYLVANIA
Dec., 1787

CONNECTICUT
Jan., 1788

NEW JERSEY
Dec., 1787

KENTUCKY
DISTRICT

DELAWARE
Dec., 1787

MARYLAND
Apr., 1788

VIRGINIA
June, 1788

NORTH CAROLINA
Nov., 1789

TENNESSEE
DISTRICT

SOUTH CAROLINA
May, 1788

GEORGIA
Jan., 1788

RATIFYING THE FEDERAL CONSTITUTION

Majority for   Majority against

Divided

the Declaration of Independence, and the revolutionary argument; the Constitution merely gave those ideas explicit, final form. The idea that government should protect life, liberty, and property was already accepted; the idea that government should be powerful enough to perform its functions was already recognized, even in the Articles (though there were sharp differences of opinion over how powerful that need be). No one at the Convention, and very few people in the states, argued for retention of the Articles without change. The question was, did the Constitution change the direction of government too much? The difference between the Articles and the Constitution lay almost wholly in the amount and quality of the authority granted to that "more perfect union."

LAUNCHING THE GOVERNMENT

Washington and Federalist Rule. After the balloting for President in January 1789, and for Congress under the terms of the new Constitution, the presidential electors met in February to choose George Washington as the first President of the United States. John Adams, who had received the smaller number of electoral ballots, was installed as Vice-President in mid-April, and on April 30 Washington, standing on the balcony of the Federal Building at Broad and Wall Streets in New York, was inaugurated as President.

For the first few months of the new administration, Congress and the President moved carefully. Congress quickly created the three executive departments of State, Treasury, and War, and Washington chose Thomas Jefferson, Alexander Hamilton, and Henry Knox to serve as their Secretaries. Congress then passed a tariff on imports and a tonnage duty on foreign vessels, both intended to raise revenue and to protect American trade. The Judiciary Act of 1789 created the office of Attorney General, a Supreme Court, three circuit courts, and thirteen district courts, filling in the outlines of the federal legal system.

Federalist Finance. Washington left the most critical problem of his first term to Alexander Hamilton, his confident young Secretary of the Treasury. Hamilton believed, as most Federalists did, that the government should play an active, even decisive role in economic affairs, so that the nation might achieve a self-sufficient, expanding economy, balanced among agriculture, manufacturing, and trade. To this end he proposed, in his *Report on the Public Credit* (1790), *Second Report on the Public Credit* (1791), and *Report on Manufactures* (1791), a firm, unified policy enforced by a strong federal authority.

Hamilton's economic program also had clear political aims. He was convinced that the new government could not last unless the Constitution were strengthened by interpretation and made responsive to changing needs, and unless the forces of wealth and property supported it. Thus he hoped to win business and financial groups to the support of the federal government, and to bind these groups to the national interest. Hamilton fashioned his program from three basic components.

The first, his *Report on the Public Credit,* laid the foundation for the Hamiltonian system. Under the previous regimes—that is, the Continental and Confederation congresses—the general government had accumulated a foreign debt of about $12 million, owed chiefly to France and Holland, and a domestic debt of about $40 million, owed to American nationals. The separate states owed a total of about $22 million more. Hamilton proposed that the federal government promise full payment of the foreign and domestic debt at par value and take over, or *assume,* the unpaid debts of the states. Since the federal government did not possess the money to pay this debt, totaling about $74 million, Hamilton recommended *funding* the entire debt; that is, in exchange for their old Continental and Confederation bonds creditors would be issued new interest-bearing bonds which would be the direct obligation of the new federal government.

No opposition was voiced against payment of the foreign debt in full, but full payment of the domestic debt at face value was another matter. On the open market these old domestic bonds had been selling at far below their original face value. Because the previous central governments had failed to meet interest payments or provide for retirement of the debt, the original owners of the bonds had lost faith in them and had sold them for whatever they could get. The purchasers were usually men of means who were willing to buy cheap on the chance that the government would make good.

Hamilton did succeed in getting Congress to make the old bonds good at face value (many congressmen were themselves bond holders), but in so doing he aroused charges from his opponents that the new government was being operated in the interest of the wealthy. Hamilton's intentions, however, were actually both honorable and farsighted: in his plan, he believed, the middle and upper classes would find a strong motive for sustaining the national government, and their confidence in the solvency and good faith of the government would stimulate business activity. In addition, the funded debt, in the form of negotiable bonds, could be used by creditors as capital to finance new enterprises.

The assumption of the state debts by the federal government also evoked vehement opposition, particularly from the Southern states, which had already paid off most of their debts. Southerners protested the use of national funds to help pay off the obligations of states with large outstanding debts, such as the New England states. Hamilton's assumption program was defeated on its first vote in the House, but he finally won in a bargain with Jefferson: in exchange for an agreement to locate the new national capital on the Potomac across from Virginia, Jefferson's congressional forces agreed to assume the debts of the states.

The second part of Hamilton's program called for the creation of a central bank, somewhat like the Bank of England, which would serve as a depository for federal funds, issue paper money (which the Treasury by law could not do), provide commercial interests with a steady and dependable credit institution, and serve the government with short-term loans. Some leaders in and out of Congress objected to this proposal on two grounds: four fifths of the bank's funds were to come from private sources, which might then control the bank's (and the nation's) fiscal policies; more important, the scheme was probably unconstitutional. Jefferson and Madison, among others, argued that since the federal government was not specifically authorized by the Constitution to create a national bank, for Congress to do so would be unconstitutional.

Hamilton, aware that the bank bill might set an important precedent, argued that Congress was authorized by the Constitution to do what was "necessary and proper" for the national good. If the proposed bank fell within this definition, as he believed it did, the Constitution gave Congress "implied powers" to act in ways not precisely enumerated in the document. He took the position "that every power vested in a government is in its nature *sovereign* and includes, by *force* of the *term,* a right to employ all the *means* requisite and fairly applicable to the attainment of the *ends* of such power. . . ."

Jefferson, to the contrary, argued that the federal government possessed only those powers explicitly granted to it in the Constitution, and that all others, as the Tenth Amendment determined, were reserved to the states. The language of the Constitution must be strictly construed. "To take a single step beyond the boundaries thus specially drawn around the powers of Congress," he wrote, "is to take possession of a boundless field of power, no longer susceptible of any definition." Neither the "general welfare" nor the "necessary and proper" clause of the Constitution, he maintained, could be so broadly interpreted as Hamilton wished. Washington and Congress, however, accepted Hamilton's argument and in 1791 created the Bank of the United States with a charter for twenty years.

The Whiskey Rebellion.   Third, Hamilton proposed to levy an excise tax on a number of commodities to supply money to the federal Treasury, for, he wrote, ". . . the creation of debt should always be accompanied by the means of its extinguishment." Among the items included in the bill, passed in 1791, was whiskey; in western Pennsylvania and North Carolina, where conversion into whiskey was a cheap and efficient way of getting grain to market, Hamilton's excise tax was therefore a tax on the farmer's most valuable cash crop. Collections fell off in this area in 1792, a few tax collectors were manhandled by irritated Pennsylvania farmers in 1793, and in 1794 a sizeable force of angry whiskey makers vowed to march on Pittsburgh to challenge federal authority at its nearest point.

Memories of Daniel Shays were still fresh in Congress, and President Washington acted quickly. He issued a proclamation ordering the Pennsylvanians to return to their homes, declared western Pennsylvania in a state of rebellion, and sent Hamilton and Henry Lee with a force of fifteen thousand militiamen to Pennsylvania. The farmers promptly scattered, but Hamilton, determined to teach the unruly frontiersmen a lesson in federal authority, saw to it that a score of the ringleaders were arrested, tried, and sentenced to death. Washington wisely pardoned them, but neither Hamilton nor Federalism was ever popular in that region again.

The Indian Frontier.   At the close of the Revolution the issue between Indian and white American remained as insoluble as ever. It seemed impossible to divert or delay the American drive westward, where the tribes stood in possession of undeveloped lands of great value. Indians were difficult to negotiate with, for few Americans understood much of Indian psychology, politics, or culture, while both red and white men were heirs of two hundred years of constant warfare. White explorers and settlers, almost from their first contacts with the Indian, developed contrasting images of him—as "noble red man" on the one hand, and "barbaric savage" on the other—which persisted in the American mind. Some Americans, particularly the educated minority, viewed the Indians' culture with respect and sympathized with their plight; like Jefferson, they hoped that Indian rights would be respected and that the tribes could be assimilated into American society. Others tended to see the Indian as irredeemably—though tragically—savage, incapable ever of learning the ways of civilization. Frontiersmen, too, had vivid recollections of Indian attacks during the French and Indian wars and fresher bitter memories of Loyalist-Indian raids in New York and Pennsylvania during the Revolution.

The new government also inherited an Indian policy that was itself divided—on the one hand, British "imperial" policy, which was to keep peace with and among the tribes, control expansion into Indian territory, and encourage Indian trade; on the other, the American colonial policy of conquest, which sought to evict the Indians from their tribal lands, move them westward, and open their former territories to settlement. Part of London's troubles with the colonies had derived from the conflict between these policies. After the Revolution the federal government was free to pursue a policy of subjugating and removing the Indians on the frontier but simply did not have the military power to enforce it. Meanwhile, the possibility of an alliance between the western tribes and the British army, still in Canada, posed a threat to the Ohio-Indiana frontier. In fact, although the British had promised at the Peace of Paris to give up their posts in the Northwest, they apparently intended to hold them as long as possible. Orders from the Colonial Office to the governor-general of Canada, one day before the proclamation of the treaty in 1784, instructed British commanders to do exactly that. Indian assistance, in this case, could be of great importance to the British.

THE PERILS OF NEUTRALITY

The French Revolution.   The outbreak of the French Revolution forced the Washington administration into the first real test of its foreign policy. A good many Americans in 1789 welcomed the news of the French uprisings as the logical outcome of their own revolution, and "in no part of the world," wrote John Marshall later, "was the Revolution hailed with more joy than in America." The execution of Louis XVI and the Reign of Terror which followed led many, however, to sober second thoughts, while the French declaration of war against England, Holland, and Spain in February 1793 introduced the difficult question of neutrality directly into American foreign policy. One segment of opinion, holding that Britain was still the United States' major enemy, favored the French cause. Others felt that British trade was so essential to American prosperity that the United States, whatever its sympathies with revolution, could not afford to offend the world's greatest naval and economic power. Still others, observing the chaos of Jacobin Paris, saw France as a threat to the security and order of society everywhere, even to Christianity itself.

When he received news of the outbreak of war between France and Britain, Washington immediately issued a proclamation in April 1793 (avoiding the word "neutrality") which guaranteed the belligerents the "friendly and impartial conduct" of the United States. America, he believed, needed peace—the opportunity to build up its strength—more than anything else. "If this country is preserved in tranquillity twenty years longer," he wrote, "it may bid defiance in a just cause to any power whatever. . . ." His proclamation, which was to influence American foreign policy for the next half century, derived from his firm conviction that the United States should avoid, at all reasonable costs, the brawlings of Europe. In 1794 Congress passed a Neutrality Act which made Washington's position the official American policy.

Strained Relations with Britain. The British navy was large, the French navy small, and the British blockade of France very effective. When the French, desperate for trade, opened up their West Indian ports to American ships, the British immediately declared that any trade with France was a military act and that ships caught at it were subject to seizure. Not only did British men-of-war confiscate American cargoes, but claiming that some American sailors were really deserters from the British navy (as, indeed, a few were), they forcibly "impressed" a number of American seamen into naval service. Still, though American ships were in danger wherever they went in Atlantic waters, wartime trade was so lucrative that many American merchants felt that the profit was worth the risk, and incidents multiplied.

Jay's Treaty. Hoping to reduce tensions, Congress passed an embargo act in 1794 which forbade British ships to call at American ports and American ships to sail in areas where they might be subject to British seizure. Since this hurt American trade more than it hindered the British navy, the embargo lasted less than two months. However, American protests induced the British to relax some of their rules, and in 1794 Washington requested Chief Justice John Jay to sail for London to discuss a treaty to settle outstanding differences.

Jay's arguments were no doubt good ones, but perhaps more important, French military successes persuaded the British that it was unwise to antagonize the United States unduly. Under the terms of Jay's Treaty (the Treaty of London, signed in 1794) the British agreed to evacuate the frontier posts by 1796; to open the British West Indies to American trade under certain conditions; to admit American ships to East Indian ports on a nondiscriminatory basis; and to refer to a joint commission the payment of pre–Revolutionary War debts and the northwest boundary dispute. However, they simply refused to discuss other important points at issue, including impressment and the Indian question, and made far fewer concessions than Jay had been instructed to get. Washington reluctantly submitted the treaty to the Senate, which ratified it by only one vote. Not only was the Washington administration severely criticized for the settlement, but Jay himself was burned in effigy in various cities.

Not all news was bad, however. Spain, badly mauled by France in the land war, signed a separate peace in 1795 and, fearful of British retaliation for its defection, needed American friendship. In the Pinckney Treaty (the Treaty of San Lorenzo), signed on October 27, 1795, Spain recognized the line of 31° latitude as the United States' southern boundary and granted the United States free navigation of the Mississippi with a three-year right of deposit at New Orleans.

EARLY POLITICAL PARTIES

The Emergence of Partisan Politics. The dispute over Jay's Treaty revealed a deep division in Washington's administration, as well as growing public opposition to a number of Federalist policies. The French Revolution, the Franco-British War, and subsequent problems in foreign relations created further political differences in Congress. By 1792 opposing factions had begun to coalesce about the two strong men of Washington's cabinet, Hamilton and Jefferson. Though John Adams had written, "There is nothing I dread as much as the division of the Republic into two great parties, each under its leader," such a split seemed inevitable. This political division, first observable in the arguments over Hamilton's fiscal program, widened noticeably throughout Washington's first administration.

The pro-Hamilton, pro-Washington group, using the name adopted by the forces favoring the Constitution during the ratification campaign, called themselves Federalists. The opposition at first called themselves Antifederalists, a somewhat unsatisfactory label but the best that could be devised at the moment.

The Antifederalists opposed the administration's program chiefly on the grounds of what they felt was its tendency to concentrate wealth and influence in a relatively small class. Certainly neither Jefferson nor his followers objected to sound currency and credit or to economic stability and prosperity; rather, they opposed the Hamiltonian methods of obtaining them—the Bank, tariffs, excise taxes (but not the assumption of state debts)—because these measures might serve to create a permanently privileged class whose interests could well become inimical to the opportunities and welfare of the greater number of people. Through Washington's first term the rivalry between the two factions increased, but despite these internal tensions the Federalists easily reelected Washington against token opposition for a second term in 1792, with John Adams as his Vice-President.

The Election of 1796. James Madison gave the anti-administration forces a better name when, in 1792, he spoke of "the Republican party," a designation (sometimes "Democratic-Republican") that shortly displaced "Antifederalist." Into this loosely organized opposition group, formed about the commanding figure of Thomas Jefferson, came such men as Monroe and Madison of Virginia, George Clinton and Aaron Burr of New York, Albert Gallatin and Alexander Dallas from Pennsylvania, Willie Jones, the North Carolina back-country leader, and others from the Middle and Southern states. Among the Federalists were Hamilton, Schuyler, and John Jay of New York, Timothy Pickering and John Adams of Massachusetts, Thomas Pinckney of South Carolina, and John Marshall of Virginia, with Washington, of course, at the head of the party.

When Jefferson, convinced that he could no longer work with Hamilton and the administration party, resigned as Secretary of State in 1793, Republican partisan politics began in earnest. Hamilton resigned from the Treasury in 1795, partly because he could not afford to neglect his law and business interests, but he still remained the most powerful Federalist leader, since Washington decided not to run again in 1796.

Washington's achievements as President have been overshadowed by his image as "The Father of His Country" and by the dramatic contest during his second term between Hamilton and Jefferson. More recently, historians have pointed out Washington's real skill as an administrator and the importance of his contributions to the skill and efficiency of the fledgling government. Since almost every act of his first term set a precedent, Washington did more than any other man to establish the tone of the presidential office and to establish the whole set of delicate relationships among the executive, the cabinet, the Congress, and the judiciary.

When Washington decided in September 1796 not to seek a third term as President, he submitted to the press a "Farewell Address" which he had written with the aid of Madison and Hamilton. In his valedictory, published in newspapers throughout the nation, Washington explained his reasons for declining to seek a third term; stressed the necessity of preserving the Union, the "main prop" of individual liberty; pointed out the obligation of all Americans to obey the Constitution and the established government "'till changed by an explicit and authentic act of the whole People"; warned of the dangers of a party system, particularly one based on a division along geographical lines; urged that the public credit be cherished; and admonished Americans to observe "good faith and justice towards all Nations."

The most enduring passages of the Farewell Address, however, are those in which Washington counseled Americans to steer clear of permanent alliances with the foreign world. Washington's admonitions for a foreign policy of neutrality have been quoted consistently by isolationists in the past century and a half to justify the dominant American policy of avoiding involvement in international politics.

> . . . The great rule of conduct for us, in regard to foreign Nations, is, in extending our commercial relations, to have with them as little *Political* connection as possible. . . . Europe has a set of primary interests, which to us have none, or a very remote relation.—Hence she must be engaged in frequent controversies, the causes of which are essentially foreign to our concerns.—Hence therefore it must be unwise in us to implicate ourselves, by artificial ties in the ordinary vicissitudes of her politics. . . . Taking care always to keep ourselves . . . on a respectably defensive posture, we may safely trust to temporary alliances for extraordinary emergencies.

After eight years in office, Washington left behind a government that possessed a reasonably good civil service, a workable committee system, an economic program, a foreign policy, and the seeds of a body of constitutional theory. Unfortunately, he also left behind a party already beginning to divide. The election of 1796 gave clear indication of the mounting strength of the Republican opposition. Thomas Jefferson and Aaron Burr campaigned for the Republicans, John Adams and Thomas Pinckney for the Federalists. The margin of Federalist victory was slim: Adams had 71 electoral votes, and Jefferson had 68. Since Jefferson had more votes than Pinckney, he became Vice-President.

Federalist and Republican. It is too broad a generalization to say that the Federalists represented the conservative, commercial, nationalistic interests of the Northeast and Middle Atlantic states, and the Republicans the more radical, agrarian, debtor, states' rights interests of the South and West. Though there is some truth to the statement, the fact is that both parties drew support from all classes in all parts of the country. It would be more accurate to say that these parties were loose combinations of certain economic, social, and intellectual groupings, held together by a set of common attitudes and convictions.

Fundamentally, they reflected two different opinions about the qualities of human nature. Hamiltonians were acutely aware of the "imperfections, weaknesses, and evils of human nature"; they believed that if men were fit to govern themselves at all, it must only be under rigid controls imposed on them by society and government. Jeffersonians, on the other hand, believed that men were by inclination rational and good; that if they were freed from the bonds of ignorance, error, and repression, they might achieve real progress toward an ideal society. Others, of course, took positions between these two extremes.

These contrasting concepts of human fallibility were reflected in contemporary political opinions about the structure and aim of government. The Federalists emphasized the need for political machinery to restrain the majority. They believed in a strong central government and a strong executive, and the active participation of that government in manufacturing, commerce, and finance. They believed that leadership in society belonged to a trained, responsible, and (very likely) wealthy class which could be trusted to protect property as well as human rights.

The Jeffersonian Republicans distrusted centralized authority and a powerful executive, preferring instead a less autonomous, decentralized government modeled more on confederation than on federalism. They believed in the leadership of what Jefferson called "a natural aristocracy," founded on talent and intelligence rather than on birth, wealth, or station. Most Republicans believed that human nature in the aggregate was naturally trustworthy and that it could be improved through freedom and education; therefore the majority of men, under proper conditions, could govern themselves wisely.

THE TRIALS OF JOHN ADAMS

The XYZ Affair.   John Adams took office at a difficult time, for the Federalist party that elected him was showing strain at the seams. Hamilton still dictated a large share of party policy from private life; he did not like Adams and had maneuvered before the election to defeat him. Adams himself was a stubbornly honest man, a keen student of government and law, but blunt, a trifle haughty, sometimes tactless.

Adams' administration promptly found itself in trouble. Within his party there was a violently anti-French group who virtually demanded a declaration of war against France, and the French, angry at Jay's Treaty and at an American neutrality that appeared to favor Britain, seemed willing to cooperate. Adams, who did not want war, sent John Marshall, C. C. Pinckney, and Elbridge Gerry to Paris in 1797 to try to find some way out. The French foreign minister Talleyrand, dealing with the American commission through three mediaries called (for purposes of anonymity) X, Y, and Z, demanded not only a loan to the French government but also a bribe, which the Americans indignantly refused. When the news of the "XYZ Affair" leaked out, the ringing slogan "Millions for defense, but not one cent for tribute!" (presumably Pinckney's reply) became a rallying point for the anti-French faction in Congress.

   The Treaty of 1800.   Capitalizing on the war fever, Congress created a Department of the Navy, built a number of new ships, armed American merchantmen, and authorized an army of ten thousand men. Though his own party leaders (Hamilton among them) argued that war with France was inevitable, Adams refused to listen, and as it turned out, the French did not want war either. After nearly a year of undeclared naval war, the French government suggested that if an American mission were to be sent to Paris it would be respectfully received. By the time the American commissioners arrived in France in March 1800, the country was in the hands of Napoleon Bonaparte, who quietly agreed to a settlement of differences. The Treaty of 1800 was not popular with the Federalists or Congress, but it was ratified; it avoided a war and also dissolved the French-American alliance. John Adams got his peace, but probably at the expense of his own and his party's victory in the coming elections.

The Alien and Sedition Acts. The popular outcry against France, and the near-war that carried through 1797–99, gave the Federalists a good chance, they believed, to cripple their Republican political opponents under cover of protecting internal security. The country was honeycombed, so the Federalist press claimed, with French agents and propagandists who were secretly at work undermining the national will and subverting public opinion. Since most immigrants were inclined to vote Republican, the Federalist Congress capitalized on antiforeign feeling in 1798 by passing a series of Alien Acts which lengthened the naturalization period from five to fourteen years, empowered the President to deport undesirable aliens, and authorized him to imprison such aliens as he chose in time of war. Though he signed the bill, Adams did not like the acts and never seriously tried to enforce them.

Congress passed the Sedition Acts, also in 1798, as the second step in its anti-Republican campaign. Under these acts a citizen could be fined, imprisoned, or both for "writing, printing, uttering, or publishing" false statements or any statements which might bring the President or Congress "into contempt or disrepute." Since this last clause covered almost anything Republicans might say about Federalists, its purpose was quite plainly to muzzle the opposition. Under the Sedition Act twenty-five editors and printers were prosecuted and convicted—though they were later pardoned and their fines returned by the Jeffersonians.

With the Alien and Sedition laws the Federalists went too far. Public opinion sided with the Republicans. The legislatures of Kentucky and Virginia passed resolutions in 1798 and 1799 (Jefferson drafted Kentucky's, Madison Virginia's) condemning the laws and asking the states to join in nullifying them as violations of civil rights. Actually none did, but the Kentucky and Virginia resolutions furnished the Jeffersonians with excellent ammunition for the approaching presidential campaign. And although the United States had no strong tradition of civil liberties, the Alien and Sedition laws helped to create one by pointing out how easily those rights of free speech and free press guaranteed by the Bill of Rights could be violated.

The Election of 1800. Washington's death in December 1799 symbolized the passing of the Federalist dynasty. The party that he led was in dire distress, divided into wrangling factions. The Republicans were in an excellent position to capitalize on a long string of political moves which had alienated large blocs of voters—the handling of the Whiskey Rebellion, Hamilton's tax policies, the Jay Treaty and Jay's negotiations with Spain in 1786, the Alien and Sedition Acts—as well as conflict and resentment within the Federalist party. As a matter of fact, the Federalists had been unable to maintain a balance between the nationalist business interests which formed the core of their support, and the rapidly growing influence of the middle and lower urban and agrarian classes of the South, the West, and the Middle Atlantic states. After Washington, who had held the party together by the force of his example, no Federalist leader found a way to absorb and control the elements of society which, after 1796, began to look to Jefferson for leadership. The clash of personalities within the Federalist camp, of course, damaged the party further.

John Adams, who through his entire term had to face the internal opposition of the Hamiltonians as well as the Republicans from without, deserves more credit than he is often given. Except for Adams' stubborn desire to keep the peace, the United States most assuredly would have entered into a disastrous war with France, and without him the Federalist party under Hamilton's control would probably have killed itself ten years sooner than it did. Adams' decision to stay out of war, made against the bitter opposition of his own party, was not only an act of courage but very likely his greatest service to the nation.

Though Hamilton circulated a pamphlet violently attacking the President, the party had no other satisfactory candidate for the election of 1800 and decided to nominate Adams again, choosing C. C. Pinckney to run with him. The Republicans picked Jefferson and Burr once more, hoping thus to unite the powerful Virginia and New York wings of the party. The campaign was one of the bitterest and most scurrilous in American history; the Republicans, who won the Middle Atlantic states and the South, held a small edge in total electoral votes. Under the Constitution, however, the candidate with the most votes was President and the next Vice-President, so that when the Republican electors all voted for Jefferson and Burr, they created a tie. This threw the election into the House of Representatives, still controlled by lame-duck Federalists. The Federalist hatred of Jefferson was so intense that many of them preferred Burr; at the same time Burr's own party wanted Jefferson, but Burr refused to step aside. Hamilton, much as he disagreed with Jefferson's principles, considered Burr a political adventurer and deeply distrusted him. He therefore threw his influence behind Jefferson, who was declared President.

CHAPTER 5

THE JEFFERSONIAN ERA
1800–1824

JEFFERSON IN POWER

"The Revolution of 1800."   Thomas Jefferson usually referred to his presidential election victory as "the revolution of 1800," though it was hardly a "revolution" in any accepted sense. It was, nonetheless, an important election, for it shifted national political authority toward the South and West and introduced a new emphasis on decentralized power and state sovereignty. It marked the first successful alliance of agrarian and urban forces later consolidated by Jackson; and since it was also the first really violent American political campaign, it set "faction" and partisanship firmly into the political process. In actual practice, however, Jefferson did surprisingly little to erase what his predecessors had done, and there was much greater continuity from the Federalist decade into his own than appeared at first glance.

Settling the Barbary Corsairs.   Jefferson's administration had hardly caught its breath before it was plunged into a vortex of swift-moving foreign affairs. The President's first problem involved the depredations of pirates from the Barbary states of North Africa (Tunis, Algiers, Morocco, and Tripoli), who had preyed on Mediterranean commerce for a quarter century, enslaving seamen and levying tribute on shipping. During their administrations, Washington and Adams paid out more than $2 million in ransom and bribes to the Barbary potentates, and Jefferson determined to end the affair. Beginning in 1803 the United States sent to the Mediterranean four naval squadrons, which in a series of brilliant actions finally forced some of the pirate states to sue for peace. A final treaty was not established until 1815, but after 1805 American rights were generally respected in the Mediterranean and the shameful practice of extracting ransom and tribute was on its way to extinction.

The Purchase of Louisiana.   In 1801 Napoleon Bonaparte recovered the territory of Louisiana, lost by France to Spain in 1763. Jefferson recognized the potential danger to the United States of this sudden shift in ownership of half the American continent from impotent Spain to imperial France. The United States could not afford to have New Orleans, he wrote, possessed by "our natural and habitual enemy," Napoleon; "The day that France takes possession of New Orleans, we must marry ourselves to the British Navy." And of course the United States needed the West if its empire was ever, as Jefferson hoped, to stretch from sea to sea.

The President therefore sent James Monroe to Paris to discuss the possible

BRITISH POSSESSIONS

OREGON COUNTRY

LOUISIANA PURCHASE 1803

UNITED STATES IN 1783

SPANISH POSSESSIONS

SPANISH POSSESSIONS

LOUISIANA PURCHASE

purchase of Louisiana; it was either buy now, Jefferson said, or fight for it later. Napoleon, for his part, did not want to face a British-American alliance in case of war and knew that, since New Orleans was almost indefensible against American attack, he would probably lose Louisiana anyway.

Napoleon therefore decided to sell, and after some haggling the United States purchased the Louisiana territory and West Florida in April 1803 for $15 million. Jefferson, though overjoyed at the bargain, was also embarrassed by the fact that nowhere in the Constitution could he find presidential authority to make it. He finally accepted Madison's view that the purchase could be made under a somewhat elastic interpretation of the treaty-making power. The brilliance of the maneuver obscured the constitutional question involved, but the "strict constructionist" doctrine was never the same again.

Whatever its constitutionality, the Louisiana Purchase was one of the most important presidential decisions in American history. At one stroke the United States became a continental power, master of the continent's navigation system, and owner of vast new resources that promised greater (and perhaps final) economic independence from Europe. It also put an end to the likelihood that the West could ever be split from the East and set a precedent for future territorial expansion.

The Problems of Political Patronage. In addition to the need for keeping a watchful eye on Europe and the Mediterranean, Jefferson had political problems at home. His cabinet, a particularly able group, included James Madison of Virginia as Secretary of State and the brilliant Swiss from Pennsylvania, Albert Gallatin, as Secretary of the Treasury. Quite aware of the utility of patronage, Jefferson quietly replaced Federalist appointments with his own, so that before the close of his first term he had responsible Republicans in positions where it counted. One of his thorniest problems, however, was that of the so-called "midnight judges" appointed by John Adams under the Judiciary Act of 1801. The act reduced the number of Supreme Court justices to five, created sixteen new circuit courts, and added a number of federal marshals and other officials. About a month earlier Adams nominated Secretary of State John Marshall as Chief Justice of the Supreme Court; then on the eve of

Jefferson's inauguration, Adams filled many of the new judicial posts with solid Federalist party men.

John Marshall was a stalwart Federalist, but beyond that he was a convinced nationalist who believed that the Constitution was the most sacred of all documents, "framed for ages to come . . . , designed to approach immortality as nearly as human institutions can approach it." He did not trust the Jeffersonians, and he entered the Court determined that none should play fast and loose with the Constitution so long as he could prevent it.

Jefferson v. Marshall. Jefferson was certain that Marshall, that "crafty chief judge," would set as many obstacles as he could in the administration's path and that the "midnight judges" would undoubtedly follow his lead. When Congress repealed the Judiciary Act of 1801, all of Adams' judges were left without salaries or duties. This, the Federalist opposition claimed, was unconstitutional. The judges had been appointed for terms of life or good behavior; therefore Congress could not in effect cancel these appointments by repealing the act.

As a test to determine the constitutionality of the repeal, William Marbury asked the Supreme Court to issue a writ of mandamus ordering Secretary of State Madison to give Marbury his legal commission as justice of the peace of the District of Columbia. This Madison refused to do. Marshall, in a dextrous opinion, used the case to promote what Jefferson did not want established—the Supreme Court's right of judicial review of legislation, which had been occasionally exercised in practice since 1796 but never firmly accepted.

In *Marbury* v. *Madison* (1803) Marshall made two points: first, that those portions of the Judiciary Act of 1789 which gave the Supreme Court the power to issue writs as Marbury requested were unconstitutional; second, (and Marshall drove this home) that it was the prerogative of the Supreme Court to review an act of Congress, such as the Judiciary Act of 1789, and to declare it constitutional or unconstitutional. The Constitution, wrote Marshall, is "the *supreme* law of the land, superior to any ordinary act of the legislative." "A legislative act contrary to the Constitution is not law," Marshall went on, and "it is the province and duty of the judicial department to say what the law is."

The Jefferson administration then launched an attack directly on the Federalist judiciary itself, using as its tool the constitutional power of impeachment for "high crimes and misdemeanors." The first target was John Pickering of the New Hampshire district court, who was apparently both alcoholic and insane. Pickering was impeached by the House, judged guilty by the Senate, and removed from office. Next, in 1804, the Republicans picked Associate Justice Samuel Chase of the Supreme Court, a violently partisan Federalist who had presided over several trials of Jeffersonian editors under the Sedition Act of 1798. In 1805, when the Senate decided it could not convict Chase, Jefferson conceded that impeachment was ineffective as a political weapon. Congress then gradually created a series of new judgeships and filled them with Republicans, a slower process but one that worked.

Marshall and the Supeme Court. Jefferson's differences with Marshall were temporarily settled, but Marshall's long tenure as Chief Justice was a most important influence on the rapid growth of the power of the federal government over the next three decades. Marshall served on the Court from 1801 to 1835, participated in more than a thousand opinions and decisions, and wrote some five hundred of them. Whenever opportunity presented itself, as it often did, Marshall never failed to affirm the doctrines of constitutional sanctity and federal supremacy. He stressed the fact that the Constitution was an ordinance of the people rather than an agreement among the states, and that the United States was a sovereign nation instead of a mere federation. By rejecting the states as creators of the Union, he weakened the states' rights (and later right-of-secession) concept of political powers.

In *Fletcher* v. *Peck* (1810) Marshall asserted the inviolability of contracts, which even a state could not break. Also in this decision, for the first time a state law was held void because it conflicted with the Constitution. *Martin* v. *Hunter's Lessee* (1816) affirmed the Supreme Court's power to overrule a state court. *McCulloch* v. *Maryland* (1819) embedded the doctrine of Congress' "implied powers" into constitutional law. In *Dartmouth College* v. *Woodward* (1819) Marshall held unconstitutional a New Hampshire law altering the charter of Dartmouth College and placing that institution, against its will, under state control. The decision established the principle that corporation charters were contracts which could not be impaired. *Gibbons* v. *Ogden* (1824) affirmed the exclusive right of the federal government to regulate interstate commerce.

In these and other opinions and decisions Marshall consistently stressed two principles: that the Supreme Court possessed the power to nullify state laws in conflict with the Constitution and that the Court alone had the right to interpret the Constitution, especially in regard to such broad grants of authority as might be contained in terms such as "commerce," "general welfare," "necessary and proper," and so on. His opinion did not always become the final version of constitutional issues, but the consistency of his attitudes, carried over a whole generation of legal interpretations, had much to do with the shaping of American constitutional law.

Opening the West.   After the Louisiana Purchase there was great anxiety to find out about what the nation had bought, more or less sight unseen. Jefferson, who had already made plans for the exploration of these newly acquired lands, persuaded Congress to finance an expedition up the Missouri River, across the Rocky Mountains, and if possible on to the Pacific. To lead it Jefferson chose his private secretary, a young Virginian named Meriwether Lewis, and William Clark, brother of George Rogers Clark, the frontier soldier.

In the spring of 1804 Lewis and Clark's party of forty-eight, including several scientists, left St. Louis for the West, mapping, gathering specimens of plants and animals, collecting data on soil and weather, observing every pertinent detail of the new country. They wintered in the Dakotas and with the help of a Shoshone Indian woman, Sacajawea, crossed the Rockies and followed the Columbia River to the Pacific, catching their first glimpse of the sea in November 1805. By autumn of 1806 the expedition was back in St. Louis. At almost the same time a party under Lieutenant Zebulon Pike was exploring the upper Mississippi and the mid-Rockies. Other explorations followed, and Louisiana Territory was soon organized on the pattern of the Northwest Ordinance of 1787 (its first state, Louisiana, entered in 1812). The West was no longer a dream but a reality. (See map, p. 98.)

The "Essex Junto." The prospect of more states being carved out of the wide new West greatly disturbed the Federalist party leaders. Ohio entered the Union in 1803, a soundly Republican state, and the probability that all the new states from the Northwest Territory, plus all those to be developed from the Louisiana Purchase, might lean politically to the Jeffersonians was profoundly worrisome. United only in their common hostility to the President, the Federalists had neither issue nor leader to counter his popularity and had little chance of finding either. The gloom was especially thick in New England, so much so that a small number of Federalists (nicknamed the "Essex Junto") explored the possibilities of persuading the five New England states, plus New York and New Jersey, to secede from the Union to form a separate Federalist republic—a "Northern Confederacy," said Senator Timothy Pickering of Massachusetts, "exempt from the corrupt and corrupting influence and oppression of the aristocratic democrats of the South."

Alexander Hamilton of New York showed no inclination to join them, so the New Englanders approached Aaron Burr. Since Burr felt it unlikely that he would be nominated for Vice-President again, he consented to run for the governorship of New York, an office from which he might lead a secession movement. Hamilton disliked Jeffersonians too, but he considered Burr a dangerous man and campaigned against him. After Burr lost, he challenged Hamilton to a duel on the basis of certain slurs on Burr's character reported in the press and killed him in July 1804.

Alexander Hamilton died as he lived, a controversial man who aroused strong feelings. His blunt distrust of "King Mob" and his frank preference for British-style constitutionalism had never endeared him to the public, but the leadership he provided for the country during the crucial postwar years had much to do with its successful transition from a provincial to a federal philosophy. Woodrow Wilson once characterized Hamilton, quite unfairly, as a great man but not a great American; it is more accurate to say that he may not have been a great man, but he was an indispensable one.

The duel ruined Burr's reputation and helped to complete the eclipse of the Federalist party. Yet Burr himself was not quite finished. After the Republicans passed him over as their vice-presidential candidate in 1804 in favor of George Clinton of New York, he apparently entered into a scheme to carve a great empire of his own out of the American West, a conspiracy which ended with his trial for treason in 1807. Although he was acquitted, everyone drawn into his plan was likewise ruined, and Burr himself was forced to flee to England to escape further prosecution for Hamilton's death and additional charges of treason. Meanwhile, the Federalist party approached the election of 1804 with its brilliant leader dead, its reputation tarnished, and neither candidates nor issues of any public value.

The Election of 1804. The election of 1804 was very nearly no contest. The Republican caucus nominated Jefferson for a second time, with George Clinton of New York as his running mate. The Federalists ran the reliable C. C. Pinckney and Rufus King of New York. Jefferson carried every state except Connecticut and Delaware, garnering 162 of the total 176 electoral votes and sweeping an overwhelmingly Republican Congress with him. His first administration ended on a high note of success—as John Randolph said later, the United States was "in the 'full tide of successful experiment.' Taxes repealed; the public debt amply provided for, both principal and interest; sinecures abolished; Louisiana acquired; public confidence unbounded." Unfortunately, it could not last.

AMERICA AND THE WOES OF EUROPE

Neutrality in a World at War.   Napoleon Bonaparte loomed large in the future of both Europe and America. Jefferson did not like him, but Napoleon nevertheless represented Jefferson's beloved France and what little was left of the legacy of the French Revolution. Against Napoleon stood England, whose aim Jefferson believed was "the permanent domination of the ocean and the monopoly of the trade of the world." He wanted war with neither, nor did he wish to give aid to either in the war that flamed up between them in 1803.

It would be an oversimplification, of course, to assume that American foreign policy of the period was governed primarily by a like or dislike of France or England. The objectives of Jefferson's foreign policy, like Washington's and Adams', were first to protect American independence and second to maintain as much diplomatic flexibility as possible without irrevocable commitment to any nation. In the European power struggle between England and France that developed after 1790, Jefferson saw great advantages to the United States in playing each against the other without being drawn into the orbit of either. An American friendship with France would form a useful counterbalance against the influence of Britain and Spain, the chief colonial powers in North and South America; a British and Spanish defeat might well mean the end of their American empires. At the same time Jefferson did not want to tie America's future to the fortunes of Napoleon, who might be an even greater threat to American freedom if he won. The wisest policy therefore lay in neutrality to all and trade with any—or, as the British wryly put it, America's best hope was "to gain fortune from Europe's misfortune."

Maintaining neutrality was as difficult for Jefferson as it had been for Washington and Adams before him. The British navy ruled the seas, and Napoleon, particularly after the Battle of Austerlitz in 1805, ruled Europe; the war remained a stalemate while the two countries engaged in a battle of proclamations over wartime naval commerce. Each side set up a blockade of the other's ports, but since neither had sufficient ships to enforce the quarantine, American vessels filtered through these "paper blockades" with comparative ease when the risk was warranted.

The British at Sea.   From 1804 to 1807 the British and French issued a confusing series of orders and decrees aimed at controlling ocean trade, with the result that American vessels were liable to confiscation by either belligerent if they obeyed the rules of the other. In addition, British men-of-war insolently patrolled the American coast to intercept and inspect American ships for contraband almost as soon as they left port; and, as if this were insufficient provocation, the British claimed the right to search American ships for British deserters.

Conditions in the British navy encouraged desertion, and doubtless a number of British sailors turned up in the American merchant marine; it was also evident that British captains were notoriously careless about matters of citizenship and in many cases simply kidnapped American sailors. Protests from the United States government about these "impressments" were loftily disregarded. Finally, in the summer of 1807 the British *Leopard* stopped the United States navy's *Chesapeake* (a warship, not a merchant vessel), killed or wounded twenty-one men, and took four sailors.

This was by any standard an act of war, and America burst out in a great roar of rage. Had Congress been in session, it almost certainly would have declared war on the spot; but Jefferson held his temper, demanded apologies and reparations, and ordered British ships out of American waters to prevent further incidents. Though the British apologized, they also reaffirmed their right to search American ships and seize deserters. The *Leopard-Chesapeake* affair rankled in American minds for years and had much to do with the drift toward war with Britain in 1812.

The Obnoxious Embargo. Jefferson and Secretary of State Madison bent every effort to avoid provocation that might lead to war. There were only two choices—war or some kind of economic substitute. The easier choice would have been war, for which Jefferson could have obtained public and congressional support; but he chose peace, aware as he was of the troubles he was stirring up for himself and his party. He pinned his hopes on "peaceful coercion," as he called it, by means of a boycott of British goods and a set of nonimportation acts which Congress passed in 1806 and 1807.

Neither was sufficiently effective to do much good. As the situation between the two nations steadily deteriorated, Jefferson asked Congress for a full-scale embargo, a logical move since Britain needed American trade, especially foodstuffs, in increasing quantities as the war progressed. In late 1807 Congress therefore passed the Embargo Act, which forbade American ships to leave the United States for any foreign port or even to engage in the American coastal trade without posting a heavy bond.

Jefferson hoped that the Embargo of 1807 would do two things: first, that it would discourage the British from seizing American ships and sailors and force them to greater regard for American rights; and, second, that it would encourage the growth of American industry by cutting off British imports.

England suffered shortages, but not enough to matter; France approved of the Embargo since it helped at second hand to enforce Napoleon's own blockade of England. American ships rotted at anchor along the Eastern seaboard; merchants went bankrupt; farm surpluses piled up. In New York, one traveler wrote, "The streets near the waterside were almost deserted; the grass had begun to grow upon the wharves." While the shipping interests suffered, however, New England and the Middle Atlantic port states began a transition to manufacturing that was soon to change their economic complexion. With foreign competition removed, capital previously invested in overseas trade was available for new factories and mills, which sprang up in profusion along the seaboard. But the future economic advantages were difficult to see in the midst of the paralyzing effects of the Embargo. Jefferson was violently attacked in the taverns and counting houses, and finally Congress repealed the Embargo. On March 1, 1809, three days before his successor Madison took office, Jefferson reluctantly signed the bill.

The end of Jefferson's second term came during the bitterest disputes over the Embargo, and the President, who had wished for some time to retire to his beloved Monticello, was relieved to accept Washington's two-term precedent and announce his retirement. His eight years of rule, begun in such high confidence, ended on a much more equivocal note. Ironically, Jefferson, the believer in decentralized government, found himself under the Embargo wielding more power over American life than any Federalist would have dreamed of. Though a "strict constructionist," he had discovered authority in the Constitution to buy Louisiana; and though a believer in states' rights, he had coerced the New England states into an economic boycott which hurt their commerce badly.

The Election of 1808. Jefferson trusted and admired James Madison and easily secured the Republican nomination for him. The Federalists nominated the tireless C. C. Pinckney again, but in spite of the Embargo and divided Republican sentiment Madison won by 122 to 47 electoral votes.

The Drift to War. James Madison, far from being a mere graceful shadow of Jefferson, was very much his own man. His role in the formation of the Republican party was a decisive one, and the political philosophy of the Jeffersonian group owed much to his thinking. He was an astute practitioner of politics as well as a profound student of it, but when he succeeded Jefferson, he inherited from him a large bundle of thorny problems. The Non-Intercourse Act, with which Madison replaced the Embargo in 1809, allowed American ships to trade with any nations except France and England; when this failed to work, Congress replaced it with Macon's Bill No. 2 (named after the chairman of the House Foreign Affairs Committee), which relieved American shipping from all restrictions while ordering British and French naval vessels from American waters. This failed to influence British policy, but "peaceable coercion" was beginning to hurt England more than the British admitted and more than Madison realized. Parliament was preparing to relax some of its restrictions even as Congress moved toward a declaration of war. It simply did not happen soon enough to change the course of events.

The War Hawks. Jefferson's "peaceful coercion" policy was probably the best that could have been pursued under the circumstances, and except for some exceedingly clumsy diplomacy abroad and mounting pressures for war at home, it might have worked. Much of the pressure came from a group of young aggressive congressmen, the first of the postrevolutionary generation of Western politicians—Henry Clay of Kentucky, John C. Calhoun and Langdon Cheves of western South Carolina, Peter B. Porter of western New York, Felix Grundy of Tennessee, and other so-called buckskin boys. Intensely nationalist and violently anti-British, this group of "War Hawks," as John Randolph of Roanoke called them, clamored loudly for an attack on Britain via Canada and on the seas.

The regions from which these "War Hawks" came believed they had special reasons to dislike England. The West fell on hard times in the years from 1805 to 1809, and it blamed the British navy rather than the Embargo. More serious, however, was the charge that the British, from their Canadian posts, stirred up the Indians and armed them for marauding raids on the American frontier. A war with England would not only settle the Indian problem, some Westerners felt, but would also open up British Canada to conquest—a company of Kentucky militia, Henry Clay thought, could easily do the job.

"Mr. Madison's War."   On June 1, 1812, President Madison asked Congress to declare war on Great Britain, listing the catalog of British offenses over the past years, none of major importance but adding up to an intolerable total. On June 18 Congress responded with a declaration of war. The vote was close in the Senate—19 to 13—and not overwhelming in the House, 79 to 49, with New England and the Middle Atlantic states against, the South and West for. Ironically, unknown to Madison, Parliament had already on June 16 revoked the orders restricting neutral trade with France— orders which had so stirred American resentment—and there were signs that the British might be willing to negotiate differences further.

The congressional vote reflected the popular attitude toward the war the Westerners wanted; at the news, flags flew at half-mast in New England, and there were minor riots in some Eastern cities. The Federalist press dubbed it "Mr. Madison's War," and so it remained. There were some, at least, who regarded it as a stab in Britain's back when that nation stood alone against Napoleon, who in 1812 was already on his way to Moscow for what seemed to be his last great conquest; as John Randolph told the War Hawks, whether one liked the British or not, the plain fact was that England remained "the only power that holds in check the archenemy of mankind."

The origins of war are never simple, and the War of 1812, especially, derived from a bewildering complexity of causes. It is not enough to say that the United States and Britain "blundered" into war through "inept diplomacy," though there was enough of that. The lingering resentments of two decades of friction, memories of impressed sailors and arrogant British captains, demands for protection of American maritime rights from men-of-war and frontier settlements from Indian marauders, the land-hunger of the expansionist Westerners—all these were factors.

Yet the chief opposition to the war came from the commercial and maritime interests of New England, whose rights had been most consistently violated; and the largest vote for war came from Georgia, Kentucky, Tennessee, and South Carolina, where sea trade was less important. As much as anything else, it seemed, the United States went to war in 1812 as a matter of national pride. Andrew Jackson of Tennessee said succinctly: "We are going to fight for the reestablishment of our national character, for the protection of our maritime citizens, to vindicate our right to a free trade, and open market for the productions of our soil because the *mistress of the ocean* has forbid us to carry them to any foreign nations."

THE WAR OF 1812

War on the Land: First Phase.   The United States was totally unprepared for war. The army, reduced to about seven thousand men, was badly equipped and poorly led.

Secretary of War William Eustis, though clearly incompetent, was not replaced until 1813; his successor John Armstrong was hardly better; and not until the quality of American generalship improved did American military affairs seem to have direction and firmness. The utter failure of the army's first move against Canada in the summer of 1812 showed that it would take a good deal more than Clay's militia company to do the job. Meanwhile British forces captured not only Detroit but also Fort Michilimackinac in upper Michigan and Fort Dearborn in Illinois, establishing virtual command of the western Great Lakes.

In the middle of these military failures, Madison was nominated for another term. An Eastern antiwar wing of the Republicans, however, nominated De Witt Clinton of New York against him, and the Federalists added their support for Clinton. Madison won, 128 to 89 electoral votes, but, significantly, Clinton carried all of New England and the Middle Atlantic states except Vermont and Pennsylvania. At the same time the Federalists doubled their delegation in Congress.

War on the Land: Second Phase. Despite its early disasters, the army kept trying for Canada. In the winter of 1812–13 American sailors commanded by Captain Oliver Hazard Perry hammered and sawed out a small fleet and in September 1813 met and smashed the British lake squadron at the Battle of Lake Erie, near Sandusky, Ohio. Lake Erie was one of the most savage naval actions of the era (Perry's flagship suffered 80 percent casualties), but after three hours of fighting, Perry dispatched his message to General Harrison commanding the forces near Detroit, "We have met the enemy and they are ours." Without control of Lake Erie, the British evacuated Detroit and fell back toward Niagara, but Harrison's swiftly advancing force caught and defeated them at the Battle of the Thames on October 5, 1813.

By reason of Perry's and Harrison's victories, the United States now commanded the Northwestern frontier. But after three unsuccessful American expeditions into Canada, a British force struck back at Buffalo, captured and burned it, and then took Fort Niagara in December 1814.

War at Sea. The American navy entered the War of 1812 with sixteen ships; the British had ninety-seven in American waters alone. The outnumbered Americans therefore limited themselves to single-ship actions and did surprisingly well. The *Constitution* ("Old Ironsides"), a forty-four gun frigate commanded by Yankee Isaac Hull, defeated the British *Guerrière* in one of the most famous sea fights in history. The big frigate *United States,* commanded by Captain Stephen Decatur, captured the British *Macedonian,* a few weeks later, but the American *Chesapeake* lost a bitter fight to the British *Shannon* in 1813.

American privateers, however, contributed most to the success of the war at sea. These swift ships ran circles around the British navy, captured or destroyed thirteen hundred British merchantmen, and even had the impudence to sack British shipping in the English Channel in full sight of the shore. They gave the American public something to crow about now and then, though the overall effect on the outcome of the conflict was negligible. The British naval blockade was quite effective, and by 1813 the majority of American ports were tightly bottled up.

War on the Land: Final Phase. Napoleon abdicated in April 1814 and was exiled to the isle of Elba in the Mediterranean. With Bonaparte gone and the French war finished, England turned its huge army of Napoleonic veterans toward American shores. The strategy of the British general staff was to make three coordinated attacks: one from the north, from Canada down Lake Champlain into New York state; a second on the coast, through Chesapeake Bay, at Baltimore, Washington, and Philadelphia; a third up from the south, at New Orleans. The end was in sight, wrote the London *Times*, for this "ill-organized association" of states, and indeed it looked like it.

The northern campaign began in July 1814. Since Lake Champlain was the vital link in the invasion route, British General Sir George Prevost wanted it cleared of American ships. In September 1814 the American lake squadron under Captain Thomas Macdonough decisively defeated the British, and without control of the lake the British drive stalled and eventually dissolved.

The British were more successful at Chesapeake Bay, where in August 1814 General Robert Ross landed a strong force that marched on Washington. The American government fled into Virginia, and after setting fire to the Capitol, the White House, and all government buildings they could ignite, the British moved on the next day toward Baltimore. Here they were stopped at Fort McHenry, whose spirited defense inspired Francis Scott Key to write "The Star-Spangled Banner." Unable to crack the Baltimore defenses, the British took to sea again for the West Indies.

The third British offensive, aimed at New Orleans and commanded by General Edward Pakenham, sailed from Jamaica in November 1814 with 7500 seasoned veterans. To oppose Pakenham, Andrew Jackson took his frontier army on a forced march from Mobile, arriving at New Orleans in time to meet the British in late December. Though neither Jackson nor Pakenham knew it, American and British representatives were already at work in Belgium on a treaty of peace. Two weeks after the Treaty of Ghent was signed on December 24, 1814, Jackson's Western riflemen almost annihilated Pakenham's army. The British lost two thousand men (including Pakenham), while Jackson's loss totaled eight dead and thirteen wounded in a battle that did not affect the war or the peace.

The Hartford Convention.   The New England Federalists never favored the war and gave it only half-hearted support. In 1814, when American prospects seemed darkest, the Federalist Massachusetts legislature called a convention at Hartford, Connecticut, to discuss "public grievances and concerns," that is, the Republican conduct of the war.

The delegates, who came primarily from the Massachusetts, Connecticut, and Rhode Island legislatures, had a great deal to discuss. Some advised amending the Constitution to clip Congress' war-making powers; some proposed a new Constitution which would limit presidential reeligibility and thus get rid of Madison; others suggested negotiating a separate peace with England. Curiously enough, the delegates, all Federalists, appealed to the doctrine of states' rights, the same doctrine which the Jeffersonians during Adams' administration had used against Federalist centralization. They argued that since the Republican Congress had violated the Constitution by declaring an unwanted war, those states which did not approve had the right to override congressional action. At the conclusion of the meeting Massachusetts and Connecticut sent commissioners to Washington to place their protests before Congress—but the commissioners arrived at the same time as the news of Jackson's victory at New Orleans, and whatever they had to say was forgotten.

A Welcome Peace. Early in 1813 Czar Alexander I of Russia offered to mediate between the United States and England since he wanted the British to be free to concentrate their full force on Napoleon. Madison sent commissioners to Russia, but Lord Castlereagh, the British foreign minister, refused to accept the czar's suggestion. Later that same year, however, Castlereagh notified Secretary of State James Monroe that he was willing to discuss differences between the two nations, and in August 1814 American and British representatives met in Ghent, Belgium.

As the meetings dragged on, it became plain that the three-pronged British invasion of the American continent would not succeed. Weary of war, both British and Americans wanted to finish it, and on December 24, 1814, the commissioners signed a peace treaty which did not mention impressment, blockades, seizures at sea, or any of the major disputes over which the war was presumably fought. Most of the critical points at issue, in fact, were left for later commissions to decide.

The Results of the War. The reactions of war-weary Americans to the news of the Treaty of Ghent, which arrived in the United States in February 1815, was swift and spontaneous. Bells rang, parades formed, newspapers broke out in headlines to proclaim the "passage from gloom to glory." Yet "Mr. Madison's War" had accomplished very little in a military or political sense. The treaty realized few if any of the aims for which the war had presumably been fought; the most that can be said is that it opened the way for future settlements, which were worked out over the next decade with Britain, Spain, and France. The war dislocated business and foreign trade, deranged currency values, and exposed glaring cracks in the national political organization.

But to the American people the outcome, ambiguous as it was, marked a turning point in patriotic self-esteem. If it had been fought as a matter of national pride, in this it had succeeded. It was true that the war might have been avoided by better statesmanship and that it might even have been fought with France on equally reasonable grounds—yet from the American point of view the War of 1812 gave notice to the rest of the world that the United States had arrived as a nation. "Who would not be an American?" crowed *Niles' Register*. "Long live the Republic! All Hail!"

A Confident Nation. The end of the War of 1812 marked the end of America's lingering colonial complex. It was hardly a "second war of independence," as some called it, but from it there did come a new spirit of national consciousness. "It has renewed," wrote Albert Gallatin, "and reinstated the national feeling and character which the Revolution had given, and which were daily lessening. The people now have more general objects of attachment. . . . They are more Americans, they feel and act more as a nation."

The war also turned Americans westward. Hitherto they had faced Europe despite their political independence of Britain. Until the War of 1812 America's major trade was foreign trade, its principal problem in foreign affairs that of maintaining neutrality in European struggles, its challenges of statesmanship nearly always those arising from foreign affairs, even its own political campaigns influenced by preferences for France or England. After the Treaty of Ghent the United States turned toward the great hazy West, where half a continent lay empty. America could now concentrate on its domestic problems with less concern for European standards, ideals, and entanglements; indifference to foreign affairs after 1814 was so great that even Napoleon's escape from Elba, his return to France, and his final defeat at Waterloo in June 1815 excited little attention in the American press. The interest of the United States centered on perfecting and expanding the nation it had constructed out of two wars and a generation of experiment. In other words, its chief task lay in developing modern America.

AMERICA MAKES A NEW START

The Aftermath of War. The most persistent postwar problems were economic. Finances during the war had been handled almost as ineptly as military affairs. Banks had multiplied profusely and without proper control; the country was flooded with depreciating paper money; prices were at the most inflated level in America's brief history. Though the shipping industry had been badly hurt by war and blockade, the value of manufacturing had increased tremendously—the total capital investment in American industry in 1816, it was estimated, was somewhat more than $100 million. The West, now producing foodstuffs and raw materials in abundance, balanced on the verge of a tremendous boom. As soon as peace was established the Republican Congress began to consider a three-point program for economic expansion: a tariff to protect infant American industry; a second Bank of the United States, since the charter of Hamilton's original Bank had expired in 1811; and a system of roads, waterways, and canals to provide internal routes of communication and trade.

A Protective Tariff. The protection of America's infant industries was a matter of first priority. New factories, encouraged by the war, had grown in great numbers, especially in the textile industry. As soon as the wartime blockade ended, British-made products streamed toward the United States, and young industries that flourished under conditions of embargo and war found it quite another matter to compete in an open peacetime market. Whereas the total value of United States imports in 1813 had been $13 million, by 1816 it had leaped to $147 million, while American manufacturers begged for protection.

Congress in 1816 passed a tariff to protect the new factories—the first United States tariff passed not to raise revenue but to encourage and support home industry. The argument over this protective tariff exposed some potentially serious sectional economic conflicts and marked the first appearance of a perennial political issue. Southern producers and New England shippers opposed the tariff, but the growing factory towns of New England supported it, as did some of the younger Southern cotton politicians, who hoped to encourage industrial development in the South. The Middle Atlantic states and the West favored it, and the Southwest divided on the issue.

Renewing the Bank of the United States.   In 1816 Congress turned its attention to the national Bank. The charter of the first Bank of the United States had been allowed to expire because the Republicans believed that, as Jefferson originally claimed, banking powers properly belonged to the states and Hamilton's centralized bank was therefore unconstitutional. The new contingent of Western congressmen were much less interested in the Bank's constitutionality than in its usefulness. Henry Clay, who had opposed the first Bank in 1811 on constitutional grounds, now supported the second Bank, he explained, because it was necessary for the national (especially Western) interest to have a stable, uniform currency and sound national credit. Therefore, Congress in 1816 gave the second Bank a twenty-year charter, on much the same terms as before but with about three and a half times more capital than the first and substantially greater control over state banks.

America Moves West.   The Treaty of Ghent released a pent-up flood of migration toward the West. In 1790 a little more than 2 percent of the population lived west of the Appalachian mountain chain; in 1810, 14 percent; in 1820, 23 percent, with the proportion still rising. The stream of migration moved west in two branches following the east-west roads and rivers, one from the South into the Southwest, the other from the northeastern states into the Northwest Territory.

There were a number of reasons for this great westerly movement. One was America's soaring population, which almost doubled in the first two decades of the nineteenth century, from 5.3 million in 1800 to over 9.6 million in 1820. Another was the discharge of war veterans, accompanied by a rush of immigrants from Europe, who moved west to look for new opportunities. Another was improved transportation: there were not many good roads to the West, but the number grew, while the Great Lakes-Ohio River waterway provided an excellent route for settlers to move into the Northwest.

The most compelling force behind the westward migration was land—the rich black bottom lands of the Southwest, the fertile forest and prairie lands of the Northwest. Governor William Henry Harrison of Indiana Territory persuaded Congress in 1800 to reduce the minimum required sale of land to a half section at two dollars an acre, with four years to pay. In 1804 Congress reduced the minimum to a quarter section, and in 1820 to eighty acres at $1.25 an acre. This was the great magnet that drew men west.

The Connecting Links: Internal Improvements.   The British wartime blockade and the westward movement exposed a critical need for roads, improved waterways, and canals. When coastal shipping was reduced to a trickle by British offshore naval patrols, forcing American goods to move over inland routes, the roads and rivers were soon choked with traffic. The Republican program of improved internal communications was especially popular in the West, but more conservative Easterners, including President Madison, doubted the constitutionality of federal assistance for roads and canals unless an amendment to the Constitution was adopted for the purpose. Calhoun and Clay could see no objections; Calhoun, in fact, proposed using the yearly bonus, paid each year by the national Bank to the Treasury, to finance some of these projects, but Madison vetoed this "Bonus Bill" on his last day in office in 1817. Many of the states, however, started building roads and digging canals themselves. President Monroe later decided that the "general welfare" clause of the Constitution provided the federal government with the necessary authority to participate, inaugurating the great canal and turnpike era of the 1820s.

The Election of 1816. Madison selected James Monroe of Virginia for his successor in the presidential election of 1816, and although some Republicans favored William H. Crawford of Georgia, the party caucus agreed to choose the third Virginian in succession for the presidency. The Federalists, disheartened by the Hartford Convention, failed to nominate an official candidate, though in some states they supported Rufus King of New York. King received only the votes of Massachusetts, Connecticut, and Delaware, and Monroe won easily by 183 to 34 electoral votes.

A tall, distinguished, quiet man, James Monroe had studied law with Jefferson and was the older statesman's close friend and disciple. He drew his advisers impartially from different sections of the country, choosing John Quincy Adams of Massachusetts as Secretary of State, William H. Crawford of Georgia as Secretary of the Treasury, John C. Calhoun of South Carolina as Secretary of War, and William Wirt of Maryland as Attorney General. Henry Clay of Kentucky, the Speaker of the House, and others of the Western group dominated Congress, with Daniel Webster of New Hampshire and other New Englanders furnishing the opposition.

The "Era of Good Feelings." Because of the virtually unchallenged Republican control of political life until 1824, these years are labeled "The Era of Good Feelings." The Federalist party was dead, and it seemed for a time that the two-party system itself was moribund. There were no European wars of consequence during the period to involve the United States, nor any crucial issues in foreign affairs. But, like all labels, this one was true only in part: feelings were "good," true, but subterranean conflicts were soon to destroy the political peace.

Sectional interests and aspirations were growing and changing. The new Northwest, as it gained stature and stability, demanded greater influence in national policy. The South, tied more and more to cotton, and New England, changing from an agricultural to a manufacturing economy, were both undergoing inner stresses that took outward political form. Specifically, these sectionalized rivalries were shortly to appear in two issues—tariffs and slavery—which terminated the good feelings and produced many new bad ones. As if to underline the temporary nature of this tenuous political peace, the Monroe administration faced immediate dissatisfaction beyond the Alleghenies.

Prosperity and Panic. After 1815 the national economy flourished mightily; the wartime boom continued, industry grew strong behind its tariff wall, and American ships carried goods and raw materials over all the world. Yet much of this prosperity had a hollow ring. Too many small Southern and Western banks had issued far too much paper money in excess of their capital reserves, and in 1818 the second Bank of the United States (which suffered from mismanagement itself) began to close out some of these "wildcat" banks by collecting their notes and demanding payment.

The purpose was fiscally sound—to force stricter control of banking practices—but the effect was disastrous. By early 1819 a number of shaky banks had already collapsed and others were about to follow; in fact, the entire national banking system, none too sound for several years, was nearly ready to topple. In 1819 more and more banks crashed, businesses failed, and a wave of losses and foreclosures swept over the nation, especially through the West. The consequences of the 1819 crisis continued to be felt until 1823; and for the part it had played in precipitating it, the second Bank of the United States and the financial interests of the East earned the undying resentment of the West.

Clashes on the Frontier. While it was clear from the first that the new American government wanted swift access to the Indians' tribal lands, Congress in 1789 assured Indians that their "land and property shall never be taken from them without their consent." And in appropriating funds to pay certain tribes for land claims, Congress tacitly recognized, as Secretary of War Henry Knox said, the Indians' right to ownership as "prior occupants." Land was the issue. Activated by that "insatiable spirit of avarice and that restless and dissatisfied turn of mind" which traveler Isaac Weld in 1800 thought characteristic of the American frontiersman, settlers paid little attention to boundaries and treaties. The Indians, reported Thomas Forsyth, who journeyed into frontier country in 1818, "complain about the sale of their lands more than any thing else"; the settler, he wrote, "tells the Indian that that land, with all that is on it, is his," and, treaty or not, "to go away or he will kill him etc." Clashes between Indian and settler were constant; Congress' postwar Indian policy was neither sufficiently definite nor sufficiently aggressive to satisfy impatient settlers, traders, and land speculators. Treaties negotiated with the tribes of the Northwest brought only temporary peace, while in the South the Creeks harassed the frontier settlements with encouragement from the Spanish.

In 1793–94 Tennessee militia, in a series of small, sharp engagements, temporarily stabilized the Southwestern frontier. In 1790 General Josiah Harmar's expedition against the Indians in the Ohio country was ambushed and scattered, and General Arthur St. Clair's larger force in 1791 did no better. Washington then gave command to General "Mad Anthony" Wayne, who took four thousand men into northwestern Ohio, where the British had authorized the construction of a fort inside American boundaries, and defeated the Indian forces at the Battle of Fallen Timbers in late summer of 1794. The next year the twelve strongest tribes ceded most of the Ohio country to the United States by the Treaty of Greenville.

Postwar Indian Policy. Despite the attraction of the Indian lands, the majority of enlightened American leaders considered the use of force to obtain them as morally indefensible; many hoped to save the Indian from what seemed to be certain extinction by finding some means of instructing him in the ways of the white man's civilization, so that he could find a place within the American system. Basically, Jefferson's policy was a continuation of the Indian policy of the colonies: have the Indian give up his tribal lands to white settlement and become a farmer, or perhaps have him move westward into new lands beyond the Mississippi. As he once told Andrew Jackson, Jefferson believed that lands should be obtained from the tribes only "by all *honest* and peaceable means."

On the other hand, Jefferson was under strong political pressure from his frontier

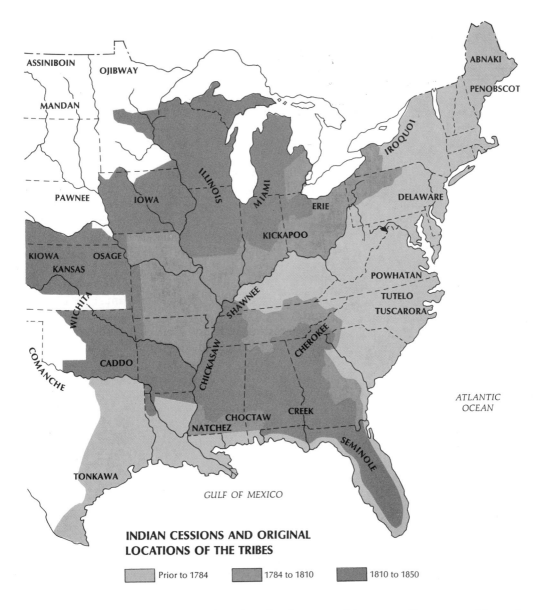

INDIAN CESSIONS AND ORIGINAL LOCATIONS OF THE TRIBES

Prior to 1784	1784 to 1810	1810 to 1850

constituencies to obtain as much Indian land as possible as quickly as possible and open it to settlement. When the French purchase of Lousiana from Spain seemed to pose a threat to the American West, Jefferson was anxious to acquire all Indian lands east of the Mississippi to consolidate the country's western boundary. After he finally bought Louisiana for the United States in 1803, he still favored his policy of Indian removal, and within the next few years the government acquired—one way or another, sometimes by dubious means—over 100 million acres of land which the

Indians were expected to relinquish at once. Conflicts between settlers and Indians became increasingly violent and frequent, and the emergence of a remarkable leader, the Shawnee Tecumseh, crystallized Indian resistance. Rejecting all American claims to Indian lands, Tecumseh and his medicine-man brother, The Prophet, organized the tribes of the Northwest into a loose and effective alliance. It was finally broken by General William Henry Harrison, governor of Indiana Territory, at the Battle of Tippecanoe in November 1811. Tecumseh escaped to join the British in Canada and reappeared with his Indians in the War of 1812. He was killed at the Battle of the Thames in 1813.

At the close of the war, with the British threat removed from the Northwest and the French from the Southwest, the federal government could at last proceed with its policy of assimilation or removal. The Jeffersonian dream of an enlightened, peaceful solution to the problem faded fast, for after 1815 the political power of those who, like Andrew Jackson, wanted to clear the Indian lands immediately was too strong to resist. In 1817 the Senate Committee on Public Lands reported it feasible to exchange public lands in the trans-Mississippi region for Indian lands, but only by voluntary consent of the tribes. Very soon, however, it became clear that voluntarism would not work and that, as John C. Calhoun wrote in 1820, all Indians "must be brought gradually under our authority and laws." "Our opinions, and not theirs," he continued, "ought to prevail, in measures intended for their civilization and happiness." In 1825 Calhoun, then Secretary of War, and President Monroe presented Congress with a plan to remove the eastern tribes into the region beyond Missouri and Arkansas, a plan opposed by those who felt such an act a betrayal of the national honor. As James Barbour, Secretary of War in the next administration, observed, the removal policy showed that "our professions are insincere; that our promises have been broken; that the happiness of the Indian is a cheap sacrifice to the acquisition of new lands." But such opposition proved inadequate, and by 1848 twelve new states had been created from what had been Indian country.

FIRE BELL IN THE NIGHT

Sectionalism and Slavery. As the tariff issue of 1816 exposed some of the sectional tensions beneath the surface of "good feelings," so the panic of 1819 revealed more. The third great issue, the question of the existence and extension of the institution of slavery, was projected into Congress by Missouri's impending statehood in 1819.

Slavery had been a submerged issue in national politics since Washington's time. In 1793, during his administration, Congress passed a fugitive slave law and later forbade the further importation of slaves, beginning in 1808, without unduly arousing sentiment in North or South; in fact, there were many in both sections who hoped that the 1808 act might lead to the eventual extinction of the entire system. In the North, where slavery was unprofitable and unnecessary, all the states had legally abolished it by 1804 (as the Northwest Ordinance of 1787 already had abolished it from the Northwest Territory), while in the South antislavery societies actively campaigned against it. Still, after 1816 there was noticeable asperity in Northern and Southern discussions of the slavery question.

The most important area of disagreement over slavery concerned its economic relationship to Southern cotton culture. Eli Whitney's invention of the cotton gin, the introduction of new strains of cotton, the expanding postwar textile market at home and abroad, and the opening to production of the rich "Black Belt" lands of the Southwest, all combined to make cotton an extremely profitable cash crop. Cotton was well on the way to becoming "King" in the South.

Cotton required a large, steady supply of cheap, unskilled labor; many believed that black slaves filled this need. At the same time, it was found that the delta lands of Louisiana and Mississippi were ideal for sugar cane, while tobacco culture moved from the coastal South into Kentucky and Tennessee. All these economies needed cheap labor. In 1800 there were about 894,000 blacks in the United States, almost wholly concentrated in the eastern South. In 1808, when the importation of slaves ceased, the figure stood at over one million, and the South's investment in slaves by 1820 was estimated to be nearly $500 million. It was perfectly clear that slavery and cotton together provided the foundation of Southern society and would continue to do so.

The Missouri Compromise. Missouri, early in 1819, counted sixty thousand persons and applied for entry to the Union as a slave state. No doubt the bill for its admission would have passed without appreciable comment, had not James Tall-

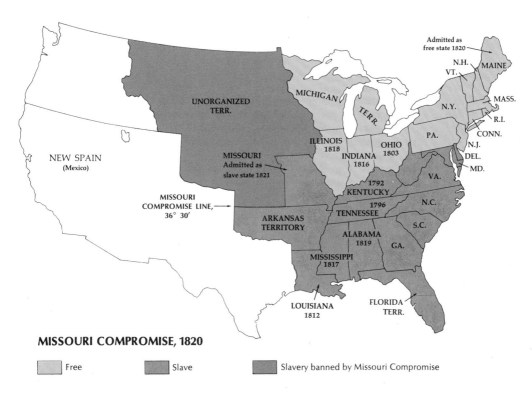

MISSOURI COMPROMISE, 1820

Free   Slave   Slavery banned by Missouri Compromise

madge, Jr., of New York introduced in the House an amendment requiring the gradual abolition of slavery in the new state as a condition of its admission. This amendment immediately exposed the heart of the issue.

As the nation moved west, the tendency had been to maintain a rough balance of power between slave- and free-state blocs in Washington. The North and Northwest, however, had gained a million more persons than the South and Southwest since the 1790 census, thereby proportionately increasing their congressional representation. The slave states were already outvoted in the House; only in the Senate were the sections equally represented, a situation which might not continue for long.

Of the original thirteen colonies, seven became free states and six slave. Between 1791 and 1819 four more free states were admitted and five slave. When Missouri applied for entrance to the Union in 1819, the balance was even. Therefore Tallmadge's amendment involved far more than Missouri's admission alone. Slavery was already barred from the Northwest Territory but not from those lands acquired through the Louisiana Purchase. Should Missouri and all other states subsequently admitted from the Louisiana Purchase lands be admitted as slave states, the balance of federal political power would be tipped toward the South and slavery. If they were to be free states, their entry favored the North and emancipation. At stake lay political control, present and future, of the Union. "It is political power that the northern folk are in pursuit of," Judge Charles Tait of Alabama wrote to a friend concerning the Missouri question, "and if they succeed, the management of the Gen'l Gov't will pass into their hands with all its power and patronage."

Tallmadge's bill finally passed the House in February, after hot and protracted debate. Congress adjourned, however, until December, and during the interval Maine, long attached to Massachusetts, applied for statehood. Sensing compromise, the Senate originated a bill accepting Maine as a free state and Missouri as slave, thereby preserving the balance. The House accepted it, but added a proviso that slavery be banned forever from the Louisiana Purchase lands above the line of 36°30'. The bill was passed and signed in March 1820, but this so-called Missouri Compromise merely delayed the ultimate confrontation of the problem of slavery, and everyone knew it. The "momentous question," wrote Jefferson from Monticello, "like a fire-bell in the night, awakened me and filled me with terror."

EVOLVING A FOREIGN POLICY

Catching Up on Old Problems. Following the Treaty of Ghent the United States and Britain gradually worked out their differences one by one. The Rush-Bagot Agreement of 1817 demilitarized the Great Lakes. The Convention of 1818 gave U.S. nationals fishing rights off the coasts of Labrador and Newfoundland, established the northern boundary of the Louisiana Purchase at the 49th parallel, and left the Oregon country, which both claimed, under joint occupation for ten years.

America and Spain, too, settled some old disputes. The United States took one section of Florida in 1810 and another in 1813. Secretary of State John Quincy Adams continued negotiations for the rest of the territory, but his diplomacy was disturbed by Florida's Seminole Indians, who kept up raids (with Spanish and British assistance) on the Georgia border. In 1818 General Jackson marched into Florida, captured two Spanish forts, and executed two suspected British agents in what is known as the First Seminole War. The posts were quickly returned to Spain, but Jackson's action helped precipitate a treaty, signed by Adams and Spanish minister Luis de Onís in February 1819, by which Spain renounced its claims to West Florida and ceded East Florida to the United States. In the Adams-Onís Treaty the Spanish also agreed to a boundary line stretching across the continent to the Pacific, redefining the Louisiana Purchase line, and dividing the old Southwest from Spanish Mexico, and gave up their somewhat vague claims to Oregon in return for a clear title to Texas.

The Monroe Doctrine. Reduced to a third-rate power and racked by internal dissension, Spain was losing its empire in Central and South America. Beginning in 1807, its colonies revolted one after another until, by 1821, nearly all had declared themselves independent republics. Sympathetic to such revolutions and alert to opportunities for new markets, the United States waited until its treaty with Spain was accepted and then recognized these republics early in 1822.

Spain, of course, continued to consider the new Latin American nations simply as Spanish colonies in rebellion. In Europe, meanwhile, Austria, Prussia, Russia, and France had formed an alliance and "congress system" for the purpose of crushing popular revolutions wherever they occurred. The United States feared that the alliance would decide to send an army to restore Spain's lost colonies, making royal Catholic Spain once more a power in the New World. Nor was the alliance the only threat to the Americas. Russia had already established trading posts in California, and in 1821 Czar Alexander's edict claimed part of the Oregon country for Alaska and barred foreign ships from a large area of the northwest Pacific.

The British, who had no desire to see Spain regain its empire or Russia expand its colonial holdings, offered to join with the United States in a declaration against any interference in the Americas on the part of the alliance, but Secretary of State John Quincy Adams convinced President Monroe and the cabinet that the United States should handle the problem alone. For one thing, Adams did not want his country, he said, to "come in as a cockboat in the wake of the British man-of-war." Furthermore, Adams and others recognized the potential value of the new Latin American republics as markets. And lastly, no one wanted to write off the possibility of American expansion southward if one or more of the new republics asked to be annexed to the United States.

President Monroe, in his annual message to Congress on December 2, 1823, therefore stated the official attitude of the United States on the issue. The Monroe Doctrine, as it came to be called, rested on two main principles—noncolonization and nonintervention.

Concerning the first, Monroe stated that any portions of the Americas were "henceforth not to be considered as subjects for future colonization by any European power." In regard to the second, he drew a sharp line of political demarcation between

Europe and America. "The political system of the allied powers is essentially different . . . from that of America," he said. "We should consider any attempt to extend their system to any portion of this hemisphere as dangerous to our peace and safety." At the same time, Monroe promised that the United States would not attempt to interfere with the internal affairs of European nations or with any of their existing colonies in the New World, such as Cuba. These ideas had been implicit in all American foreign policy since Washington's Farewell Address, but Monroe's message restated in precise terms the classic American principles of hemispheric separation and avoidance of foreign entanglements that had motivated the diplomacy of his predecessors. His enunciation of American domination over half the globe seemed "arrogant" and "haughty" to European statesmen, nor were the Latin American republics particularly pleased with such doubtful protection. Both knew, whether Monroe or the American public cared to admit it, that it was the British navy and not the Monroe Doctrine that barred European expansion into the Americas.

The Triumph of Isolation. The Monroe Doctrine simply articulated what Americans had believed since the beginnings of their foreign policy—that there were two worlds, old and new, contrasted and separate. The Old World of England and Europe seemed to Americans regressive, corrupted, plagued by wars and ancient hatreds. The New World was thought to be democratic, free, progressive, hopeful. The objective of the United States, reflecting these attitudes, was to keep these worlds apart, lest the "taint" of the old besmirch the "fresh future" of the new.

The first generation of American statesmen, from Washington to Monroe, unanimously insisted that the United States should, whenever possible, avoid entanglements in Old World politics or problems. At the same time it was perfectly clear to them that the United States could not exist without European trade and that, since the major European powers still held territorial possessions in the New World, it would be extremely difficult to avoid some sort of implication in their almost continuous wars. The foreign policy of every President from Washington to John Quincy Adams was shaped by this constant tension between the dream of isolation and the reality of involvement.

Still, there were certain accepted positions on foreign affairs that the United States throughout the period believed it must maintain—freedom of the seas, freedom of trade, neutrality in European disputes, national integrity, and, above all others, the promotion of the cause of liberty throughout the world. In practice, American diplomats found it hard to work out solutions within this somewhat rigid framework. Did maintenance of freedom of the seas, for example, justify involvement in a European war? Would American assistance to other nations' revolutions justify entanglement in European affairs, even for the best of motives? Should American policy, when it coincided with that of a European power, be pursued jointly? Ought the United States to assume responsibility for internal affairs of democracy in other American republics?

In attempting to answer these and similar questions, the makers of American foreign policy during the early years of the Republic followed rather closely the principles laid down by Washington and the first generation. Fortunately for them,

Europe was so preoccupied with its own power conflicts that American diplomacy had time to temporize and room to make a few mistakes. Still, every statement about foreign affairs after 1796 derived from the fundamental American assumption that the United States was detached from Europe and must remain so, always free to pursue its special ends.

CHAPTER 6

THE EMERGENCE OF
A NATIONAL CULTURE

THE DEVELOPMENT OF AN AMERICAN CREDO

The Circumstances of Creation. The period between 1783 and 1824 was a time of extraordinary political, economic, and social revolution. This was the age which saw the close of the American Revolution, the ratification of the Constitution, and the development of the two-party system of government. It was the age of George Washington and Thomas Jefferson, of the Louisiana Purchase and the Lewis and Clark expedition, of the War of 1812 and the growth of textile and iron industries, of Henry Clay and John C. Calhoun, of the Missouri Compromise and the Monroe Doctrine. In Europe it was the age of the French Revolution and of the rise and fall of Napoleon, of the Romantic Movement and the Industrial Revolution.

In launching a new system of government, Americans looked ahead with a strong sense of hope and experiment. They were sanguine about the future, for they had no significant record of failure to disillusion them. They were impatient of "established" institutions or traditions, for they had just established some of their own and disestablished a good many British ones. Though their society did not grant the Declaration's "unalienable rights" to slaves and Indians, nor full political and social equality to all classes of other Americans, nonetheless—thoughtful Americans believed—it afforded more freedom to its citizens than any other.

This pride in what they had accomplished, joined to their anti-British feelings, made Americans aggressively self-confident. Triumphant in their newly won independence, they became less aware of their social, cultural, and religious indebtedness to Great Britain. Having rejected all the prejudices, superstitions, and errors of the Old World, so Americans felt, they were ready to outdistance it in every sector. In retrospect, however, it is clear that the bonds of British and European inheritance were not to be cut so sharply and that the old pattern of transplantation and adaptation continued with the influx of both immigrants and ideas from across the Atlantic.

American Nationalism. The train of events was propitious for the growth of American nationalism. For one thing, many democratic and humanitarian tendencies were accentuated or set in motion during the Revolution and the early national period. Large Loyalist estates were confiscated and divided; small business and manufacturing were stimulated; church establishments were attacked; slavery, imprisonment for debt, and humiliating punishments were regarded with growing disfavor; the idea of universal education at state expense was voiced. Americans were far from being of one mind about these matters, but they did believe that they could, by honest effort and the fortunate circumstances of their society, forge ahead in ways that the nations of the Old World could not. The Americans were a "new" people, as Crèvecoeur put it; they were ready to teach the rest of the world, and were no longer content to be taught.

Indeed, Americans considered the United States to be superior to England and Europe in every way; it was, they hoped, the model of a new kind of New World. "Americans are fanatically proud of their own wild country," remarked an English traveler during the period, "and love to disparage the rest of the world." It was America's mission to lead other nations to revolution against the forces of ignorance and oppression or, as Joel Barlow wrote, "to excite emulation throughout the kingdoms of the earth, and meliorate the conditions of the human race." It was America's responsibility to extend the concepts of liberty, equality, and justice over all the earth; this, said James Wilson at the Constitutional Convention, was "the great design of Providence in regard to this globe."

In order to accomplish its mission, it was considered imperative that Americans cultivate their Americanness, emphasize their differences with Europe, develop their own culture in terms of their own national purpose. "Every engine should be employed to render the people of the country national," wrote Noah Webster, "to call their attachment home to their own country." If the United States was to succeed as an experiment in self-government, the men who governed themselves must have deep faith in it. The patriotic impulse was considered essential to the creation of a national character.

THE FRAMEWORK OF THE AMERICAN MIND

The structure of ideas within which Americans achieved their independence was provided by two great intellectual movements, the Age of Reason and the Age of Romanticism. The United States itself, almost purely a creation of the eighteenth century, emerged at a time when the Western world was shifting from one system of thought to another, each involving quite different views of man, the world, and the deity beyond them.

The Transit of the Enlightenment. The American colonies were children of the Age of Reason, or the "Enlightenment." John Locke, the English political philosopher, wrote a charter for the Carolinas; Rousseau and Montesquieu were friends of Franklin; Sir Isaac Newton and Cotton Mather were contemporaries; Voltaire was still living when the Continental Congress signed the Declaration of Independence. The Enlightenment, not the Puritanism of New England, provided the first *nationalized* pattern of American thought.

The Age of Reason rested upon three major principles: the perfectibility of men; the inevitability of progress; and the efficacy of reason. It emphasized the scientific method over the theological, reason over faith, skepticism over tradition and authoritarianism. The thinkers of the Enlightenment believed that by subjecting himself, his society, the past, and the universe itself to rational analysis, man could discover certain general laws which would supply him with precise, definitive explanations of human and natural activity. With this knowledge, men could so direct their energies and construct their institutions that their progress would be swift and sure. The Americans who chose the path of revolution, and who, after its successful conclusion, accepted the challenge of making a new nation on new principles, reflected these attitudes.

The Nature of the American Enlightenment. There was an American Enlightenment, but it was late, eclectic, and singularly American. Eighteenth-century America was not merely an extension or a reflection of contemporary Britain or Europe. First of all, there was a culture lag in the transmission of patterns of thinking from one side of the Atlantic to the other. The Founding Fathers worked with ideas fifty to one hundred years old by European standards, on another continent, for different purposes—and mixed with them later borrowings and adaptations. The Romanticists—Goethe, Wordsworth, Coleridge, Schiller, and Kant—were writing at nearly the same time that Americans were still quoting the men of the Age of Reason—Newton, Locke, and Montesquieu.

Second, Americans chose from British and European thought only those ideas they needed, or those in which they had special interest. They adopted Locke's justification of a century-old English revolution as vindication of their own, for example, and used French "radicalism," aimed at Gallic kings, to overthrow a tyranny that really did not exist. The Americans thus bent the Enlightenment to American uses.

The Arrival of Romanticism. The rise of Romanticism disturbed the orderly patterns of the Age of Reason. During the latter years of the eighteenth century, philosophers and critics in America and Europe became increasingly uncomfortable within the framework of thought erected earlier by Newton, Locke, and Pope. No longer content with a rationalism and classicism which, it seemed to them, had hardened into traditionalism, they took renewed interest in ideas about the deity, the universe, and man which had been relatively neglected by the earlier eighteenth century. These ideas were developed and extended into a loose, quasi-philosophical system which spread through Europe and America, causing men on both sides of the Atlantic to question seriously some of the attitudes of the Enlightenment and to alter their conceptions of nature, human nature, and society. Many of these "Romantic" ideas were not new, nor were they ever assimilated into a unified system, but the climate of opinion that characterized the intellectual activity of Americans and Europeans from the closing decades of the eighteenth century to the middle of the nineteenth was coherent and consistent enough to warrant calling the period the Age of Romanticism.

The Romantic view of society rested on three general concepts. First, on the idea of organism, that things were conceived as wholes, or units, with their own internal laws of governance and development. This held true both for individual men and for societies. Second, on the idea of dynamism, of motion and growth. Beliefs and institutions were assumed to be fluid, changing, capable of manipulation and adaptation. Third, on the idea of diversity, of the value of differences of opinions, cultures, tastes, societies, characters—as opposed to the uniformitarian norms of the Enlightenment. To the Age of Reason, conformity meant rationalism; diversity meant irrationality and therefore error. To the Romantic, a consensus seemed much less important than the judgment of the individual, and diversity seemed "natural" and "right."

The men who fought the Revolution, wrote the Constitution, and set the Republic on its way were products of the Age of Reason and derived their intellectual inspiration from it. The next generation of leaders, those who took over direction of the nation from the Founding Fathers, were men shaped less by the Enlightenment than by the new arrangement of ideas. What Americans thought about their state, their arts, the organization of relationships within their politics and society, and about themselves and the natural world around them, was powerfully influenced by this emergent Romanticism.

The Professionalization of Science. The intellectual impact of the Enlightenment manifested itself most clearly in the advancement of American science in the later eighteenth century. The colonies had been settled in the scientific age of Galileo and Newton; American intellectuals were never far from the center of the great scientific revolution that marked the European Enlightenment, and, like other educated men of their times, lived by contemporary scientific attitudes. They believed that all problems responded to scientific investigation; that the universe was mechanistic, governed by constant natural laws which were discoverable by human reason; that all knowledge was fundamentally scientific; and that the inductive method of thinking was quite possibly the only trustworthy method of arriving at truth. These beliefs, derived from Newtonian science, furnished the most coherent pattern by which the affairs of man and nature might be explained; from science, the leaders of American thought believed, they might find solutions to the problems of human society.

The Revolution suspended practically all scientific activity, but immediately after it, as Dr. Amos Eaton wrote, "A thirst for natural science seemed to pervade the United States like the progress of an epidemic." The nation was especially fortunate in receiving a number of brilliant immigrants and refugees during and after the war. Thomas Cooper, geologist and economist, came from England, as did Joseph Priestley, one of the world's greatest chemists; Pierre du Pont de Nemours, a noted chemist, arrived from France. Meanwhile, the United States possessed a number of highly competent scientists among its native born. President Jefferson was a scientist of repute himself, and the Lewis and Clark expedition which he sent westward in 1804 was one of the most significant scientific projects in American history.

Though long neglected by the colleges and universities, the study of science began to appear in the curriculum, usually as astronomy, chemistry, or physics. Indeed, science itself was becoming a profession rather than a hobby for interested amateurs. The tremendous growth in the amount of scientific knowledge, and the equally great impact of that knowledge on contemporary life, meant that there was no longer a place for the "natural philosopher" who took all scientific knowledge as his province. The day of the oldtime jack-of-all-trades like Dr. Samuel Latham Mitchill of Columbia, who ranged through chemistry, medicine, mathematics, botany, zoology, and poetry, was nearly over.

American scientists readily admitted that they had made no major contributions to scientific theory and that Europe and England still dominated the various fields. Yet their achievements were not negligible, especially in identifying and classifying the flora and fauna of their continent and in exploring the extent of its resources. And Americans were confident that their own great scientific contributions would inevitably come.

Creating American Law.   The laws which had governed the American colonies had come from three main sources: decisions of the king; acts of Parliament or boards of trade; and common law—that is, written or unwritten English law embodied in judicial decisions, precedents, and usage. Legal codes and procedures in the colonies had been substantially the same as in the mother country, and colonists had expected and substantially received the same legal rights as Britons at home. The requirements of American environment and experience had naturally made adjustments and modifications necessary—as, for example, in laws of land tenure and of navigation—but American law, at the instant of separation in 1776, was English law and the system of courts and justice thoroughly British. The *Commentaries* (1771–72) of Sir William Blackstone, professor of law at Oxford, defined, explained, and systematized natural law with such clarity that they were particularly influential on American legal thinking at the time.

The act of independence theoretically canceled every law in every state, though in practice, of course, the states took over the existing legal structure and continued to use the laws they had, changing the source of authority. But as these states wrote constitutions and formed governments, they also addressed themselves to the problems of designing for American purposes a legal system of their own out of the mass of materials—English common law, continental law, natural law, colonial acts and precedents, and so on—which they had inherited.

There were two possible approaches: to establish a completely new American code or to remake the colonial legacy into a system of basically English but functionally American law. A very few (like the Kentuckian who "wished to make it a penal offense to bring an English lawbook into the country") favored abandoning British law, but the force of the English tradition and two centuries of history was far too strong for any such drastic revisions. Furthermore, British commercial and common law, hammered out over centuries of experience, met American requirements extremely well.

Though Britain provided form, direction, and detail for the early development of the American legal system, it did not fit every need. The ideals of British law reflected an old, settled, hierarchical society rather than the fluid, individualistic, open society of a new country. Thus lawyers and courts made a number of changes in translating the British system into American terms. American courts tended to simplify the complexities of British legal machinery, which was largely uncodified, and to organize constitutional and statute law into written codes. Americans also relied much more on juries, in both civil and equity cases, than was true of British practice. The unsettled state of the American courts and the scarcity of experienced judges after the Revolution led to a greater reliance on jury decisions, which appealed to a frontier people who believed in republican equality. Until late in the nineteenth century American juries retained much greater powers at law than those normally granted juries in England.

The revolutionary generation, however, did not wholly trust courts and lawyers. It had fresh memories of royal judges and admiralty courts and of the large number of colonial judges who had remained Loyalist. The confusion of postwar economic conditions threw thousands of citizens into the courts, where, it was popularly believed, the poor man always lost. During the years that produced Shays' Rebellion (see p. 78) "the mere sight of a lawyer," one of them wrote ruefully, "was enough to call forth an oath or a muttered curse."

The people generally placed confidence less in courts than in state legislatures, since legislatures were the lawmaking bodies chosen by the public at large. Early legislatures did not hesitate to act on this assumption. They summoned judges before them for questioning, reversed court decisions, probated wills and handled estates, passed special laws meting out justice, and usurped many of the functions of the courts. But gradually, as time passed, the law gained greater public confidence and lawyers greater responsibilities in the governing of American society. The most distinctive trends in American law from the close of the Revolution until 1830 were the gradual emergence of equality between the judiciary and the legislative branches in American governments and the increasing influence of lawyers in American life.

The excesses of some of the state legislatures during the Confederation disillusioned many sober Americans, and public confidence soon began to shift from state capitals to courts. Because other institutions were unpredictable or slow to develop, citizens turned to the courts for help, providing tremendous opportunities for lawyers in postrevolutionary society. "Scarcely any question arises in the United States," commented the French traveler Alexis de Tocqueville in 1835, "which does not become sooner or later, a subject of juridical debate." In an era when the explication and interpretation of constitutions and statutes furnished the keys to political and economic power, the legal profession possessed great advantages.

Meanwhile, law as a profession was gaining respectability and evolving standards of proficiency and conduct for itself. Instruction was carried out in private schools and in a few colleges and universities; by 1800 all states except Kentucky, North Carolina, and Virginia had fixed standards of legal training. The profession of law, wrote Charles Brockden Brown in 1790, "is withal, in this country, one of the roads to opulence, and the most certain path to political importance and fame."

The "Scottish Philosophy."   The necessities of life in the revolutionary and early republican periods demanded men of action rather than speculative philosophers. Americans were too busy shaping a revolution, creating a government, and constructing a society to spend much time in probing or systematizing their assumptions. To them philosophy was often a way of rationalizing the things they intended to do. As a result, Tocqueville remarked that nowhere in the world was less attention paid to philosophy than in the United States. Although he exaggerated the case, it was true that American philosophy was highly derivative of British and French sources, practical rather than speculative and either theologically or politically oriented.

The major strain of American philosophy during the revolutionary era was Lockean empiricism, which based all knowledge on experience and which fitted in admirably with the political and scientific interests of the times. When Locke's popularity faded in the United States (as it did in Britain), Americans found a replacement in the philosophy of "common sense" recently developed in Scottish universities.

According to the Scottish school, the human mind possessed the ability to make what Thomas Reid called "original and natural judgments" which "served to direct us in the common affairs of life, when our reasoning faculty would leave us in the dark." These judgments, he continued, "make up what is called the *common sense of mankind,*" providing men with "first principles" on which they may agree to act and furnishing them a kind of moral and social stability. The "Scottish philosophy" did not rest on subtle argument or pedantic jargon; it seemed to settle bothersome problems by reference to an understandable consensus. Its basic optimism fitted American needs admirably, especially its assumption that all men, whatever their condition, possessed an inherent moral sense which could be strengthened and improved by proper education and application. The American democratic experiment had to be posited on some such faith in the common man's judgment to make the decisions, political and otherwise, so important to his society, and the principles of "common sense" provided reason to believe that the average individual possessed a natural ability to fulfill those obligations which America placed upon him. It furnished a way of establishing the philosophical validity of those "self-evident" truths on which the American system rested; it was a straightforward and sensible method of looking at life and considering its problems, one which could be easily codified, illustrated, and taught. Such a mode of thought, wrote the Reverend John Gros of Columbia College, gave "rules for the direction of the will of man in his moral state, such rules to serve for the guidance of the individual, community, and nation."

The Scottish approach became the official philosophy of late eighteenth- and early nineteenth-century America, accepted almost unanimously as the proper way to direct and control one's thinking and acting. By 1810 the majority of courses in "Moral Science" or "Natural Philosophy" taught in every institution of higher learning were founded on common-sense principles. Between 1790 and 1860 there were few educated Americans who were not familiar with the concepts of the Scottish school. These ideas influenced the development of American thought considerably during the nineteenth century.

The Secularization of Theology. At the time of the Revolution there were approximately three thousand churches in the United States. The majority of these were Calvinist and belonged to the Presbyterians and Congregationalists, whose differences lay less in creed than in matters of church government. The Anglican Church was seriously divided by the Revolution, supplying, on the one hand, the largest number of Loyalists of any church and, on the other hand, the majority of the signers of the Declaration of Independence. The Methodists, whose first missionaries had arrived only in 1769, were growing rapidly, as were the Baptists, though both were still relatively small and dispersed. Lutheran and Reformed church membership lay chiefly in German- and Dutch-settled areas. The small Catholic population was concentrated primarily in Maryland; in 1782 there were still fewer than twenty-five priests in America.

During the Revolution the states immediately set about to establish proper relationships with the various churches. Since each former colony had its own religious history and since it was plain that no single church could satisfy a diverse, expanding population that already worshipped under seventeen different creeds, the legislatures wisely chose to allow, as New York's did, "free enjoyment of the rights of conscience." The Continental Congress, and later the Constitutional Convention, both reaffirmed the prevailing belief that religion, as Jefferson phrased it, was "a matter which lies solely between man and his God." Most of the state constitutions contained clauses or bills of rights guaranteeing freedom of worship on much the same terms as the federal Constitution.

Also during the war years each legislature, in one way or another, provided for a clear separation of the churches from state authority, with the exception of New Hampshire, Connecticut, and Massachusetts, where the Congregationalists successfully resisted disestablishment for another thirty to fifty years. In Virginia, Jefferson saw the passage of the Statute for Religious Freedom in 1786, which he counted among his proudest accomplishments. Nevertheless, there was still widespread doubt whether religious freedom and toleration could be fully extended to everyone. For full civil and political rights a number of states required religious tests or qualifications which discriminated against Catholics, Jews, and nonconformist Protestant sects. Most of these, however, had disappeared by 1830.

Ministers of the postwar years generally believed American Protestantism to be in "a low and declining state." The Presbyterian Assembly of 1798 noted "a general dereliction of religious principles and practice among our citizens," and congregations were often restive with authority and impatient of the old doctrines. In 1800 even the powerful Congregational and Presbyterian churches could count less than 10 percent of the people of New England and the Middle Atlantic states as church members, and all the major Protestant sects were split by argument and dissension. None of the older Calvinist groups, in fact, had been able to make the necessary adjustments to the great new surge of scientific information, and none had kept direct touch with the secular, optimistic, republican spirit of the time.

Nor was this all. The churches faced another threat in the form of a religio-philosophical movement transported from England and Europe in the latter decades of the eighteenth century under the name of deism. Rooted in the Enlightenment's faith in reason and science and closely in tune with the secular, rationalistic temper of the period, deism had a strong appeal to intellectual and political leaders such as Franklin, Jefferson, Paine, Barlow, and Freneau. Cutting away the twisted intricacies of Calvinistic doctrine, the deists proclaimed God's benevolence, man's rationality, goodness, and free will, and nature's order, harmony, and understandability. If men would but live by these beliefs, said Ethan Allen of Vermont, "they would . . . rid themselves of blindness and superstition, gain more exalted ideas of God, and make better members of society."

Against the deists the orthodox theologians put up a sturdy defense, but against the inroads of another "heresy," unitarianism, they had less success. Partly imported from England and partly the legacy of the Great Awakening of the earlier eighteenth century, unitarianism was so named because it rejected the idea of the Trinity and emphasized the human personality, rather than the divinity, of Jesus. "Liberal" unitarian doctrines, which placed far greater trust in man and his abilities to discern religious truth, interested more and more orthodox Calvinist parishioners and ministers after 1790. Harvard College, the traditional fortress of New England Calvinism, surrendered to the "liberals" in 1805. The "Conference of Liberal Ministers," called in 1820 to furnish leadership for those dissatisfied with Calvinistic orthodoxy, six years later became the American Unitarian Association, a separate group of 125 churches, among them twenty of the oldest Calvinist churches in New England.

There were indications, as early as the 1790s, that the religious evangelism of the Great Awakening of a half century before might once again provide a revitalizing force within the orthodox Calvinist churches. The Methodists and Baptists especially produced a number of evangelist preachers, but revivalism was never really popular in Presbyterian and Congregational circles. On the frontier, however, the evangelists' simple, direct, and emotionally satisfying version of Christian faith was well adapted to the needs of the pioneer community. There the camp meeting took on great importance, and by 1800 traveling preachers had spread revivalism through western Pennsylvania, Kentucky, Ohio, and Tennessee. Famous exhorters such as James McGready and Barton Stone, preaching a vivid religion of hellfire, rigid morality, and salvation, attracted huge crowds. At the great Cane Ridge camp meeting of 1801 in Kentucky, between ten thousand and twenty thousand people heard forty evangelists preach over a six-day period. Such meetings spread across the country—Methodist Bishop Francis Asbury counted four hundred of them in 1811, chiefly in the South and West—and continued through the 1850s.

While frontier evangelism sometimes encouraged emotional excess, it helped bring stability and order to new communities, increased church membership, and gave churches great influence in social and political affairs. Calvinism itself was powerfully affected by the impact of this "second Great Awakening," which, in addition to exerting a strong democratizing force on religion, emphasized individualism, morality, and social action. The new Romanticism, by reason of its insistence on the individual, the validity of his emotions, and his ability to make things better, also contributed significantly to the impetus of revivalism. From the religious enthusiasm generated by this "Awakening," churches became involved in reform causes such as temperance, social welfare, prison reform, and eventually the abolition of slavery.

Free and Equal Men. Thomas Jefferson put into the Declaration the phrase that "all men are created equal." Those who signed the Declaration apparently agreed that this was part of that body of "self-evident" truth enumerated in the document and supported by natural law. Equality and liberty, the Declaration implied, were coexistent. *Liberty* was the more easily defined; *equality* was more difficult, and the need for defining its meaning was imperative.

Neither Puritans nor Virginians came to the colonies looking for equality. The company settlers searched for more wealth than they had, while the Puritans brought with them the elements of an aristocratic theology. Both carried to the new country many of the distinctions of the British social system. But Calvinism also pointed in another direction: it rejected much of the church hierarchy, believed in the priesthood of all believers, and introduced elective methods into portions of church policy. Later, philosophers of the Enlightenment included the principle of equality within their listings of "natural rights," and men such as John Locke and Jean Jacques Rousseau added wider dimensions to the term's meaning.

More important, however, the idea of equality had a strong practical basis in the American colonial experience. The wilderness stripped a man of the distinctions of civilization and put him on an equal footing with his fellows. Indians, disease, starvation, and other hazards of frontier life killed an earl's or a tinker's son with equal disregard. The lack of fixed organization in a new society made it possible for men to be both free and equal in an actual, visible sense; social mobility allowed a man to change his status, within limits, rather rapidly. The equality forced on American society by the frontier was the most compelling fact about it.

Colonial and republican society, like England's, was built on stratifications which no one questioned. Everyone recognized, a Virginian wrote in 1760, that there were "differences of capacity, disposition, and virtue" among men, which divided them into classes. Yet these strata were broader and more vague than England's. Colonial society possessed the whole range of criteria for class distinctions, including wealth and property, dress, manners, speech, and education, but these carried less weight than they did abroad. There was not so much doffing of caps, bowing or curtseying, and pulling of forelocks; British General Carleton complained that it was hard to uphold "the dignity of the throne and peerage" in American society. Few foreign travelers failed to remark on the fluidity of American classes, much of it the result of broad economic opportunities offered by an expanding society.

After 1783, when Americans faced the necessity of implementing the terms of the Declaration, almost every leader gave attention to the problem of equality and of how to make it an integral part of the new nation's life. Jefferson's "glittering generality," as John Adams called it, provided an inspirational rallying cry for revolution, but to construct a government in a disjointed postwar society required a definition of what *equality* meant in practical terms. Some, like Fisher Ames, believed the doctrine "a pernicious tool of demagogues"; others, like Thomas Paine, thought it "one of the greatest of all truths" in political theory. Franklin, while remarking that "Time, Chance, and Industry" created social and economic distinctions, believed that men were equal in "the personal securities of life and liberty." Jefferson and John Adams discussed the matter in their old age, concluding, in Jefferson's phrase, that there was a "natural aristocracy" of "virtue and talents," but that there was also an equality of rights belonging to all men. (Or, as Nathaniel Ames said succinctly in his popular

Almanac, "Men are by nature equal, but differ greatly in the sequel.") Generally, the leaders of the postwar generation agreed that the new nation needed a government in which the better and more able men governed, and also one in which the rights of all men were equally protected and the equal rights of all men maintained. On this basis the nation began to build its society, with the implications of the term *equality* still to be explored more fully by future generations.

Race, Equality, and the Social Problem. Thoughtful Americans were well aware of the anomaly of slavery in a society predicated on man's "natural rights" and the contradiction of a revolution waged to "free" men who held others in bondage. There was no dearth of opposition to the system: between 1776 and 1804 seven states passed legislation for emancipating slaves. Jefferson included an antislavery clause in his instructions to the Virginia delegates to the Continental Congress and tried unsuccessfully to place an antislavery provision in the Virginia constitution of 1776; revolutionary leaders Charles Carroll and William Pinkney also unsuccessfully sponsored an antislavery bill in the Maryland legislature in 1789. But while slavery was a matter of legal condition, it was also a matter of race, which made a great difference when emancipation legislation and the black slave's future status in an overwhelmingly white society were discussed.

Anthropological theories of race were not well developed until the eighteenth century, when continuing contact with Indians and blacks forced Europeans to speculate about the different kinds of men, their origins, and their qualities. Eighteenth-century scientists, who arranged all life forms in systems, considered man a *species* and different races as *varieties* of that species. The species, created by God to occupy a particular place in the design of nature, existed within fixed, immutable limits. The varieties of races were the result of geography, climate, and other factors, which produced differences within the species but did not alter its boundaries. Beginning with the Biblical account of the creation of Adam, anthropologists postulated that at one time all men had been alike but that different environments had changed them into members of related races, differing in color, size, hair, and other characteristics. Though color was not a wholly satisfactory criterion for identifying these varieties of man, it provided the most visible and logical basis for classifying them.

There were also those who believed—with Biblical support—that the different races were the result not of environmental influence but of a second creation; and later there were still others who believed that each race originated in one of a series of separate creations. Whatever the theory, it was generally agreed that there were five biologically identifiable groups of men: Caucasian or white; Mongolian or yellow; Malayan or brown; "American" or red; and Ethiopian or black. Whether or not these races were equal in abilities—or, if not, possessed the potential to be made so—became a question of major importance to the Enlightenment.

Some anthropologists believed that since all men, whatever their color, were created as members of the same species, they had the same abilities and, through education, favorable environment, and other means, could reach equality. Among the American writers who belonged to this optimistic school, one of the most influential was Professor (later President) Samuel Stanhope Smith of Princeton. Others disagreed, arguing that the races of men were separate and not necessarily equal species. Thomas Jefferson, in *Notes on Virginia* (1786), took the view that certain races, particularly the red and the black, probably did not possess the proper potential for progressive change and that while their status might be improved, it was doubtful they could attain actual equality. He later modified his ideas, expressing the hope that blacks would someday be "on an equal footing with the other colors of the human family."

As the debate over race continued into the nineteenth century, Jefferson's hope seemed increasingly less likely of realization. Anthropologists on both sides of the Atlantic tended to assume that each race had inherent and quite separate traits; they were not equal, nor could they be made so. Most authorities ranked them in descending order as white, yellow, brown, red, and black, on the basis of pseudoscientific evidence subject to much debate. Acceptance of this theory of racial abilities dominated American thinking about race over the next half century and both shaped and justified national policy toward Indians and blacks.

Woman's Place in Society. The legal status of women during the eighteenth century remained much as it was in earlier colonial days. Unmarried women were considered the wards of relatives, married women their husbands' chattels. A wife's rights to property were closely limited: she could not make a will, sign a contract, or witness a deed without her husband's permission. Divorce for a woman, no matter what the provocation, was so difficult in most colonies as to be next to impossible; almost all professions and trades were closed to women; and, of course, they could neither vote nor hold office, a handicap they shared with some males. In the eyes of the law, as Blackstone tersely put it, "The husband and wife are one, and that one is the husband." Not only the law but the church supported this view. According to both Catholic and Protestant clergy, woman's subordinate place in society was established by those intellectual and physical limitations placed upon her at her creation and forever fixed by her weaknesses as a daughter of Eve.

Nonetheless, the American woman held a higher status in this new and flexible society than it might appear. In city or country, woman's work—spinning, weaving, sewing, making shoes, soap, candles, clothing, and much else—was absolutely necessary to the maintenance of the home and the functioning of society. Nor were such mundane tasks the extent of her obligations. The development of the child-centered family, which began in the Renaissance, powerfully influenced the position of the woman within the home during the eighteenth century. With it came the idea that the family—not society at large—had the crucial task of preparing the young—socially, intellectually, and spiritually—to enter society. This belief placed major responsibility on woman as supervisor of home and teacher of children. By the early nineteenth century men were ready to agree that, from this point of view, women's function in society was equal to—possibly superior to—their own. Herein lay the beginnings of a reevaluation of women's place in the world.

Colonial women were not restricted to purely domestic duties. The contemporary system of household manufacturing provided opportunities for them to learn a craft and become part of the home labor market. They also helped their husbands in their work, ran the farm or shop when the men served in the militia or went to sea or hunted game, and often took over management of farm or shop when husbands died. Thus Franklin's sister-in-law Ann ran her husband's print shop after his death, and John Singleton Copley's widowed mother kept her late husband's tobacco store. Chronic labor shortages made female labor much more acceptable in America than in Europe. The growth of the textile industry was particularly influential in opening the way to the employment of women outside the home: extending them the privilege of working fourteen hours a day at a loom raised a number of questions about their lesser status. Other trades began to accept women workers until, by the early 1830s, Harriet Martineau could list seven kinds of employment currently approved for females— teaching, sewing, typesetting, bookbinding, domestic service, textile mill work, and running a boarding house.

Women's Rights and Revolution.   The Revolution itself encouraged new ways of thinking about women's status. The Daughters of Liberty, though not so well publicized as the Sons, aided in the boycott of British goods and the harassment of Loyalists. Not only did the departure of men to serve in the army and the government create vacancies that women had to fill, but the whole drift of the revolutionary argument worked to their benefit. If all men were endowed with natural and unalienable rights, were not women, too? Strong-minded women like Mercy Warren and Margaret Winthrop and Abigail Adams (not to mention the legendary Molly Pitcher, who joined her husband's artillery crew at the Battle of Monmouth) were likely to ask such questions, while Judith Sargent Murray was demanding that an American woman be treated as "an intelligent being" with interests beyond "the mechanics of a pudding or the sewing of the seams in a garment." Enlightened males like Franklin, Paine, and Benjamin Rush joined her in asking for a reconsideration of women's rights.

Meanwhile, the winds of feminist thought abroad blew westward across the water: Americans read Godwin and Condorcet and especially Mary Wollstonecraft's *Vindication of the Rights of Women* (1792). Women's rights became a topic of discussion in magazines and in drawing rooms everywhere. Charles Brockden Brown's tract *Alcuin* (1798) was intended to serve as the American *Vindication,* and several of his novels, notably *Ormond,* explored issues raised by the feminist debate. Judith Sargent Murray could thus confidently predict in 1798 the advent of "a new era in female history."

This was not soon forthcoming. Despite the liberalizing influences of Revolution and Enlightenment, conservative elements provided powerful opposition. What feminist leaders asked for was primarily the right to self-development through education, in which they believed lay the key to legal rights and ultimate social equality. And even for equal education the struggle was hard, for they faced the entrenched tradition of female inferiority, the belief that woman's "sphere" was within the home and that (as Jean Jacques Rousseau had written) "the whole education of women ought to be relative to men." Although men like Burr and Jefferson believed in educating their daughters in something more than the polite and domestic arts, most Americans considered women's minds to be incapable of contending with subjects like law, philosophy, science, and theology. Emma Hart Willard, herself an accomplished mathematician, first cracked the wall (with the help of Governor DeWitt Clinton and others) by establishing in 1821 at Troy, New York, the first endowed school for women equal to those for men—Troy Female Seminary. A few others appeared during the twenties and thirties, but it was left to the next generation to give the women's rights movement measurable momentum.

THE QUEST FOR A NATIONAL CULTURE

A Native Art. Having gained political independence, Americans sought their own culture for a way to express—in literature, drama, and the arts—the fundamentals of their civilization.

Critics, editors, and authors agreed on the need for a native, original, indigenous art—as Noah Webster wrote, "America must be as independent in *literature* as she is in politics"—but it was easier to demand art than to produce it. For one thing, a great deal of creative energy was diverted into business and politics. Politics, Samuel Miller explained in his *Retrospect of the Eighteenth Century* (1803), had a tendency to stifle culture; furthermore, as Washington Irving pointed out, the United States, lacking "the charms of storied and poetical association . . . , and the accumulated treasures of age," had no usable past to stir the artist's fancy.

Since the United States had no tradition of literary patronage among the wealthy, there were no really professional American authors, nor was authorship financially rewarding. For this reason Henry Wadsworth Longfellow's father warned him against being a poet, for "there is not wealth and munificence enough in this country to afford sufficient encouragement and patronage to merely literary men." And last, there was the practical matter of the lack of an adequate copyright law in the United States, which made it extremely difficult for a book published in America to compete with a cheap, pirated English edition.

The Literary Discovery of America. The first step toward cultural independence was to declare America's freedom from English and European domination. The second was to define the circumstances and standards by which the United States could produce a distinguished literature of its own. The author must have something American to write about and a defined, recognizable native manner of writing it. True, Timothy Dwight admitted, the United States lacked "ancient castles, ruined abbeys, and fine pictures." But on the other hand the American artist possessed a number of things that neither British nor other European artists possessed.

The American artist had the Indian, the frontier, and a brief but eminently usable past. After 1790 every author of note made at least one attempt to use the American frontier or American history in a major work, though not until James Fenimore Cooper's novel *The Spy* (1821) did any of them find a way to handle the material with success. In addition, American artists possessed ample material for studies of manners, what dramatist James Nelson Barker called "the events, customs, opinions, and characters of American life." The American scene, wrote William Cullen Bryant, displayed "an infinite variety of pursuits and subjects, [an] endless diversity and change of fortunes." All that one needed to exploit it, he concluded, was "sagacity and skill."

The greatest artistic resource was, of course, the land itself—American nature, vast, unspoiled, fascinating in its variety and grandeur. Out of these things, American artists believed they could produce something aesthetically valuable, morally true, and uniquely expressive of American life. To create it the artist must, Charles Brockden Brown urged, "examine objects with his own eyes, employ European models merely for the improvement of his taste," and build his art out of "all that is genuine and peculiar in the scene before him." This, then, was the aim of the first generation of American artists.

Patterns in American Prose.   The distinguishing characteristic of developments in literature produced during the period from 1783 to 1830 was the growing popularity of the novel, the poem, the essay, and the drama, and the decline of such once-popular forms of writing as the sermon, the journal, the travel narrative, and the autobiography. This reflected in part the increased level of appreciation and sophistication of American society and in part a greater effort by American writers to enter into the mainstream of contemporary literary fashions.

The essay, modeled chiefly after the work of the great British essayists, attracted a number of talented Americans, among them Washington Irving, who became famous with the appearance of *The Sketchbook* (1819–20).

The novel in America still faced public and ecclesiastical suspicion, and most critics did not consider it an art form worthy of serious effort. Nevertheless, the demand for fiction increased rapidly, magazines printed novels by the score, and libraries stocked greater numbers of them each year. The most popular ones copied the sentimental novels of the English author Samuel Richardson. William Hill Brown's *Power of Sympathy* (1789), Susannah Rowson's *Charlotte Temple* (1791), and others like them ran through numerous editions as Americans wept over the predicaments of virtuous young ladies besieged by rascally villains.

A few novelists turned to satire: Royall Tyler's *Algerine Captive* (1797) and Hugh Henry Brackenridge's *Modern Chivalry* (1792–97) poked fun at politics, fashions, sentimentalism, and almost every other aspect of contemporary life. The Gothic novel of suspense and terror found a gifted American practitioner in Philadelphia's Charles Brockden Brown, whose *Wieland* (1798) and *Ormond* (1799) were uneven in quality but indicative of genuine talent.

Most popular of all, however, was the historical romance, patterned on the works of Sir Walter Scott, whose novels enjoyed a tremendous vogue in early nineteenth-century America. Dozens of American novelists imitated him, but none successfully fitted the Scott formula to the American scene until James Fenimore Cooper wrote *The Spy* (1821), *The Pioneers* (1823), *The Last of the Mohicans* (1826), and thirty other novels. When Cooper's buckskin hero Natty Bumppo walked into American fiction and leaned on his long rifle, the American novel came of age.

Meanwhile, another American, Washington Irving, had included several pieces of short fiction in his *Sketch Book.* Two of these, "Rip Van Winkle" and "The Legend of Sleepy Hollow," provided a pattern for a new literary form, the short story, and their central characters quickly became a part of the American cultural heritage. Irving's popularity, combined with Cooper's, furnished a decisive answer to English critic Sydney Smith's sneer in 1820, "Who reads an American book?"

Poetic Literature in the New Republic. Poetry found hard going in the period after the Revolutionary War. There were plenty of young men interested in writing verse, but the way of the poet was difficult in a world torn by two wars with England, a near-war with France, bitter political rivalries at home, and a whole new political system a-building. Some young men of talent, like Joel Barlow, tried their hands at "epics" and retreated to politics; John Trumbull, one of the cleverest, went into law; Timothy Dwight, whose poetic gifts were considerable but of doubtful quality, turned to theology and education. Out of the flood of American verse—usually imitating the English classical poetry of Pope, Dryden, Gray, or Goldsmith—that washed over the closing decades of the eighteenth century, very little remained as a lasting contribution to an American poetic tradition.

This was not the case with Philip Freneau, the first authentic poetic voice to be heard in the United States. His poems, dealing with nature, beauty, the past, and personal experience, show genuine poetic gifts. The delicacy and skill of his lyric verse were unmatched by any American poet of his day—and by few British.

American Building: British, Greek, or Roman? The Enlightenment, as befitting an Age of Reason, preferred spare, clean harmonious designs derived from Greek and Roman building over the intricate and ornamented baroque and medieval styles inherited from the seventeenth century. There were very few professional architects in the United States at the time of independence, and most existing public buildings were almost wholly copied from designs imported from Britain. The typical colonial style was, therefore, a modification of Georgian, made popular in England by Inigo Jones and the Adam brothers. After the Revolution there was an immediate demand for buildings to serve the new state and federal governments and a corresponding need for professional architects. The current vogue for things Greek and Roman, as well as the prevailing English style, created two distinct architectural traditions—a modified Georgian style, exemplified in Philadelphia's State House, or Independence Hall, and a Romanized style characteristic of the Middle and Southern colonies, best illustrated by Jefferson's Virginia State Capitol at Richmond.

The two greatest practitioners of these architectural styles were Charles Bulfinch of Boston and Thomas Jefferson of Virginia. Deeply impressed by the British style, Bulfinch developed an American version of it, called the Boston or "Federal" style, which emphasized simplicity and balance, with cleanly symmetrical brickwork, graceful doorways separating equal numbers of sash windows, white trim, and classical cupolas. He rebuilt Faneuil Hall in Boston, designed capitols for Boston, Hartford, and Augusta, built a number of churches, and served for a time as architect in charge of the national Capitol in Washington. His influence may still be seen in the small towns of Ohio, Michigan, and Illinois, or wherever New Englanders migrated in the next fifty years.

Jefferson believed that the United States needed to develop an architectural tradition of its own, free of British influence and worthy of a young, great nation. Perceiving an analogy between the grandeur of the classic past and the future of the Republic, he drew on his study of Roman remains in Europe, and of French and Italian adaptations of the classic style, to create an American tradition well illustrated by his plans for the University of Virginia. His home at Monticello, on which he worked for forty years, was his crowning achievement and is one of the gems of American architecture.

After Jefferson, the classical tradition was further modified by Benjamin Latrobe, whose source was Greek, not Roman, and who with his followers helped to initiate what soon became the Greek Revival era in American architecture. The Federal, classical, and Greek Revival styles, though they added grace, beauty, and charm to the American scene, still could not yet be called wholly American architecture.

Musicians and Painters.   The eighteenth-century colonists loved music as ardently as their English contemporaries. French and German immigrants, too, brought their musical tastes to America, and after 1800 such cities as New York, Philadelphia, Boston, and Charleston supported good orchestras, musical societies, studios, and academies. However, American composers and musicians could hardly hope to match their powerful European contemporaries or to compete with the talented, trained immigrants who came to America from the finest European orchestras and schools.

As for popular music, eighteenth-century colonists imported large numbers of songbooks from England; "singing meetings" were common diversions; and "singing schools" trained not only church choirs but secular choruses, some of professional skill. After the Revolution, publishers put together "songsters" or "musical miscellanies" by the hundreds, including such songs as "The Blue Bell of Scotland," "Drink to Me Only with Thine Eyes," "Yankee Doodle," "Auld Lang Syne," and many others that became enduring favorites. These collections (such as the 1808 *Missouri Songster,* which Lincoln remembered using as a boy) proliferated after the 1790s and served as the main source of American popular music over the next century.

Samuel Miller, in his *Retrospect of the Eighteenth Century* (1803), admitted apologetically that American art had as yet produced no great painters, though he could point with pride to Benjamin West, John Singleton Copley, Charles Willson Peale, Gilbert Stuart, and John Trumbull. These painters, all born into the prerevolutionary generation and rooted in an English and European tradition, looked to Paris, Rome, and especially London for instruction and inspiration. Yet they were men of considerable talent, whose work was admired abroad as well as at home. West, whose forte was historical painting, became court painter to England's King George III and successor to Sir Joshua Reynolds as president of the British Royal Academy. A painter in the so-called grand style, he specialized in huge canvasses of such famous events as "The Death of General Wolfe." Copley, though one of West's students, avoided the heroic and excelled in skillful, sensitive, and perceptive portraits, becoming probably the best portrait painter in London. Peale not only painted well but founded the first museum in the United States (1786), organized the first public art exhibition in the country (1794), and in 1805 helped establish the Pennsylvania Academy of Fine Arts.

Gilbert Stuart, another pupil of West's, dominated American portrait art for nearly thirty years, producing the amazing total of 1150 portraits. His realistic, luminous style and his feeling for the person behind the painting made him the best painter of the period in the genre. His "Washington," which appears on a well-known postage stamp, is an example of Stuart at his best. Trumbull, strongly affected by West's manner, became head of the American Academy of Arts in 1817 and exerted considerable influence on American taste and critical standards for many years.

The Course of American Culture. During the period from 1787 to 1830 the arts in the United States, from literature through painting, were in large part derivative, imitative, dependent upon Britain and Europe for standards and inspirations. Literature showed much more of an American disposition than painting, architecture more than music. Artistic production on the whole was increasingly nationalistic in spirit, and the artists were seriously committed to the use of American materials and the expression of American attitudes. Though still suffering from a colonial complex, lacking confidence in their own tastes and ideas, fearful of not conforming to traditional, time-tested artistic norms, they nevertheless hoped to create a new, distinctive, independent culture within the framework of a unified American experience. What the United States wanted was a Golden Age of its own, built out of American materials and ideals, couched in artistic terms and derived from aesthetic theories that could be accepted with confidence and performed with pride. Real cultural independence was yet to come.

BIBLIOGRAPHY

General studies of the early national period include Edmund S. Morgan, *The Birth of the Republic** (Chicago: University of Chicago Press, 1956); Marcus Cunliffe, *The Nation Takes Shape, 1789–1837** (Chicago: University of Chicago Press, 1959); and Charles M. Wiltse, *The New Nation, 1800–1845** (New York: Hill and Wang, 1961). R. R. Palmer, *The Age of Democratic Revolution,** 2 vols. (Princeton: Princeton University Press, 1969, 1970) places American events within the larger European context. Thomas D. Clark, *Frontier America* (New York: Charles Scribner's Sons, 1969) and Louis B. Wright, *Culture on the Moving Frontier** (New York: Harper & Row, 1955) provide insight into frontier life in the later eighteenth and early nineteenth centuries. John A. Krout and Dixon Ryan Fox, *The Completion of Independence** (Chicago: Quadrangle, 1971) and Russel B. Nye, *The Cultural Life of the New Nation** (New York: Harper & Row, 1963) treat social and cultural developments. See also the latter chapters of

Howard Mumford Jones, *O Brave New World!** (New York: Viking, 1972), Russel B. Nye, *American Literary History 1607–1830** (New York: Alfred A. Knopf, 1970), John C. Burnham, ed., *Science in America** (New York: Holt, Rinehart, and Winston, 1971), and Daniel Boorstin, *The Americans: The National Experience** (New York: Random House, 1967) for additional studies in cultural history.

Carl Becker, *The Declaration of Independence** (New York: Alfred A. Knopf, 1959) remains the classic treatment of the ideological backgrounds of revolutionary philosophy. Merrill Jensen, *The Articles of Confederation,** 2nd ed. (Madison: University of Wisconsin Press, 1959) and *The New Nation** (New York: Random House, 1965) have had great influence in shaping interpretations of the Confederation period. The standard account of the Constitutional Convention is Max Farrand, *The Framing of the Constitution** (New Haven: Yale University Press, 1913); A. T. Prescott, *Drafting the Federal Constitution*

(Baton Rouge: Louisiana State University Press, 1941) reorganizes Madison's notes for convenient study and discussion. Clinton Rossiter, *1787: The Grand Convention** (New York: Mentor, 1968) is thorough, while Merrill Jensen, *The Making of the American Constitution** (New York: Anchor, 1969) is an excellent brief treatment. Robert L. Schuyler, *The Constitution of the United States* (New York: Peter Smith, 1952) is also useful.

An important study that has influenced historical thinking for a half century is Charles A. Beard, *An Economic Interpretation of the Constitution,** rev. ed. (New York: Macmillan, 1935). The Beardian economic thesis, however, has been challenged by Robert E. Brown, *Charles Beard and the Constitution** (New York: W. W. Norton, 1965) and Forrest McDonald, *We the People: The Economic Origins of the Constitution** (Chicago: University of Chicago Press, 1958). Jackson Turner Main, *The Antifederalists* (Chapel Hill: University of North Carolina Press, 1961) and Celia Kenyon, ed., *The Anti-Federalists** (Indianapolis: Bobbs-Merrill, 1966) are studies of the opponents of the Constitution. Louis M. Sears, *George Washington and the French Revolution* (Detroit: Wayne State University Press, 1960) and Paul A. Varg, *Foreign Policies of the Founding Fathers** (Baltimore: Penguin Books, Inc., 1970) are valuable.

John C. Miller, *The Federalist Era** (New York: Harper & Row, 1963) is an excellent general survey of the period. Leonard White, *The Federalists: A Study in Administrative History** (New York: Macmillan, 1965) and *The Jeffersonians** (New York: Macmillan, 1965) analyze the respective administrations as political operating units. Shaw Livermore, Jr., *The Twilight of Federalism* (Princeton: Princeton University Press, 1962) covers that party's rise and fall. Stephen Kurtz, *The Presidency of John Adams** (New Jersey: A. S. Barnes, 1961) and Alexander De Conde, *The Quasi-War** (New York: Charles Scribner's Sons, 1966) deal with the Adams administrations. Charles M. Wiltse, *The Jeffersonian Tradition in American Democracy** (New York: Hill and Wang, 1960) is a thoughtful consideration of Jeffersonian ideas, while Merrill D. Peterson, *The Jeffersonian Image in the American Mind** (New York: Oxford University Press, 1963) is a provocative study of Jefferson's impact on the American self-concept. Adrienne Koch, *Jefferson and Madison: The Great Collaboration** (New York: Ox-

ford University Press, 1964) traces the development of political theory and practice through both men's administrations. Marshall Smelser, *The Democratic Republic: 1801–1815** (New York: Harper & Row, 1968) and Noble E. Cunningham, Jr., *The Jeffersonian Republicans in Power** (Chapel Hill: University of North Carolina Press, 1958) concern the Republican administrations. Two special studies throw light on the Alien and Sedition Acts: James M. Smith, *Freedom's Fetters** (Ithaca: Cornell University Press, 1956) and John C. Miller, *Crisis in Freedom** (Boston: Little, Brown, 1964).

George Dangerfield, *The Era of Good Feelings** (New York: Harcourt Brace Jovanovich, 1952) is the best general history of the pre-Jacksonian decades, while Herbert J. Clancy, *The Democratic Party: Jefferson to Jackson* (New York: Fordham University Press, 1962) is concisely considered political history. Also important for an understanding of the period is Dangerfield's *Awakening of American Nationalism 1815–1828** (Evanston: Harper & Row, 1965). Bradford Perkins, *Prologue to War: England and the United States 1805–1812** (Berkeley: University of California Press, 1961), Francis S. Beirne, *The War of 1812* (Hamden, Conn.: Shoe String Press, Inc., 1949), and Harry L. Coles, *The War of 1812** (Chicago: University of Chicago Press, 1965) all treat the War of 1812.

The materials of the period are rich in biography. Dumas Malone's life of Jefferson has reached four volumes, *Jefferson and His Time** (Boston: Little, Brown, 1948–70). The definitive biography of Washington is Douglas Southall Freeman's *George Washington* (New York: Charles Scribner's Sons, 1948–57), while John C. Miller, *Alexander Hamilton** (Evanston: Harper & Row, 1959) is the best single volume on his Secretary of Treasury. Irving Brant's six-volume *James Madison* (Indianapolis: Bobbs-Merrill, 1948–61) and William P. Cresson, *James Monroe* (Chapel Hill: University of North Carolina Press, 1946) cover the lives of Jefferson's successors; Gilbert Chinard, *Honest John Adams** (Gloucester, Mass: Peter Smith, 1933) remains the best biography. Samuel F. Bemis, *John Quincy Adams and the Foundations of Foreign Policy* (New York: Alfred A. Knopf, 1949) is the classic treatment of foreign relations during Adams' times, and Bemis' *John Quincy Adams and the Union* (New York: Alfred A. Knopf, 1956) is an excellent one-volume biography. Dexter

Perkins, *A History of the Monroe Doctrine* (Boston: Little, Brown, 1955) is a definitive study. There is no modern biography of John Marshall, though Albert Beveridge's *Life of John Marshall*, 4 vols. (Boston: Houghton Mifflin, 1916–19) remains a sound source of information.

An excellent general history of the women's rights movement is Eleanor Flexner, *Century of Struggle* (Cambridge, Mass.: Harvard University Press, 1959); see also Robert E. Riegel, *American Woman: A Story of Social Change* (Rutherford, N.J.: Farleigh Dickinson Press, 1970) and the documents edited by William L. O'Neill, *The Woman Movement* (Chicago: Quadrangle Press, 1971). General studies of American Indians are Ruth Underhill, *Red Man's America* (Chicago: University of Chicago Press, 1953) and Clark Wissler, *Indians of the United States* (New York: Doubleday, 1966). Edward Spicer, *A Short History of the Indians of the United States* (New York: Van Nostrand, 1969) and William T. Hagan, *American Indians* (Chicago: University of Chicago Press, 1961) take somewhat different views of the Indian in American history. Reginald Horsman, *The Frontier in the Formative Years, 1783–1815* (New York: Holt, Rinehart, and Winston, 1970) deals with the postrevolutionary Indian wars. Two useful collections of documents are Jack D. Forbes, *The Indian in America's Past* (Englewood Cliffs, N.J.: Prentice-Hall, 1964) and Wilcomb E. Washburn, *The Indian and the White Man* (Garden City, N.Y.: Doubleday, 1964). American attitudes toward Indians are treated historically by Roy H. Pearce, *The Savages of America* (Baltimore: The Johns Hopkins University Press, 1965). For summaries of racial theory in America, see Oscar Handlin, *Race and Nationality in American Life* (New York: Doubleday, 1957), Thomas F. Gossett, *Race: The History of an Idea in America* (New York: Schocken Books, 1965), and the documents edited by Louis Ruchames, *Racial Thought in America* (Amherst, Mass.: University of Massachusetts Press, 1969).

*Denotes a paperback.

3

democracy
and
Manifest destiny

THE EIGHTEENTH-CENTURY BRITISH STATESMAN EDMUND BURKE ONCE PARtially defined a political party as "a body of men . . . united upon some particular principle in which they all agreed." But whatever validity that definition may have had in eighteenth-century England, it must be used cautiously in reference to the two-party system of a country as economically and regionally diversified as the United States. While rival parties can sometimes be defined in terms of their *tendencies* toward one view or another on major issues, each party draws on a wide spectrum of interests, some of them seriously conflicting with what is considered the dominant philosophy of the party.

This fact has been illustrated throughout our political history. In the 1960s and 1970s, for example, Hubert H. Humphrey of Minnesota and George C. Wallace of Alabama often represented diametrically opposite policies and principles. The same also may be said of South Dakota Senator George S. McGovern and Washington Senator Henry M. Jackson. Yet all these men were repeatedly elected to high office as Democrats.

In the Republican party of the 1950s, President Dwight D. Eisenhower looked with disfavor upon Wisconsin Senator Joseph R. McCarthy, differing on some fundamentals as well as on many tactics. During long careers in the Senate, Barry Goldwater of Arizona and Jacob Javits of New York have been ranged against each other on principle after principle. Yet Eisenhower, Goldwater, Javits, and McCarthy are four names that certainly would be included on any roster of prominent Republicans in the 1950–70 span.

Some critics, currently and in the past, have cited such anomalies among the weaknesses of the American party structure. On the other hand, the fragmentation of parties abroad (fourteen parties in the Third French Republic, and twenty-six in the Second Spanish Republic, with no party in a majority and hence no party responsible) time after time has spelled frustration and failure. Thus, a political party in the United States might best be defined primarily in terms of purpose—its purpose being to win and exercise power by gaining control of the government.

The years 1824–48—often called the Jacksonian Era—were a time well made for unusual alliances of political forces. The commercial-industrial interests of the Northeast, predominately Whig, were allied with influential planters of the Deep South as well as with leaders in the West. Jackson, a Tennessee plantation owner and a Democrat, drew followers from every source—Western farmers, Northeastern laborers, New York and Pennsylvania businessmen, persons from all walks of life. However, more than changing political alignments contributed to the instability of the times. Americans were taken by the fever of progress—material and political—to a degree unknown before.

To find consistency in the political actions of Democrats and Whigs is difficult, chiefly because change was so typical and so constant. Daniel Webster, for example, began his career as a champion of New England shipping interests in favor of free trade. But after the War of 1812, with the growth of domestic manufactures, Webster caught the spirit of industrial progress, and by the late 1820s he had become an aggressive advocate of protective tariffs fostering young American industry. Because the new businessmen were pioneering unknown paths, Webster and like-minded Whigs of the 1830s and 1840s felt they needed all the government aid they could get, including not only a protected market but also a sound banking system which would provide a stable currency and ample, expandable credit.

Henry Clay, too, changed his convictions with the changing times. Reared as a youth in the Virginia environment of Jeffersonian agrarianism, he migrated to Kentucky and was awakened to new Western economic ambitions. Clay, a spokesman of Western Whigs, believed in a nationalistic program—his so-called "American System"—which, by means of internal improvements, a liberal policy of public-land sales, a central bank, and tariffs, would reduce America's dependence on foreign trade and provide a home market for the exchange of the North's manufactures and the West's agricultural products.

According to Whiggery, government aid to the business community would ultimately promote the economic progress and well-being of all Americans. However, it should be recalled that the Whig party also embraced prominent Southern planters, whose reliance on cotton exports and low-cost imports caused them to oppose the nationalistic views of their Northern confreres. The fact that the South, a slaveholding and staple-producing section, was "different" from the rest of the country prompted its leaders to take anguished turns in their search for adjustment. John C. Calhoun of South Carolina began as a "War Hawk" nationalist during the days of Jefferson and Madison but later became a defender of states' rights in defiance of federal "authoritarianism"; he shifted from the Democrats to the Whigs and back to the Democrats.

Andrew Jackson, a popular military hero, was looked upon as a champion of the plain people and an enemy of "privilege" that accorded advantages to one class or section over others. Often arbitrary in method, Jackson was nevertheless basically pragmatic in most of his principles. He favored what he called a "judicious" tariff; he approved or opposed internal improvements on the merits of each individual case; and, finally, he and his Democratic followers seemed more aware than were the Whigs of the potential dangers of "monopolies" like the Bank of the United States. Whether successful or not, Jackson tried to apply salutary restraints on aggressive businessmen, speculative Westerners, and states' rights extremists in an age when America was rushing headlong on an expansionist and industrialist course.

No period in American history has been subjected to more contradictory interpretations than 1824–48. This is especially true of the two Jackson administrations. Until the 1890s, most books on the subject berated Jackson himself and repudiated Jacksonian Democracy. Many of them reflected the thoughts and fears of conservative Americans in the Gilded Age and, accordingly, were especially hostile to the spoils system and "King Mob."

Then in 1893 came the historian Frederick Jackson Turner, praising the American frontier and hailing the "fierce Tennessee spirit who broke down the traditions of conservative rule . . . and, like a Gothic leader, opened the temple of the nation to the populace." Turner represented a new American scholarship, rooted in the graduate schools. He influenced other scholars, some of whom accepted Turnerian views while others—disagreeing in whole or in part—were inspired to probe for fugitive facts adding up to fresh conclusions.

Was the pre-presidential Jackson aristocratic rather than democratic? Is Jackson's Eastern-urban-labor support to be underscored? Was Jackson's Indian policy indefensible? Was the Bank struggle mainly a controversy between rival groups of New York and Philadelphia financiers and their political associates? Is Jackson to be blamed for bringing on the Panic of 1837 and the ensuing depression? All these queries have been answered affirmatively, and also negatively or with qualified affirmations, by students of the era. The most recent scholarship strongly inclines toward denial. But there is no present consensus and there probably will be none in the near future.

A second major historiographical category has to do with Texas, the Mexican War, and the extension of permanent American settlement to the Pacific Ocean. The U.S.-Mexican resort to arms was central in this respect, and no study of the subject has been more influential than Justin H. Smith's *The War with Mexico* (1919), which won both the Pulitzer and Loubat prizes. In 1971, when there were at least 766 books and articles on the Mexican War, specialists still described Smith's work as "a monument of historical scholarship." Nevertheless, because of Vietnam and New Left re-revisionism, it is likely that Smith's pro-Polk and pro-American points of view will be challenged more in the future than they have been in the past.

FOR THOUGHT AND DISCUSSION

1. In his day Andrew Jackson was considered by many Americans to be a President of the "people." What is a President of the people? To which Presidents would you apply the label? Why?

2. Which political leaders—then and now—would you most closely identify with the "Establishment"? *What* "Establishment"?

3. Who benefited from a higher tariff in 1824–48? Who suffered as a result of it? Who benefits and who suffers from protectionism today?

4. To what extent were the acquisition of Texas and the war with Mexico militarist? imperialist? racist? (Are you applying current standards or the standards of the mid-nineteenth century?)

5. One reason given for expanding the boundaries of the United States in the 1840s was that European powers were threatening to take over Western territories. Much of current American policy is also explained in terms of protection and defense. Should such explanations be automatically accepted? automatically rejected?

6. The year before Melville's *Moby Dick* received a cool reception from readers, *Fern Leaves from Fanny Fern's Portfolio* sold 100,000 copies. Is the gap between great writers and best sellers inevitable?

establish JusTice

CHAPTER 7

GROWTH OF DEMOCRATIC GOVERNMENT 1824–48

END OF THE OLD REPUBLICAN PARTY

The Election of 1824. The sands of political allegiance never shifted more swiftly than in the last year and a half of James Monroe's administration. Although the Federalist party continued to exist for a while in enclaves like Delaware, nearly all men called themselves Republicans, including the four leading candidates for the presidency in 1824. Two, Secretary of State John Quincy Adams and Secretary of the Treasury William H. Crawford, were members of the Monroe cabinet. They were pitted not only against each other but also against House Speaker Henry Clay and the famous hero of New Orleans, "Old Hickory," General Andrew Jackson.

For sixteen years the congressional caucus of the Republican majority had chosen the party's presidential candidates. During Monroe's second administration, however, the caucus system had met with increased opposition. The public looked on the caucus as an undemocratic procedure, dominated by aristocrats and not without its dictatorial aspects. There was growing conviction, also, that it was not in the nation's best interests for the newly elected President to feel that he owed his office to Congress. Politicians, aware of public opposition to the caucus, moved toward dissociating themselves from it; when the Republican caucus was held in February 1824, only 66 of 216 Republican congressmen attended.

The caucus selected Crawford of Georgia for the presidency, but its decision was scorned by Crawford's rivals and their many followers. The partisanship of the days of Jefferson was fast giving way to factional feuds. In a number of states, either the legislature or state conventions nominated their own "favorite sons"; there was a popular vote in only three quarters of the states. New England supported Adams of Massachusetts. Most of Crawford's strength was in the Southeast. Kentucky, Missouri, and Ohio looked to Clay of Kentucky, while Pennsylvania, most of the West, and some of the Southeast rallied behind Jackson of Tennessee. Secretary of War John C. Calhoun of South Carolina had early dropped out of the race, seeking the vice-presidency instead.

The real contest in the presidential election of 1824 was between Jackson and Adams: Jackson received approximately 153,000 popular votes to Adams' 108,000 and 99 electoral votes to Adams' 84. But Crawford and Clay, with 41 and 37 electoral votes respectively, split the total sufficiently so that neither Jackson nor Adams could claim a majority. Constitutional procedure now called for the decision to be referred to the House of Representatives. Here each state had one vote, and the three candidates with the most electoral votes—Jackson, Adams, and Crawford—remained in the running.

House Speaker Clay, no longer a presidential candidate, held the balance of power in the House decision. Although he earlier had instigated an anti-Adams campaign in the West, Clay personally disliked Jackson more than Adams and feared him as a future Western rival. Clay therefore decided to support Adams, and as a result the Secretary of State's victory was virtually assured. Adams was elected on the first ballot on February 9, 1825.

The new President promptly appointed Clay his Secretary of State, and just as promptly Jacksonians angrily charged that a "corrupt bargain" accounted for both Adams' election and Clay's appointment. John Randolph of Roanoke called it "the combination, unheard of till then, of the Puritan [Adams] with the blackleg [Clay]." There probably was an implicit—if not explicit—understanding between Adams and Clay, but no evidence exists to demonstrate corruption.

One of the often unseen pivots of history is discernible in the election of 1824. Adams was almost exclusively a New England candidate until the New York General Assembly gave him twenty-six of New York's thirty-six electors. This was the result of tricky maneuvering by Adams' Albany managers, who were able to divert from Clay several of the electoral votes he had counted upon. If Clay instead of Crawford had been the third candidate, it is possible that the popular Speaker of the House of Representatives would have appealed to his fellow representatives more than either Adams or Jackson.

THE J. Q. ADAMS INTERLUDE

Adams in the White House. President Adams projected a bold domestic program. In his first annual message he called for a national university (first proposed by Washington), a naval academy, a national astronomical observatory, a uniform national militia law, a uniform bankruptcy law, and an orderly, federally financed system of internal improvements. Most of these ideas were highly imaginative, and had his program gone into effect, the second Adams might today be considered one of the most constructive Presidents in our history.

Constructive accomplishments of many kinds, however, simply were not forthcoming. From the outset Adams made little effort to push his policies once he had enunciated them. A principal cause of this failure was Adams' view that the executive should abstain from what he considered undue interference in the legislative branch. As a consequence, numerous White House proposals, made year after year, were never introduced in Congress as legislative bills or resolutions. In addition, Adams had certain personal defects which prevented his being a natural leader. Aloof and unpleasant toward many associates, he disliked public contact and was incapable of appearing to good advantage when little knots of admirers gathered to greet him on his limited travels. Though a man with his diplomatic background should have overcome such traits, he was ungracious and petty in the most minor human relations.

Off to an inauspicious start during the first half of his term, Adams was hopelessly handicapped after 1826 by a congressional coalition which fought him at every turn. Jacksonians would not forget that a "deal" had made Adams President despite the electorate's clear preference for Jackson. Sectional hostilities were increasing, and states' rights adherents opposed Adams' bold plans to increase the federal government's authority. Political idealists might praise Adams for injecting so little partisanship into his conduct of the country's business, but his popularity and effectiveness suffered for this very reason. And his opponents played politics to the hilt, especially after they came to dominate Congress.

It was in the area of tariff debates and tariff votes that sectionalism and partisanship were most rampant. One reason for the passage of the Tariff of 1824, enacted while President Monroe was still in office, had been its inclusion of duties on raw wool and other farm products. These schedules were attractive to the West, but Eastern manufacturers of woolen textiles complained that their profits diminished because raw materials were so expensive. What would have been the Tariff of 1827 provided a "solution" of the wool and woolens controversy, supposedly acceptable to the Northeast and the Northwest; this tariff, however, was defeated in the Senate by Vice-President Calhoun's vote. The Tariff Bill of 1828, concocted in an effort to embarrass Adams and help elect Jackson as his successor, had numerous illogical features from an economic point of view, including higher duties on raw materials than on manufactures. Unexpectedly passed, then signed by Adams and suitably labeled the "Tariff of Abominations," it was offensive to a wide variety of individuals, sections, and interests—and particularly to the Southeast.

Internal Improvements and Foreign Policy. One of Adams' greatest disappointments was Congress' refusal to develop a systematic national public works program. Congressional appropriations followed no logical pattern, and local interests and legislative logrolling left undone some of the most necessary projects. Despite this slapdash approach, however, internal improvements were significant. Rivers were dredged and harbors made more serviceable; more federal appropriations were voted for these two purposes in Adams' four years than in the previous thirty. Lack of funds had forced a stop to work on the National Road in 1818; congressional appropriations permitted construction to resume in 1825, however, and by mid-century this important highway stretched from Cumberland, Maryland, to Vandalia, Illinois.

It might be supposed that a President with John Quincy Adams' background in diplomacy would leave a memorable record in foreign affairs, but he achieved nothing on a par with his success as Secretary of State in getting Russia to agree to Alaska's southern boundary. The United States failed to obtain from Great Britain the right of free navigation of the St. Lawrence River. American shippers had to resort to a roundabout trade when the ports of the British West Indies were closed to Yankee merchantmen as tightly as they had ever been. Old claims against France for damages arising out of the wars of the French Revolution were no nearer settlement in 1829 than in 1825. And though delegates were sent to the Congress of Panama in 1826, one

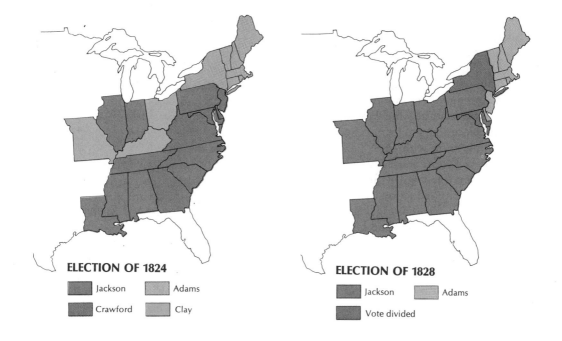

ELECTION OF 1824

- Jackson
- Adams
- Crawford
- Clay

ELECTION OF 1828

- Jackson
- Adams
- Vote divided

died en route to Panama, the other arrived too late, and the mission to the Latin American conference accomplished nothing.

In the entire field of foreign relations, Adams could point with pride only to an unprecedented number of minor treaties and to the renewal in 1827 of the Anglo-American agreement covering joint occupation of Oregon. Aside from these exceptions his administration was a negative interlude in American history.

JACKSONIAN DEMOCRACY TRIUMPHANT

The Election of 1828. Even if Adams' personality had been more attractive, his attitude more gracious, and his leadership stronger, he would have had difficulty in any political contest with the forces arrayed against him. As early as 1825 the general assembly of Tennessee placed Andrew Jackson on the track for the 1828 presidential race. Military glory was Jackson's most obvious asset, but the Tennesseean also was identified in Western minds with frontiersmen's desires for increased recognition by the United States government.

Moreover, Jackson had impressive allies. Vice-President Calhoun, an outstanding South Carolinian who had been Monroe's Secretary of War, did little to conceal his antipathy towards Adams. An important addition to the Jackson high command was Senator Martin Van Buren of New York. Formerly a Crawford lieutenant, the ingratiating Van Buren worked dexterously with Calhoun and others to effect a powerful combination of Southern and Northern Democratic-Republicans opposing Adams and favoring Jackson.

In the 1828 election, backers of both Adams and Jackson indulged in discreditable tactics. Pro-Adams journalists made much of Jackson's reputation for military high-handedness. They dragged the name of Mrs. Jackson through gutters of partisan filth by reminding voters that her divorce from another man had not been final back in the 1790s when she became Jackson's wife. This was a legal technicality which had no proper place in politics; emphasis on it infuriated Jackson and may have had something to do with Mrs. Jackson's death soon after the election.

Pro-Jackson editors, however, were no innocent bystanders when the mud was slung. They retaliated with the accusation that Adams, when minister to Russia, had encouraged the seduction by Czar Alexander I of an American servant girl who worked in Adams' St. Petersburg legation. And, of course, they continued to harp on the "corrupt bargain" that had landed Adams in office four years earlier.

More important issues were not entirely ignored. Since the country had not reached the period of national conventions and platforms, there was no formal enunciation of principles: but Jackson's name was bracketed in some minds with proposals for tariff reform, and that of Adams—fairly or unfairly—with the Tariff of Abominations. Critics of the second Bank of the United States hoped that Jackson, as President, would oppose it. Some advocates of the construction of roads and canals and the dredging of rivers and harbors seemed to prefer Adams because he had spoken out in favor of federal appropriations for these purposes. Yet there was no unanimity here; other such advocates, chiefly Southerners, believed Jackson would support internal improvements more heartily than did Adams. Old Republicans, of the variety Randolph had led in the Senate, saw danger in Adams' ideas about a national university, observatory, naval academy, and the like. Were these not projections of a trend toward a consolidated national state? If so, they feared, the South might eventually be downtrodden by an aggressive North.

If such opinions were held by some serious citizens, "Hurrah for Jackson!" was the rallying cry that appealed to most Americans. About three times as many people participated directly at the polls in 1828 as four years before, and the results were recorded with somewhat more care. Jackson, the Democratic-Republican candidate, scored a smashing triumph with approximately 647,000 popular votes to 508,000 for Adams. In the electoral college the margin was two to one, with 178 votes for Jackson and 83 for the National Republican.

"King Mob." Jackson's inauguration in March 1829 was accompanied by a demonstration unparalleled in American history. The thousands of people assembled in Washington behaved well enough outside the Capitol while Jackson read his inaugural address. But when the time came for the White House reception, "King Mob" took over. Men, women, and children crashed, trampled, and crushed their way in muddy boots and shoes into and through the mansion. Only when someone thought of placing refreshments on the White House lawn did the crowd move outdoors.

Ex-Federalists and National Republicans were shocked by this public demonstration; they talked darkly of a reenactment of French Revolution excesses on American soil. Actually, the scene had been more a matter of bad manners and an explosion of pent-up energy than anything else. The base of governmental support had broadened appreciably in the past few years, but no excesses other than social ones upset the evolutionary development of an increasingly democratic state. Nevertheless, when the multitude faded away shortly after inauguration day, the symbol of "King Mob" remained as a counterweight to "King Caucus" of old.

Reorganization of the Cabinet. The Democratic-Republican party of 62-year-old President Jackson charted its administrative course in an atmosphere of confusion. Though Van Buren became Secretary of State, several cabinet members were more closely identified with Vice-President Calhoun than with either Jackson or Van Buren.

Almost at once there erupted one of those odd controversies which occasionally have influenced American political history. Secretary of War John H. Eaton, a Jackson appointee who had long been on intimate terms with the new President, had recently married a young widow whose comeliness was said to have attracted him before her first husband's death. The story goes that Mrs. Calhoun and the wives of Calhoun's cabinet friends took the lead in snubbing Mrs. Eaton. Jackson resented the social chill, associating it with the shameful treatment of his own late wife during the campaign.

Van Buren, who endeared himself to Jackson by siding with the Eatons, offered to resign from his cabinet post, knowing that a cabinet reorganization would enable Jackson to be rid of the problem. Eaton followed Van Buren's example, and in the spring of 1831 Jackson requested resignations from all the remaining cabinet members except one. Calhoun's supporters were excluded from the succeeding cabinet, while Van Buren retained the confidence of Jackson, who promptly named him minister to Britain.

Changing Problems, Changing Arguments. Meanwhile, a more fundamental division between Jackson and Vice-President Calhoun developed over two other issues. First, the President was greatly disturbed by the discovery that, years before, Calhoun had favored his being court-martialed for his conduct during the Seminole War of 1818. Second and more significant, Jackson hotly disapproved of Calhoun's contention that a state had the right to nullify a federal statute. It was concerning this "nullification" question that the smoldering antipathies of the two ranking officials of the country flared into the open.

The nullification stand of the Vice-President and his fellow South Carolinian, Senator Robert Y. Hayne, resulted from their state's opposition to the tariff tendencies of the United States—especially to the Tariff of Abominations. They believed that while the industrial Northeast benefited, the agricultural South was damaged by the rising customs duties.

Economic conditions in the Southeast were steadily worsening. The extension of cotton planting to the rich bottom lands of Alabama, Mississippi, and Louisiana had expanded production of the staple, and cotton prices consequently dropped. Many planters in the Southeast, threatened with ruin by their inability to compete on relatively poor soil, pulled up stakes and took their slaves to the Southwest for a fresh start. The consequent loss of population compounded the Southeast's financial difficulties. There were also political reverberations, since fewer people would mean smaller representation in Congress for South Carolina and similarly affected states.

Calhoun had lately joined Hayne and other South Carolina politicians in the conviction that most of their state's troubles could be traced to the tariff. In 1828, while running for reelection to the vice-presidency as a Jackson adherent, Calhoun secretly wrote the "South Carolina Exposition." This document, published without his name, declared protective tariffs unconstitutional. It went on to assert the right of any state to "nullify" or prevent the enforcement within its boundaries of an unconstitutional act of Congress. Calhoun's authorship of the "Exposition" was not generally known in 1830, but his new position was becoming clear in some minds, including Jackson's. And the Vice-President carefully coached the less brilliant Hayne when the latter eloquently defended the extreme states' rights position in a dramatic Senate debate with Senator Daniel Webster of Massachusetts. As Massachusetts had become more industrialized and accordingly adopted a high-tariff policy, Webster had abandoned his low-tariff convictions (he opposed the Tariff of 1824), and in 1830 he was a high-tariff advocate. Moreover, Webster identified Massachusetts' changed economic attitude with a political nationalism that contrasted with the growing sectionalism of South Carolina; in so doing, he sought to equate economic interest with patriotic virtue.

The famous Senate debate of 1830 arose as the result of a resolution by Connecticut Senator Samuel A. Foot, which had as one aim a restriction of the sale of public land. The land question was a vital matter to congressmen from the West. Current land laws, in effect since the early 1820s, provided for (1) a minimum purchase of eighty acres, (2) a minimum price of $1.25 an acre, (3) no credit system, and (4) exceptions which recognized but did not wholly satisfy Western insistence on lower land prices and the preemption principle that favored squatters rather than specu- lators. Already in the air were proposals for liberalizing land policies. Eastern laborers joined Western farmers in favoring such liberalization, and Southerners saw an advantage in linking Western land desires to Southern low-tariff hopes; thus the opposition to Foot's restrictive resolution was not limited to any single section.

Senator Thomas H. Benton of Missouri resoundingly assailed the Foot Resolu- tion. Benton saw it as a scheme of New England manufacturers, fearful of losing factory operatives to the lure of the West, to make cheap land inaccessible and so keep their workers in the East. Hayne went to Benton's support but took a different tack. If Foot's proposition were put into effect, he said, future prices of Western land would be high. The income would then constitute "a fund for corruption," adding to the power of the federal government and endangering the independence of the states. There- upon Webster launched his first reply to Hayne. Denying that the East was illiberal toward the West, the erstwhile sectionalist from Boston proclaimed his nationalism.

Hayne again spoke, reminding his hearers of New England's anti-Union attitude during the War of 1812. Where, he asked, were New England nationalists then? Had not residents of Webster's section, plotters of the Hartford Convention, favored the same constitutional arguments contained in the "South Carolina Exposition"? The Northeastern sectionalists of old, Hayne insisted, currently avowed theories which they formerly had decried. Their sincerity, he implied, was open to grave doubts. And their past words and tactics hovered as reminders of appalling inconsistencies.

After Hayne spiritedly elaborated on the extreme states' rights point of view, Webster answered him in what is widely regarded as the greatest speech ever delivered in Congress. In New England, he said, what Hayne had discussed was consigned to a bygone time. New Englanders were thinking not of the past but of the present and the future. Vital now was the well-being of America as a whole. Nothing could be more preposterous than the idea that twenty-four states could interpret the Constitution as each of them saw fit. The Union should not be "dissevered, discordant, belligerent." The country should not be "rent with civil feuds, or drenched . . . in fraternal blood." It was delusion and folly to think of "Liberty first, and Union afterwards." Instead, "dear to every true American heart" was that blazing sentiment—"Liberty and Union, now and forever, one and inseparable!"

Although generations of young Americans memorized the peroration of Webster's "Second Reply to Hayne," there was at least as much logic—of the sort premised on the recorded performances of the various sections—on Hayne's side. Hayne was both consistent and persistent over a period of six years, but Calhoun (who soon overshadowed Hayne as the personification of antinationalist sentiment) was as inconsistent as Webster and as illogical on the basis of his long-established position. Both in the "Exposition" and in subsequent documents, Calhoun contributed to his state's cause the thoughts and theories of a resourceful mind. Still, modern scholarship cannot ignore the circumstances under which Calhoun and Webster made their shifts. Under the pressure of politico-economic necessity, each now occupied the other's previous position.

Calhoun and Jackson succeeded Hayne and Webster in the public spotlight during the spring of the same year, 1830, when a Jefferson birthday banquet was held in Washington's Indian Queen Hotel. Jackson offered fellow Democratic-Republicans a toast: "The Federal Union, it must be preserved!" Calhoun countered with a toast of his own: "The Union, next to our liberty, most dear!" The disparate sentiments were not lost upon the diners. The President had hurled down the gauntlet. The Vice-President had picked it up. After that, their relations became ever more strained, and before Jackson's first term ended, Calhoun had resigned the vice-presidency.

Two Controversial Vetoes. Jackson sternly opposed the Bank of the United States and objected to most proposals to use federal funds for internal improvements. The improvements question bulked large in 1830, when Congress passed a bill authorizing subscription of stock in a private company constructing a road between Maysville and Lexington, Kentucky. Jackson vetoed the proposition on the ground that the Maysville Road lay wholly in one state and therefore was not entitled to financial support from Washington.

Jackson's action was highly controversial. Henry Clay and many other transportation-minded Americans charged the President with being an impediment in the march of progress. But the veto was well received by Southern strict constructionists and by others resentful of what they deemed undue interference by the federal government in purely state affairs. Moreover, Jackson's selection of a Western road as a target of his disapproval pleased internal-improvements men in New York and

Pennsylvania, who had locally financed their own projects and saw no reason why people in other regions should get the kind of Washington help they themselves had failed to obtain.

Jackson was hostile to the Bank of the United States for at least four reasons. First, he held the Jeffersonian strict-construction view, maintaining that Congress was not empowered by the Constitution to incorporate a bank outside the District of Columbia. Jackson also doubted the expediency of the Bank, accusing it of not having established a sound and uniform currency. His third objection was that the Bank played politics in election campaigns and influenced congressmen by lending them money or placing them on its payroll. Finally, Old Hickory had an ingrained suspicion of the note issues of all banks—with the Bank of the United States the most notorious offender because it was far and away the most powerful.

Actually, under Nicholas Biddle's leadership the Bank of the United States had made important contributions to American economic stability. Regardless of what Jackson said, it did provide a sound currency, and its monetary standards and the financial power it wielded often exerted a salutary effect on the fluctuating currencies of state banks—many of which were dangerously weak. The charge of political activity and legislative influence was, for the most part, warranted. Jackson came to consider the Bank a monopoly, but though government deposits were exclusively entrusted to it, the Bank was not a monopolistic enterprise in the customary sense of the term.

The Bank's charter had four years to run in 1832, but Clay, now a United States senator, was in full accord with Bank President Biddle's desire to see the institution rechartered long in advance of the legal deadline. Clay pushed a Bank Bill through both houses of Congress; then, chosen by the National Republicans as their standard bearer in opposition to Jackson's reelection, he strove to make the Bank the main issue in the campaign. Jackson lost no time in vetoing the rechartering act in July 1832. Thus he and Clay set the stage for a showdown on the issue.

The Election of 1832. It can be argued that Clay was handicapped in his presidential race by the existence of an Anti-Masonic third party which considered the Masonic fraternity an aristocratic threat to democratic institutions and objected to both Jackson and Clay because they were Masons.

The Anti-Masons nominated William Wirt of Maryland, himself ironically a Mason and for twelve years Attorney General under Monroe and Adams. The National Republicans' choice was Clay, while the Democratic-Republicans (now beginning to be called Democrats) of course were for Jackson, with Van Buren as his running mate. In most states the anti-Jackson following was concentrated behind either Clay or Wirt, with the other man staying out of the contest. But even with this tactical advantage, neither Clay nor Wirt had a very good chance to oust the well-liked Jackson. Furthermore, the Bank issue did not aid Clay any more than criticism of Masonry helped Wirt.

Not all historians agree on the exact size of the popular vote. It is clear, however, that Jackson won easily; his popular vote was approximately 687,500 against 530,000 for Clay and Wirt combined. Jackson was victorious in nearly the entire South and West, plus the "big" states of New York and Pennsylvania. In the electoral college,

Jackson scored 219 to Clay's 49 and Wirt's 7. South Carolina, still voting through its legislature, refused to back any of the regular candidates and cast eleven protest ballots for John Floyd of Virginia.

"KING ANDREW"

Crisis Over Nullification. No sooner was the 1832 election decided than South Carolina brought the nullification controversy to a head. The issue immediately in question was the Tariff of 1832, which lowered customs duties but not enough to satisfy critics in Charleston and Columbia. The newly elected state legislature, composed predominantly of "nullifiers," ordered a special state convention to deal with the problem. The convention met in Columbia in November and took three major steps: it declared the tariffs of 1828 and 1832 null and void within South Carolina; it called on the state legislature to prohibit collection of duties in the state after February 1, 1833; and it warned that South Carolina would secede if the federal government used force to collect duties.

Jackson responded to South Carolina's saber-rattling by dispatching naval and military units to that state and by issuing a stirring Nullification Proclamation, which declared in part:

> I consider, then, the power to annul a law of the United States, assumed by one State, incompatible with the existence of the Union, contradicted expressly by the letter of the Constitution, unauthorized by its spirit, inconsistent with every principle on which it was founded, and destructive of the great object for which it was formed.

Possible bloodshed was averted when Senator Clay of Kentucky sponsored a compromise tariff bill providing for a gradual reduction of duties year by year until 1842. Though the protectionist New England and Middle Atlantic states bitterly opposed such a tariff reduction, Congress passed the compromise bill and Jackson signed it on March 2, 1833. On the same day, a Force Bill—giving Jackson congressional authority to use arms to enforce collection of customs—became law.

The Compromise Tariff of 1833 was much more reasonable by South Carolina's standards than preceding tariffs had been. The Columbia convention met once again and withdrew its nullification ordinance, but as a face-saving gesture the convention nullified the Jackson's Force Bill. The President regarded this last defiant act as of little practical significance. Both sides now considered the issue closed, and both claimed victory.

The United States Bank. Jackson, interpreting his success in the 1832 election as a mandate from the voters to continue action against the Bank of the United States, decided to remove federal deposits from the Bank gradually and deposit them in selected state banks. An order to this effect was issued on September 26, 1833, and when Secretary of the Treasury Duane refused to carry it out, Jackson replaced him with Roger B. Taney, until then the Attorney General. By the end of the year twenty-three state banks—dubbed "pet banks" by anti-Jacksonians—had been selected as depositories.

Jackson's move against the Bank met with considerable political opposition, and his policy was attacked in Congress. In December 1833 Henry Clay introduced Senate resolutions to censure both the Treasury action and the President for having "assumed upon himself authority and power not conferred by the constitution and laws, but in derogation of both."

When those resolutions were adopted, Jackson formally protested that the Senate had charged him with an impeachable offense but denied him an opportunity to defend himself. The Senate, however, rejected Jackson's protest and, as a further measure of defiance, would not approve Taney's nomination as Secretary of the Treasury. Only after a three-year Senate battle did Jackson's supporters succeed in having the resolution of censure expunged from the Senate record.

Hard Money and Land. Jackson's Bank policy contributed to a series of severe nationwide economic reverses. Even though the administration withdrew federal funds from the United States Bank only gradually, using them to meet current expenses while depositing new revenue in "pet banks," the Bank's decline was sharp enough to touch off an economic recession in 1833–34. Nicholas Biddle's actions aggravated the situation: to make up for the lost federal deposits and to force congressional reconsideration of the Bank's charter, Biddle took the unnecessarily harsh step of calling in outstanding loans, thus creating demands for credit from state banks which they could not meet. Only under strong pressure from businessmen and from the governor of Pennsylvania did Biddle at last reverse his policy.

The country pulled out of the economic doldrums and almost immediately headed into a dangerous inflationary spiral. State banks used their newly acquired federal funds for speculative purposes. Then, too, the federal government greatly increased its sale of public land, inadvertently encouraging the most reckless speculators.

Although political leaders were divided in their reaction to the inflationary trend, Jackson agreed with Senator Benton's prediction that "the present bloat in the paper system" could foreshadow another depression. On July 11, 1836, Jackson chose to issue a Specie Circular, which provided that after August 15 all public lands purchased from the federal government were to be paid for in gold or silver, with one exception: until December 15 actual settlers were permitted to use paper money (state bank notes) to purchase parcels of land up to 320 acres. Jackson's sudden policy reversal sharply curtailed western land sales and weakened public confidence in the state banks. It encouraged the hoarding of specie (hard money) and was a factor in bringing on the Panic of 1837.

The western land problem figures repeatedly in congressional debates from Jackson's day to Lincoln's and beyond. Benton and other Westerners favored the policy of "graduation," by which prices for the less desirable portions of the public domain would be reduced from $1.25 an acre to $1.00, 50 cents, or less, depending on the length of time they had been on sale. Westerners also wanted a policy of preemption, by which genuine settlers would have the first chance to buy land at the minimum price.

Although Congress passed no graduation bill until 1854, a temporary Preemption Act in 1830 authorized settlers to buy up to 160 acres of public land at a minimum price of $1.25 an acre. The act was renewed regularly and remained in force until 1842. Not to be confused with preemption was Henry Clay's advocacy of "distribution." In 1833, the Kentuckian drove through both the House and Senate a bill stipulating that most of the revenue derived from public-land sales be distributed among all the states, with a smaller fraction earmarked for states where the sales took place. That was a typical example of Clay's desire to appeal politically to two sections at once. Jackson, however, pocket-vetoed the bill, thwarting his adversary and identifying himself further with the actual settlers of the Northwest and Southwest.

Jackson's Foreign Policy. Jackson's handling of foreign affairs was at times as forthright and unconventional as one might expect of an old border captain. The only real diplomatic crisis of his two terms concerned spoliation claims against France for depredations on United States commerce during the Napoleonic wars. Adams and preceding Presidents had failed to collect, but at Jackson's urging France agreed to pay $5 million in a series of indemnity installments. The first $1 million was due in 1833; when the French made no payment then or the following year, Jackson urged Congress to authorize reprisals on French property unless the money were speedily sent. For a few months there appeared to be danger of war, but French officials finally saw that the President meant business. Payment of the debt began in 1836.

Jackson also faced the problem of whether to recognize the independence of Texas (see p. 174). Because it was a potential slave state, Jackson trod carefully in order not to inflame the American people over the slavery issue and possibly jeopardize Van Buren's presidential hopes in the election of 1836. Jackson was fearful also of angering Mexico, which insisted that the United States enforce its neutrality statutes. Though there was no question about Jackson's personal sentiment—his sympathy for the Texan revolutionists was strong—he withheld recognition from the Texas republic until the very day he left office in 1837.

The Supreme Court. Andrew Jackson's most enduring influence on the Supreme Court came indirectly through the justices whom he elevated to the bench. When he retired, five of the sitting judges were his appointees. The number included Roger B. Taney, who succeeded John Marshall as Chief Justice on the latter's death in 1835.

Among the principal early decisions under Taney was *Briscoe* v. *The Bank of Kentucky* (1837), which reduced the application of constitutional limitations on state banking and currency matters. More famous is *Charles River Bridge* v. *Warren Bridge* (1837), which stressed community responsibilities of private property and modified the contract doctrines of Marshall. In *Bank of Augusta* v. *Earle* (1839), the Chief Justice denied that corporations had all legal rights of natural persons. He also held that while corporations could take part in interstate commerce, any state had the right to exclude another state's corporations. In later cases there sometimes was a lack of agreement or consistency regarding the commerce power on the one hand and the states' internal police power on the other. This is traceable in part to the Court's changing personnel after Jackson's presidency, and in part to the alterations in Taney's own ideas.

For many years, it was the fashion to be hypercritical of Taney's Supreme Court record. Continuing on the tribunal until he died during the Civil War, he became very unpopular in the North because of his position in favor of states' rights and because of the Dred Scott decision in 1857 (see pp. 228–29). Actually, the judicial philosophies and influences of Marshall and Taney had many similarities. Taney and most of his associates believed that the growing power of corporations needed supervision by states in the public interest. But they were not unsympathetic toward property rights as such, and modern authorities on judicial history see no sharp break between most constitutional interpretations of the two able jurists.

Evaluation of Jackson's Administration.   Any President as active and dominant as Jackson is bound to arouse adverse criticism and to inspire praise bordering on idolatry. The Tennesseean's enemies did not hesitate to call him every unpleasant name in the book. They depicted him as "King Andrew," a would-be tyrant with slight regard for the ways of free men and with a ruthless determination to impose his will on the American people. On the other hand, Jackson's friends (and they were a majority) loved him personally and held his governmental talents in the highest esteem.

In the perspective of the years, Jackson's record shows marked differences from issue to issue. Although moderation is not traditionally considered a characteristic of Jackson, he was essentially a moderate on the tariff issue; his attitude toward land policy was generally temperate; and though he did not block all internal improvements financed with federal funds, he was apt to be conservative or reactionary (depending on one's point of view) on projects in that category.

Most scholars are agreed that Jackson's greatest mistake was his hostility to the Bank of the United States and that his Specie Circular represented a miscalculation in timing if not in principle. On the other hand, Jackson's foreign policy was successful, and his nationalism was tellingly asserted in opposition to the nullifiers.

A slaveholder with the manners and tastes of a Southern planter, Jackson was limited by his lack of formal education and was especially handicapped in economics. But he had an acute awareness of public preferences and the public interest. He also had an instinct for reaching the "plain" people and for identifying their desires with his own. A simple man with a fighting heart, Jackson was no democratic doctrinaire. He was wedded neither to indigenous abstractions nor to imported systems of dialectics. Jackson judged each issue on its merits—as he understood them—and contributed vigorous leadership to every cause he championed. Scholarly consensus is that as President he was great or near-great.

DEMOCRATS AND WHIGS

The Election of 1836.   As Jackson's second term neared its end, Vice-President Martin Van Buren was the Democratic presidential nominee. The opposition, now called the Whig party, tried to throw the contest into the House of Representatives by sponsoring several candidates on a regional basis. Van Buren faced Daniel Webster in the Northeast, Ohio's William Henry Harrison in the Northwest, and Tennessee's

Hugh L. White in the South. These three Whigs won 14, 73, and 26 electoral votes respectively; South Carolina gave its 11 votes to the anti-Jacksonian Willie P. Mangum of North Carolina. Their combined total of 124 was well under Van Buren's figure of 170. The Whig popular vote of 739,000 failed to match Van Buren's 765,000. So while the Whig's made gains, the 1836 regional scheme fell apart, and again the Democrats were victors.

The Panic of 1837. The "Little Magician" or "Red Fox of Kinderhook," as Van Buren was nicknamed, proved to be an unlucky President. A New York lawyer of ability and a politician who up to now had proved himself adroit in difficult situations, Van Buren found himself confronted by an economic disaster beyond his control. In May 1837, only two months after Van Buren's inauguration, a New York bank panic signaled the start of one of America's deep depressions. In part, the trouble stemmed from an English financial crisis during which many British creditors canceled their American investments. Yet Jackson and Van Buren drew much of the blame. Some of Jackson's "pet banks" were among those that went to the wall. And while the Specie Circular checked speculation in western lands, it curtailed the activities of financiers who had been supplying funds to speculators.

The depression affected the lives and fortunes of people in every part of the country. Widespread unemployment developed in seaboard cities of the Northeast, spreading into interior communities and fanning out to the south and west. Bread lines and soup kitchens relieved the hunger of poor families, including thousands of recent immigrants. Farmers received low prices for their crops. Factories closed. Laborers walked the streets. Canal and railroad projects ground to a halt. In 1839 the worst of the depression seemed to be over, but another decline occurred later that same year, and good times did not return to America as a whole until 1843.

In the meantime, Van Buren's fine display of statesmanship belied his reputation as a crafty politician. Beginning in 1837, he induced Congress to agree to a temporary issue of short-term Treasury notes; these amounted to $47 million in the next six years and enabled the government to meet its obligations. He also advocated an independent treasury, where federal funds could be safely retained without running pet-bank risks or resorting to another Bank of the United States. Most Whigs and some Democrats opposed the banking bill on the grounds that removal of federal funds from the state banks where they were depostied would restrict credit at a time when credit was sorely needed. The Independent Treasury Act finally was passed in 1840, but Van Buren's victory was short-lived: the next year, under the Tyler administration, the act was repealed, and for the next five years the Whig majority in Congress defeated Democratic efforts to reestablish this "subtreasury system."

The *Caroline* Affair. Another problem of the Van Buren regime concerned a spat along the Canadian border. In 1837 Canadian insurgents, dissatisfied with London's rule, fled to an island in the Niagara River, where American Anglophobes reinforced them with recruits and arms. The American steamer *Caroline* was employed in the supply service.

Canadian soldiers, crossing to the American side of the Niagara, set the *Caroline* afire and turned her adrift. Because of the high state of excitement, there was danger of mob invasions in either direction, and the slaying of an American citizen on the night the vessel burned seriously complicated the situation. Three years later a Canadian deputy sheriff named Alexander McLeod was arrested in Lockport, New York, and indicted for murder and arson in connection with the *Caroline* affair. There was loose talk of war, and on both sides of the border additional sums were appropriated for the strengthening of boundary defenses. Even after McLeod was acquitted by a New York court in 1841, the case seemed an unpromising preliminary to the Webster-Ashburton negotiations of the next year.

Tippecanoe and Tyler Too.   During Van Buren's presidency, Webster and Clay continued to be prominent in the senatorial spotlight. Webster's oratorical ability was as outstanding as ever, and Clay distinguished himself as a parliamentary leader. The Whigs have logically been equated with mercantile and banking classes, but it was their substantial rank-and-file support that enabled them to elect so many governors and congressmen.

Northern Whigs favored the creation of a new national bank and advocated a high tariff and federally financed internal improvements. If their anti-Jackson and anti-Van Buren confreres of the South did not agree about the tariff and the bank, the common bond linking all Whigs was the issue of "executive tyranny." Less domination by the President and more authority vested in Congress were aims which Southern and Northern Whigs shared. They also capitalized on economic distress and were as one in their criticism of Van Buren as the 1840 election approached.

The Whigs played their cards cannily in the 1840 test of skill. In the first place, their standard-bearer was neither Clay nor Webster—able men who had many friends, but also many enemies—but William Henry Harrison of Ohio. Harrison had run well in 1836 and had won a measure of military glory in the dim past at the Indian Battle of Tippecanoe. Second, the Whigs turned to their own advantage a journalist's taunt that

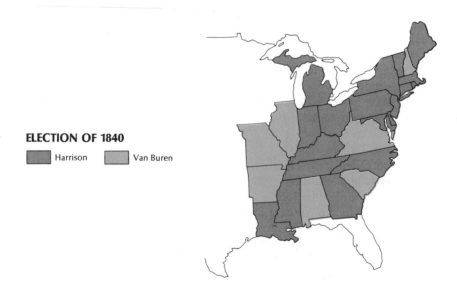

ELECTION OF 1840

■ Harrison   ■ Van Buren

Harrison was unfit for the presidency. "Give him a barrel of hard cider, and settle a pension of two thousand a year on him," the newsman sneered, "and [take] my word for it, he will sit the remainder of his days in his log cabin by the side of a 'sea coal' fire, and study moral philosophy."

Yes, the Whigs replied, their nominee was a man of the people who preferred a log cabin and hard cider to the frippery of red-whiskered Van Buren. In reality, Harrison dwelt in a mansion near Cincinnati, and he was an aristocratic Virginian by birth and rearing. But log cabins, barrels of cider, coonskin caps, and even live coons became Harrison symbols.

For the vice-presidency the Whigs had chosen John Tyler of Virginia, a former states' rights Democrat who now was a spokesman for the minority Southern element within the Whig party. The Whigs' most typical campaign verse still remains the best known of all jingles associated with elections:

> What has caused the great commotion,
>   motion, motion,
> Our country through?
> It is the ball a rolling on
> For Tippecanoe and Tyler too—
>   Tippecanoe and Tyler too,
> And with them we'll beat
>   little Van, Van, Van.
> Van is a used up man.

As expected, the Whigs were victorious in 1840. Harrison's electoral showing was impressive (234 to Van Buren's 60), and his popular vote was 1,274,000 to 1,127,000 for the Democrat. Although the Whig margin was not vast in a number of critical states, it was large enough: Van Buren carried only New Hampshire and Illinois north of the Mason-Dixon line.

President Without a Party.   The sweet taste of triumph soon turned bitter in Whig mouths. Inaugurated in March 1841, the 68-year-old Harrison died after a single month in office. Tyler, the first man to reach the presidency through the death of his predecessor, shared few of the ideas of the dominant Whig group in Congress. Twice he vetoed attempts to revive the Bank of the United States. Twice he vetoed Clay-sponsored tariffs. Thrice he defeated distribution to the states of proceeds from public-land sales. All members of Harrison's cabinet, which Tyler inherited, resigned after six months, with the exception of Secretary of State Webster.

Before Webster entered the State Department, the *Caroline* affair was not the only border incident fanning the flames of international misunderstanding. There was also the undeclared Aroostook War, caused by conflicting claims to the Aroostook River region on the undefined Maine-New Brunswick boundary. Ten thousand Maine troops were committed in 1839 to the defense of a large area subject to dispute. At length, an American general and New Brunswick's lieutenant-governor negotiated a truce.

As the crisis eased, the British government at long last saw the need for determining what portions of the disputed area should be acknowledged as belonging respectively to New Brunswick and to the U.S. Secretary Webster met in a series of conferences with England's envoy, Lord Ashburton. In their treaty of 1842, New Brunswick received 5000 square miles out of 12,000. The treaty was resented and Webster's popularity forever damaged in Maine, which felt itself short-changed. Nevertheless, the Webster-Ashburton Treaty did help to achieve order and peace.

John Tyler found himself in the unenviable position of a President without a party. He did agree with Northern Whigs that the Independent Treasury law should be repealed, and this was done in 1841. But his vetoes of Clay's tariff measures made him an apostate in their eyes. The Tariff of 1842, which Congress reluctantly passed and Tyler signed, was but mildly protective. Tyler also approved a General Preemption Act and cooperated more and more with Democrats, whose nomination he hoped to obtain in 1844. Northern Whigs and border-staters like Clay rued the day when "Tyler too" had been tapped to run with "Tippecanoe."

Return of the Democrats.   Fresh issues exerted a vital impact on the election of 1844. Some had to do with the West, others with chattel slavery. Texans had won independence from Mexico in 1836 (see p. 174); now there was considerable sentiment for the annexation of the Republic of Texas by the United States. Southerners particularly favored such a step, while expansion-minded Northerners hoped that Oregon would be wholly occupied by Americans instead of being divided between the United States and Britain.

Henry Clay's 1844 presidential nomination by the Whigs came as no surprise. But Van Buren was shunted aside by the Democrats because he was thought to be anti-Texas, and little attention was paid to Tyler as a candidate since he was not a reliable party man. Instead, delegates to the Democratic national convention nominated James K. Polk, the first "dark horse" presidential nominee.

A former governor of Tennessee and speaker of the House of Representatives, Polk seemed thoroughly at home on the Democratic platform, which euphoniously but none too accurately described the desired Western policy as "the reannexation of Texas" and "the reoccupation of Oregon." Whigs made light of Polk's qualifications. "Who *is* James K. Polk?" they asked. But Polk's campaign strategy proved more effective than that of Clay, who tried to straddle the Texas dilemma and was impaled on the horns of equivocation.

Into the close contest came James G. Birney, heading the antislavery Liberty party, who siphoned off Clay votes in New York and caused its electors to go to Polk. This made the difference. Polk received 170 electoral votes, Clay 105. The popular outcome much more narrowly favored the Tennesseean, whose 1,338,000 supporters outnumbered Clay's by only 38,000.

Features of American Democratic Growth.   The years 1824–48 were characterized by an increase in the number of elected officeholders, by a relative decrease in appointed officials at the state and local levels, and by some reflection of the popular will by the Supreme Court. There was far greater participation in government than had been the case in prior eras. By the time the period was well launched, all states except one chose presidential electors by popular vote. The popular vote itself steadily increased from campaign to campaign, not only because the population was greater but because such barriers as religious and property qualifications were gradually lowered on a state-by-state basis.

The development of democratic government was not without its growing pains. One of the most criticized aspects of the political scene was the "spoils system," by which governmental posts were allotted as "spoils" of victory to members of the party triumphant at the polls. Under Monroe and Adams a small coterie of federal clerks and minor administrators had held offices on what amounted to a lifetime good-conduct basis. Jackson removed a number of these perennials because they had played the partisan game against him, because they were corrupt and inefficient, or because he wanted to make room for partisans of his own. In 1832 Senator William L. Marcy, a Jackson adherent, had remarked, "To the victor belong the spoils of the enemy"; and Jackson's enemies applied the phrase "spoils system" to Jackson's program of rewarding his political supporters with public office.

During his entire presidency Jackson removed only a fifth of those holding office in 1829, but he did take a decisive step toward perpetuating an undesirable system. Although Jacksonians defended the policy as the quickest and surest path to reform, for every Adams man like embezzler Tobias Watkins, Jackson's party contributed a scamp of its own—such as collector Samuel Swartwout of the port of New York, who defaulted for more than a million dollars.

National political conventions, which came into being with an Anti-Masonic assembly held in 1831, were thoroughly established in the political structure by the end of Jackson's second term. Sometimes they have resulted in the choice of second-rate candidates for first-rate posts, but in the main the decisions of conventions have been sound, and they were and are more directly representative and democratic than "King Caucus" ever was. After momentarily striking a pose of aloofness from Jacksonian electioneering tactics, Whigs imitated their rivals by adopting slogans and symbols similar to Democratic ones. And for over a century styles of campaigning were patterned, to an appreciable degree, on the 1840 ballyhoo techniques promoting "Tippecanoe and Tyler Too!"

During Jackson's administration the personal advisers on whom the President relied came to be known as the "kitchen cabinet"—because they ostensibly conferred with Jackson more intimately than did members of his official cabinet. Later chief executives have followed Jackson's example by surrounding themselves with capable but unofficial counselors whose advice supplemented—or supplanted—that of department heads. It is doubtful that the "kitchen cabinet" would have originated as and when it did if Jackson had not owed his election in part to Calhounite Deep South support, which at least two cabinet members personified and on which he chose not to rely once his administration was under way.

It would be a mistake to minimize the role of the West in the period 1824–48. Public lands, the tariff, internal improvements, the United States Bank, and almost all other issues were of interest to Westerners. The West had its own viewpoint or viewpoints of a predominantly sectional variety, yet it also exerted a nationalizing influence. The Southwest had much in common with the Northwest, and Jackson the

Southwesterner proved himself a foremost nationalist who was supported as consistently in the Northwest as in any other portion of the country.

It is to the West that the camera of history turns during Tyler's final weeks and all of Polk's White House residence. During Polk's administration the territorial limits of the nation were vastly expanded by settlement of the Oregon controversy with Great Britain (1846), the annexation of Texas (1845), and the Mexican War (1846–48). These events will be discussed in Chapter 8 within the context of Western expansion.

WESTWARD EXPANSION AND ECONOMIC GROWTH 1824–48

THE BACKGROUND OF EXPANSION

Manifest Destiny. New York magazine editor John L. O'Sullivan proclaimed in 1845 that it was "the fulfilment of our manifest destiny to overspread the continent allotted by Providence for the free development of our yearly multiplying millions." O'Sullivan's exuberant words reflected the optimism of fervid nationalists that the American banner soon would wave over all of North America and beyond. For the exponents of Manifest Destiny, even the addition of Texas, New Mexico, California, and the Oregon country to the nation would not be enough; God had destined the people of the United States to extend its sovereignty over Canada, Alaska, Mexico, Cuba, other West Indian islands, and Hawaii.

The dream of Manifest Destiny was less fantastic than it may now appear: it was no less realistic to contemplate the annexation of Canada or Cuba than to dream of extending American sovereignty to Alaska or Hawaii. Furthermore, in the light of America's impressive achievements since 1776, nearly anything seemed possible in the next half century. In 1803 the Louisiana Purchase had doubled the area of the American republic. By 1830 commerce with Europe was flourishing, trade with Asia was burgeoning; adventurers were extracting fortunes from China; and wealthy speculators were willing to invest in almost any feasible enterprise.

Dreams of Manifest Destiny were both an augury of future hemispheric expansion and a concomitant of the westward expansion which was taking place between 1824 and 1848. It was during this period that the Indian barrier was surmounted and the immense areas of the new Southwest and the Far West were added to the United States. It was a period which saw a rapid influx of European immigrants into the United States. Between 1830 and 1850 more than two million Europeans—most of them impoverished farmers or manual workers—crossed the Atlantic. Many were of the new German and Irish wave of immigrants. Between 1830 and 1850 the population of the United States as a whole almost doubled, from about 12.9 million to over 23 million.

Although much of the emphasis on the theme of expansion was frankly materialistic, and some would be called racist today, idealistic motives were present, too. Protestant and Catholic missionaries, active in Oregon and elsewhere, hoped for numerous Indian converts. Many Americans took pride in the contrast between freedoms flourishing in their own country and oppressions evident in foreign lands. There was widespread concern that the intrigues of European imperialists would endanger the opportunities and liberties of ordinary Americans. Rumors spread that Britain and other powers were scheming to influence the internal and diplomatic policies of the Republic of Texas, to acquire Hawaii, and to control the Bays of San Francisco and San Diego as well as Puget Sound. (Some of the rumors had more substance than skeptics realized.) Would not encroachments of inimical courts and kings imperil the future of American democracy? Might they not also limit areas otherwise available for millions of oppressed Europeans, still hoping to come to American shores? Surely, it was God's and America's way to counter and remove the threat through a constructive program of rapid expansion. This was the sincere conviction of idealistic believers in Manifest Destiny.

The Indian Barrier. In 1830 the nation's undisputed land and water area covered more than 1,780,000 square miles. In addition, more than 12,000 square miles in the far Northeast and approximately half a million square miles in the far Northwest were claimed by both Washington and London. Substantial numbers of Americans were living in Texas, which then was still part of Mexico, on land which the Mexican government and granted to Moses Austin and his son, Stephen F. Austin.

In 1830, however, most pioneers were less concerned with Mexican Texas or with Anglo-American boundary differences than with the nearer Indian barrier. The pressure of frontiersmen and their families pushed tens of thousands of Indians west of the Mississippi River. In ninety treaties—some less honorable than others—signed during Jackson's presidency, the Indians reluctantly accepted new western lands in lieu of their old homes.

North of the Ohio River there was relatively little trouble for the white American—or suffering for the red—when what was left of the Shawnees, Wyandots, Delawares, and Miamis moved to western reservations. The most dramatic example of resistance by Northern Indians in the 1830s was an exception to the rule. This involved a resolute Sauk, Black Hawk by name, who believed that a treaty ceding the Rock River region of southern Wisconsin and northwestern Illinois to the hated whites had been signed under conditions of trickery. Black Hawk reluctantly moved his people to the west bank of the Mississippi, but in 1832 he led them back to southern Wisconsin in search of fertile farm land. The ensuing Black Hawk War, won by the whites that summer, marked the end of organized Indian resistance in the Old Northwest. Westward migration of Sauk, Fox, Winnebago, and other tribes increased. Within six years both Wisconsin and Iowa became territories; within sixteen years they became states, as settlers from the East populated the country of red men now dispossessed.

 In the judgment of many white men, Southern Indians generally were making more progress toward "civilization" than those being prodded westward north of the Ohio. Sequoya, inventor of the Cherokee syllabary, enabled thousands of Cherokee adults and children to read and write. And the Cherokees, Chickasaws, Choctaws, Creeks, and Seminoles are known in history as the Five Civilized Tribes. Some of them, notably the Seminoles and Creeks, did not always prove civilized if placidity is a criterion. But there is small wonder that enlightened and virile leaders could not invariably remain placid in light of the white men's tricks and treachery.

The Indian Springs Treaty of 1825, involving Creek land in southern Georgia, was so unfair to the Indians that the U.S. Senate rejected it. Often treaties were said to be the result of corrupt deals in which Indian "leaders" sold out to the whites in return for handsome rewards; but they did the job of securing land for the white man. The Treaty of Dancing Rabbit (1830) relinquished nearly eight million Choctaw acres in Alabama and Mississippi, and in the next decade other substantial cessions were made. Many Cherokees and other Indians were forced to move west. Not a few died along the way on what has been called the "Trail of Tears," suffering not only indignities but agonies on the long trek from their homes.

Not all Southern tribes submitted passively to the whites' intrusions. Osceola, a Florida Seminole subchief, so resented the Treaty of Payne's Landing, which authorized removal of the Seminoles to west of the Mississippi, that he is said to have plunged his knife into the document when he was expected to sign it with his "X."

Resistance on the part of Micanopy, Alligator, Osceola, and other Indians—supported by some runaway slaves—culminated in the Second Seminole War. In 1835 the Seminoles ambushed and massacred 107 of the 110 officers and men of Major Francis L. Dade. Taking full advantage of Florida's maze of inland rivers and swamps to hide their women and children, they harassed United States troops, then rushed back to cover. Osceola was seized and imprisoned when, under a flag of truce, he came for an interview with an American general. He died in a military prison, but the war—the bloodiest and most expensive of all our conflicts with Indians—continued until 1842. Although there are Seminoles in Florida in our own time, most of the original tribesmen were forced to surrender or were tricked into capture by the whites. Usually they settled in the Indian Territory of present-day Oklahoma.

The Pathfinders. By the 1830s, with the removal of the Indians, the trans-Appalachian West was a great complex of newly admitted states, and already people were moving beyond the Mississippi River. Missouri had been admitted as a state as early as 1821, and Arkansas followed in 1836. The wilderness beyond the Mississippi provided attractive commercial opportunities for aggressive American frontiersmen. The lucrative fur trade in the Northwest, for example, had early drawn rugged trappers and traders to that area.

The most successful of the early fur traders was German-born John Jacob Astor, who organized the American Fur Company in 1808 with the intention of establishing a monopoly of the fur trade throughout the West. Astor's acquisitive instincts, ruthlessness, enormous capital, and efficient administration helped him take over Great Lakes and Mississippi valley trading posts which originally belonged to other companies. In the 1820s he pushed west and northwest, absorbing the Columbia Fur Company in the Oregon country and ruthlessly crushing rival trappers and traders.

Astor's business methods met with severe criticism on the frontier. An army officer had this to say: "Take the American Fur Company in the aggregate, and they are the greatest scoundrels the world ever knew." But Astor, undaunted by criticism,

**WESTERN
EXPLORATIONS**

continued to prosper. In 1834 he withdrew from the fur business to concentrate on New York City real estate.

William Henry Ashley of St. Louis was another who made a fortune from furs in the Northwest. Ashley's Rocky Mountain Fur Company originated the revolutionary "rendezvous" method of fur trading, by which company agents, instead of trading with the Indians, bought furs directly from white trappers at an annual "rendezvous" in the mountains. From 1822 to 1826, Ashley and the rugged trappers on his payroll pushed north and west, penetrating the country of hostile tribes and trapping beaver there.

When Ashley retired he sold his Rocky Mountain Fur Company to Jedediah S. Smith, the "Knight in Buckskin" whose explorations greatly fostered American interest in the Far West. In the autumn of 1826 Smith led the first American overland

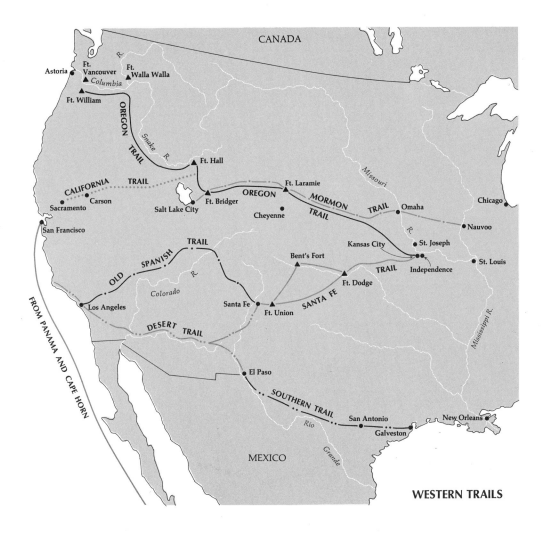

Map labels:

CANADA

Astoria • Ft. Vancouver ▲ Columbia — Ft. Walla Walla ▲

Ft. William ▲

OREGON TRAIL

Snake R.

Ft. Hall ▲

CALIFORNIA TRAIL

Carson •

Sacramento •

Salt Lake City • Ft. Bridger ▲ OREGON TRAIL

Cheyenne •

Ft. Laramie •

MORMON TRAIL

Omaha •

Missouri R.

Chicago •

Nauvoo •

San Francisco •

TRAIL

OLD SPANISH TRAIL

Colorado R.

Kansas City • St. Joseph •

Bent's Fort ▲

Ft. Dodge ▲

TRAIL

Independence •

St. Louis •

Los Angeles •

Santa Fe • Ft. Union ▲ SANTA FE

DESERT TRAIL

FROM PANAMA AND CAPE HORN

El Paso •

SOUTHERN TRAIL

San Antonio •

Galveston •

New Orleans •

Rio Grande

Mississippi R.

MEXICO

WESTERN TRAILS

expedition from Missouri to California. He carved an amazing career as "mountain man" and plainsman. Another fabulous character was Jim Bridger, who may have been the first white man to see Salt Lake. Still another was Thomas Fitzpatrick, the noted guide and genuine friend of grateful Indians.

Smith, Ashley, Bridger, Fitzpatrick, and the employees of the Astor interests all were experts with the knife, the rifle, and the trap; but, more important, they contributed significantly to frontier expansion and marked the path for others.

Perhaps the most famous explorer among his contemporaries—so famous that he was known as the "Pathfinder" and won the Republican nomination for President in 1856—was John C. Frémont. Son of a French émigré schoolteacher, Frémont early in life formed a strong taste for meeting and mastering wilderness challenges. It was in 1838–39, when employed on a survey of the broad plateau between the upper

Mississippi and upper Missouri Rivers, that this army officer got his real start as a geological observer, mapmaker, and scientific reporter. In the 1840s he led several expeditions to the West, exploring the Oregon Trail, the Sierra Nevada, California, the Colorado River, and the Rio Grande. His well-written reports, avidly read in the East, stimulated further emigration to the West.

The Santa Fe Trail. Santa Fe, in the Mexican territory of New Mexico, also provided attractive commercial opportunities for enterprising Americans. Though the volume of American trade in Santa Fe never was large, it was economically significant because American merchants were able to dispose of goods at handsome profits and because they brought away silver in an era when the specie was at a premium.

William Becknell of Arrow Rock, Missouri, initiated the Santa Fe trade in 1821, when he sold his goods for ten to twenty times what they would have brought on the banks of the Mississippi. Venturesome American merchants and farmers followed Becknell's example, carrying goods along the 800-mile Santa Fe Trail from Independence, Missouri, to the great bend of the Arkansas and into New Mexico. Though the trip was arduous, confronting caravans with the dangers of rattlesnakes, heat, and storm, only eleven whites are reported to have been slain by Indians on the trail before 1843—a figure which illustrates that the Santa Fe Trail was less dangerous than it sometimes has been depicted.

The Oregon Trail. Mention of the Oregon Trail also conjures up visions of caravans moving west, but in this case the wagon trains carried not merely merchants but farmers and other permanent settlers. Back in Jefferson's time, Lewis and Clark had traversed part of what was to become the celebrated route to the Pacific Northwest. Other hardy spirits followed, adding discoveries of their own.

The Oregon idea was not difficult to sell to land-hungry Americans. Oregon at that time was jointly occupied by the United States and Britain. The Hudson's Bay Company, an English concern, had long been established on the Columbia. Church interest heightened when such American Protestant missionaries as Jason Lee, Samuel Parker, and Dr. Marcus Whitman went out to Oregon. Thus national pride, missionary zeal, the lure of cheap lands, and the favorable reputation of the region all played a part in enticing thousands to Oregon.

As in the case of Santa Fe, Missouri communities like Independence and St. Joseph were takeoff spots for the Oregon-bound. For a couple of days, the two routes coincided. Then, as one went south, the other bent north. Out across various rivers including the Platte, and beyond to Fort Laramie, the covered wagons and pack trains of those seeking homes in the Northwest wound their way in the 1840s. On to Fort Bridger and along the Snake they proceeded to Whitman's mission. At last they saw the storied Columbia and reached Astoria, or wherever they were going. The Oregon Trail stretched two thousand miles—two and a half times the length of the Santa Fe journey.

Western Army Posts. The exploits of the mountain trappers, the Santa Fe traders, and the Oregon pioneers should not tempt us to overlook the tremendous contributions of the professional soldiers. From the 1820s well into the 1840s, the United States army never was large, but its role in aiding the settlement of the West can hardly be exaggerated. Speculators and homesteaders were more likely to bring their families to areas when the military was nearby. Army posts in time became villages, towns, and cities. It was not unusual for a retired officer to become a respected civilian in a new community. Soldiers brought steamboats to Western rivers, constructed sawmills, and built their own forts. They farmed adjacent fields, introduced cattle, and gave the lie to the widely credited legend that a "Great American Desert" existed between the Mississippi and the Rockies.

When it came to exploration, the army similarly played its part. Every adventure-minded American boy has heard of Kit Carson, who first came to fame as a trapper, an Indian fighter, and Frémont's guide. So colorful are the reputations of the Carsons and the Bridgers that well-organized infantry and cavalry expeditions into unknown or unfamiliar country seem relatively humdrum despite their importance. There were dozens of occasions when army officers advanced into river valleys or mountain fastnesses about which Washington had only vague notions.

WINNING OF THE WEST

A National Question. As long as the westward movement was confined to a few explorers and commercial adventurers, Washington could act indecisively and put off any attempt to reach terms with London and the Mexican empire in regard to territorial disputes in the West. But as American settlers poured into the Far West and the Southwest, setting up communities and then local governments, the United States government could no longer temporize. The dispute with Britain over the boundaries of the Oregon country had to be settled. And the aspirations of fellow Americans living in Texas had to be heeded. What had been social and economic developments in the West had by the 1840s risen to the level of national political questions.

The Oregon Dispute. The "Oregon country" was a great deal larger than the present state of Oregon. It was bounded roughly by the "Great Stony" Mountains on the east, the Pacific on the west, California on the south, and Alaska (then Russian) on the north. When informed men chatted about Oregon in the era after the War of 1812, they referred to a wondrously varied land with towering mountains and fertile valleys, swift-coursing rivers and magnificent forests. Details, however, eluded even the best-posted of commentators; lack of surveys made it impossible to define its area precisely.

Early in the nineteenth century both Russia and Spain laid claim to sections of Oregon. But Spain bowed out of the picture in 1819, and Russia in the next decade acknowledged 54° 40' as Alaska's southern line. Britain and the United States were left in contention over the Oregon country.

Both countries laid claim to the area between the Columbia River and the line of 49° latitude to the Pacific; it was this area—the northwestern two thirds of the present state of Washington—which was the principal bone of contention. Britain based its claims on the exploration, discovery, and occupation of the region by British subjects. American claims also were based on exploration and occupation, including Captain

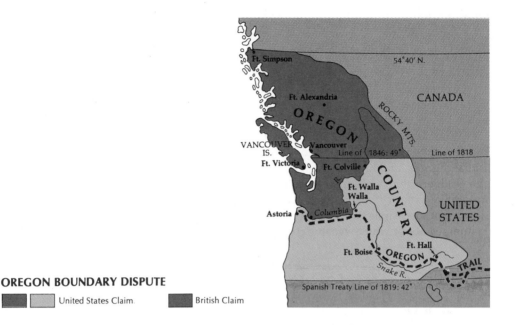

OREGON BOUNDARY DISPUTE

[ ] [ ] United States Claim.   [ ] British Claim

Gray's original discovery of the Columbia River in 1792, the Lewis and Clark expedition of 1804–1806, and the American missionaries and settlers who inhabited the area in the 1830s and 1840s.

During Anglo-American negotiations in 1818 the United States proposed the boundary line of 49° to the Pacific Ocean, but Britain was unwilling to relinquish its claims to the Columbia River, the "St. Lawrence of the West." Unable to reach a satisfactory agreement, the two nations settled upon a treaty of ten-year joint occupation. In 1827 the treaty was renewed for an indefinite period, with the provision that either party could terminate it on a year's notice.

Neither in 1818 nor at any other time until 1845 did the United States or Britain provide for civil government in Oregon. No marshal, no sheriff, no jury, no judge was empowered to carry out legal procedures. No laws could be executed because none had been enacted, there being no enacting authority. Often men took justice, or what they deemed was justice, into their own fallible hands. A missionary, without the shadow of authority, might name a constable or a magistrate. There were times when American traders and trappers tried alleged culprits for murder and other crimes. But maintenance of order, while frequently successful, was unofficial at best. Indians did not become subject to the slightest American official authority until 1843, when President Tyler appointed Oregon's first Indian agent.

That was the year when the first large body of American immigrants arduously entered the Willamette valley. It was also then that a committee, composed of American pioneers and their French-Canadian neighbors, took a stand at Champoeg favoring the establishment of a provisional government. Once the government came into being, it was almost immediately effective. Men of stamina and initiative determined to do in Oregon what Washington agencies had not done.

Soon the "Oregon fever" had hit the eastern United States, and British settlers in Oregon began to find themselves vastly outnumbered. This rapid influx of Americans prompted both Britain and the United States to try once again for a peaceful boundary settlement.

Soon after the Democratic victory in the election of 1844, the newly elected President Polk, faced with the possibility of war with Mexico, once again proposed to Great Britain the boundary line of 49°. When the British minister in Washington peremptorily rejected the American offer, the United States on April 26, 1846, gave the required one year's notice to terminate the joint-occupation treaty of 1818. Later that year the British government, realizing that the United States meant business, decided to settle for the 49° line. Britain submitted a draft treaty to this effect to the United States; Polk submitted the treaty to the Senate, which approved it on June 12 and formally ratified it a week later.

The Anglo-American settlement did not meet with unanimous approval in the United States: Northwestern exponents of Manifest Destiny and antislavery men charged that they had been betrayed by a South which, smugly complacent over the annexation of all of Texas, had been satisfied with less than all of Oregon. But the Oregon Treaty did have the important effect of preventing a possible third war between the United States and Great Britain at a time when the United States was involved in a war with Mexico over the question of Texas.

Settlement of Texas. In the 1820s and 1830s a number of Americans—mostly Southerners—took Mexico's liberal colonization law at face value and migrated to Texas. With the help of slaves and cotton gins they farmed the fertile soil and conducted business under the aegis of Stephen Austin and other *empresarios* who had contracted with the Mexican government to settle a certain number of families in Texas in return for grants of land.

In three centuries the Spanish government had brought only four thousand subjects to Texas. Now the population of the Austin communities alone expanded from 2000 in 1828 to more than 5500 three years later. By 1836 more than 25,000 white men, women, and children were scattered between the Sabine River and San Antonio de Bexar. Colonists from the United States far outnumbered those of Spanish ancestry.

Friction between Mexicans and Americans in Texas was probably inevitable. Mexicans, long accustomed to Spanish procedures, naturally were unprepared for the kinds of administrative and legislative responsibilities so readily assumed by the immigrants. Blunt and self-assertive Americans in Texas were certain that their way of life was freer, healthier, happier, and in all ways superior to that of the Mexicans. They looked upon themselves individually and collectively as proper agents to impose reform and progress on what they deemed to be a benighted society, handicapped for generations by superstition and sloth. The average newcomer failed to recognize the spirituality and gentility of Spanish culture and criticized the Mexican peasants for being illiterate and ignorant of his world. Americans also overlooked the equally pertinent truth that both Mexican peasants and their grandee overlords were sensitive and proud.

Americans in Texas were distressed by gyrations in Mexican policy and the uncertainty of their own status. The Mexican government appeared indifferent to educational needs and law enforcement, and it did nothing to strengthen the Americans' hopes that Texas might be separated from the state of Coahuila, to which it had long been joined. This neglect, as well as divergent attitudes toward religion and slavery, contributed to a drift that widened the gulf between the native Mexicans and the immigrants from the north.

War for Independence. In Mexico City, meanwhile, a growing trend toward dictatorial rule reduced the likelihood of conciliation. The master spirit of despotism was Antonio Lopez de Santa Anna, who became president of Mexico in 1833. Santa Anna, "the Napoleon of the West," was ambitious, adept at intrigue, and an able field commander as long as fate favored him. As president he ruthlessly crushed every semblance of liberalism in Mexico's central government and then turned his attention to Texas, where Americans were vehemently protesting his abandonment of the eleven-year-old "enlightened" Mexican constitution. The Texans' protests culminated in a proclamation of independence from Mexico on March 2, 1836.

Four days later Santa Anna and his Mexican troops swept into Texas and massacred every one of the 188 Americans at the Alamo mission in San Antonio. Davy Crockett, Jim Bowie, and William B. Travis were among the American heroes who died defending the Alamo. That same month, at Goliad on the south bank of the San Antonio River, the severely wounded James Walker Fannin surrendered his tiny command to Mexican General José Urrea, with the understanding that the Texans would be accorded the humane treatment normally extended to prisoners of war. Instead, acting under Santa Anna's orders, Urrea mercilessly executed most of the prisoners in cold blood, with Colonel Fannin the last to go. If the shots that killed them were not heard 'round the world in the tradition of Concord bridge, "Remember the Alamo!" and "Remember Goliad!" long served as rallying cries in Texas.

During the war for Texan independence the young republic's forces were in the capable hands of General Sam Houston. This robust native of Virginia had moved in his youth to Tennessee, fought under Andrew Jackson in the War of 1812, studied law, and served as congressman and governor of Tennessee. He settled in Texas after Jackson sent him there to negotiate an Indian treaty in 1832.

Houston demonstrated his leadership at the Battle of San Jacinto on April 21, 1836—not quite two months after the Texans' stunning defeats at the Alamo and Goliad. His troops surprised and defeated Santa Anna's forces and captured the Mexican dictator himself. Houston forced Santa Anna to sign the Treaty of Velasco, by which Mexico agreed to withdraw its forces from Texas and to recognize the Rio Grande as the southwestern boundary of the new Republic of Texas.

The Republic of Texas. Soon after the Texans declared their independence from Mexico, they submitted a formal proposal for annexation to the United States, but the proposal was rejected by President Van Buren, who feared precipitating a serious sectional controversy over the extension of slavery into that area. Thus the young republic, under the leadership of Presidents Sam Houston (who served two nonconsecutive terms) and Mirabeau B. Lamar, proceeded to develop its own foreign and domestic policies. One of its first problems was Mexico's refusal to recognize its independent status. Because Santa Anna had signed the Treaty of Velasco under duress, while a prisoner of war, the Mexicans denied its validity. Thus, though both Europe and the United States officially recognized Texan independence, Mexico withheld recognition.

Though the sizable volunteer army of the San Jacinto campaign was disbanded in 1837, Texas maintained armed troops against the danger of another military campaign by Mexico. The Texas Rangers, loosely organized until then, were developed into a tight-knit corps. And the Texas navy made itself felt in the Gulf of Mexico; as late as 1843, Texan sailors fought against Mexican steam warships.

Maintenance of the navy and defenses against marauding Indians demanded more money than Texas had. The republic's civil government also desperately needed financial support. Though bond issues were floated with varying degrees of success, the fiscal structure never was very solid in the period of the republic.

Nevertheless, Texas prospered. Its population grew rapidly, most of the immigrants continuing to be Americans. Large in territory and rich in untapped resources, Texas was regarded with covetous eyes by those American politicians who viewed it as a promising field for expansion, exploitation, and the extension of slavery.

Annexation of Texas. Presidents Jackson and Van Buren had been concerned about the North's opposition to the annexation of Texas. Jackson favored annexation and was more outspoken about it after he retired from the presidency. Van Buren marked time, but neither Tyler nor Polk had qualms about working toward annexation. Although both were slaveholders, neither seems to have been thinking primarily about considerations of slavery. (Polk's diary gives abundant evidence to this effect.) Both couched their motives in terms of expansion: Would it be to the country's advantage to undergo curtailment of the federal domain? This was substantially the same question Jefferson had asked himself in 1803 with reference to the Louisiana Purchase—and, like Jefferson, Tyler and Polk answered with a ringing "No!"

But antislavery elements in the North viewed the situation differently. Most Northerners—excluding the tiny minority of abolitionists—agreed with their Southern brothers that the Constitution protected slavery where slavery then existed. Extension of slavery into the West, however, wafted dark clouds of trouble into the skies; the addition of Texas as a slave state was opposed by many citizens north of the Mason-Dixon line.

Early in 1844 President Tyler, anticipating the presidential campaign of that year, sent a treaty for the annexation of Texas to the Senate. When the Senate rejected it by a vote of 35–16, Tyler recommended that Texas be annexed by joint resolution of both houses of Congress, since a joint resolution could be passed by a simple majority in both houses plus the President's signature, in contrast to the two-thirds Senate majority needed for treaty ratification. Congress adjourned before the measure could be brought to a vote, but when the second session convened on December 2, 1844, Tyler again urged a joint resolution to annex Texas. This time the resolution passed both House and Senate, and Tyler signed it on March 1, 1845. Under the terms of the resolution, Texas was offered statehood with the understanding that its territory might be subdivided into not more than four states. The Missouri Compromise line of 36° 30' was extended westward to permit slavery in Texas.

Before the annexation resolution was passed, there had been hints and fears of British involvement in the fate of the Texas Republic. It was to England's, as well as to Mexico's, interest to see that Texas stayed out of the United States; a pending arrangement whereby Texas would ship cotton directly to Liverpool, for example, would mean the tightening of mutually advantageous Anglo-Texan economic ties. The London government tried to induce Mexico to recognize Texan independence on the condition that the Lone Star Republic would not become part of the United States. Mexico did assent to this proposal in May 1845, and Texans had a choice of being annexed to the United States or negotiating such a treaty with Mexico. The Mexican offer had come too late, however; now that annexation to the United States was its for the taking, Texas found this alternative the more desirable.

War with Mexico.   Already irate over Texas' independence, the Mexican government became exceedingly resentful when, in 1845, its erstwhile possession was formally annexed by the United States. Mexico had threatened to declare war on the United States if Texas was annexed; now it withdrew its minister to the United States and severed official relations with the American government.

In June 1845 President Polk ordered General Zachary Taylor and his troops into Texas to defend the territory; Taylor set up camp on the south bank of the Nueces River, about 150 miles from the Rio Grande. In November Polk dispatched John Slidell to Mexico on a special mission to discuss the outstanding issues between Mexico and the United States. Slidell was to propose that the United States assume the $2 million in claims of American citizens against the government of Mexico, in return for Mexico's recognition of the Rio Grande as the southwestern boundary of Texas (Mexico claimed the Nueces River as the southwestern line). Polk also authorized Slidell to offer $5 million for New Mexico or $25 million for both New Mexico and California.

When the new Mexican government under President José J. Herrera refused to receive Slidell, Polk ordered Taylor to proceed to the Rio Grande. There, on April 25, 1846, Taylor's troops were attacked without warning by Mexican contingents, and Congress declared war on the Republic of Mexico.

The Battles of Palo Alto and Resaca de la Palma followed; the first was an inconclusive artillery duel, the second a smashing American victory. These opening engagements of May 1846 were followed by the major encounters of Monterrey the next September and Buena Vista in February 1847. General Zachary Taylor, bearing battlefield and theater responsibility in the Monterrey area, displayed great gallantry and was popular with his men. However, he did not make much progress in the direction of Mexico City, partly because Polk transferred most of the seasoned soldiers from Taylor's command to that of Major General Winfield Scott.

It was Scott, who, landing at Vera Cruz in March 1847, made that Gulf port his supply base and advanced inland to the mountain pass of Cerro Gordo, where he

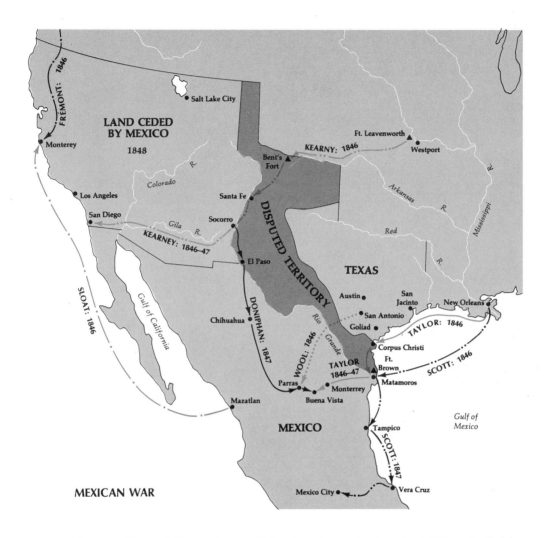

MEXICAN WAR

routed Mexican General Santa Anna. Other battles took place in 1847, and all, like Taylor's four encounters, were American victories. Scott entered Mexico City in September, but it was bloodsoaked Buena Vista more than half a year before that would make Taylor the next President.

Although the United States declared war on Mexico in May 1846, the news did not reach California for a number of weeks. Meanwhile, a group of California settlers, aided by explorer John C. Frémont and by American naval officers, had revolted against Mexican rule and proclaimed California an independent republic. They raised a flag on which a grizzly bear, a red star, and the legend "Republic of California" were juxtaposed. When news that the United States had declared war against Mexico was received, however, the significance of the Bear Flag Revolt was greatly diminished.

In the summer of 1846 Colonel Stephen W. Kearny and a detachment of about

1700 troops took possession of Santa Fe in the name of the United States. Polk subsequently ordered Kearny to take charge of American operations in California. The American elements, previously led by Commodore R. F. Stockton, were brought together under Kearny, and by autumn of 1846 the conquest of California was complete.

Treaty of Guadalupe Hidalgo. In April 1847 President Polk, eager to end the fighting as quickly as possible, delegated Nicholas P. Trist, chief clerk of the State Department, as peace commissioner to Mexico. Trist's instructions were to negotiate a treaty recognizing the Rio Grande as the southwest boundary of Texas and ceding to the United States for $15 million all Mexican territory between the Rio Grande and the Pacific Ocean above the latitude of El Paso. The United States also would assume the claims of United States citizens against Mexico up to $3.25 million.

Once in Mexico, Trist badly bungled the negotiations and was peremptorily recalled by Polk. Trist, however, refused to return to Washington and, with no official authority, signed on February 2, 1848, a treaty which incorporated all the provisions of his annulled instructions. Polk was furious at Trist's disobedience, but he immediately sent the treaty to the Senate for ratification. Though the Treaty of Guadalupe Hidalgo was denounced by two vocal minorities—those who had demanded the cession of all of Mexico and those who wanted none of the southwestern territory—it was ratified by the Senate on March 10, 1848. The United States found itself in possession of the mammoth region which includes the present states of California, Nevada, and Utah, most of Arizona and New Mexico, and parts of Colorado and Wyoming. It also found itself with a considerable number of Spanish-speaking residents, many of whom had lived there for generations.

Eruption of the Slavery Issue. Northern reactions to the War with Mexico were even more intense than Northern reactions to Texas' annexation. No matter how moderate they had previously been, antiextension Northerners began to heed the abolitionists' propaganda that a vicious "slave power" must be checked. According to this version of affairs, the South, having dominated the federal government since its establishment, now was afraid that population growth in the North and the proliferation of free states in the Northwest would destroy its political advantage. Therefore, it was argued, this nefarious "power"—arrogant, determined, and utterly unscrupulous—sought to strengthen itself by spreading an evil which enlightened men righteously deplored. The threat would affect the Southwest (as a result of the Mexican War), the West as a whole, and Northern states as well. The "slave power," the argument continued, would try to annex every Mexican mile and Central America and the West Indies in the bargain.

At the same time, there were Southerners who saw the North as the fundamentally culpable aggressor section. The pamphlets of abolitionists stirred up blacks, they asserted; slave insurrections had resulted and would continue to result from senseless agitation. Antislavery virulence had long been limited to a few Northern hotheads, but now the zealotry was epidemic. Northerners petitioned to do away with slavery in the District of Columbia and on federal property in the South. The same intolerance had been manifested in opposition to annexing Texas. And did not

Northern states abysmally fail to live up to constitutional commitments when they repeatedly refused to enforce the Fugitive Slave Law of 1793? So ran the Southern arguments.

As the world has often seen in situations where emotion interferes with reason, there were exaggerations on both sides rather than complete departures from truth. On the one hand, there simply was no "slave power" in the abolitionist sense of the term. There was no unanimity of Southern opinion as to policies. From Jefferson's day through Jackson's to Polk's, all Southern officeholders in high places had not been of one political mind. Chief Justice Taney, for example, did not invariably hand down Supreme Court opinions resembling those of Chief Justice Marshall. Taney was a Marylander and Marshall a Virginian, yet their legal tenets and those of other Southerners were poles apart. Contrary to what was charged in certain circles, there was no widespread Southern *or* Northern conspiracy.

In the 1840s, the issues of slavery and antislavery, expansion and containment became intermeshed. If the Civil War had never taken place, we might not now be inclined to stress North-South antipathies respecting the West. But since the war did occur, it is evident that the relationship of the slavery question to the West involved problems loaded with political dynamite.

Filling Out the West. While settlement of Texas and the Oregon country was proceeding apace, other areas were luring pioneers westward in search of land or mineral wealth. Some who had started out on the Oregon Trail bound for the Northwest changed their destination to California. The path to California followed the Oregon Trail to the Continental Divide where, turning southwestward, it became the California Trail and led through the Sierra Nevada into California.

Before 1840, only fur traders penetrated to California, and whaling ships stopped there for supplies occasionally. In the early 1840s some farmers began to move into the Pacific Coast valleys, but when war with Mexico broke out in 1846, there were only about seven hundred Americans in California. The discovery of gold at Sutter's Mill near Sacramento in 1848 started the "gold rush," which brought the total population of the area to ninety thousand by 1850, when California became a state. The gold seekers came by sea around Cape Horn, or by sea after an overland crossing of Mexico or Central America, or by various overland routes across the North American continent. The transcontinental journey was chosen by most immigrants, an estimated forty thousand using it in 1849 alone.

By the 1850s there were two frontiers in America, one moving westward beyond the Mississippi and the other moving eastward from California and Oregon into the Rocky Mountain area. The first settlement to fill this gap was made by the Mormons, who moved to Utah in 1847. This religious group had been organized by Joseph Smith in New York state in 1830. They had moved to Ohio in 1831 and to Illinois in 1839 to escape persecution, and then, for the same reason and under the leadership of Brigham Young, they decided to move to a desert valley around the Great Salt Lake, where they hoped to find peace. They had some misfortunes and near disasters in the first few years but eventually became prosperous.

With the close of the Mexican War the Mormons lost the nominal Mexican

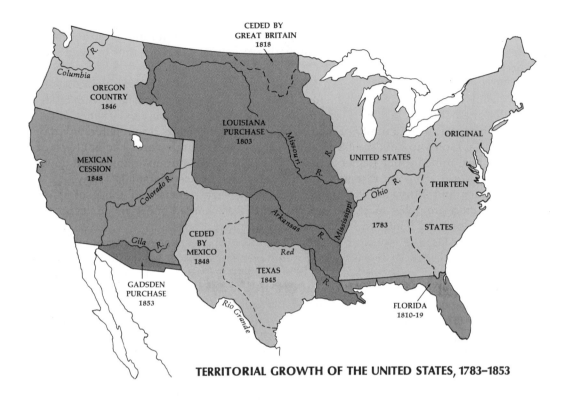

CEDED BY
GREAT BRITAIN
1818

Columbia R.

OREGON
COUNTRY
1846

LOUISIANA
PURCHASE
1803

Missouri R.

ORIGINAL

UNITED STATES

MEXICAN
CESSION
1848

Colorado R.

THIRTEEN

Ohio R.

Arkansas R.

Mississippi R.

STATES

1783

Gila R.

CEDED
BY
MEXICO
1848

Red

TEXAS
1845

GADSDEN
PURCHASE
1853

Rio Grande

R.

FLORIDA
1810-19

TERRITORIAL GROWTH OF THE UNITED STATES, 1783–1853

jurisdiction under which they had been free to do as they pleased. Congress organized the Mormon lands into Utah Territory in 1850, naming Brigham Young as territorial governor. By 1860 there were forty thousand persons in Utah, but it was not admitted as a state until 1896 because the Mormon church did not renounce the practice of polygamy until 1890. For a few years after 1849 the Mormons profited substantially from the sale of supplies to gold seekers on the way to California.

The treaty ending the war with Mexico filled out the present continental limits of the United States with the exception of a strip of land in what later became southern New Mexico and Arizona. It was purchased from Mexico in 1853 because it was thought to provide the best route for a railroad to California. With the Gadsden Purchase, the American "empire" was complete from Atlantic to Pacific.

THE ECONOMICS OF EXPANSION

The West and the Transportation Revolution.   From the beginning of human life on earth, man has lived in close association with rivers and streams. Waterways were the natural routes over which men moved both themselves and their goods, for rivers cut through wildernesses men could not penetrate. Therefore, when the settlers moving into the American frontier were forced to return to the most primitive conditions of living, rivers naturally became their first important means of inland transportation.

One of the great drawbacks to river transportation is that the river does not always go where the traffic needs to go. That became true in the United States as soon as the territory west of the Appalachian Mountains was opened for settlement. Rivers descended eastward from the Appalachian watersheds to the Atlantic or westward to meet the Ohio and Mississippi, but no waterway connected East and West. Thus the great enthusiasm for building national roads during the "Turnpike Era" from 1800 to 1830 was occasioned partly by the fact that they were to connect the Ohio River system with the Atlantic coastal rivers. However, transportation of goods between West and East over these road and river routes was prohibitively expensive except for light and very valuable merchandise. The best outlet for the bulky Western produce was not eastward but southward on flatboats down the Ohio and Mississippi Rivers to New Orleans. To try to propel flatboats back up the river against the current, however, was still impractical; manufactured products needed by Western settlers—such as guns, ammunition, traps, axes, plows, tools, and even shoes and cloth—still had to come in overland from the East.

Because America's immediate economic problem was the need to move goods over great distances inexpensively, the new steam power developed in England in the eighteenth century was applied in America to water transportation even earlier than to industry. Beginning with John Fitch in 1786, a series of American inventors worked on the problem of driving a boat with steam, culminating with Robert Fulton's commercial success in powering his *Clermont* up the Hudson River in 1807. In the following decade steamboats were successfully tried on the Ohio and Mississippi Rivers. By 1829 there were 200 steamboats in operation on the Western rivers, and by 1842 the number had reached 450. A decade later there were considerably over 1000. Partly because of the special needs of the West and partly because early steamboats were too fragile for ocean use (trans-Atlantic steamer service was not frequent until mid-century), more steamboats were in service on the Mississippi River system than anywhere else in the world. Pittsburgh, Cincinnati, and Louisville began as river towns, and New Orleans became one of America's greatest ports.

Meanwhile, in an attempt to avoid the roundabout route through New Orleans, Northerners turned their attention to canal building, which had been so successful in England in the 1760s and 1770s. The first such waterway of great importance was New York's Erie Canal, connecting the Great Lakes and the Hudson River (and thus the port of New York). Upon its completion in 1825, freight charges from Buffalo to New York City were cut from $100 to $10 a ton, the time of the trip from twenty days to six. Migrants began to use the canal to gain access to the West; Buffalo, Cleveland, Detroit, Chicago, and other cities began to sprout around the Great Lakes; and the area began to fill up with settlers just as the Ohio valley had earlier. As a result of the canal trade, New York City grew rapidly in wealth and population, becoming the greatest port on the Atlantic seaboard. The nation was propelled into the "Canal Era" (1825–40), with other sections from Illinois to Massachusetts trying to imitate the success of New York.

Yet rivers and canals had their shortcomings. During winter, frozen waterways could not be used in the North; rivers followed inconvenient courses, and canals could not be built in rough or hilly country. The railroads would overcome all these limitations.

Steam-powered rail locomotives had already won success in England when the Baltimore and Ohio Railroad instituted the first few miles of American rail service in 1830. Soon other short lines were built elsewhere, and by 1840, 2808 miles of track had been laid. Ten years later the mileage had more than tripled, to 9029 miles, and by 1860 it had tripled again, to 30,626 miles (as compared to industrial Britain's 10,410 miles). The railroads, which connected the Atlantic coast to Chicago and St. Louis by the 1850s, for the first time provided the West with exactly the kind of transportation it needed. Western products, no matter what their bulk, could now be moved regardless of weather or terrain directly to Eastern markets for overseas shipment. Manufactures from the East and abroad could come in freely. Traffic on the rivers and canals declined. With the coming of the rails, the commercial and industrial East and the agricultural West were tied more closely together by common economic bonds.

The Northeast and the Industrial Revolution.   Under the impact of continually expanding trade, each section of the country underwent a characteristic economic evolution of its own. New England, for example, the section which achieved the lead in population in the colonial era, was the first to pass from agriculture to commerce and industry. The absence of good soil for agriculture and the abundance of good harbors adjacent to ample supplies of pine and hardwood had turned its people to shipbuilding, fishing, and overseas commerce in colonial days. It was no accident, too, that the Industrial Revolution should have entered America through New England, for towns well located for commerce were also attractive for manufactures. Mills and factories need to be near shipping points.

Other circumstances contributed to the growth of industrialism in the Northeast. In the early stages of the Industrial Revolution, streams were still a must for turning the water wheels that drove the machinery of mills and factories, and the Northeast was favorably endowed with water power. In Chapter 5 we saw how the Embargo and the War of 1812, in restricting overseas trade, had driven idle commercial capital into investment in domestic industry. The tremendous potentialities of trade with the West, facilitated first by the Erie Canal and then by the railroads, provided further incentive for the manufacture of industrial products. Finally, even after steam had replaced water power in industry, manufacturing continued for a time to be located where capital and labor were already concentrated—in the Northeast.

The rise of industrialism in the northern United States had economic and social consequences of such a revolutionary character that it has been called—as in England—the Industrial Revolution. It revolutionized the nature of business organization, of labor, of population distribution, and of the life and welfare of all Americans.

The Corporate Revolution.   The arrival of industrialism meant the beginning of the growth of large factories and large railroad networks. And as the size of businesses increased, the old methods of organizing and financing business enterprises by means of individual ownership or partnership became inadequate. The costs of maintaining trading ships or small mills did not exceed the personal fortune of individuals, but with the coming of railroads and large-scale manufactures, the enormous costs of buildings, equipment, and stock began to run into millions of dollars, far beyond the financial resources of even the wealthiest person, and the risks were too great to be undertaken singly. As a consequence, entrepreneurs turned increasingly to the corporate form of enterprise.

The chief disadvantage of the partnership was its "unlimited liability" for business debts: if the firm failed, creditors could force the sale of the owners' personal property, as well as their business property, to satisfy claims. The partnership, therefore, usually comprised a very few individuals who knew and trusted one another and who were willing to take the risks together. Moreover, the partnership had no permanence; it dissolved and the company collapsed when any single member took it into his mind to withdraw. The corporation, on the other hand, is a separate legal entity or "person," distinct from its owners. An owner may sell his stock in the corporation without the assent of the other owners, and the corporation remains *permanent.* Most important is the feature of "limited liability." If the corporation fails, the owners are liable to lose only what they paid for stock in the corporation; the creditors have no claim on their personal resources. Finally, by the issuance of stock, the corporation can draw on the contributions of literally thousands of investors and accumulate the large amounts of capital needed for big industry.

In spite of its advantages, the corporate form was not without its opponents in the Jacksonian period. Jackson, Jefferson before him, and even the father of free enterprise or laissez faire, the English economist Adam Smith, had attacked corporations as according "exclusive privilege" and limiting "free competition." But what they were attacking was the kind of incorporation that was known before the 1830s. Corporation charters had been obtainable only by special enactment of a legislature and had usually been granted for some specific enterprise that had to be run as a monopoly in order to be profitable. Thus turnpikes, canals, bridges, and banks— enterprises of a semipublic character—were often conducted under charters granting exclusive privileges. Part of Jackson's hostility toward the Bank of the United States can be traced to its monopolistic character. And even less clearly beneficial to all the public was the construction of industrial establishments.

However, the wider markets in the West and the new technical processes made increased capital so necessary to industry that corporation charters were sought more and more in spite of possible public opposition. Moreover, to make incorporation democratic and consonant with Jacksonian equal-rights principles, Whigs and like-minded Democrats urged "general incorporation laws" (as distinct from special legislative grants) which would make corporation charters available to all who could meet certain legal requirements. Beginning in the 1830s and continuing into the 1840s and 1850s, corporations began to proliferate under the new system of general laws.

The Whig party, which generally favored business interests (as would later its successor, the Republican party), had advocated free incorporation as a method of inaugurating a kind of "democratic" capitalism; that is, business would no longer be dependent upon rich men but could gather the combined resources of countless small investors. However, this multiplication of ownership eventually resulted in a revolutionary change in the nature of business organization. As the number of stockholders or owners in a corporation rose into the thousands and as they were dispersed about the country, actual management or "control" of the company fell into the hands of individuals who were not dominant owners or perhaps not even stockholders at all. Under the system of individual proprietorship or partnership, ownership and control had been in the hands of the same person; the corporate system began the process of divorcing ownership from control and of creating a vast class of investors dependent, insofar as their profits were concerned, on the actions of others, of corporate managers. The inherent danger was that the managers might not act in the interests of the owners. In former days when the owner managed his own business, an owner who defrauded the company defrauded himself. With the separation of ownership and control, the "insiders" or managers could systematically loot a company for their own profit. Said a contemporary observer concerning the stock market scandals of 1854:

> The spring trade of '54 opened gloomily. . . . In June it was discovered that the Parker Vein Company had flooded the market with an immense and unauthorized issue of stock. The first of the next month New York was startled by the intelligence that Robert Schuyler, President of the New York and New Haven Railroad, had been selling some 20,000 illegal shares at par,—and was now a defaulter for two millions. Almost simultaneously it was ascertained that Alexander Kyle, Secretary of the Harlem Railroad Company, had made an issue of forged stock to the amount of $300,000. Other developments of breaches of trust came flocking from the inland cities.[1]

Scandals, very fortunately, represented only one phase of America's part in the Industrial Revolution. Another phase, at least equally significant, was the entirely new evaluation of the forces that affected the location of industry.

The Rise of Industrial Populations. Many years before the steam engine was developed, the almost complete reliance on water power resulted in scattering manufacturing among a large number of small or medium-sized towns, for the capacity of any given dam site was limited. The triumph of steam reinforced the tendency of manufacturing to concentrate in large cities.

Industrial employment brought new problems not imaginable in the previous handicraft period of individual workshops. In America, as in England, people did not know how to cope with the problems of health and safety in the new factories because never before had such problems existed; even in England factory laws were not introduced until the 1840s. Moreover, congested living quarters in the growing industrial cities of New England and the Middle Atlantic states often resulted in a deplorable lack not only of sanitation but also of the minimum requirements for decent human existence. Hours of work were usually long, wages low, and schools for the children of workers inadequate. Workers could afford little for housing. The idea of public transportation had not been developed, so employees had to live within walking distance of their place of employment. All these conditions worked together to

---

[1]James K. Medbury, *Men and Mysteries of Wall Street* (Boston: Fields, Osgood, 1870), p. 309.

produce a type of housing for industrial workers which could become slums of the worst sort.

Perhaps the greatest evil was the increasing employment of children. While the earlier hand industries required skilled male workers, the new steam-driven machines required such minimal skill to operate that women and children could perform the simple but arduous and monotonous tasks of factory work. On the other hand, conditions were perhaps not so disagreeable as they were in England, and there were bright spots on the American industrial landscape. The novelist Hawthorne in one of his rambles about the New England countryside remarked on the bright, cheerful faces looking out through the factory windows, and the factory girls of Lowell, Massachusetts, were known for their neat dress and published a literary weekly. But these pleasant scenes were fast fading into the past.

Urban industrialism resulted not only from new production techniques and new Western markets but also from increased efficiency in agriculture: improved farm methods and farm machinery permitted more people to be siphoned off into industrial production. In addition, a good many immigrants settled immediately in the cities. As a result, between 1820 and 1850 the cities grew much faster than the population as a whole. In 1820 only one person in fourteen lived in a city of 2500 or more; in 1850 nearly one person in six lived in such a city. This meant an increase of more than fivefold in the population of cities, while the whole population had increased just over twofold during those years.

The rapid growth of industrial cities in the North dismayed many Americans, who associated crowded cities and the factory grind with a Europe of decadence and oppression. The great majority of Americans were still rural, still untouched by conditions developing in the Northeast; but those who watched the cities fill with immigrants and develop slums, vice, and crime were deeply disturbed. The traditional Jeffersonian vision of America—the land of democratic simplicity—seemed to be threatened by new problems of industrial complexity.

The Rise of Labor. Among the first to react to these unsatisfactory conditions were the workers themselves. The rise of industry was followed by the rise of unionism. Usually it was the skilled artisans of the building trades and other industries who made the most effective protest. The unskilled workers, who were the worst off, contributed little to the support of movements from which they would be the greatest beneficiaries.

The oldest labor organizations in America date back to the late eighteenth century, when various skilled craftsmen banded together to obtain higher wages, shorter hours, and other benefits from their merchant-artisan employers. But it was not until the late 1820s and the 1830s that aggressive union activity began with the establishment of strong craft unions in Philadelphia, Boston, New York, Providence, and other cities. An attempt was even made in 1834 to form a National Trades Union, but though the group held conventions for several years, the effort failed to achieve an enduring result. The most successful of the early unions were local groups which were primarily political in their objectives, working especially hard for various social reforms like free public schools. Aided by favorable public opinion, labor was able to make substantial gains by legislative action. By the middle of the nineteenth century the idea of free public education, at least through the primary grades, was pretty generally accepted. Beginning in the late 1840s, a number of important states began to establish the ten-hour day as the legal maximum work day. But it was usually possible for a worker to make a special contract with his employer to work longer, and economic necessity frequently drove him to do so, nullifying the effect of the statutory provision. Nevertheless, such laws represented a gain for labor, since they helped to establish the idea of a ten-hour limit.

Finally, in the 1850s, unions less interested in political activity than in "bread-and-butter" issues (wages, hours, and working conditions) gathered momentum. During this period, the first permanent national unions of separate trades were set up, beginning with the National Typographical Union in 1852.

The appearance of solid and enduring national unions was a sign of the end of America's industrial adolescence. Many more decades were to pass before economic conditions would convince even a substantial minority of American workers or employers that unions were a good and permanent element in industrial relations. The individualistic tradition and conditioning of both workers and employers, and an excess of labor, prevented that result sooner. But national unions were here to stay, and their very existence testified to the arrival of a new period in American economic history.

The South and King Cotton.   While the commercial and industrial North and the agricultural West were closing together in common economic bonds, the South remained exclusively agricultural and largely dependent upon Europe and the outside world to absorb its products. Basically, the South was pulling away from its earlier common interests with other parts of the country and tying itself to an international market economy, in which it became the specialized producer of seven eighths of the world's cotton fiber.

However, certain financial obstacles prevented the South from completely freeing itself from dependence on the North. A growing demand for slaves meant continually rising prices for them. To buy land and slaves for the expansion of cultivation required new increments of capital, which the planter class—a leisure-loving economic aristocracy—simply could not provide for itself. The new capital, therefore, had to be acquired in the financial markets of the North and Europe in competition with an expanding and increasingly productive mechanized industry. The shipping and sale of cotton tended to be handled by mercantile agencies in the principal Northeastern seaports, because the highly specialized shipping requirements of the Southern economy could not be met efficiently except in conjunction with the more general trade of the major ports. Southern ports did not offer such possibilities of pooling cargo and warehouse space, and Southerners complained that their own business was taken away from them by Northern merchants who obtained the profits of the cotton trade and kept the Southern planters dependent upon them for mercantile credit.

Nevertheless, the South continued to follow its policy of determined divergence from the economies of the other sections of the nation and continued to seek a free world market. Not all white men living in the South were in agreement on means and methods, but the most vocal elements felt there was only one way in which their section could escape economic submission to the North and West. Only through secession from the Union, they were convinced, could the Southern states avoid being damaged by future economic policies which would destroy slavery and the plantation system. So they chose the path of secession, a path that took them not only to the termination of the institutions they had sought so long to save but also to the most destructive event in our national history—the Civil War.

CHAPTER 9

THE AMERICAN RENAISSANCE

AMERICAN TRAITS

The Frontier Individualist. No other trait of the Jacksonian American was more marked than what we might call his "frontier individualism." There was grubbiness on the frontier. There could be narrow-mindedness. And this individualism was not necessarily "nonconformist," that is, marked by willingness to act differently from one's fellow Americans; most Americans, indeed, took the cue for their behavior from the majority. But in the main, men who invaded the wilderness and established settlements in the West looked upon themselves as economically self-reliant and capable of almost any exertion or achievement. They developed versatility, robustness, and resilience, together with the physical courage which was expected of the frontiersman.

In part, these character tendencies were a heritage from colonial times, when bravery and imagination characterized the Atlantic frontiersman. In part, they resulted from the recent immigrants' impression that the way to get ahead was to make a virtue of necessity and emulate the older Americans. A third reason lay in the nature of the country—particularly in its combination of incessant, often cruel demands and boundless opportunities.

American Nationalism. Closely linked to this "rugged individualism" of a largely economic sort was the social trait of national pride. In the half century preceding 1830, the United States had made astounding progress. The victory of Yorktown, the Constitution, the Bill of Rights, the Louisiana Purchase, the Battle of New Orleans, the Missouri Compromise, and the Monroe Doctrine were landmarks passed within the memory of many living citizens. The increase of the population, growth of the national domain, and development of cities and industries were only a few of the reasons for Americans' sense of gratification.

As earnestly as any other interpreter, the nationalistic historian George Bancroft put into words the story of America's glory. In his *History of the United States,* which began appearing in 1834, the scholar lauded the colonial past in terms of divine origin and lofty mission. In politics Bancroft was a partisan Democrat, and his volumes were criticized on the score that every page "voted for Jackson." Bancroft expressed in his history what fellow Democrats like John L. O'Sullivan of New York and Robert Rantoul of Boston wrote in their essays and what other Americans echoed in Fourth of July orations.

Romanticism Revisited. The growth of democratic government during the Jacksonian period reflected a new emphasis on the value of the individual, or the "common" man, apart from his role as an atom in the complex structure of society. This rising ideal of individual worth was a prominent feature of American Romanticism, another leading cultural trend of the pre-Civil War period. Although the Romantic view of society has been discussed in Chapter 6 (see pp. 122–23), a review of its characteristics will help to explain American intellectual and cultural development from 1824 to 1848.

Romantic writers and artists placed new emphasis on imagination, emotion, experimentation, informality, the appreciation of external nature, and the capturing of transient—rather than static—aspects and moods of life. They tended toward the picturesque, the exotic, the sensuous, and the supernatural. In contrast to men of the Enlightenment, who had emphasized reason and intellect, the Romanticists believed that human intuition and poetic sensibility were more likely to lead man to truth. They viewed society as an evolving organism susceptible to refashioning and improvement, and their goal was the "liberation" of man—the full development of his individual potentialities.

The Romanticists' view of society as an evolving organism susceptible to improvement led naturally to the growth of reform movements against customs and institutions which they felt were hindrances to individual development. Since the Continental nations had not yet achieved representative democracy, European efforts at reform were often political; but because Americans found in their own nation the necessary political foundations for rapid progress toward perfection, American Romanticists tended to concern themselves less with political reform than with social and humanitarian reforms and the cultivation of the arts. For example, the period saw great emphasis on the temperance movement, extension of social and political rights to various classes and to women, the first important work with the handicapped and mentally ill, and a vocal attack on the Southern institution of slavery. The various reform movements of the pre-Civil War era are analyzed in Chapter 12.

RELIGION, PHILOSOPHY, AND THE ARTS

The Unitarian Influence. The Romanticist's emphasis on the innate value of the individual and the importance of self-development was closely related to the religious view of man held by the loosely knit Unitarians, who had challenged the doctrines of the strict, theocratic Puritans of New England (see pp. 54–58, 126–28).

Unitarians accepted some of the traditional Christian revelation, but only so far as that revelation was in accordance with man's reason. They rejected the Calvinistic belief in the doctrine of election, since such a belief implied that God was arbitrary; instead, Unitarians stressed God's benevolence. They believed that Christ was divine in the sense in which all men are divine. Theirs was a reaction against both the formalism of Congregationalists and the fire-and-brimstone evangelism of the Great Awakening (see p. 61), though one also finds definite links between the latter and

Unitarian individualism. Christ's life represented to the Unitarians an example to be emulated by men who were already innately good and spiritually free.

An intellectual and spiritual bridge between the Unitarianism of 1800–1820 and the transcendentalism of the 1830s was provided by William Ellery Channing. Implicit in his ideas was the prominence of the individual—independent, yet one with God—spiritually obliged to "transcend" his individualistic self by intimate identification with the Deity. Although Channing had been reared in the creed of Calvinism, he came to deny the doctrine of original sin and to believe strongly in freedom of the will.

Channing himself helped in the formation of the American Unitarian Association in 1825. This was ironic, because he personally deplored "the narrow walls of a particular church"—that is, an organized church, which the very establishment of an association seemed to imply. Indeed, under the association's aegis, a Unitarian ministry and church membership did develop, and far more attention than Channing approved of was paid to such formalities as creeds, church offices, and church organization.

The revolt against this trend took two forms: one type of "dissent from the dissenters" was that of Ralph Waldo Emerson; a second was that of Theodore Parker. Each of these ministers was convinced that religion should be a vital personal experience, hinging upon inspiration rather than upon forms and doctrines. The manner of the two men, however, differed drastically. Parker, an activist, viewed himself in the role of "conscience to the nation." His harsh language caused resentment among the conservative majority of Unitarian ministers and laymen. He denied such things as miracles and denounced popular ignorance and corrupt leadership, demanding that "we worship, as Jesus did, with no mediator, with nothing between us and the Father of all." Parker, trained in philosophies and sciences, urged theology to embrace scientific methods of inquiry.

Emerson and Transcendentalism. Transcendentalism has been defined philosophically as "the recognition in man of the capacity of knowing truth intuitively, or of attaining knowledge transcending the reach of the senses." Jesus "spoke of miracles," Emerson pointed out, for Jesus "felt that man's life was a miracle, and all that man doth, and he knew that this his daily miracle shines, as the character ascends." But churches' interpretation of "the word Miracle," Emerson added, not only gave a false impression but was "not one with the blowing clover and the falling rain."

The allusion to clover and to rain, as miracles, symbolizes Emerson's and other transcendentalists' reliance upon external nature as well as man's nature for revelations of divinity. Emerson viewed the many different aspects of the universe as diverse manifestations of one all-encompassing central spirit, which he called the Over-Soul. The individual man, according to Emerson, could become a channel for the higher truths of the Over-Soul if he would only develop his intuitive powers to the fullest. A logical result of Emerson's doctrine of the Over-Soul was his belief in self-reliance, as expounded in his famous essay of that name.

When he wrote about self-reliance, Emerson's meaning was that man and the universal spirit could achieve a direct, exalted relationship one with the other. Another transcendentalist, George Ripley, expressed it in a slightly different way. Transcendentalists, he said, "value literature not as an end, but as an instrument to help the solution of problems that haunt and agitate the soul. . . . They become students of God unconsciously; and secret communion with the divine presence is their preparation for a knowledge of books, and the expression of their own convictions."

The philosophy that Emerson taught was essentially a variety of idealism—idealism as distinct from materialism. Broadly speaking, idealism and materialism are opposing philosophies—an idealist being one who believes that the basic reality is spiritual and the materialist being one who believes that the basic reality is physical or material. The temper of the times in which Emerson lived—which accorded prime attention to nation building, the exploitation of resources, and scientific thought—aided and abetted a materialistic view. Yet Emerson became one of the outstanding idealists of modern times. He was no mere ivory-tower thinker, however. His idealism was applied. He was concerned ultimately with the conduct of life. He felt in both a practical and an idealistic way that man can draw upon a power greater than his own. He suggested the presence of a spiritual energy in the universe and the availability of this energy to man in facing the tasks of life.

Communitarianism. Perry Miller, the late Harvard scholar, underscored the element of revolt in transcendentalism. Emerson and his disciples, said Miller, appeared to members of the older generation of the 1830s and 1840s to be "throwbacks to the messy emotionalism and the dangerous mysticism" of an earlier time. Thus there was a generation gap or, in Miller's words, a "rift between the generations" that sounds very familiar to Americans of the 1970s.

One relationship of transcendentalists to the day-to-day life of their era had to do with "communitarianism." Much of the enthusiasm for communal living, however, had come from Britain and the Continent long before Emerson's first book, *Nature*—the bible of the early transcendentalists—was published in 1836. The idea was for a limited number of people to live together in a little community, wholly or mainly self-sufficient in terms of economics, culture, and religious worship, and more or less separated from the general society surrounding it. These communities could be either religious or secular. Among the Christian communitarians were the Shakers, who established settlements in New England, New York, Kentucky, and elsewhere, and who believed in separation from the world, simplicity of language, celibacy, and an austere way of life. Religious communities also were founded by the Mormons as well as by several Adventist sects.

Secular communitarianism resembled the Christian kind in that the purpose was to join people together in order to face collectively the challenge of the frontier or to solve collectively the hazards of living in an industrialized society. Among the better-known experiments were New Harmony in Indiana, the North American Phalanx in New Jersey, and Brook Farm and Fruitlands in Massachusetts. Secular and religious communitarianism usually shared such features as vegetarianism, prohibition of alcoholic beverages, equitable sharing of labor, and community ownership and control of property. While most of the secular communities had their philosophical bases in the social contract theories of the eighteenth century, Fruitlands and Brook

Farm are worthy of special mention—for these are identified with transcendentalism.

Both these Massachusetts communities were composed largely of people who sought an atmosphere conducive to transcendental thinking, transcendental discussion, and cultivation of the intuitive faculty in a place set apart from a society intent upon materialistic gain. Emerson's influence was distinctly, if indirectly, felt in both communities though he never became closely identified with either except through his writings and his pupils. Like most such secular experiments, neither community lasted long—perhaps because of an absence of the explicitly Christian zeal which, in the case of the Mormons and the Shakers, proved a reliable source of community strength.

Henry David Thoreau. As the leading spirit of the transcendentalist movement and of self-reliant individualism, Emerson significantly influenced communitarianism. As a disciple of nature, he encouraged a back-to-nature movement and counseled men to live in simplicity, according to the prescriptions of nature. Compared with Henry David Thoreau, however, he was merely a theorist. Emerson was "civilized," dignified, and prosperous; he lived in a good house in Concord and wore good clothes. Thoreau was ascetic, primitive, "eccentric" in comparison. It was he who most thoroughly put Emerson's mandates of individualism and plain living into practice. Fourteen years younger than Emerson, Thoreau graduated without distinction from Harvard College in 1837, taught school, helped his father manufacture lead pencils in the early 1840s, did odd jobs in the Emerson household, and in general was a jack-of-all-trades, engaging in fence building, house painting, carpentering, gardening, berry picking, and surveying.

Thoreau's greatest experiment in plain living, or living close to nature, was his two-year residence in a shack on the edge of Walden Pond near Concord, Massachusetts. Here he dwelt among the woodland birds and beasts, read and wrote with few distractions, and in large part shunned the established social order. "I went to the woods because I wished to live deliberately," Thoreau wrote, "to front only the essential facts of life. . . . I had not lived there a week before my feet wore a path from my door to the pondside. . . . How worn and dusty, then, must be the highways of the world, how deep the ruts of tradition and conformity!" From this experience at the pond came Thoreau's famous work, *Walden,* published in 1854.

Independence and self-reliance dominated Thoreau's life. He refused support of any organized church: "Men call me a skeptic, but I'm only too conscientious to go to church." So strongly did he oppose slavery that he actively helped the "underground railroad" to convey runaway slaves to the freedom of Canada; and he spent a night in jail rather than pay a small tax in support of a government that prosecuted what he considered an unjust war against Mexico in order to extend slave territory into the Southwest. Out of this latter experience came his essay "Civil Disobedience," perhaps the most famous political essay ever written in America and one which Henry S. Canby called "Gandhi's textbook in his campaign of passive resistance against British government in India." In it Thoreau inveighed against any government that did not conduct itself in accordance with high moral principle and declared it a citizen's duty to deny support or allegiance to a government that one deeply felt to be wrong. It can be said in Thoreau's favor that such an attitude is essential to the health of a democracy; it is the opposite of that apathy—so destructive of an effective public opinion—which prevents the citizen from exerting himself to take a stand and allows contests of great moment to go by default. Thoreau was not antisocial; he merely took his duties as a citizen more seriously than most Americans.

The Boston Brahmins. The period from the triumph of Jacksonian democracy to the Civil War was one of the greatest eras in American literary development. It has been called "The Golden Day," "The New England Renaissance," and "The Flowering of New England." Boston, as the cultural center of New England, was the home of a social and intellectual aristocracy that did much to make literature "respectable" in an era preoccupied with politics, technology, and economic advancement. Oliver Wendell Holmes, the most articulate spokesman of this group, applied the label "Brahmin caste of New England" to the small, cultivated, and exclusive class into which he had been born and which he typified. Holmes and other well-known members of the Brahmin caste—including Henry Wadsworth Longfellow and James Russell Lowell—contributed a great deal to New England ideals of culture and scholarship.

The Brahmin conception of literature was that it should be lofty, pure, and noble; they recoiled from the sort of literary unpleasantness which characterized the writings of Hawthorne and Melville. And as with literature, so with life: the Brahmins—Holmes and Longfellow, in particular—strove consistently to erect barriers against unpleasant or perplexing social and philosophic questions. They neither wanted nor expected such Romantic utopias as were visualized by Emerson, Thoreau, and the founders of communitarian experiments like Brook Farm. Rather, they were benevolent toward their fellowmen, yet satisfied to savor the pleasant intellectual life of Cambridge and Boston. Holmes considered Boston "the thinking center of the continent, and therefore of the planet."

Nathaniel Hawthorne. The New England writer who most brilliantly opposed transcendentalist tendencies was Nathaniel Hawthorne of Salem, Massachusetts. He was the chief inheritor, in literature, of the old Puritan tradition; and his writings—particularly his novel *The Scarlet Letter* (1850)—embodied Puritan ideals and the Puritan way of life. His seventeenth-century ancestors had been Puritan magistrates charged with persecuting Quakers and condemning the "witches" at Salem court, and he felt deeply his connection with these forebears. Despite his disapproval of their bigotry and cruelty, he recognized the ancestral tie: "Strong traits of their nature," he said, "have intertwined themselves with mine." Thus in opposing the Emersonian view, Hawthorne was essentially criticizing both the optimism inherent in transcendentalism and the reform movements abetted by transcendentalism on the grounds that man is innately sinful, that evil is an ever present reality, not an illusion to be brushed aside, and that self-reliant individualism alone does not save man from destruction. Hawthorne is a striking example of the persistence of the Puritan point of view in an age of liberalism and progressivism.

Unlike Emerson, who denied that evil existed in an ultimate form, Hawthorne not only acknowledged evil but made it central in his stories, sketches, and novels. *The Scarlet Letter* deals with secret guilt, the effects of a disgraceful crime on man and woman, and the need for expiation through confession or love. In *The House of the Seven Gables* (1851) evil appears as a hereditary taint visiting the sins of the fathers on the children in a study of degeneration and decay. *The Blithedale Romance* (1852) was, in part, a satire on Brook Farm—the villain showing how the zealotry of a reformer can become enmeshed with unconscionable ambition and thus serve evil rather than good.

Herman Melville. Another writer close to Hawthorne in his concern with the "deep mystery of sin" and his revulsion against the contemporary currents of optimism was Herman Melville, a novelist neglected during his own lifetime but "rediscovered" in the 1920s by post-World War I critics to whose mood of disillusion-ment *Moby Dick* had powerful appeal. Born in New York and reared in the Berkshires of Massachusetts, Melville as a youth shipped as a sailor on a merchantman plying the Atlantic and later on a whaler traveling the South Seas, and on these voyages he saw firsthand a world of violence, crime, brutality, and misery.

Unlike Emerson but like Hawthorne, Melville was a philosophical pessimist who found it difficult to accept many of the assumptions of Emersonian Romanticism. However, he had arrived at his pessimism along intellectual avenues that differed from Hawthorne's in at least three key ways: (1) while Hawthorne cherished Calvinist values, although ever critical of them and all others, Melville rebelled against the religious conservatism which he had known in his home as a boy; (2) both in Liverpool and in the South Seas, Melville was shocked by the rough and cruel ways of "civilized" men—brutalities which neither Hawthorne nor Emerson had ever experienced at first hand; (3) whether or not the restless and questing nature of his mind sprang wholly from these causes, he lacked the resignation of Hawthorne just as he lacked the optimism of Emerson. Said Hawthorne in reference to a meeting with Melville in England in 1856:

> Melville, as he always does, began to reason of providence and futurity, and of everything that lies beyond human ken, and informed me that he had "pretty much made up his mind to be annihilated"; but still he does not seem to rest in that anticipation; and, I think, will never rest until he gets hold of a definite belief. It is strange how he persists—and has persisted ever since I knew him, and probably long before—in wandering to-and-fro over these deserts, as dismal and monotonous as the sand hills amid which we were sitting. He can neither believe, nor be comfortable in his unbelief; and he is too honest and courageous not to try to do one or the other.

Melville's dilemma was the dilemma of many other serious modern minds in an age of materialism.

Southern Romanticism and Realism. The South produced many writers during the period of sectional controversy that preceded the Civil War, yet it took little part in the American literary renaissance that had its center in New England. Put increasingly on the defensive, the South tended more and more to withdraw from intellectual contact with the North. As many Southerners became convinced that the institution of slavery must be maintained and permitted to spread, political and economic leadership in the South passed to men who no longer felt the need to apologize for slavery; instead they attempted to defend it—indeed, to praise it. Southerners tended to idealize the cotton plantation as a happy feudal domain where slaves were humanely ruled by highborn gentlemen. They pointed to the Greek ideal of democracy, in which *inequality,* rather than *equality,* was recognized as the fundamental condition of nature. In such a society the competent and worthy individuals, acting in the interest of all, voluntarily assumed the care and direction of the incompetent. This theory, in effect, denied the eighteenth-century idea that all men had certain natural rights.

Because of this emphasis on the pleasantness of feudal life, the dominant Romantic literary influence in the South from the mid-1830s to the mid-1840s was the fiction of the English novelist Sir Walter Scott. Scott's re-creation of the Middle Ages, his knights in shining armor, his defenders of glamorous ladies in distress, the pageantry of his scenes, and the exemplary character of his heroes accorded with Southern notions as to what Southern chivalry was and always would be—in contrast to Northern commercialism and reformism.

A number of American writers attempted to create romantic and idyllic pictures of life in the "feudal" area of the old South. One of the first and best of such novels was John P. Kennedy's *Swallow Barn* (1832), a depiction of Virginia rural life in the 1820s. Kennedy strung together sketches of plantation aristocracy on an episodic thread so thin that the plot is minimal. Substantially all the characterization and what little action develops are only marginally "true to life." Thus the master of Swallow Barn is genial, generous, and bland; his relatives and friends are virtuous and benevolent; their hospitality is bountiful; and the Negroes are cheerful. *Swallow Barn* enjoyed an enviable vogue during the 1830s, but the South it depicted existed largely in the author's imagination.

Indeed, the South was not all gentility and plantation virtue. The Old Southwest—Arkansas, Louisiana, Tennessee, Mississippi, Alabama, and parts of Georgia—still had its small farmers and reckless frontiersmen; and these became the subject of wildly humorous yarns by a series of frontier writers, including Augustus B. Longstreet, J. J. Hooper, George Washington Harris, and William T. Thompson. Writing with a keen awareness of the bumptious comedy inherent in the backwash of the frontier and aiming to depict authentically the rascally people, the speech, customs, and scenery of these regions, they produced tales characterized by a robust realism found nowhere else in Southern—or Northern—literature of the times.

George Washington Harris' fictional character Sut Lovingood is a good example of the breed of men inhabiting the pages of these Southwestern humorists. Sut, a lanky mountaineer and a self-confessed "nat'ral born durn'd fool," loves liquor and women but hates Yankees and circuit-riding preachers, whom he describes as "durn'd, infurnel, hiperkritical, potbellied, scaley-hided, whisky-wastin'." His adventures are full of mischief-making and comic situations.

As if things in America were not big enough, the storytellers of the Southwest loved the boast and brag of the "tall tale":

I'm that same David Crockett, fresh from the backwoods, half-horse, half-alligator, a little touched with the snapping-turtle; can wade the Mississippi, leap the Ohio, ride upon a streak of lightning, and slip without a scratch down a honey locust; can whip my weight in wild-cats—and if any gentleman pleases, for a ten-dollar bill, he may throw in a panther. . . .[1]

Chauvinism, boastfulness, and exaggeration here all reflected the influence of the vast wilderness on American thinking and on reading tastes. Recently historians have become more and more convinced that the "starting point of a truly American literature" can be located on the Western frontier more logically than in the East.

Edgar Allan Poe. Raised as a foster child in Virginia, Edgar Allan Poe can be treated nevertheless only partially as a Southerner. In his personal life he was—or wanted to be—a conservative Southerner, and consequently he opposed the New England group; moreover, he supported the works of Southern writers and even praised the Southern defense of slavery. But his writings rarely reveal a Southern tone or setting. In his tales he was more strikingly influenced by the "Gothic" tradition in English fiction—the kind of fiction that used certain stock properties like old castles, decayed houses, dungeons, secret passages, ancient wrongs, supernatural phenomena, and the like. Poe was not concerned with portraying contemporary scenes or providing moral reflections on life; he believed that poetry, for example, should exist for its own sake, never as an instrument of instruction. It may be that no other American has maintained more consistently that literature exists primarily and perhaps solely to entertain. But Poe did not take this function lightly. In his own poetry and prose he applied the theories of literary technique that he expounded in his critical writings.

Fenimore Cooper. The disparity between the dream of a peaceful, democratic society in the virgin wilderness and the reality of frontier life is frequently reflected in American thought and literature of the Romantic Age. The real Western frontier posed many problems of adjustment for its settlers. Life was harsh and there was little time for social amenities; land speculation, political corruption, and immorality were common in the poorly organized towns of the West. In short, the real frontier bore little resemblance to the literary legend or to the popular tall tale.

The first major writer of fiction to exploit the literary potential of the frontier was James Fenimore Cooper, whose series of "Leatherstocking Tales" both romanticized the wilderness and conveyed the loss many Americans felt when they became aware of the crude fashion in which the frontier was being settled. For instance, Cooper convincingly expressed the tragedy of the American Indian, pushed out of his ancestral lands by the advancing white man.

Although modern critics often lampoon his didacticism, stock characters, heavy-handed style, and strained and starchy dialogue, at his best Cooper was a captivating

---

[1]Vernon Louis Parrington, *Main Currents in American Thought,* II (New York: Harcourt Brace Jovanovich, Inc., 1927), p. 176.

storyteller with a talent for both description and perceptive social criticism. The Leatherstocking Tales represent a romantic view of the West, just as Sir Walter Scott's novels romanticized with charm and skill the people and places of a lost Europe. Cooper's West, however, was mainly confined to upper New York State before 1800; he himself never saw the prairie, never neared the Rocky Mountains, never crossed the Mississippi River.

Arts and Sciences. If literature was the form in which Americans did their finest artistic work in the Jacksonian period, an exception existed in the case of the drama; of American playwrights before the Civil War, the less said the better. And while inspiring hymns were written, mostly in the Northeast, and the spirituals of Southern slaves contributed to the unfolding of a distinctively American music, there was nothing like the achievements of contemporary European composers.

American sculptors, however, had a remarkable vogue both in Europe and at home. Among the most famous sculptors were Hiram Powers, an Ohioan whose *Greek Slave* was greeted with admiration in London, and Thomas Crawford of New York, whose *Armed Freedom* surmounts the Capitol in Washington, D.C. The heroic classic poses—the equestrian statues and idealized portrait busts—were esteemed in that nationalistic age.

If American architecture was largely derivative, many stately and beautiful structures were erected during the age of Jackson. The columns of Greek Revival and Roman Revival dwellings and business buildings continued to demonstrate the influence of Jefferson and Benjamin Latrobe. In the 1840s, however, the Romantic approach made itself felt in the Gothic style, which revived features of the architecture of the Middle Ages. Two well-regarded architects, Alexander J. Davis and Richard Upjohn, designer of Trinity Church in New York City, both primarily represented the Gothic Revival.

As in architecture, so in other arts and in some of the sciences; the United States still leaned on Europe for much of its leadership. Thus John James Audubon, the ornithologist and painter whose *Birds of America* is a classic, was born in the West Indies and reared in France. Duncan Phyfe, famous for the grace of the furniture he produced in New York, came to America from Scotland. Louis Agassiz, a native of Switzerland who joined the Harvard faculty, did as much as anyone else to arouse American interest in zoology and geology. Young Americans of promise, like Longfellow and Holmes, went to Germany and France for graduate study. In philanthropy, the Old World pointed the way; Washington's Smithsonian Institution was endowed by an Englishman. The most highly esteemed performing artists appearing in the United States were an Austrian ballet dancer, a Norwegian violinist, a Swedish soprano, and British actors and actresses.

Not all cultural contributions came from abroad. Although the most successful portrait painter, Thomas Sully, had come to the United States from England as a boy, the canvases of the American-born artists Matthew H. Jouett and Chester Harding also were deservedly popular. Too, "storytelling" or anecdotal painting—in which common human situations were depicted nostalgically or humorously—was growing in public favor. Scenes of life on the farm or of raftsmen poling their flatboats upstream or of the prairie schooners and Indians of the West appeared in the work of George Caleb Bingham, William Sidney Mount, and Alfred Jacob Miller. Romanticism and American pride in the land combined to produce a group of painters known as the Hudson River School, which romantically portrayed the wilderness of forests, mountains, and streams.

Despite the fact that deep research was not within the reach of most teachers, the period witnessed numerous advances along scientific and other scholarly lines. Benjamin Silliman, professor at Yale for over fifty years, published *Elements of Chemistry* in 1830 and wrote learnedly on subjects ranging from gold deposits to sugar planting. Other pioneers were Elisha Mitchell, geologist and botanist at the University of North Carolina; Edmund Ruffin, Virginia soil chemist; and Matthew Fontaine Maury of the navy, who was his generation's outstanding expert in navigation and oceanography.

Applications of scientific thought to industry brought about socioeconomic changes. Samuel F. B. Morse, an admirable portrait painter, invented the telegraph. Charles Goodyear discovered the process afterwards known as the vulcanization of rubber. From the mind and skill of Samuel Colt came the first practical firearm with a revolving chamber, and Elias Howe is given credit for the first sewing machine. During this period, medical and dental pioneers in Georgia and New England helped ease the suffering of future millions by applying anesthesia to surgery. William Beaumont, an American army doctor on the Michigan frontier, was the first physician to study gastric digestion in a living patient. And Holmes, the poet who was also a physician, saved the lives of countless mothers and babies by telling the world with scientific evidence that antiseptics could prevent puerperal fever. Meanwhile, it was hard to say whether the lithographs of Nathaniel Currier or the daguerreotypes of Mathew B. Brady delighted larger numbers of their fellow Americans. George Ticknor at Harvard was the American trailblazer in the study and teaching of modern foreign languages. In the historical field, William H. Prescott was publishing his monumental works on Mexico and Peru, and another first-rate historian, Francis Parkman, was writing *The Oregon Trail* and *The Conspiracy of Pontiac*.

The lighter side of cultural life developed with gaiety and zest. The stage was at its best in New York, but Philadelphia had three theaters, and Boston five. Road companies visited smaller cities and towns and even performed in barns and log houses. There were plays and musicals on boats in Western waters. Among indigenous American entertainments was the minstrel show with its interlocutor and end men, banjos, bones, and tambourines; both American and European audiences cheered minstrels like Daniel Emmett, the singer and composer who subsequently gave "Dixie" to the South. Americans already were humming the tunes of Stephen Collins Foster, the Pennsylvanian who immortalized Florida's "Swanee" River and evoked sentiment or sentimentality with the strains of "My Old Kentucky Home." Love of the spectacular as well as of good music led men, women, and children to line the pockets of Phineas T. Barnum, who sponsored tours for Jenny Lind, "the Swedish

Nightingale," and amazed gaping compatriots with his museum of curios—from the woolly horse and bearded lady to the celebrated midget "General Tom Thumb."

Both limitations and achievements in the arts and sciences naturally reflect the society in which they develop. Social priorities in turn are at least partly dependent on the economy, which in the United States of 1828–48 was still fundamentally agricultural albeit with a strong commercial trend and in the North ever increasing industrialism. Most Americans were either self-made people or eager to attain that status. Nearly all who were not still members of farm or plantation families were only two or three generations removed from European peasantry or American farm life. If the principal purpose of an aspiring citizenry is to free itself from handicaps old and new, its logical initial goal is independence from economic thralldom. The invisible shackles of the average farmer, like the visible chains of slaves, had to be broken before emancipated man could enjoy the leisure needed for widespread cultural excellence.

Economically, Americans were wonderfully assisted by a combination of conditions available to them in unique proportions: (1) a remarkable climatic range, appropriate for a great variety of enterprises; (2) the accessibility of free, or at least cheap, land and labor; (3) an untapped wealth of raw materials; (4) security from foreign military attack. This last factor enabled Americans to concentrate their energies on making the most of the other three. From a European cultural standpoint, however, American society was inadequately developed. Most European masterpieces in music, drama, painting, sculpture, and architecture had been created not only in urban environments but at royal and ecclesiastical courts and in the capital cities where those courts were located. There was then no American equivalent for this traditional form of encouragement. Washington and nearly all state capitals were underdeveloped communities except in a political sense. Nor had the United States yet evolved its own successful democratic substitute, fellowships, for long-established royal and noble patronage to subsidize talent.

The wonder was that, in so short a time span since the signing of the Constitution, one could find such substantial cultural growth. At the close of 1848, only six decades had elapsed since the eventful months of ratification. Much had been achieved in the sciences, arts, and, notably, letters. And the intellectual, artistic, and scientific progress of the most recent twenty years had been decidedly the most distinctive in American history until then. Authors, artists, and scientists already were giving eloquent and sustained proof of the richness and variety of American life and thought.

AMERICAN WOMEN

In the United States at mid-century many women spent their lives at hard, repetitive labor in frontier cabin, isolated farmhouse, or urban home. But the involvement of women in so many other phases of the American experience leads us to ask why so little attention has been paid to her in history books. The principal answer is that, while she was usually freer and more esteemed in America than in Europe, she was long denied the right to vote, to hold public office, or to attain other posts of leadership.

As wives, as mothers, as valued members of their communities, women were respected by relatives and neighbors, but fame and even prominence were deemed unladylike. It was true that exceptions like Abigail Adams and Dolley Madison had been widely known and recognized as persons of ability when their husbands reached the presidency, and some other women had become arbiters of fashion or leading local sponsors of good works. But it was not until the 1830s and 1840s that pioneering moves in a variety of fields demonstrated how versatile and effective women could be.

Thus Elizabeth Blackwell, struggling against prejudice, won her medical degree and became a physician. Sarah and Angelina Grimké, of a prominent South Carolina family, went north to work for the abolition of slavery. Dorothea Dix, a Massachusetts girl, grew up to crusade throughout the country for humane treatment of the insane. Under the tutelage of Samuel Gridley Howe, the blind deaf-mute Laura Bridgman of New Hampshire learned to read. As author, editor, and literary critic, Margaret Fuller was well known in intellectual circles. Harriet Tubman, a black woman, guided fellow blacks from slavery to freedom. All these women may be termed trailblazers.

Two general movements, then just getting under way, would ultimately affect large numbers of women regardless of the handicaps which law and custom had imposed. Lucretia Mott and Elizabeth Cady Stanton labored for women's rights, and Mary Lyon and Emma Willard were two of the many striving to improve educational opportunities for girls. (See p. 132.) With the single exception of the antislavery drive, no other reform germinating in the period had a greater ultimate effect on American society than the improvement and extension of women's roles.

SLAVERY AND DEMOCRACY

When Eastern writers like Thoreau and Melville turned their attention to the Southern states, they were far less concerned with the books of Southern authors than with the institution of slavery. Yet, with some rare exceptions, cultured and creative Easterners entered the antislavery cause on a wave of popular sentiment; few of them pioneered actively in the movement for abolition of the South's "peculiar institution."

In the 1820s, relatively humble men like the Philadelphia Quaker Benjamin Lundy were in the vanguard of the abolition fight. But in Boston in 1831 a Massachusetts journeyman printer named William Lloyd Garrison founded *The Liberator,* a violently abolitionist paper. Garrison could see no good in the legal sanctions which protected slavery in half the country. There was perhaps a reflection here of transcendentalists' respect for all men; certainly there was no relationship to the Jacksonians' emphasis on making all white men voters. According to Garrison's concept of Christianity, slavery was sinful. Its sinfulness, not its unfairness nor its economic inefficiency, motivated *The Liberator's* editor. Fanatical in his single-track idealism, he attacked the Constitution of the United States as "a convenant with death and an agreement with hell." It was hardly surprising that neither Emerson nor Hawthorne nor Holmes would underwrite such extremism in a day when John Quincy Adams, himself antislavery but no Garrisonian, described the Abolition party as small and shallow.

From 1833 on, the New England Quaker, John Greenleaf Whittier, contributed poems as well as prose and organizing ability to the abolitionists' campaign. Longfellow in 1842 published a few antislavery poems but never became a Garrison adherent. Lowell wrote for the *National Anti-Slavery Standard.* Other younger authors—Thoreau, Melville, and Walt Whitman—were repelled by slavery and said so. Then, while the conservative Holmes and Hawthorne continued to abstain from the agitation, Emerson swung around in the 1850s to laud John Brown (see p. 230) and to compare his gallows to the cross of Jesus. It is not astonishing to find Parker, Channing, and other Unitarians of their individualistic bent among the most out-spoken antislavery recruits. Nor does it seem strange that Harriet Beecher Stowe, author of *Uncle Tom's Cabin* (1852), was the daughter, wife, and sister of Calvinist ministers—and a woman abundantly aware of her own powerful New England conscience. Mrs. Stowe contended that *Uncle Tom's Cabin,* which depicted the separation of families, maternal loss, and other evils inherent in slavery, was inspired by God. Inspired or not, it turned out to be the greatest work of propaganda ever written by an American. Southern fiction, produced by way of reply, had no comparable punch.

The ablest Southern arguments were in the sphere of nonfiction and came mostly from politicians and educators. Many slaveholders agreed with John C. Calhoun and William Harper of South Carolina and Thomas R. Dew of Virginia that—instead of being harmful—slavery was a positive good. Other Southerners merely saw—or thought they saw—a practical necessity of retaining the slave labor system. When *The Impending Crisis of the South,* a book attacking slavery on economic grounds, was published in 1857, its author, Hinton R. Helper of North Carolina, was violently assailed by Southern spokesmen for spreading slanders against their section. On the other hand, the writings of a Virginian, George Fitzhugh, were warmly praised by some of the men who denounced Helper. In *Sociology for the South,* Fitzhugh said slavery was a social, political, and economic blessing—and avowed that men trying to eliminate it were blind to Southern realities.

JUDGMENT OF A VISITOR

Tocqueville's America.   The antislavery crusade was only one aspect of the reform spirit manifest throughout the North (see pp. 264–69). As slavery and abolition interests held no monopoly on Americans' conversations and activities, foreign visitors did not limit their observations to the subject. Indeed, many travelers evinced more abiding interest in other features.

Some visitors from abroad went home to publish scathing reports of what they had found in the United States. Depicted as great tobacco chewers, habitually spitting with inferior aim, Americans were described by these critics as not only crude, dirty, provincial, and unphilosophical but vain and boastful in the bargain. Hypocrisy and unctuousness were included in some congeries of criticisms. "Grog parties commence with prayer" and "terminate with benediction" while "devout smokers say grace over a cigar," a Scotsman reported to his readers. And an equally caustic Englishwoman declared that she "would infinitely prefer sharing the apartment of well-conditioned pigs" to confinement in a Mississippi steamboat's cabin.

Hostile observations, including those of the novelist Charles Dickens, often came from foreigners who landed with plainly visible chips on their shoulders and refused to give suitable recognition to any favorable features. Other pungent remarks were penned by sensationalists in the hope of selling more books at home, or were tossed off in what was construed as the spirit of fun. Certain it is that numerous Americans took much of the criticism far too seriously, failing to differentiate between irresponsible and unjustified attacks on the one hand and sober, searching analyses on the other.

Alexis de Tocqueville, a young French magistrate and member of a noble family, spent nine months in the United States in 1831 and 1832. Although his official purpose was to study the penal system, Tocqueville's noteworthy contribution to political science, sociology, and history was *Democracy in America* (1835). The Frenchman concluded that American democracy was functioning successfully; that its success depended chiefly on separation of church and state and on the absence of centralization; that American political morality was important; and that American democracy was not for export to Europe until such time as Europeans elevated their standards of governmental morality.

Tocqueville was particularly struck by what he saw as an American tendency toward the practical, an avoidance of traditions, and an optimistic hope that in the new social system men would be able to progress rapidly toward perfection. One of his principal theses was that the American system of government derived from a dominant principle—the will of the people—which had been felt all during the nation's history and, in Jackson's time, was presenting its consequences, good and ill, for reflection.

The French magistrate, who stayed long enough to look around thoroughly and to reflect on what he saw and heard, was by no means oblivious to the problems involved in the questions of slavery and race. "The most formidable of all the ills which threaten the future existence of the Union," he wrote, "arises from the presence of a black population upon its territory; and in contemplating the cause of the present embarrassments or of the future dangers of the United States, the observer is invariably led to consider this as a primary fact."

Social mobility was a feature of American life that intrigued Tocqueville. He believed that, with one exception, such mobility would prevent both class stratification and extreme social conflict resulting from it. This exception he found in black-white relationships. If and when Southern blacks "are once raised to the level of freemen," he predicted, "they will soon revolt at being deprived of almost all their civil rights; and as they cannot become the equals of the whites, they will speedily show themselves as enemies." Northern whites, he observed, "avoid the Negroes with increasing care in proportion as the legal barriers of separation are removed."

Tocqueville was not without other doubts concerning the American experiment. He saw a potential danger to freedom of the individual in the possibility that majorities would crush minorities or nibble away at minority rights. He also thought he discerned a trend toward mediocrity in popular leaders and in American culture—this in a country where Emerson, Thoreau, Hawthorne, Melville, Walt Whitman, and Abraham Lincoln all were living when Tocqueville's book went to press. Still, while the French visitor guessed wrong at times, he was remarkably correct in the aggregate.

BIBLIOGRAPHY

Volumes 4 and 5 of Edward Channing's *A History of the United States,* 6 vols. (New York: Macmillan, 1905–25), chronicle the growth of democratic government from 1824 to 1848. For a briefer assessment of the period by an expert in political theory, see Charles M. Wiltse, *The New Nation:1800–1845** (New York: Hill and Wang, 1961). Chilton Williamson, *American Suffrage from Property to Democracy, 1760–1860** (Princeton: Princeton University Press, 1960) contains specific data on voting which had never before been compiled.

The most famous discussion of democracy in the Jacksonian period is contained in the French observer Alexis de Tocqueville's *Democracy in America,** 2 vols., published in several editions since 1835–40. Arthur M. Schlesinger, Jr., won a Pulitzer Prize for *The Age of Jackson** (Boston: Little, Brown, 1945). Claude Bowers vividly describes *The Party Battles of the Jackson Period* (New York: Octagon Books, 1965). For other interpretations of the age of Jackson, see: Glyndon G. Van Deusen, *The Jacksonian Era: 1828–1848** (New York: Harper & Row, 1959); Leonard D. White, *The Jacksonians** (New York: Free Press, 1965); Marvin Meyers, *The Jacksonian Persuasion** (Stanford: Stanford University Press, 1957); Richard P. McCormick, *The Second American Party System** (Chapel Hill: University of North Carolina Press, 1966); Edward Pessen, *Jacksonian America: Society, Personality, and Politics** (Homewood, Ill.: Dorsey Press, 1969);

Peter Temin, *The Jacksonian Economy** (New York: W. W. Norton, 1969); and Lee Benson, *The Concept of Jacksonian Democracy** (Princeton: Princeton University Press, 1961).

John W. Ward, *Andrew Jackson: Symbol for an Age** (New York: Oxford University Press, 1962) places emphasis on nonpolitical aspects of the Jackson period. Marquis James, *Andrew Jackson,* Vol. II, *Portrait of a President** (New York: Grosset and Dunlap, 1956) is a sympathetic account of "Old Hickory" and his political career. James Parton, *The Presidency of Andrew Jackson,** Vol. III of *The Life of Andrew Jackson,* Robert V. Remini, ed. (New York: Harper & Row, 1967) has an illuminating introduction by Remini. Remini's own writings include *Martin Van Buren and the Making of the Democratic Party** (New York: W. W. Norton, 1970), *The Election of Andrew Jackson** (Philadelphia: J. B. Lippincott, 1963), *Andrew Jackson** (New York: Harper & Row, 1969), and *Andrew Jackson and the Bank War** (New York: W. W. Norton, 1968).

Charles S. Sydnor, *The Development of Southern Sectionalism, 1819–1848** (Baton Rouge: Louisiana State University Press, 1968) is a scholarly treatment of this important Southern trend. A detailed discussion of the important nullification controversy will be found in Chauncey S. Boucher, *The Nullification Controversy in South Carolina* (Westport, Conn.: Greenwood Press, 1969). A more recent interpretation is found in William W. Freehling, *Prel-*

ude to Civil War: The Nullification Controversy in South Carolina, 1816–1836* (New York: Harper & Row, 1966). Jackson's anti-Bank policies are discussed in Ralph C. H. Catterall, The Second Bank of the United States (Chicago: University of Chicago Press, 1903; reprint, 1960) and in Thomas P. Govan, Nicholas Biddle: Nationalist and Public Banker, 1786–1844 (Chicago: University of Chicago Press, 1959).

Robert G. Gunderson has written a delightful account of events surrounding the election of 1840 in The Log-Cabin Campaign (Lexington: University of Kentucky Press, 1957). Robert J. Morgan deals with Tyler's presidency from the viewpoint of a political scientist in A Whig Embattled (Lincoln: University of Nebraska Press, 1954). John Tyler's White House bride, the vivacious and very young Julia Gardiner, lives again in Robert Seager, And Tyler Too (New York: McGraw-Hill, 1963). Bray Hammond, Banks and Politics in America from the Revolution to the Civil War* (Princeton: Princeton University Press, 1957) is valuable for political-entrepreneurial interpretations of the period. Douglass C. North, The Economic Growth of the United States, 1790–1860* (New York: W. W. Norton, 1966) is recommended. And few basic books are fresher or more provocative than Henry Cohen, Business and Politics in America from the Age of Jackson to the Civil War: The Career Biography of W. W. Corcoran (Westport, Conn.: Greenwood Publishing Corporation, 1971).

Bernard De Voto, Year of Decision: 1846* (Boston: Houghton Mifflin, 1961) is a dramatic treatment of Western developments. Commercial interests and westward expansion are discussed in Norman A. Graebner, Empire on the Pacific (New York: Ronald Press, 1955). Frederick Merk, Manifest Destiny and Mission in American History* (New York: Vintage Books, 1963) and The Monroe Doctrine and American Expansionism, 1843–1849 (New York: Alfred A. Knopf, 1966) are products of a major authority's mature scholarship. Frederick J. Turner, Frontier and Section* (Englewood Cliffs, N. J.: Prentice-Hall, 1961) is an important collection of essays by an oft-cited master.

For a discerning reevaluation of the West in history and literature, see Henry N. Smith, Virgin Land* (New York: Vintage Books, 1957). Walter P. Webb, The Great Plains* (New York: Universal Library, 1957) is a regional study by an authority. A classic of the frontier, Josiah Gregg's Commerce of the Prairies,* abridged ed. by Milo M. Quaife (Lincoln: University of Nebraska Press, 1967) presents the retouched account of a Santa Fe trader. Other scholarly and readable surveys of the period of Western expansion are Grant Foreman, Five Civilized Tribes* (Norman: University of Oklahoma Press, 1971) and Indian Removal (Norman: University of Oklahoma Press, 1969); William T. Hagan, American Indians* (Chicago: University of Chicago Press, 1961), John F. Stover, American Railroads* (Chicago: University of Chicago Press, 1961) and Paul W. Gates, The Farmer's Age, 1815–1860* (New York: Harper & Row, 1968).

Students who enjoy the biographical approach to history may wish to read all or parts of Samuel F. Bemis, John Quincy Adams, 2 vols. (Alfred A. Knopf, 1949, 1956); Charles M. Wiltse, John C. Calhoun, 3 vols. (New York: Russell & Russell, 1970); Glyndon G. Van Deusen, The Life of Henry Clay* (Boston: Little, Brown, 1937); R. L. Rusk, The Life of Ralph Waldo Emerson (New York: Columbia University Press, 1957); Charles Sellers, James K. Polk, 2 vols. to date (Princeton: Princeton University Press, 1957, 1966); Charles H. Foster, The Rungless Ladder: Harriet Beecher Stowe and New England Puritanism (New York: Cooper Square Publishers, 1954, reprint, 1970); Holman Hamilton, Zachary Taylor, 2 vols. (Hamden, Conn.: Archon Books, 1966), or Claude M. Fuess, Daniel Webster, 2 vols. (New York: Plenum Publishing Corporation, 1968). For the colorful details of political campaigns from 1824 through 1848, see Volumes 1 and 2 of Arthur M. Schlesinger, Jr., ed., History of American Presidential Elections, 4 vols. (New York: Chelsea House, 1971).

Volumes 5, 6, and 7 of a pioneer work in the field of social history, John B. McMaster's A History of the People of the United States, 8 vols. (New York: Farrar, Straus, & Giroux, 1964), deal with social currents in the first half of the nineteenth century. Social and economic aspects of the Jacksonian era are discussed in Carl Russell Fish, The Rise of the Common Man, 1830–1850* (Chicago: Quadrangle Books, 1971). Van Wyck Brooks, The Flowering of New England* (New York: E. P. Dutton, 1936) treats New England literary developments in detail. Also recommended are Chapters 11–16 in Volume 1 of

Harvey Wish, *Society and Thought in America,* 2 vols. (New York: David McKay Co., 1950), and especially Chapters 18–46 in Robert E. Spiller et al., eds., *Literary History of the United States,* 2 vols. (New York: Macmillan, 1963). For an Englishwoman's view of Jacksonian America, see Frances Trollope, *Domestic Manners of the Americans** (New York: Vintage Books, 1832, reprint, 1970).

Otis A. Singletary, *The Mexican War** (Chicago: University of Chicago Press, 1960), Robert S. Henry, *The Story of the Mexican War* (New York: Frederick Ungar, 1960), and William R. Hogan, *The Texas Republic** (Austin: University of Texas Press, 1969) satisfactorily cover those topics. A valuable assessment of transportation, manufacturing, and the wage earner is contained in George R. Taylor, *The Transportation Revolution, 1815–1860** (New York: Harper & Row, 1968). *Fluctuations in American Business, 1790–1860* (New York: Russell & Russell, 1969) by Walter B. Smith and Arthur H. Cole is an invaluable reference work.

For works on slavery and the racial problem, see the bibliography at the end of Part IV.

*Denotes a paperback.

4

A
House
Divided

By 1850 THE UNITED STATES HAD ATTAINED THE SIZE AND THE PHYSICAL resources of a powerful nation, but it was not yet a nation in the full sense. In fact, there was some doubt as to whether it was a nation at all, or whether it could become one.

Nation or not, however, the United States had grown with remarkable speed. Within a space of forty-seven years this country had moved its western border from the Mississippi River to the Pacific Ocean and had almost trebled its area. What had begun as a string of states along the Atlantic coast had now become a transcontinental two-ocean republic, looking out toward Hawaii, Alaska, and the Far East, as well as toward Europe.

This rapidly expanding republic had made great progress in solving some of the problems that had to be solved if the United States was to be both a democracy of free citizens and a nation with strength among nations. In previous history the governments of large countries had been made strong at the expense of individual freedom and local self-government. Political strength for an empire had meant tyranny for its people, and freedom had meant weakness. But America had escaped the choice between internal tyranny and external weakness through the device of a federal system, which left many domestic questions for local action while throwing the collective weight of all the states behind the action of the Union in matters which concerned them as a group. Under this arrangement, freedom did not involve weakness, and strength was not gained at the sacrifice of democratic self-rule. Freedom and local responsibility on the one hand and strength and collective power on the other were effectively reconciled.

America had also enjoyed remarkable success in maintaining a cohesion which at first seemed threatened by the sheer dimensions of continental expansion. When distances were great enough to make communication and the exchange of goods too difficult, too slow, or too expensive, governments which tried to span them had tended to break in pieces unless they concentrated all power in absolute rulers. But in America the development first of turnpikes and canals and then of steamboats and railroads—not to mention the telegraph—was making travel and communication swift and the movement of goods cheap and easy. Consequently, the country was acquiring greater cohesion even as it was growing larger.

Even so, at mid-century it was still uncertain whether nationalizing forces would complete the forging of a nation, or whether their very pressure could cause a disruption of the rather loose-jointed Union. Indeed, the fact that stronger ties were developing brought the question to a crisis more sharply, for the growth of federal power led many Americans to believe that their country ought to maintain uniform values throughout the Union and enforce basic American ideals in all the states. When this concept led to an attack upon slavery, which was a basic institution of labor in the Southern states, these states were prompted, in turn, to defend a theory that ultimate power lay in the states and not in the Union, that the Union was a voluntary association of separate and autonomous states rather than a consolidated nation of states welded into a single unit, and that the states could go out of the Union by their separate act just as they had come into it.

The effort of the Southern states to put this idea into operation led to a four-year Civil War (1861–65), which constituted the greatest internal crisis in American history. The waging of the war settled the question of the nature of the American system. The Union became a single nation, consisting of member states with a diminished power to deal with essentially local affairs. After the war, the Civil War amendments imposed limitations upon the states and thus wrote into the Constitution the ultimate ascendancy of the federal authority in the Republic.

The victory of the Union had vested in the central government immense potential strength which would remain largely untapped until the twentieth century. The emancipation of the slaves had broadened the application of democracy and had reaffirmed—at least in principle—the worth of each human being and his right to freedom. But unfortunately this affirmation was only in principle; and in the decades after the "Reconstruction" which followed the Civil War, the whole nation acquiesced in the segregation and disfranchisement of black Americans. Thus a vital problem of democracy in the realm of race relations was left unsolved, to arise again in acute form in the twentieth century.

Like all men everywhere, the men of the Civil War generation could hope only to solve the problems of their own time. By fighting the war, they did solve a major problem in a way that was crucial for the future of America. But they shared the irony which overtakes each generation—namely, that even the solutions they achieve involve unforeseen challenges for the values they defend. The preservation of the Union meant also the triumph of industrial America, and this triumph meant that Americans were moving into a different world—a world where the cherished values of democracy, of freedom, of individualism, and of the general welfare would have to be reinterpreted and reaffirmed in a new kind of republic not only stronger and greater but also infinitely more complicated than the one that the Founding Fathers had established or that Abraham Lincoln had fought a war to save.

The historiography of the Civil War and Reconstruction offers a vivid example of how interpretations of the past reflect preoccupations and attitudes of the present. By 1890 most white people in both North and South agreed that while slavery had been wrong and Northern victory in the war probably a good thing, Reconstruction was a disastrously ill-advised attempt to elevate freed slaves to positions of equality and power for which they were not qualified. The national consensus in favor of white supremacy formed the basis of most historical treatments of Reconstruction until the 1950s. According to these treatments, vengeful Republicans forced black suffrage upon a prostrate South that for more than a decade reeled helplessly under the corrupt and ignorant rule of carpetbaggers, scalawags, and blacks. Goaded to a just fury, white Southerners turned upon their tormentors and finally overthrew the "Black Republicans" in 1877 to redeem the South from plunder and ruin.

In the 1930s and 1940s some historians extended this interpretation backward in time to include the causes of the Civil War. They portrayed the South as the victim of vicious abolitionist propaganda and demagogic antislavery politicians who stirred up sectional hatred. Slavery, in this view, was a benign institution that would have gradually and peacefully evolved into freedom if Northern agitators had not provoked a war that, while abolishing slavery, so embittered race relations in the South that reconciliation was postponed for generations, if not forever.

A fundamental revision of these interpretations accompanied the civil rights movement of the 1950s and 1960s. This revision had been anticipated, of course, by some earlier scholars, especially black historians such as W. E. B. Du Bois and Carter G. Woodson. The new interpretations drew parallels between the abolitionists and Radical Republicans of the Civil War generation and the civil rights workers of the 1960s, between Southern slaveholders or the Reconstruction Ku Klux Klan and the Citizens Councils or the Klan of the 1960s. Instead of an avoidable and tragic conflict, the Civil War became an inevitable clash between irreconcilable ideologies that accomplished a desirable social revolution—emancipation. Instead of a vengeful effort to humiliate a beaten foe, Reconstruction became an admirable attempt to create an interracial democracy in the South, an attempt that nevertheless failed because it did not go far enough in the direction of redistributing wealth and power in the South.

These conflicting interpretations illustrate that history is not what *happened*, but rather what historians *say* about what happened. The past, like the present, is complex and ambiguous; we can never know all of it and must be content with flashes of insight that illuminate small corners of reality. Historians must ask questions of the past, but their answers (and indeed the questions themselves) will be colored by their own biases and limitations as fallible human beings.

FOR THOUGHT AND DISCUSSION

1. How might the nation have solved the problem of slavery without war?

2. In their willingness to break the law and in other respects, what groups of protesters in recent years have most resembled the abolitionists?

3. Was Reconstruction a nightmare of suppression, corruption, and plunder or a fulfillment of the American dream of equality? Did Southern whites, Northerners, or the freed slaves bear most of the responsibility for the collapse of Reconstruction governments?

4. Can Lincoln fairly be called a racist?

5. What were the long-term consequences of slavery for American blacks? For American whites?

6. Does the treatment of immigrants from the mid-nineteenth century on, coupled with the animosity of white immigrants toward black Americans, make the pecking order a more appropriate metaphor for our society than the melting pot?

insure domesTic

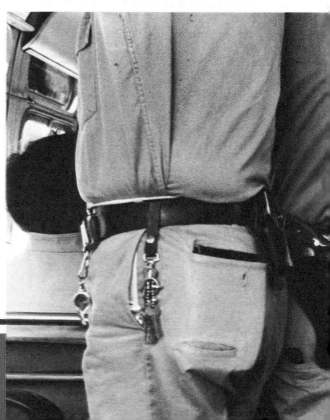

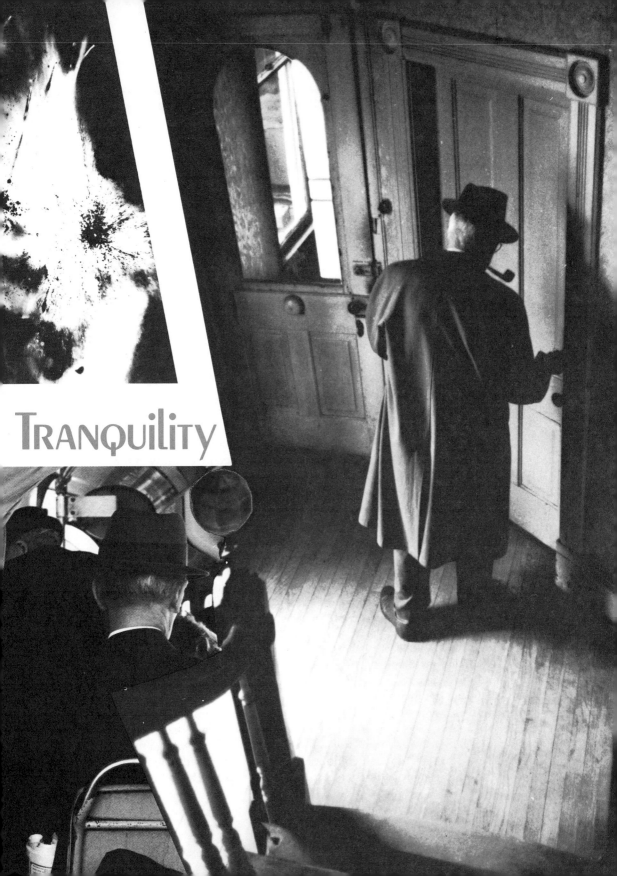

Tranquility

CHAPTER 10

THE SECTIONAL CRISIS 1848–61

THE ORIGINS OF SECTIONALISM

The Transcontinental Republic. Between 1846 and 1848, with the settlement of the Oregon question and the Treaty of Guadalupe Hidalgo, the United States became in the full sense a two-ocean transcontinental republic. Except for Alaska, Hawaii, and a small segment of Arizona which would be acquired by the Gadsden Treaty in 1853, the country had reached its present territorial limits. Growth had been remarkable; within forty-five years the western boundary had moved from the Mississippi River to the Pacific Ocean.

In one sense, the acquisition of the Southwest marked a fulfillment of American nationalism. No other nation on earth had grown so rapidly, and no people were prouder of their nation than the Americans, who boasted incessantly of the superiority of republican institutions. Yet, ironically, the climax of national growth also brought with it a crisis of national unity, for it precipitated a bitter rivalry between two dissimilar sections of the country—areas divided by the Mason-Dixon line and the Ohio River.

The problem of geographical rivalries was not a new one in the United States. In a country larger than all of western Europe, with immense diversity of soil, terrain, and climate, conflicts had arisen more than once between the economic interests of one area and those of another. In fact, American history has been full of such conflicts, and they have often been marked by a division between East and West. This was true, for instance, in the contest over the Bank of the United States in the time of Jackson, and again in the battle between the advocates of the coinage of silver and the defenders of the gold standard in 1896. The theme of sectional rivalry has been so persistent that historians sometimes dispute whether the deepest antagonisms in American history have been between conflicting social classes or ethnic groups or religious denominations or between conflicting sections.

Thus, the sectional crisis between North and South, which approached its climax between 1848 and 1860, was in no sense unique, but it did reach a unique pitch of intensity. Usually, competing sectional forces have sought only to gain advantage over one another within a Union which both accept, but on this occasion the South became so alienated that it made a titanic effort to withdraw from the Union.

The Southern Way of Life. Historians have never been able to agree on any one factor as the primary cause of this division, but they do agree in recognizing a cluster of contributing factors. As far back as the seventeenth century, North and South had developed along dissimilar lines. Virginia, Maryland, and the colonies to the South had based their economy on crops which were limited to latitudes of warm climate and a long growing season. Tobacco, the first of these to be introduced in the colonies, was followed by rice and indigo in Carolina, sugar in Louisiana, and, most important, by cotton throughout the lower South. For the cultivation of these crops the plantation had evolved as the economic unit of production, and within the plantation system the labor supply had grown to consist of blacks imported from Africa as slaves. Slave labor did not become dominant until the eighteenth century, but even before the American Revolution, slaves had come to outnumber free persons in the plantation districts. In 1850, 32 percent of the South's total population was held in slavery, and in South Carolina and Mississippi a majority of the population consisted of slaves.

Slavery. Slavery presented a supreme paradox, for while the slave was a human being, he was also a piece of property. The complex relationships between masters and slaves reflected this paradox. On the one hand, most white Christians recognized the slave's humanity and believed that he had an immortal soul to be saved (of course the idea of a better life after death could also be useful in diverting slave unrest into religious zeal). The law viewed slaves as human beings by making them liable to punishment for serious crimes. Some masters insisted on a wedding service for slave couples even though they could not legally be married. On plantations where blacks and whites mingled closely in everyday life, relations of intimacy and affection often developed. Even the proslavery stereotype of the "happy and carefree" slave, a reflection more of the white man's wishful thinking than of reality, was a backhanded way of admitting the slave's right to human happiness.

On the other hand, the slave was a chattel—a piece of property. He could be bought, sold, mortgaged, bequeathed by will, or taken in payment for debt if his master became bankrupt. He could not legally marry, nor own property, nor, in most states, be taught to read or write. A master might let him have a family, earn money, and even buy his freedom, but until he was free, money, wife, and children could all be taken from him at any moment.

The evils of slavery can be looked at in several ways. Many abolitionists condemned slavery primarily for its physical harshness—the flogging and branding of slaves, the separation of mothers and children at the auction block, the brutal labor conditions, especially for slaves who had been "sold down the river" to work in the sugarcane fields, and the low standard of diet, clothing, and housing. Slaves experienced much cruelty and hardship no doubt, but many slaves were kindly treated. The worst feature of slavery was probably its psychological effect upon the slave, a point increasingly emphasized by abolitionists. The slave's extreme dependence on his master retarded his maturing and, in some cases, "infantilized" his personality. The male slave could not be an adequate husband and father, because he could not protect his woman and his children. The female slave was more or less accessible sexually to men of the master class.

Of course this does not mean that all slaves were "infantilized" or that they were totally dependent. White men who operated successful plantations knew that they needed efficient labor, and no labor is efficient unless it is voluntary. Slaves could sometimes win better treatment by "dragging their feet" or hiding out in the woods for a day or two, just at the peak of the harvest, when labor was needed most. The overseer might flog them, but he could not afford to lose their labor, and he would not keep his job as overseer if he had too much trouble with the slaves.

Moreover, despite repression the slaves sustained a vigorous black culture largely independent of surrounding white institutions. Natural leaders in the slave quarters often became eloquent preachers in the "invisible institution" of the black church, whose congregations worshipped apart from whites (sometimes secretly) in spite of laws to the contrary. Some of these preachers, especially Gabriel Prosser in 1800 and Nat Turner in 1831, plotted armed insurrections to strike for freedom. The slaves created the most original and moving music in antebellum America—the spirituals— which expressed their longing for freedom as well as their resignation to sorrow, and evolved after the Civil War into the blues and eventually jazz. Recent research suggests that while slavery made stable family life difficult, a majority of slaves nevertheless formed strong ties of kinship and family. Thus although bondage crippled many of its victims morally and psychologically, the countervailing force of a positive black culture provides an impressive example of survival in the face of adversity.

If slavery had detrimental effects upon the slaves, it also had serious effects upon the Southern whites. They lived very much on the defensive, ever fearful of slave insurrection and ever conscious that slavery was condemned throughout most of the civilized world. As a result they isolated themselves more and more, imposing an "intellectual blockade" to keep out not only abolitionist ideas but any social ideas involving very much freedom or change. To defend their system, they idealized the society as romantic and chivalric—and, at its best, they realized their ideal in the attainment of a real aristocracy. But the paternalistic tradition was maintained at a high cost, for it tended to make society static and to prevent change.

The Southern system, its rural life and its slave labor, had led to the development of a somewhat conservative temper, a marked stratification of social classes, and a paternalistic type of society. The power of every landowner to rule his own workers on his own plantation had prevented the growth of a strong public authority. As a result, violence was frequent, and qualities of personal courage and physical prowess were especially valued. For instance, the practice of dueling, which had died out in the North, still prevailed. The taboo against women working outside the home was far stronger than in the North; even women schoolteachers in the South were often Northerners.

The Northern Way of Life. It would be a mistake to think of the North as presenting a total contrast, for the majority of people in the free states also engaged in agriculture and lived a rural life. But the Northern economy and Northern life were more diversified. In the absence of a valuable export crop such as tobacco or cotton, New England Yankees had turned early to commerce as a means of securing money to buy the imports they needed. During the Napoleonic wars, when their commerce was disrupted and the supply of imported manufactures was cut off, they had begun a manufacturing industry. As manufacturing grew, cities grew with it. Prosperity and rapid economic growth fostered a belief in progress and innovation quite different from the more traditional (or static) attitudes of the South. Although the factory system brought with it a certain amount of exploitation of labor through low wages, the fact that all men were free made for greater mobility, greater equality, more democracy, and less sharply defined social stratification than in the South. The North grew to value the commercial virtues of thrift, enterprise, and hard work, in contrast to the more military virtues which held a priority in the South.

Such differences as these can easily be exaggerated, for a great deal of frontier Americanism prevailed in both the North and the South. Evangelical Protestantism was the dominant religion of both sections. The materialistic pursuit of wealth motivated cotton planters as well as Yankee industrialists. To a European, all Americans seemed bumptiously democratic, and in Southern politics the Whig party, favored by most planter aristocrats, could not have competed against the Democratic party at all unless it had adopted the democratic symbols of the log cabin, the coonskin hat, and the cider barrel.

THE BASES OF SECTIONAL ANTAGONISM

Regional dissimilarity, however, need not lead to conflict. In the United States today, states of the farm belt differ greatly from those of the Atlantic seaboard, but we tend to think of these differences as making the areas complementary, rather than antagonistic to each other. The antagonism which drove North and South to war in the mid-nineteenth century, therefore, needs to be explained.

Economic Causes. In one sense the antagonism was economic, for the dissimilar economic interests of the North and the South caused them to favor opposite economic policies and therefore to clash politically. Essentially, the South, with its cotton economy, produced raw materials for a textile industry centered in Britain. Accordingly, the South sold on the world market, and in return it needed to buy its manufactured goods where they were cheapest, which was also in the world market, and to keep down taxes and governmental costs as much as possible.

For the North, the need was different. Eastern manufacturers, who could not produce as cheaply as the British, needed a tariff to protect them against ruinous competition (or to increase their margins of profits), and Western grain farmers who had no good way of sending their crops to market needed turnpikes and canals ("internal improvements"). Henry Clay, when he devised his American System, had perceived the possibilities in an alliance by which the Northwest would support the protective tariff needed by the Northeast, and the Northeast would support the internal improvements needed by the Northwest. Not only could each gain its objective, but also each would serve as both a market and a source of supply for the other. Eastern cities would consume Western grain and provide manufactures for the West, while the grain belt would buy manufactured goods from the cities and provide foodstuffs for them.

But the South failed to fit into this scheme. For the South, internal improvements meant only that the South would be paying part of the governmental costs of a program from which it did not benefit, and, indeed, which diverted trade away from the South's own Mississippi River system, which drew trade southward toward New Orleans. The tariff meant only that the South would be prevented from buying its manufactures from those who bought its raw materials and would be forced by law to pay a higher, tariff-supported price for its manufactures. As the Virginian, John Randolph of Roanoke, had angrily declared, "we shall only pay more for worse goods."

Because of these economic factors, North and South tended to vote against each other on questions of tariff, internal improvements, and the extension of the power of the central government in general. Their rivalry had reached a crisis at the time of the Nullification Controversy in 1833, when South Carolina was ready to defy federal law (see p. 155). The crisis had been averted only when other Southern states had not supported South Carolina. The South as a whole resented federal economic policies but never opposed them to the point of breaking up the Union, to which most Southerners felt strong patriotic loyalty.

The Growth of the Slavery Issue. A deeper cause of division, however, was the institution of slavery. Until the 1770s slavery had scarcely been regarded as a moral question at all—except by the Quakers—and pious Yankee shipowners of stern Puritan faith had engaged in the slave trade to Africa just as readily as Southern tobacco and rice planters had bought slaves for labor. As late as 1780 there was no division into slave states and free states; slaves were held in every state of the Union, and they were less numerous in the North only because they were less profitable there. But in the late eighteenth century (during the Age of Reason, or the Enlightenment), slavery came under attack from believers in natural law, human equality, and the rights of man. At the same time, emphasis in the churches shifted from a limited concern with the personal salvation of the individual to a fuller application of Christian teaching in relation to human society. Thus, the savage penal code of earlier times was modified, various social reforms were adopted, and slavery came under attack.

The states from Pennsylvania northward shared in this movement against slavery. By 1804 all of them had adopted laws for the gradual or immediate emancipation of their slaves, and in 1808 Congress had prohibited the importation of any more slaves from Africa. For a time it appeared that the South might also participate in this movement. Southern Enlightenment leaders like Jefferson condemned slavery in the abstract; antislavery societies were active in the South; and the restriction of slavery to the rice and tobacco economy, which was static and no longer very profitable, meant that the Southern economy as a whole did not depend on slave labor. But Jefferson never freed more than a handful of his own slaves; the Southern antislavery societies devoted their efforts mainly to encouraging the emigration of free blacks; and the tenor of Southern antislavery sentiment, apart from the Quakers and the early Methodists, was one of anguished handwringing over an inherited evil rather than vigorous action for its abolition.

The introduction of cotton injected greater vitality into the slave system. In one generation, the cultivation of short staple cotton spread across the lower South from middle Georgia to the banks of the Brazos in Texas. Every decade from 1800 to 1860 the value and the volume of the crop doubled. In this dynamic and expanding economy, the price of slaves rose and fell with the price of cotton. Slavery went with cotton into the new areas, and by 1820 it was completely interwoven into the whole Southern system.

While this was happening, the humanitarian crusade against slavery in Great Britain (which abolished slavery in the West Indies in 1833), in France (which abolished it in 1848), and in the Northern states (where the abolitionists became increasingly militant in their denunciations) led the South to a defensive reaction. By 1830 Southern leaders were no longer saying, as some had said earlier, that slavery was an evil but was too deeply rooted to be abolished at once. Instead, they were beginning to assert that slavery was a positive good. They defended it with claims that it had been sanctioned in the Bible; that the Negro was biologically inferior to the white; that the exploitation of Negro workers by the slavery system was not so harsh as the exploitation of white workers by a wage system in which the worker received only a bare subsistence when he was working and no subsistence at all when he was not; and that, since social divisions were inevitable, assigning leadership to one class and subordination to another was better than having an endless struggle between classes.

Soon the South became so defensive about criticism that it would not tolerate the expression of antislavery opinion. An intellectual blockade, as it has been called, was imposed upon antislavery ideas. Meanwhile, in the North, the growth of reform activity and humanitarian feeling created a more and more widespread conviction that slavery was morally wrong.

In spite of this disagreement on the ethics of slavery, several factors prevented a clash over the question. To begin with, slavery was widely regarded as a matter for the states locally rather than for the federal government nationally. (South Carolina's nullification attempt can be seen as a challenge to the government's authority in this area as well as in setting tariffs.) At that time, people regarded the federal system more as a loose association of states and less as a consolidated nation, and they were willing to leave many important questions to state action. Further, it was generally understood that the Constitution, in its "three-fifths" and fugitive slave clauses (see p. 83), protected the South's right to practice slavery. It was on the basis of such provisions that the Southern states had agreed to join the Union.

Apart from the question of legal or constitutional obligation, many Americans took the position that the harmony of the Union was simply more important than the ethics of slavery—that the slave question must not be permitted to weaken the Union and that the abolitionists were wrong to keep up constant agitation on an issue which caused sectional antagonism. The abolitionists, who were in the minority, felt that the Union was not worth saving unless it was based upon freedom.

The Question of Extending Slavery. All this meant that as long as the institution of slavery was confined to the existing slave states, few Northerners were willing to act against it, and it was not an explosive question politically. But when the question of extending slavery to new areas arose, the opposition was far more determined. As early as the Ordinance of 1787, the old Congress under the Articles of Confederation had agreed to exclude slavery from the region north of the Ohio. Not only were sincere antislavery men determined to "contain" slavery, as we might now express it, but also many people who cared nothing about the evils of slavery wanted to reserve unsettled areas for white men only, and many others wanted to bring these new areas to the support of the North in the economic struggle between North and South. The South, conversely, was equally convinced that the growth of the country should not be all on the side of the North, reducing the South to a defenseless minority. This feeling made the South unwilling to concede even the areas where there was little prospect of extending slavery.

Because of these attitudes, the acquisition of any new area, the organization of any new territory, and the admission of any new state had always involved a possible flare-up over the slavery question. There had been such a crisis in 1820, when Missouri applied for admission to statehood as the first state (except Louisiana) to be formed out of the Louisiana Purchase. In the same way, the prospect of acquisition of territory from Mexico as a result of the Mexican War brought on a more protracted and more serious crisis beginning in 1846.

A few months after the beginning of the Mexican War, President Polk asked Congress to appropriate $2 million to be used in negotiating for land to be acquired from Mexico at the termination of the war. Many Northern Democrats were at this time angry with Polk, partly because he had supported a low tariff and partly because they felt he had violated the promise on which he was elected. His platform, calling for the "reoccupation" of Oregon and the "re-annexation" of Texas, and for "all of Oregon or none," had put the question of expansion on a bisectional basis by promising Oregon, sure to be free territory, for the North, and Texas, which already had slavery, for the South. But after becoming President, he had compromised on Oregon, accepting the boundary at the 49th parallel instead of at 54° 40', while pushing expansion toward the southwest to the fullest extent by waging war with Mexico.

The Wilmot Proviso and the Calhoun Resolutions.   This was the state of affairs when David Wilmot, a Democrat from Pennsylvania, introduced a resolution in the House of Representatives that slavery should be prohibited in any territory acquired with the $2 million Polk requested. This free-soil resolution passed the House, where the North was stronger, but failed to pass in the Senate, where the South was stronger. The disagreement of Senate and House marked a deadlock in Congress which lasted for four years, blocked the organization of governments for the new areas, and caused a steady increase in sectional tension.

In 1848, at the end of the Mexican War, the victorious United States acquired the present states of Nevada, California, and Utah, most of Arizona and New Mexico, and parts of Colorado and Wyoming by means of the Treaty of Guadalupe Hidalgo; in this treaty also, Mexico relinquished all claims to Texas above the Rio Grande. In the same year gold was discovered in California, and by 1849 the Gold Rush was in full swing. The need for organizing the new land was urgent, and the territorial question became the foremost issue in public life. At one extreme on this question stood Wilmot and the "free-soilers," both Whig and Democrat, who demanded the exclusion of slavery from the new areas by act of Congress. At the other extreme, most Southern Whigs and Democrats adopted the position of John C. Calhoun. Calhoun argued that the territories were owned in common by all the states (rather than by the federal government, which was only a joint agent for the states) and that all citizens had an equal right to take their property (including slaves) to the common territory. Therefore, Congress had no power under the Constitution to exclude slavery from any territory.

The Doctrine of Popular Sovereignty. Political leaders who wanted some kind of adjustment or middle ground were not satisfied with either Wilmot's or Calhoun's alternative, one of which conceded nothing to the South, the other nothing to the North. They sought a more "moderate" position, and some of them advocated an extension of the Missouri Compromise line at 36° 30' to the Pacific. But most of them were more attracted by a proposal sponsored by Lewis Cass, senator from Michigan, for what was called "popular sovereignty" or "squatter sovereignty." Cass contended that the fairest and most democratic solution would be to let the people in the territories decide for themselves whether they would have slavery, just as the people in the states had already decided. Cass' proposal offered an attractive means for keeping the slavery question out of federal politics, but it contained one ambiguity which he adroitly refused to clarify: it did not specify *when* the people in the territories should make this decision. If they could make the decision as soon as the territory was organized, free soil could be attained by popular vote as easily as by congressional vote. According to Calhoun, popular exclusion would be just as wrong as congressional exclusion, for it would mean that Congress was giving to the territory a power which Congress did not have and therefore could not give. But if the voters in a territory could decide on slavery only when they applied for statehood, this would mean that popular sovereignty left the territories open to slavery quite as much as Calhoun's position did.

Far from reducing the amount of support for popular sovereignty, however, this ambiguity actually added to the attractiveness of the doctrine: antislavery men argued that popular sovereignty would result in free territories, while proslavery advocates contended that it guaranteed slavery a fair chance to establish itself during the period before statehood.

THE COMPROMISE OF 1850

While these various positions on the territorial extension of slavery were being developed, the impasse in Congress continued. For three entire sessions covering most of the Polk administration, nothing could be voted for California or the Southwest, and it was only after long delay that an act to organize Oregon Territory without slavery was adopted.

In 1848, when the two national parties faced this question in a presidential election, both of them evaded it: the Democrats by nominating Cass, on a platform which still did not say whether the people of a territory could prohibit slavery during the territorial period; the Whigs by nominating a military hero, Zachary Taylor, who had never been in politics, without any platform whatever. In the election campaign, which was a kind of contest between frank evasion and concealed evasion, Taylor was triumphant. He became President in 1849.

Early Secessionist Sentiment. Meanwhile, the House of Representatives had repeatedly voted in favor of Wilmot's principle of free soil by congressional action. The seeming imminence of a free-soil victory had, in turn, aroused bitter resentment in the South, and for the first time many Southerners began to think of withdrawing from the Union if Congress voted to prevent them from taking their slaves into areas they had helped to win and to pay for. By 1848, Southerners in Congress were beginning to speak rather freely of disunion. After Taylor was elected, Southerners realized that, although he was a Louisiana slaveholder, he was not going to block free-soil legislation, and they began to organize Southern resistance. In October 1849 a state convention in Mississippi called for a convention of Southern state delegates to meet at Nashville, Tennessee, the following June to work out a united Southern position. Five Southern states officially elected delegates to such a convention, and representatives were unofficially chosen from four others.

Thus, when Taylor's first Congress met in December 1849, the need for organizing the area acquired from Mexico was urgent, and the relations between North and South were at a crisis. This crisis became more acute when Taylor announced his support for admitting California directly to statehood, without going through a territorial stage, and his intention to support the same plan for New Mexico in due course. Technically, this plan bypassed the question of congressional exclusion, but in substance it would represent a free-soil victory, for the proposed states seemed fairly certain to be free states. At this prospect Southern protests were intensified, and though historians today disagree as to whether the country was close to disunion, certainly many prominent leaders at the time feared that it was.

The Clay Compromise Proposals. Among these leaders fearing disunion was Senator Henry Clay of Kentucky. As a spokesman of the border states, which were always anxious to promote sectional harmony, and as one who had played a leading part in arranging the compromises of 1820 and 1833, Clay was a natural leader of compromise. Although a Whig, he was at odds with President Taylor. Accordingly, Clay came forward, early in the congressional session of 1850, with an elaborate compromise designed to cover the slavery question in all its national aspects. Clay's plan called for: (1) admitting California as a free state; (2) organizing the rest of the Mexican cession into two territories, Utah and New Mexico, which were to decide for themselves whether slavery should be permitted or abolished; (3) awarding New Mexico part of the area on the upper Rio Grande claimed by Texas, but compensating Texas through federal payment of the Texas debt contracted before annexation; (4) abolishing the sale of slaves in the District of Columbia but guaranteeing slavery itself in the District; (5) enacting an effective law to compel the return of fugitive slaves who had escaped into the free states.

Clay's proposal brought on a long, brilliant, and famous series of debates in Congress. Clay himself made an immensely eloquent appeal for his plan as a means of

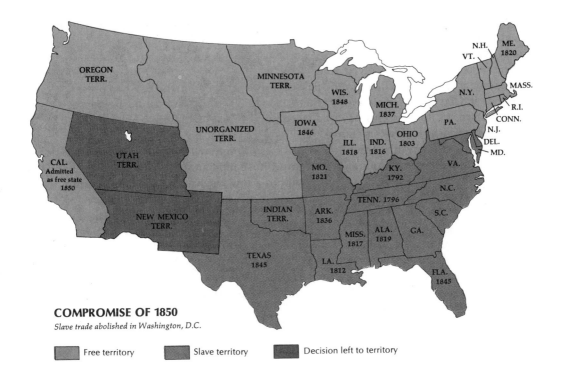

COMPROMISE OF 1850

Slave trade abolished in Washington, D.C.

◻ Free territory   ◻ Slave territory   ◻ Decision left to territory

saving the Union. Calhoun, who did not support the compromise directly, helped it indirectly by coming into the Senate almost in a dying condition to warn solemnly of the danger to the Union and the determination of the South to maintain its rights. The most important speech of the session was made by Daniel Webster, who was Clay's only peer as an orator and who was generally regarded as an antislavery man. On the seventh of March, Webster announced his support of the compromise and made a powerful argument that slavery was naturally excluded from the West by climatic, physical, and agricultural conditions and that there was no need to bring on a crisis by adopting an antislavery law, such as the Wilmot Proviso, to accomplish what had already been settled by physical environment. "I would not re-enact a law of God," said Webster, impressively, "I would not reaffirm an ordinance of nature."

Despite great oratorical support, Clay's "omnibus bill," incorporating all his proposals in one measure, faced heavy opposition. President Taylor was waiting to veto it, and in July it was cut to pieces on the floor by a process of amendment in which Northern and Southern extremists voted together to prevent its passage. Clay—old, worn out, and badly discouraged—went off to Newport for a rest.

The Douglas Strategy. Even before this vote was taken, however, the tide had turned. President Taylor died. His successor, Millard Fillmore, favored the compromise and immediately began to exert presidential influence to support it.

Meanwhile, Stephen A. Douglas, a young and vigorous senator from Illinois, took over the management of the compromise forces in Congress. Douglas was not a great orator, but he was a supremely effective rough-and-tumble debater, a man of immense energy ("a steam engine in breeches" was the phrase), and a most sagacious political tactician. He perceived that there was not a clear majority in favor of the compromise and that it could not be passed in the form in which Clay had presented it, but that if Clay's proposals were taken up one by one, each could be passed by a combination of those who favored the compromise and those who favored the particular measure. (For instance, California would be admitted by a majority composed of compromise men and antislavery men, while the Fugitive Slave Act would be adopted by a combination of compromise men and proslavery men.) Douglas applied this strategy so effectively that within a few weeks Clay's entire program was enacted into law.

The adoption of the "Compromise of 1850" ended the crisis. It also broke the long deadlock and gave badly needed political organization to California and the Southwest. Because it brought a great sense of relief to those who had feared for the safety of the Union, it was hailed as a great and final settlement which defused the slavery issue once and for all as a source of discord in the Union.

The Fugitive Slave Act.   In fact, the Great Compromise of 1850 settled far less than it appeared to settle. For Utah and New Mexico it still left open the explosive question Lewis Cass had so carefully avoided: could the citizens of the territory outlaw slavery in the territory? More important, while laying to rest the explosive issue of the Wilmot Proviso, it brought to life the even more explosive issue of the fugitive slave. For the question of the slave in the territories was a legal and abstract question—a question of what was later called "an imaginary Negro in an impossible place"—but the question of the runaway slave was dramatic and real, involving a human creature in quest of freedom who was being hunted down by his fellow man. Finally, the compromise had never commanded a real majority and had been enacted only by finesse. The Southern states accepted it somewhat reluctantly, but Georgia spoke for the rest of them when its legislature voted resolutions that if the compromise were not fully enforced, Georgia would withdraw from the Union. In fact, while the Southern disunionists were agreeing not to demand secession at this time, the Southern unionists were almost forced to agree to the *principle* of secession in order to get the secessionists to agree not to exercise it. Meanwhile, in the North the antislavery forces were pouring their denunciations upon the Fugitive Slave Act and upon Daniel Webster for supporting it. Perhaps never before in American politics had political invective been so bitter.

For a time, the fugitive slave question raised a terrific furor. To appreciate the uproar, one must understand that the law contained a number of very extreme features. It denied trial by jury in the case of alleged fugitives and provided for their cases to be decided by a special federal commissioner. Further, it paid the commissioner a fee that was higher in cases where he returned the alleged fugitive to slavery than in cases where he set him free; though this arrangement was defended on the ground that there was much more paper work in one case than the other, it led to severe criticism. Still further, the law stipulated that any citizen could be called upon to participate in the enforcement process, which meant that antislavery men must not only permit the capture of fugitives but might possibly be made to help in their capture.

Apart from these features of the law itself, the act aroused criticism because in operation it applied not only to slaves who were then running away but also to any slaves who had ever run away. There were many fugitives who had lived quietly in Northern cities for many years and who had been quite safe from arrest under the relatively ineffectual Fugitive Slave Law of 1793, but now, under the act of 1850, they found themselves in real danger. In 1851 a black who had lived in Indiana for nineteen years was torn from his family and sent into slavery. Throughout the North, blacks were terrorized by the law, for those who were not fugitives had reason to fear being kidnapped quite as much as actual runaways had reason to fear being arrested. Consequently, a wave of migration to Canada set in, and several thousand blacks moved to Ontario.

Resistance Against the Fugitive Slave Law.   A series of fugitive slave episodes followed which kept the country at a high pitch of excitement. In Boston, leading citizens openly asserted their intention to violate the law, and in October a "vigilance committee" headed by one of the foremost citizens of Boston, the Reverend Theodore Parker, smuggled two undoubted slaves out of the country. Four months later a crowd, mostly black, seized a prisoner, Shadrach, from the courtroom and spirited him away to Canada. Finally, in April 1851 the government succeeded in returning a slave from Boston, from which city it was boasted that no slave had ever been returned, but this was accomplished only after mobs had surrounded the courthouse for several days. Only once again was a slave, Anthony Burns, returned from Boston; in his case a mob stormed the courthouse in an effort to rescue him, and a large military force was required in order to prevent his rescue.

In other cities, also, rescues and attempted rescues kept the pot boiling, and the fugitive slave question became for a time the foremost issue of the day. Yet the excitement and emotion which the issue generated have made it hard to get at the facts about whether the escape of slaves from the South was numerically significant. On the one hand, Northern antislavery men boasted of their resistance to the law and claimed that they were operating a vast "underground railroad" which had helped 80,000 slaves to escape their pursuers. On the other, spokesmen of the South, indignant at the open violation of the law, complained bitterly that 100,000 slaves had been abducted over a forty-year period. These were probably inflated figures; the underground railroad was more extensive in legend than in reality and more important as a weapon of psychological warfare than as an escape route for slaves. It also appears that in many parts of the North the Fugitive Slave Act received public support and effective enforcement.

There is no doubt, however, that the fugitive question dramatized the issue of slavery to a spectacular degree. The human being in quest of freedom, pursued by man-hunters, was an immensely moving figure, and by changing the focus of the slavery question from the legal status of an imaginary chattel in a remote territory to the human plight of an individual human being in a nearby street, the Compromise of 1850 had, perhaps, created more tension than it relieved.

It is by no means an accident that *Uncle Tom's Cabin* (1851–52), the classic literary protest against slavery, was published less than a year after the enactment of the fugitive law; that the book's most dramatic scene was that of the fugitive slave girl, Eliza, crossing the icebound Ohio River as she was being pursued by a slave trader; or that the book, one of America's all-time best sellers, wrung sympathy and tears from countless people who had never previously been moved by the abolitionists.

Support of the Compromise: The Election of 1852. If the Fugitive Slave law dramatized the issue of slavery, the crisis preceding the Compromise had dramatized the issue of Union. Many Northerners who thoroughly disapproved of slavery felt that the question of Union was more important and must have priority. Consequently, despite fugitive slave episodes, the Compromise received strong support throughout the country, and though there had not been a clear majority in favor of adopting it, there was certainly a clear majority in favor of maintaining it.

The firmness of public support for the Compromise showed up clearly in the election of 1852. As it approached, Millard Fillmore, who had signed the compromise acts while serving out the term of Zachary Taylor, aspired to a term of his own. But in the party convention Northern Whigs blocked the effort of Southern Whigs to nominate Fillmore and forced the nomination instead of General Winfield Scott, who had captured Mexico City in the Mexican War. Scott was the Whigs' third military hero, and they hoped that, like Harrison and Taylor, he would get to the White House on his military record. The adoption of a platform revealed a deep division among the Whigs: though the majority secured the adoption of a plank accepting the Compromise of 1850, including the Fugitive Slave Act, as a final settlement, the opposition was very strong and consisted mostly of delegates who supported Scott. Scott, who was pompous and politically clumsy, tried to get out of this dilemma by saying merely, "I accept the nomination with the resolutions attached," but it was clear that he was not a thoroughgoing supporter of the Compromise.

The Democrats settled their differences between rival candidates by agreeing upon a dark horse, Franklin Pierce of New Hampshire, who had served with gallantry in the Mexican War. Pierce later proved a weak man, but he was an attractive candidate—handsome and pleasing in his manner—and the Democrats gave him united support on a platform that proclaimed the finality of the Compromise.

The position of the two parties gave the voters a fairly clear choice on the question of compromise—Pierce and his party were united on it, the Whigs were not—and the voters exercised their option in a decisive way. They gave Pierce the largest plurality any President had received up to that time, and he carried all but four states—two in the North, two in the South. The defeat smashed the Whig party, which was already badly divided between the "Cotton Whigs" of the South and the "Conscience Whigs" of the North, and though many important figures—including Abraham Lincoln—remained in the Whig organization somewhat longer, it was never a national party after 1852. This meant that only one national party—the Democratic—was left, which in turn meant that there was now only one remaining political organization in which Northern and Southern leaders were still seeking to smooth out sectional disagreements for the sake of party victory.

KANSAS AND NEBRASKA

The Douglas Bill. Pierce's campaign had promised harmony for the Union and finality for the Compromise, but his administration brought just the opposite. His first Congress had barely met in December 1853, when the territorial question arose again in a new form. Stephen A. Douglas wanted to organize territorial government for the region west of Iowa and Missouri. This area lay within the Louisiana Purchase, and since it was north of 36° 30', it had been closed to slavery by the Missouri Compromise of 1820. Douglas, therefore, at first introduced a bill to organize free territories.

But Southern senators voted against his legislation and thus blocked it. They did this in part because they knew that Douglas wanted to promote a transcontinental railroad west from Chicago or some other Northern terminus to the Pacific. They were equally eager to run such a road west from New Orleans; there was simply no reason for them to give their votes to organize another free-soil territory for the purpose of facilitating a Northern railroad. Douglas felt that he had to have their votes, and thus in January 1854 he was led to take the fatal step of agreeing to change his bill so that it would leave the status of slavery in the Kansas-Nebraska region to be settled by popular sovereignty. Douglas made the plausible argument that what he advocated was nothing new and that the legislation of 1850 had already replaced the principle of geographical division with the principle of popular sovereignty.

KANSAS-NEBRASKA ACT, 1854

- Free territory
- Slave territory
- Slavery question to be decided by people

"Appeal of the Independent Democrats." In a widely disseminated tract entitled "Appeal of the Independent Democrats," antislavery men rejected Douglas' argument with furious indignation. They insisted that the act of 1850 applied only to the Mexican cession and was thus merely supplementary to the Missouri Compromise. The South, they asserted, was violating a sacred pledge; in 1820 it had promised to recognize freedom north of 36° 30' in return for the admission of Missouri, and now it was defaulting on the agreement. This argument was not entirely accurate, for, to mention but one point, a majority of Southern congressmen had voted against the act of 1820 to begin with. But the act had stood for thirty-four years, and Douglas was at least reckless, if not wrong, to tamper with it.

The furious blast of indignation that greeted his amended Kansas-Nebraska bill must have told him that he had made a major blunder. But Douglas was bold, aggressive, and tenacious. After committing President Pierce to his bill, he staged an all-out parliamentary battle for enactment. His own resourcefulness in debate enabled him repeatedly to throw his attackers on the defensive, and he conducted a brilliant campaign by which he succeeded in forcing the bill through both houses of Congress.

The Election of 1854. Douglas' success came at a terrible price. He himself had correctly foreseen that the repeal of the Missouri Compromise would "raise the Hell of a storm," but he had not foreseen, as he later said, that he would be able to travel to Chicago by the light of his own burning effigies. Six months after the act was adopted, the congressional elections of 1854 were held. The Whigs were too weak to capitalize on the public reaction; the Republican party had not yet emerged; but the Democrats suffered a stunning setback in the North.

Bloody Kansas. The worst thing about the new Kansas-Nebraska Act was that, even at the price of causing the bitterest kind of sectional hostility, it did not create a real basis for stability in the new territory. It merely changed the terms of the contest, for Douglas and many Northern Democrats believed that popular sovereignty could make Kansas and Nebraska free territories just as well as congressional action could, while proslavery leaders took the repeal of the Missouri Compromise to mean that slavery should prevail in at least one of the two new territories.

Both antislavery and proslavery groups prepared to rush supporters into Kansas to defend their respective positions there. From Missouri, proslavery men, known as Border Ruffians, had a way of riding over into Kansas on election day to vote and to intimidate the free-soilers and then riding back to Missouri. In New England, antislavery men organized an Emigrant Aid Society to send free-soil settlers to Kansas, and though the society never officially purchased weapons for these settlers, the leaders of the society bought rifles with separate funds to arm the emigrants against the proslavery men.

It would have taken a strong President to keep order in Kansas, and Pierce was not strong. He appointed a succession of able governors for the territory, but he would not vigorously support them when they needed his backing. Affairs therefore went from bad to worse. After the proslavery men had stolen an election and Pierce had given recognition to the government thus elected, the free-soil men formed another government of their own. Kansas then had two governments—a proslavery one at Lecompton, legal but not honest; an antislavery one at Lawrence, honest but not legal.

It is a great mistake to think of frontier Kansas as inhabited entirely by men who went there as missionaries for slavery or for freedom. Many settlers were simply land-hungry frontiersmen like those who swarmed into all new territories. Such men were always quick to violence, and all the shooting that took place in Kansas was not because of slavery. But the slavery issue did accentuate the violence and give a pattern to the lawlessness of the frontier.

Thus, with President Pierce denouncing the free-soil government for its illegality, the proslavery forces secured an indictment of the free-soilers by a grand jury which was, of course, of the proslavery men's own choosing. With this indictment an armed mob, or "posse," as it called itself, marched on the free-soil headquarters at Lawrence, where they destroyed the printing press and burned or looted a good deal of property. Four days later John Brown, a free-soiler who carried his views to fanatical lengths, avenged the sacking of Lawrence by leading a body of men to Pottawatomie Creek, where they took five unarmed proslavery settlers from their homes in the dead of night and killed them. These events were part of an escalation of terror and violence in "Bleeding Kansas"; probably two hundred men met violent deaths before a new territorial government used federal troops to restore order four months later.

"The Crime Against Kansas." Meanwhile, the intensity of sectional ill will was both illustrated and heightened by an occurrence in Washington. Charles Sumner, an antislavery senator from Massachusetts, delivered an oration entitled "The Crime Against Kansas" in which, in addition to castigating the slave power as bitterly as he could, he spoke in extremely personal terms about the elderly Senator Andrew P. Butler of South Carolina. He alluded, for instance, to "the loose expectoration" of Butler's speech. A nephew of Butler's in the House of Representatives, Preston Brooks, went to the Senate chamber when the Senate was not in session, found Sumner seated at his desk, and beat him severely with a cane. For several years thereafter Sumner was incapacitated, either by the blows which he received or, according to the best modern medical opinion, by his psychological reaction to the assault. The public significance of this affair, however, lay less in the attack itself than in the fact that a large part of the Northern press made a martyr of Sumner and pictured all Southerners as barbarians, while the South made a hero of Brooks and typed all Yankees as rabid fanatics.

The Character of Franklin Pierce. By this time the Pierce administration was ending as a disaster because of the weakness of the President and the extent to which he let himself be dominated by Southern influence. After failing to prevent repeal of the Missouri Compromise, Pierce might still have saved the peace of the country if he had stood firm for real popular sovereignty in Kansas. But he had instead backed a proslavery regime which was palpably fraudulent, had allowed violence to go unrestrained, and had finally given his support to the idea of statehood with a proslavery government. At this point Stephen A. Douglas had broken with the administration and was fighting hard in Congress to defeat this proslavery government. Thus the political division at this point was less between free-soil and proslavery forces than between the honest application of popular sovereignty and the perversion of it.

Indeed, Pierce had backed the South at almost every point. He had negotiated the Gadsden Purchase (1853) for the acquisition from Mexico of what is now the southernmost part of Arizona because the land in question was strategic for the construction of a transcontinental railroad by the southern route from New Orleans. He had permitted three of his diplomatic emissaries in Europe to meet at Ostend, Belgium, in October 1854 to propose American annexation of Cuba by purchase or, if that failed, by "wresting it from Spain." Cuba had almost 200,000 slaves and would strengthen the power of slavery. (This "Ostend Manifesto," however, aroused such worldwide indignation that the administration was forced to repudiate it.) Moreover, the administration did nothing effective to prevent expeditions by adventurers, called filibusters, who invaded Latin countries from American shores. One such expedition from New Orleans against Cuba failed, and another, led by William Walker against Nicaragua, was temporarily successful.

ON THE EVE OF WAR

The Election of 1856.   At the end of Pierce's term even the Southern Democrats knew that he could not be reelected. The Democrats nominated James Buchanan of Pennsylvania, who, as minister to England, had been out of the country at the time of the Kansas-Nebraska Act (although as one of three authors of the Ostend Manifesto, he was particularly acceptable to the South). Buchanan was Secretary of State under Polk and a veteran of American politics—an old Public Functionary, as he called himself. To run against him, a remnant of the Whigs nominated Millard Fillmore, but the principal opposition came from a new party—the Republicans—formed by "Conscience" Whigs and anti-Nebraska Democrats and springing up very rapidly after 1854. This new party passed over its regular leaders to nominate the dashing but politically inexperienced young explorer of the Rocky Mountains and the Far West, John C. Frémont. In the election that followed, Buchanan carried all the slave states (except Maryland, which voted for Fillmore) and four free states, thus winning the election. But the majority of the North was now backing a party which denounced slavery, along with polygamy (a jab at the Mormons in Utah), as a "relic of barbarism" and which had no organization whatever throughout half the Union.

It is questionable whether, by this time, anyone could have brought the disruptive forces of sectional antagonism under control, but certainly Buchanan could not do it. His cabinet, like Pierce's, was dominated by Southern Democrats, and in February 1858 he forfeited his claims to impartial leadership by recommending the admission of Kansas to statehood under the proslavery and fraudulent Lecompton Constitution. Douglas and other Northern Democrats resisted; thus Douglas lost the Southern support which he had won in 1854, and the Democratic party became deeply divided.

The Dred Scott Decision.   Meanwhile, the Supreme Court handed down a decision which may have been intended to restore sectional peace but which had exactly the opposite effect. This ruling concerned a Missouri slave, Dred Scott, who had been carried by his master first into the free state of Illinois and then into Wisconsin Territory, which was within the Louisiana Purchase north of 36° 30′ and was therefore, under the Missouri Compromise, free territory. After he had been carried back to Missouri, Scott sued for his freedom, and the case was eventually carried up on appeal to the Supreme Court. The justices divided in various ways on several questions that were involved, but essentially the five justices from slave states held that Scott was still a slave, while the four from the free states divided two and two. The principal opinion was rendered by Chief Justice Roger B. Taney, who stated that, during colonial times, blacks had "been regarded as beings so far inferior that they had no rights which the white man was bound to respect." As a description of the conditions which had existed, this statement was substantially correct, but it was widely quoted as expressing Taney's own attitude and was used against him mercilessly. The majority of the court held that a man born a slave was not a citizen and therefore could not bring suit in federal courts. In strict logic, therefore, the court need not have ruled on the other questions Scott raised, but it went on to state that even if he could have sued, he still would not have been free, for the Missouri Compromise was unconstitutional; Congress had no power to exclude slavery from the territories.

In a literal sense the Dred Scott decision added nothing new, for it merely declared void a law which had already been repealed by the Kansas-Nebraska Act three years earlier. But in another sense, it had a shattering effect: it strengthened a conviction in the North that an evil "slave power," bent on spreading slavery throughout the land, was in control of the government and must be checked. It justified Southerners, on the other hand, in believing that the free-soilers were trying to rob them of their legal rights. It struck a deadly blow at the one moderate position—that of popular sovereignty—which lay between the extremes of free-soil and proslavery contentions. If, as the Court ruled, Congress had no power to exclude slavery from a territory by its own act, certainly it could not give a power which it did not possess to the territorial legislature, and without such power there could be no effective popular sovereignty. It made compromise by act of Congress almost impossible. The decision also convinced many free blacks that they had no future in a country that denied them citizenship. It intensified the growing mood of black nationalism and spurred movements for emigration to Haiti or Africa.

The Lincoln-Douglas Debates. The effect of the Dred Scott decision in popularizing sectional extremism showed up clearly in 1858, when Stephen A. Douglas ran for reelection to the Senate from Illinois and was challenged to a series of debates by his Republican opponent, Abraham Lincoln. Lincoln, a former Whig, was deeply opposed to slavery. He regarded it as morally wrong—"if slavery is not wrong then nothing is wrong"—and he insisted that the Dred Scott decision be reversed. Slavery must be kept out of the territories and placed "in the course of ultimate extinction." But he was by no means an abolitionist. He did not advocate racial equality, and he recognized both the complexity of the slavery question and the fact that slavery was protected by constitutional guarantees which he proposed to respect—even to the enforcement of the fugitive slave law. Lincoln defined the dilemma the Dred Scott decision had created for Douglas and for all moderates. If slavery could not be legally excluded from the territories, how could the people of the territory, under popular sovereignty, exclude it?

Douglas replied at Freeport, Illinois (the "Freeport doctrine"), that unless a territory adopted positive laws to protect slavery by local police regulations, slavery could not establish itself; and thus by merely refraining from legislation, lawmakers could keep a territory free. This answer was enough to gain reelection for Douglas, but it cost him what was left of his reputation as a national leader with strong bisectional support. At one time, Southerners had applauded him for repealing the slavery exclusion of the Missouri Compromise, but now they saw him as a man who was supporting the free-soilers in Kansas and who was advocating a theory which would deprive the South of rights guaranteed by a decision of the Supreme Court.

John Brown's Raid.   If the Dred Scott decision brought to a climax the Northern feeling that freedom was being dangerously threatened by a sinister conspiracy of the "slave power," John Brown's raid on Harper's Ferry created an even more intense feeling below the Mason-Dixon line that abolitionist fanaticism posed an immediate danger to social order and even to human life in the South. After the "Pottawatomie massacre" in Kansas, Brown had dropped out of sight, but during the night of October 16, 1859, he suddenly descended, with a band of eighteen men (including five blacks), on the town of Harper's Ferry, Virginia, seized the federal arsenal there, and called upon the slaves to rise and claim their freedom. Within thirty-six hours Brown was captured, and he was later tried and hanged. But his act had touched the South at its most sensitive nerve—its fear of the kind of slave insurrection that had caused immense slaughter in Santo Domingo at the beginning of the century and had periodically threatened to erupt in the South itself, especially at the time of the Nat Turner revolt in 1831 and the Gabriel Prosser and Denmark Vesey plots of 1800 and 1822. Southern alarm and resentment would perhaps have been less great if the North had denounced Brown's act—as many Northerners, including Lincoln, did—but the fact soon came out that Brown had received financial backing from some of the most respected figures in Boston, and the day of his execution became one of public mourning in New England. John Brown was called Saint John the Just, and Ralph W. Emerson declared that Brown would "make the gallows glorious like the cross."

The Election of 1860.   By this time, developments were rapidly moving toward a crisis. For more than a decade, sectional dissension had been destroying the institutions which held the American people together in national unity. In 1844 it had split the Methodist church; the Baptist church had divided into separate Northern and Southern bodies in 1845. Between 1852 and 1856, sectionalism had split the Whig party, and as matters now stood, the Democratic party was the only major national institution, outside of the government itself, which still remained. In 1860, with another presidential election at hand, the Democratic organization, already strained by the tension between the Buchanan and the Douglas Whigs, also broke apart.

The Democrats.   Meeting at Charleston, the Democratic convention divided on the question of the platform. Douglas Democrats wanted a plank which promised in general terms to abide by the decisions of the Supreme Court but which avoided explicit expression of support for slavery in the territories. Southern Democrats, led by William L. Yancey, a famous orator from Alabama, wanted a categorical affirmation that slavery would be protected in the territories. When the Douglas forces secured the adoption of their plank, Yancey and most of the delegates from the cotton states walked out of the convention. The accusation was later made that they did this as part of a deliberate plan or conspiracy to break up the Union by splitting the Democratic party, letting the Republicans win, and thus creating a situation which would cause the South to secede. But, in fact, many of those who bolted were hoping to force Northern Democrats to come to terms or to throw the election into Congress, where there was a chance that the South might have won. For weeks, desperate efforts were made to reunite the Democrats, but in the end the Northern wing of the party nominated Douglas and the Southern wing nominated John C. Breckinridge of Kentucky, Vice-President under Buchanan.

Some of the conservative successors of the Whigs, now calling themselves Constitutional Unionists, nominated John Bell of Tennessee for President and Edward Everett for Vice-President on a platform that said nothing about the territorial question, and called only for "the Constitution, the Union, and the enforcement of the laws."

The Republican Victory. The principal opposition to Douglas, it was understood, would come from the Republicans, whose convention was meeting at a new building called the Wigwam in Chicago. The leading candidate before the convention was William H. Seward, U.S. senator from New York, who had been the leading Republican for some years. But his talent for coining memorable phrases—"a higher law than the Constitution" and "the irrepressible conflict between freedom and slavery"—had won him a reputation for extremism, and the Republicans, who smelled impending victory after the Democratic split, decided to move in a conservative direction in order not to jeopardize their prospects. Accordingly, they nominated Abraham Lincoln, who had made his reputation in the debates with Douglas but who had never been militant on the slavery question. To balance this nomination they made Hannibal Hamlin, a former Democrat from Maine, their vice-presidential candidate.

To attain victory, the Republicans needed only to hold what they had won in 1856 and to capture Pennsylvania and either Illinois or Indiana, which Buchanan had carried. As the election turned out, they won every free state except New Jersey (part of which went to Douglas), while Breckinridge won all the slave states except Virginia, Kentucky, and Tennessee (which went to Bell) and Missouri (which went to Douglas). Douglas ran a strong second in popular votes but a poor fourth in electoral votes, while Lincoln was in the curious position of winning with only 39 percent of the popular vote. His victory resulted not from the division of his opponents, however, but from the fact that his strength was strategically distributed. His victories in many of the free states were narrow, and he received no votes at all in ten Southern states. Thus his popular votes had maximum effectiveness in winning electoral votes.

Secession. Lincoln's victory at last precipitated the sectional crisis which had been brewing for so long. As we can now see in the light of later events, Lincoln was moderate-minded and would have respected the legal rights of the South even though he deplored slavery. But to the South, fearful of Northern aggression, his victory was a signal of imminent danger. Here was a man who had said that a house divided against itself could not stand and that the Union could not continue permanently half slave and half free. To the South he denied rights in the territories which the Supreme Court

Separated from Va. 1861
Admitted 1863

Richmond:
Confederate
capital,
June 1861-
Apr. 1865

Ft. Sumter:
Bombardment began
Apr. 12, 1861

Montgomery:
Confederate capital,
Feb.-June 1861

THE UNITED STATES ON THE EVE OF CIVIL WAR *(Dates of secession are given under state names)*

Free states

Border slave states that did not secede

Slave states seceding before firing on Ft. Sumter, Apr. 12, 1861

Slave states seceding after firing on Ft. Sumter, Apr. 12, 1861

(slavery abolished in territories: 1862)

had said the South possessed. He was supported by swarms of militant antislavery men. And his victory clearly represented the imposition of a President by one section upon the other, for 99 percent of his vote was concentrated in the free states.

In view of these facts, proponents of Southern rights felt that the South must act before it slipped into the position of a hopeless minority, at the mercy of men who had approved of John Brown. Therefore, states' rights leaders invoked the doctrine that each state had retained its sovereignty when it joined the federal Union and that, in the exercise of this sovereignty, each state, acting through a special convention like the conventions that had ratified the Constitution, might secede from the Union. Putting this doctrine into action, South Carolina called a convention that adopted an Ordinance of Secession on December 20, 1860. By February 1, 1861, Mississippi, Florida, Alabama, Georgia, Louisiana, and Texas had followed. The secession of the lower South was complete.

The Failure of Compromise. The actual arrival of disunion, which had been dreaded for so long, evoked strenuous efforts at compromise—especially by leaders in the border slave states, where loyalty to the Union was combined with sympathy for the South. From Kentucky, Senator John J. Crittenden, heir to the compromise tradition of Henry Clay, introduced proposals in Congress to revise and extend the Missouri Compromise line by constitutional amendment. Virginia took the lead in convening a Peace Convention, with delegates from twenty-one states, which met in Washington in February. Congress actually adopted a proposed amendment which would have guaranteed slavery in the states that wanted to keep it; this amendment was submitted to the states for ratification before the war came and made it obsolete. But concessions on the territories were the only terms that might possibly have conciliated the South, and this was an issue upon which Lincoln was not willing to yield at all. As a result, compromise failed and the rift widened. By the end of February the seven Gulf Coast states had formed a new government, the Confederate States of America, with a capital at Montgomery, Alabama, and with Jefferson Davis of Mississippi as President.

Fort Sumter. Thus, when Lincoln was inaugurated on March 4, 1861, he was faced by a new Southern republic where seven states of the Union had been. This new Confederacy had seized federal post offices, customs houses, arsenals, and even federal forts, with the exception of Fort Sumter in Charleston harbor and Fort Pickens in Pensacola harbor. From North Carolina to the Rio Grande, these were the only two places where the Stars and Stripes still flew. There was great speculation at the time as to what position Lincoln would take, and there has been great dispute among historians since then as to what position he actually *did* take. Certainly he made it absolutely clear that he denied the right of any state to secede and that he intended to preserve the Union. But whether he intended to wage war in order to preserve it is not so clear. There were eight slave states (Virginia, North Carolina, Kentucky, Tennessee, Missouri, Arkansas, Maryland, and Delaware) still in the Union. Lincoln was extremely eager to keep them loyal; so long as they remained in the Union, they might help to bring the other slave states back. This split among the slave states represented a failure on the part of the secessionists to create a united South. Thus Lincoln had every reason to refrain from hasty action.

If he had been able to maintain the federal position at Fort Pickens and Fort Sumter, or even at one of them, he apparently would have been prepared to play a waiting game. But less than twenty-four hours after becoming President he learned that Major Robert Anderson, commander at Fort Sumter, was running out of supplies and would soon have to surrender unless food were sent to him. Lincoln apparently gave serious consideration to the possibility of surrendering Sumter, and if he had been able to reinforce Fort Pickens and to make it the symbol of an unbroken Union, he might have done so. But attempts to reinforce Pickens were delayed, and on April 6 Lincoln sent a message to the governor of South Carolina that supplies would be sent to Sumter. If they were allowed in, no reinforcement would be attempted.

Historians have disputed whether this was a promise not to start shooting if supplies were allowed or a threat to start shooting if they were not allowed. But the Confederate government decided that the supplies could not be allowed, and before dawn on April 12, 1861, Confederate batteries opened a bombardment that forced Fort Sumter to surrender after twenty-six hours of furious shelling. This bombardment marked the beginning of a war which lasted four years and which was, with the exception of the Napoleonic wars, the greatest military conflict the world had seen up to that time.

"CAUSES" OF THE CIVIL WAR

Ever since 1861, writers have disputed what caused the Civil War and whether it was an "irrepressible conflict" in the sense of being inevitable. Southerners have argued that the war was fought not over slavery but over the question of states' rights; several of the Confederate states, they point out, seceded only when the others had been attacked. Economic determinists have contended that the Northern public never would support the abolitionists on any direct question (which is certainly true), that Lincoln did not even venture to issue the Emancipation Proclamation until the war had been in progress for a year and five months (which is also true), and that the conflict was really between an industrial interest which wanted one kind of future for America and an agrarian interest which wanted another. Other historians, going a step beyond this, have pictured the North and the South as two "diverse civilizations," so dissimilar in their culture and their values that union between them was artificial and unnatural. In the 1940s another group of writers, known as revisionists, emphasized the idea that Northerners and Southerners had formed distorted and false concepts of each other and that they went to war against these images rather than against the people they were really fighting. The war, they argued, grew out of emotions, not out of realities.

Every one of these points of view has something to be said for it. The causes of the Civil War were certainly not simple. But though each of the explanations points to something other than slavery, it is significant that the factor of slavery was involved in all of them. It is true that the South believed in the right of the states to secede whereas the North did not, but this belief would have remained an abstraction and never been acted upon if the Republican crusade against slavery had not impelled the South to use the secession weapon. It is also true that the economies of the North and of the South were very different, but the United States has always had certain great regional diversities in economy—for instance between the urban, industrial Northeast and the rural, grain-producing Middle West—and these diversities have not led to war.

It is hard to believe that without slavery the general dissimilarities of North and South—their economic divergence, their specific disagreements on issues like the tariff, or even their social and cultural separateness—would have been brought into such sharp focus as to precipitate a war. That North and South could live together in harmony despite great dissimilarities was proved by experience before 1846 and again after 1877. Furthermore, when one speaks of a "distinctive Southern civilization," one is speaking to a very great extent of slavery, for slavery lay at the foundation of the plantation system, which was the very heart and center of Southern society. Finally, it is true that in the 1850s extremist leaders came to the fore and each section formed an emotional stereotype rather than a realistic picture of the other. But this is a process which always occurs as antagonism deepens.

The point is that slavery furnished the emotional voltage that led to deep distrust and dislike in each section for the people of the other. In his second inaugural, Abraham Lincoln said, "All know that slavery was somehow the cause of the war." The operative word in his statement was "somehow," for the war was not in any simple sense a fight between crusaders for freedom all on one side and believers in slavery all on the other. Robert E. Lee, to name but one Southerner, did not believe in slavery at all, and many a Northern soldier who was willing to die, if need be, for the Union was deeply opposed to making slavery an issue of the war. But both antislavery Southerners and proslavery Northerners were caught in a web which could never have been woven without the issue of slavery.

Could this issue have been settled without war? Was the crisis artificial? Was the territorial question a contest over "an imaginary Negro in an impossible place"? Was war really necessary in a situation where it seems doubtful that a majority of Southerners wanted to secede (only seven out of fifteen slave states seceded before the firing on Fort Sumter) or that a majority of Northerners wanted to make an issue of slavery? (Lincoln had only 39 percent of the popular vote, and he promised security for slavery where it was already established.) Were the American people, both North and South, so much alike in their religion (overwhelmingly evangelical Protestant), their speech (an American variant of English), their ethnic descent (mostly from British, Irish, and German stock), their democratic beliefs, their pioneer ways, their emphasis upon the values of self-reliance and hard work, their veneration for the Constitution, and even their bumptious Americanism—were they so much alike that a war between them could and should have been avoided? This question raises the more general question whether disagreements are any less bitter when the parties disagreeing share much in common.

What was happening in America was that the center of gravity was gradually shifting from a loosely organized agricultural society to a modern industrial society with much greater concentration of power. As this happened, the government was being transformed from a loose association of separately powerful states to a consolidated nation in which the states would be little more than political subdivisions. In America's startling growth the North had outstripped the South and the equilibrium that previously existed between them had been destroyed. The proposal of the victorious Republicans to confine slavery—and in this sense to exclude the South from further participation in the nation's growth—dramatized this shift in equilibrium. It seems most unlikely that the South would ever have accepted the political consequences of this basic change without a crisis, especially since Southern whites greatly feared the possibility that a preponderant North in control of the federal government might ultimately use its power to abolish slavery. The brooding presence of race permeated this issue. Slavery was more than an institution to exploit cheap labor; it was a means of controlling a large and potentially threatening black population and of maintaining white supremacy. Any hint of a threat to the "Southern way of life," which was based on the subordination of a race both scorned and feared, was bound to arouse deep and irrational phobias and to create a crisis. Whether this crisis had to take the form of armed conflict and whether this phase of armed force had to occur precisely when it did, or might have come a month, or a year, or a decade sooner or later, would seem to be a matter for endless speculation.

CHAPTER 11

CIVIL WAR AND RECONSTRUCTION
1861–77

THE BLUE AND THE GRAY

The "American" War.   The American Civil War lasted four years, from April 1861 to April 1865. It was fought over more than half of the United States, for battles took place in every slave state except Delaware, and Confederate forces made incursions into Pennsylvania, Ohio, West Virginia, Kansas, and (raiding from Canada) Vermont.

From a total of 14 million free males, 2.8 million were in uniform—two million for the Union and 800,000 for the Confederacy—a higher proportion than that in any other American war. The Union total included 180,000 black soldiers—almost one in ten of the manpower in the Union Army—and more than 20,000 black sailors. Either as battle casualties or as victims of camp maladies, 618,000 men died in service (360,000 Union troops and 258,000 Confederates); more than one soldier in five lost his life—a far heavier ratio of losses than in any other war in our history.

Partly because the cost was proportionally so heavy, and partly because the Civil War was distinctly an American war, this conflict has occupied a place in the American memory and the American imagination which other wars—more recent, greater, and more crucial in terms of survival—have never held. On both sides, men were fighting for what they deeply believed to be American values. Southerners were convinced that their right to form a Confederacy was based on a principle of the Declaration of Independence—that governments derive their just powers from the consent of the governed. Northerners were equally zealous to prove that a democracy is not too weak to hold together, and that, as Lincoln said, the principle of self-government is not an absurdity.

The Resources of North and South.   In later years, after the Confederacy had gone down to defeat, men said that the Lost Cause, as Southerners called it, had been lost from the beginning and that the South had been fighting against the census returns. In many respects this seems true, for the South was completely outnumbered in almost all the factors of manpower and economic strength which make up the sinews of modern war. The eleven Confederate states (not counting Kentucky and Missouri, which were divided) had a white population of 5,450,000, while the nineteen free states had 18,950,000. These figures leave out both the population of the four border slave states of Missouri, Kentucky, Maryland, and Delaware and the slave population of the Confederate states. Slaves strengthened the Confederate war effort indirectly, since by serving as workers they could release some of the whites to serve as soldiers.

The Union was far ahead of the Confederacy in financial and economic strength, too. It had a bank capital two and a half times as great as that of the South. It led the South in the number of manufacturing enterprises by three and a half to one; in the number of industrial workers by six to one; and in the value of its manufactures by five and a half to one. In railroad mileage, it led by approximately two to one.

But against these ratios of strength must be placed the fact that the Union was undertaking a vastly more difficult military objective. It was seeking to occupy and subdue an area larger than all of western Europe. This meant that armies had to be sent hundreds of miles into hostile territory and be maintained in these distant operations. This necessity involved the gigantic task of transporting the immense volume of supplies required by an army in the field and defending long lines of communication, which would be worthless if they were cut even at a single point. In wars prior to the Civil War, armies had depended upon the use of great wagon trains to bring supplies. As the supply lines lengthened, the horses ate up in fodder a steadily increasing proportion of the amount they could haul, until there was scarcely any margin left between what the supply lines carried and what they consumed in carrying it. During the Civil War, for the first time in the history of warfare, railroads played a major part in the supply services. If these more efficient carriers of goods had not changed the whole nature of war, it is questionable whether invading armies could ever have marched from the Ohio to the Gulf of Mexico. Ten years earlier the United States had not possessed the railroad network which supplied the Union armies between 1861 and 1865. At an earlier time the defensive position of the South would have been far stronger.

But even with railroads, superior munitions, and superior industrial facilities, the military tasks of the Union were most formidable. America was a profoundly civilian country. The peacetime army numbered only sixteen thousand, and few people on either side had any conception of the vast problems involved in recruiting, mobilizing, equipping, training, and maintaining large armies. It was an amateur's war on both sides, and many of its features seem inconceivable today. Most of the troops were recruited as volunteers rather than by conscription. There were no conscription laws in operation until the war was more than half over, and when these laws were adopted, their real purpose was not to put recruitment on a conscription basis but rather to stimulate volunteering. Even when conscripted under the Union's law, a man could still gain exemption by paying a fee of $300 or by hiring a substitute. Conscription was applied only in localities which failed to meet their quotas, and thus communities were impelled to pay "bounties" to encourage men to volunteer. This resulted in the practice of "bounty-jumping"—a man would enlist, collect his bounty, desert, enlist again in some other locality, collect another bounty, and desert again.

Volunteers often enlisted for limited periods, and when their terms of enlistment expired, there was nothing to prevent them from quitting the service and going home, even if the army in which they were enrolled was on the eve of battle. Volunteer units in most cases elected their own officers, up to the rank of colonel, and they frequently preferred officers who were not strict in matters of discipline.

Preparation for military service was negligible. Physical examinations for recruits were a farce. Men were placed in positions of command without prior training as officers, and recruits were often thrown into combat without any basic training as soldiers. This was, to a great extent, a do-it-yourself war.

THE WAR IN THE FIELD

The Virginia Front. From the very outset of the war, attention was focused on the Virginia front. After fighting had begun at Fort Sumter and the states of the upper South had joined the Confederacy, the Confederate government moved its capital to Richmond, Virginia, about one hundred miles south of Washington. With the two seats of government so close together, the war in the East became a struggle on the part of the Union to capture Richmond and on the part of the South to defend it.

Between Washington and Richmond a number of broad rivers—the Potomac, the Rappahannock, the York, the Chickahominy, and their tributaries—flow more or less parallel with one another from the Allegheny Mountains in the west to Chesapeake Bay in the east. This grid of rivers afforded a natural system of defense to the South and presented an obstacle course to the North. Southern armies on the defensive could lie in wait for their attackers on the south banks of these streams, as they did at Fredericksburg or at Chancellorsville. If the Southern army was driven back after going on the offensive, it could recross to safety, reorganize, and recoup, as it did after Antietam (Sharpsburg) and Gettysburg.

For four years the principal army of the North, the Army of the Potomac, struggled against the principal army of the South, the Army of Northern Virginia, over this terrain. Here each side placed its foremost commander: Robert E. Lee headed the Army of Northern Virginia after Joseph E. Johnston was wounded in 1862, while Ulysses S. Grant was brought east to take overall command of Union armies in 1864 after his great successes in the West. Public attention centered primarily upon these campaigns, and they have continued to receive more than their share of attention in history.

During the first half of the war, the Union met with a long succession of disappointments and defeats on the Virginia front. In July 1861, when both armies were still raw and unseasoned, the Union sent General Irvin McDowell south with the slogan "Onward to Richmond" and with expectations of an easy victory. But when he encountered the Confederate armies of Generals Pierre Beauregard and Joseph E. Johnston at Manassas Junction (the first battle of Bull Run), he was defeated, and his army, which was too green to absorb a defeat, lost all organization and retreated in panic to Washington. McDowell was replaced by George Brinton McClellan, who had campaigned successfully in West Virginia—a little man of supremely self-confident manner who was inevitably compared with Napoleon. McClellan possessed real ability as an organizer, and he had the good sense to realize that he must make his troops into

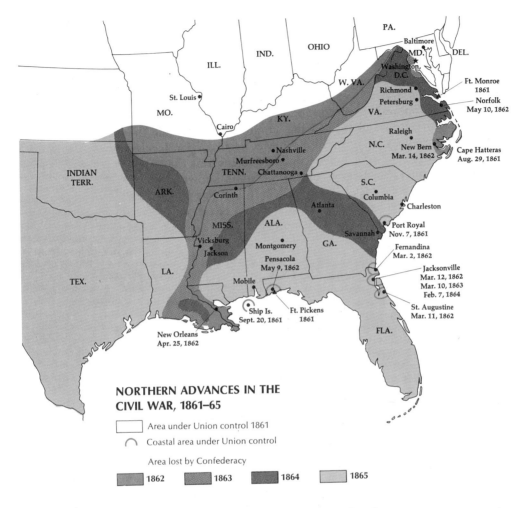

**NORTHERN ADVANCES IN THE
CIVIL WAR, 1861–65**

☐ Area under Union control 1861
⌒ Coastal area under Union control

Area lost by Confederacy

☐ 1862   ☐ 1863   ☐ 1864   ☐ 1865

an army before he took them campaigning. Consequently, there was no more major fighting on the Virginia front for almost a year. When McClellan did at last move in April 1862, he persuaded President Lincoln to let him transport his troops by ship to a point (Fort Monroe) on the Virginia coast within striking distance of Richmond. From this point he proposed to move up the peninsula between the York and the James rivers (hence called the Peninsula Campaign) and to capture the Confederate capital.

McClellan's plan was a brilliant solution to the difficult problem of supply, for he could now bring provisions to his army by ship without fear of Confederate raiders getting to his rear and cutting his lines. But the plan had one important drawback: it left, or appeared to leave, Washington exposed to the Confederates. President Lincoln therefore insisted on withholding, for the defense of the capital, part of the troops that McClellan wanted, and McClellan, who was never willing to fight unless he had a sure thing, refused to push the offensive without these troops.

While these developments were in progress, the Confederate commander, Joseph E. Johnston, was badly wounded and was replaced by Robert E. Lee. Lee, a Virginia aristocrat, mild of speech and gentle of manner but gifted with a daring that was terrible to his adversaries, quickly perceived that he could play upon the Union's fear that Washington was too exposed. Accordingly, he sent his brilliant subordinate, Thomas J. ("Stonewall") Jackson, on a raid up the Shenandoah Valley, appearing to threaten Washington and causing the administration to hold there defensive troops which had previously been promised to McClellan. When Jackson returned from his raid with phenomenal speed, Lee's reunited forces took the offensive against McClellan's original forces in a series of engagements known as the Seven Days' Battles (June 26-July 1, 1862). McClellan fought hard and was not decisively defeated, but he lost his nerve, moved back to a base on the James River, and sent Washington a series of hysterical messages that the government had deserted him. Lincoln, who had never

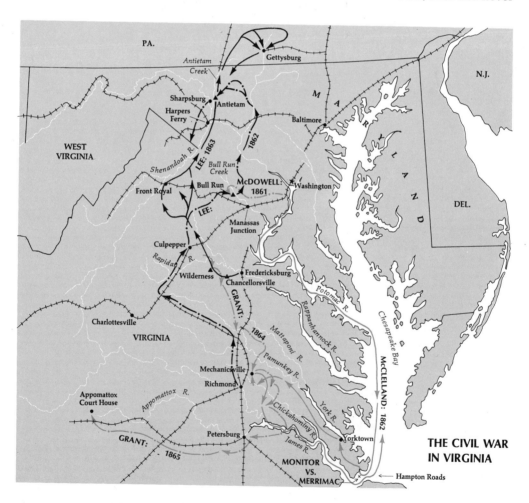

THE CIVIL WAR
IN VIRGINIA

fully accepted the basic idea of operating by sea, removed him from command and placed most of the troops under John Pope, who had gained a reputation in the West.

Pope promptly ran afoul of the Lee-Jackson combination at the Second Battle of Manassas (the second battle of Bull Run) in August 1862, and McClellan was restored to command and given a second chance. When Lee marched north, crossed the Potomac, and advanced into Maryland, McClellan shadowed him. Again Lee divided his forces, sending part of his army to capture Harper's Ferry. But even when a copy of Lee's secret orders fell into McClellan's hands and he knew exactly what to expect, he still did not move quickly or decisively. After a supremely hard-fought engagement at Antietam (Sharpsburg), Lee withdrew, undefeated and unpursued, to the south bank of the Potomac. Lincoln again replaced McClellan, this time with Ambrose E. Burnside.

In December 1862 Burnside made an unimaginative frontal attack across the Rappahannock at Fredericksburg, Virginia, against prepared Confederate defenses. Fighting the Confederates on ground of their own choosing, he sustained terrible losses and was replaced by Joseph Hooker. Hooker seemed a man of boldness and decision, but in May 1863, when he was trying to cross the Rappahannock at Chancellorsville, Lee and Jackson caught him with his army straddled across the river. The Confederates won another victory, but Hooker saved his army and the South paid a fearful price: Jackson was accidentally shot by a Confederate and died of his wound a few days later.

Hooker remained in command until Lee launched a second offensive against the North, this time into Pennsylvania. When Lee escaped from Hooker on the northward march, Lincoln again changed commanders, turning this time to George Gordon Meade. Meade's army and Lee's army met at Gettysburg, though neither side had planned it that way, and on July 2 and 3, 1863, the South made its supreme effort. The little town in Pennsylvania became the scene of the greatest battle ever fought in North America. Lee, facing Meade across a valley, threw his troops against the Union positions in a series of bold attacks, the most famous of which was Pickett's Charge. But Meade was too strong to be dislodged. Lee's forces, which had been fearfully punished, waited for more than a day to receive a counterattack that never came and then marched south. Meade did not pursue until too late, and ten days after the battle Lee recrossed the Potomac unmolested. The Army of Northern Virginia had still never been driven from a battlefield, but its great offensive power was forever broken.

The War in the West.   On July 4, 1863, the day on which Lee began his uncontested withdrawal, another Confederate general, John C. Pemberton, at Vicksburg, Mississippi, surrendered an army of about thirty thousand men—the largest that has ever been captured in North America. The man to whom he surrendered was Ulysses S. Grant, and the event marked the culmination of a series of campaigns in the West which had been much more decisive in their results than the eastern campaigns.

The whole region beyond the Alleghenies was far vaster and more broken up geographically than the Virginia theater, and the campaigns in the West never had a single focus as they did in Virginia. Operations along the Mississippi were scarcely coordinated with operations in the central and eastern parts of Tennessee and

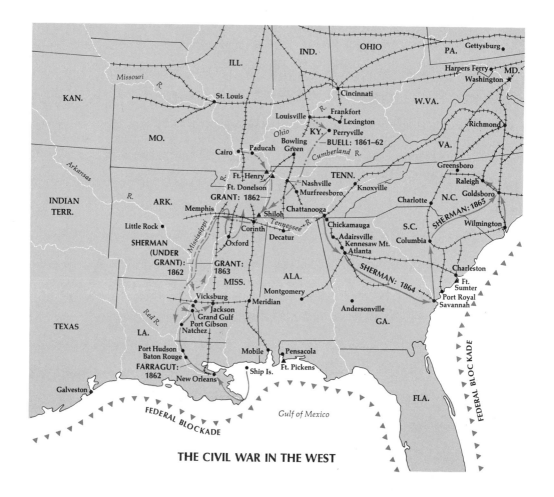

THE CIVIL WAR IN THE WEST

Kentucky, and neither of these was synchronized with activities "west of the River" in Missouri, Arkansas, most of Louisiana, and Texas. Essentially, however, it was the objective of the Union to gain control of the Mississippi and thus to cut off the western wing of the Confederacy. In this way Confederate armies would be deprived of reinforcements and supplies—especially of Texas cattle—which they vitally needed. A further division of the Confederacy would be undertaken by driving southeast through Kentucky and Tennessee, cutting vital Confederate rail connections at Chattanooga in eastern Tennessee, and continuing thence into the heart of the Confederacy, across Georgia to the sea. Such an operation would cut off the Gulf Coast region from the Atlantic seaboard and leave only Virginia, the Carolinas, and part of Georgia to support a hopeless cause.

It took three years and eight months for the Union to carry out these plans, but they began sooner than the great campaigns in Virginia. In February 1862, Grant, a man who had left the army in 1854 as a failure because of excessive drinking, successfully captured two forts, Henry and Donelson, in western Kentucky, which controlled the Tennessee and the Cumberland Rivers. Unlike the streams of Virginia, which cut across the paths of advancing armies, each of these rivers flowed in a "U" shaped course from the southern Appalachians southward into northern Alabama (in the case of the Tennessee) or central Tennessee (in the case of the Cumberland) and then, reversing their course, almost due north to the Ohio River. Control of these river highways gave Grant easy entry deep into the South. On the Cumberland, Nashville, the capital of Tennessee, fell to the Union as soon as Fort Donelson was captured, and by April Grant had advanced up the Tennessee almost to the border of Mississippi. In that same month, when all was still very "quiet along the Potomac," the Union army and navy, by skillful combined operations, captured New Orleans, the largest city of the Confederacy.

After these early successes, the Union forces found themselves blocked for some time. A Confederate army under Albert Sidney Johnston struck Grant unexpectedly at Shiloh, Tennessee, on April 6, 1862, drove his army to the edge of the Tennessee River, and might have destroyed it if Johnston had not been killed in action. When Grant was later able to resume the initiative, he turned his attention to the Confederate stronghold at Vicksburg, where towering bluffs command the Mississippi. Deep in enemy country, Vicksburg was rendered almost impregnable by vast swamps, a succession of steep hills, and by the river itself. After making a series of unsuccessful moves against this natural fortress, Grant at last hit on the bold and unorthodox plan of moving down the west side of the river, crossing below Vicksburg, abandoning his lines of communication, and living off the country during a final drive against the Confederate defenses. It was by this plan that he finally captured Pemberton's entire army at Vicksburg on July 4, 1863, and gained complete control of the Mississippi artery.

Grant Takes Command. After Vicksburg, in March 1864, Lincoln brought Grant east to serve as general-in-chief and to take personal charge of the Army of the Potomac (Meade was not removed but was under Grant's command).

By this time the Confederacy, outnumbered from the beginning, was fearfully handicapped by losses of men which could not be replaced as Union losses could. Grant, recognizing this handicap, settled upon a plan of operations that was far less brilliant than his operations in the West, but no less decisive. By steadily extending his flanks, he forced the Confederacy to extend also and to make its lines very thin; by continuing pressure, he gave his adversaries no rest. Lee resisted with immense skill, and Grant sacrificed men so freely in the Campaign of the Wilderness (May 5–6, 1864) that his losses exceeded the total number of men in Lee's army. In June 1864, after being terribly punished at the Battle of Cold Harbor, Grant decided to move his base to the James River (as McClellan had done two years earlier), to attack from the south. He succeeded in this maneuver and thus pinned Lee's forces at Petersburg, which is actually south of Richmond. With Petersburg under siege and Lee no longer mobile, it was only a question of time, but Lee held on for nine long months while Richmond remained the Confederate capital.

Sherman's March.   While Grant and Lee faced each other across the trenches at Petersburg, the Confederacy was being cut to pieces from the rear. Grant had first cut it at Vicksburg on the Mississippi, and the next cut was to take place from central Kentucky and Tennessee. By the end of 1863 the Union armies had won control of eastern Tennessee through a series of battles, principally at Chickamauga and at Missionary Ridge outside Chattanooga. When Grant left for Virginia, William T. Sherman, a trusted subordinate, was left to face the Confederate forces under Joseph E. Johnston in the mountains of north Georgia.

Johnston, "retreating general" but a resourceful obstructionist, blocked and delayed Sherman at every step, all the way to Atlanta. There he was removed because of his unwillingness to take the offensive, and John B. Hood was put in his place. Hood made the mistake of challenging Sherman in a general engagement and was so badly defeated that Sherman, after taking Atlanta on September 2, 1864, was able to march unopposed across Georgia to the sea. Sherman reached the port of Savannah on Christmas 1864, while Grant was still outside Petersburg.

Appomattox.   From this time, the South was completely fragmented and the Confederacy's cause was hopeless. But Johnston, having returned to his command in the Southeast, held together a force which retreated across the Carolinas, with Sherman pursuing and burning Columbia, South Carolina, as he pursued. Lee, meanwhile, held against steadily increasing odds at Petersburg. By April 1865, however, the inevitable defeat could be put off no longer. Petersburg fell and Richmond was evacuated. Lee met Grant on April 9 at a farmhouse near Appomattox Court House, and in a moving scene surrendered the Army of Northern Virginia to Grant, who accorded generous terms and told his troops not to cheer because, he said, "the rebels are our countrymen again." Johnston also surrendered at Greensboro, North Carolina, before the end of the month, and the Confederate government, which had fled south after the fall of Petersburg, simply evaporated.

THE WAR BEHIND THE LINES

The Problems of the Confederacy.   Writers on the Civil War have piled up a vast literature—one of the largest bodies of literature on any historical subject—detailing the military aspects of the war: the battles and leaders, the campaigns and maneuvers, the strategy and tactics. This military record, however, does not fully explain the outcome of the war. For, in terms of strategy and tactics, the Confederate performance equaled that of the Union and, on the Virginia front, surpassed it until the last year of the war. The final result was registered on the battlefield, but the basic factors which caused Confederate defeat lay behind the lines. Essentially, the Confederacy failed to solve the problems of organizing its society and its economy for war. It faced these problems in a particularly difficult form, and when it proved unable to solve them, it went down to defeat.

One basic handicap of the Confederacy lay in the fact that while the North had an industrial economy that was invigorated by war, the Southern economy was based on cotton production, which was dislocated and almost paralyzed by the war. In the North, war stimulated employment, and while wages failed to keep pace with inflation, civilian morale was generally high except among the underpaid urban poor. In the South, economic conditions deteriorated so badly that what may be called economic morale declined even while fighting morale remained good. During the spring of 1863 "bread riots" occurred in Richmond and several other Southern cities.

Essentially, the Confederacy, with its rural and agricultural society, needed two things. First, it needed access to the products of European—especially British—industry. Second, it needed to stimulate production of food, of horses, and of strategic supplies within the South. Ultimately, it was unable to meet any of these needs.

In order to be able to draw on British industry, the Confederacy needed to have buying power in the European market and to be able to ship goods freely to and fro across the Atlantic. Once war broke out, Lincoln proclaimed a blockade, which meant that federal naval vessels would try to seize the merchant vessels of any neutral country bringing goods to Confederate ports. But Southerners thought that the blockade would not work, partly because there were not enough Union ships to enforce it and even more because they believed in what has been called the "King Cotton delusion." They were firmly convinced that cotton was an absolute economic necessity to Britain, because textiles were the heart of British industry, and without cotton this industry would be prostrated; Britain's factories would stand idle; its workers would be unemployed and would literally starve. When this started happening, the British government would decide to intervene to get cotton, and the British navy, which still dominated the seas, would break the blockade.

Southerners were so confident of this idea that they were quite willing to see the British supply of cotton cut off for awhile. In the first months of the blockade, while it was still largely ineffective, they deliberately kept their cotton at home instead of sending a part of it abroad to be held in British warehouses so that it could later be sold to give them funds for the purchase of supplies. Thus, their only important economic asset, a store of cotton which was worth ten times as much as the gold supply of the Confederacy, was never put to constructive use.

The Importance of Sea Power. This faith in cotton ultimately proved to be a fallacy for several reasons. Britain succeeded in getting a certain amount of cotton elsewhere; British antislavery sentiment generated a strong resistance to taking steps that would help the Confederacy; and Britain was pleased to see America adopting a doctrine of international law concerning the right of blockade which she had always advocated and which was bound to be favorable to a nation with large naval power. But most of all, British industry was not paralyzed because Northern wartime purchases stimulated it. Britain, as a neutral, enjoyed an economic boom from supplying war materials to the Union—a boom very similar to the booms which the United States later enjoyed in 1914–17 and 1939–41 as a neutral supplying war materials to Britain.

Consequently, Britain and France, which was following Britain's lead, never did give diplomatic recognition to the Confederate government, although they did recognize the existence of a state of war in which they would be neutral. This meant that they would treat Confederate naval vessels as warships and not as pirates. The

British recognition of belligerency was much resented in the United States, but in fact the real danger for the Union cause lay in the possibility of diplomatic recognition of the Confederacy, which would probably have resulted in British efforts to break the blockade. Such efforts would, in turn, have led to war with Britain. But this recognition, for which the Confederacy waited so anxiously, never came.

In November 1861 Confederate hopes were high when an eager Union naval officer, Charles Wilkes, stopped a British ship on the high seas and took off two Confederate envoys to Britain, James Mason and John Slidell. Britain, at this point, actually prepared to fight, but President Lincoln wisely admitted the error and set the commissioners free. Meanwhile, the blockade steadily grew tighter. One Confederate port after another was sealed off. Small Confederate vessels, built for speed and based in the Bahama Islands, continued to delight the South by running the blockade freely and bringing in cargoes of goods with high value in proportion to their bulk. But their volume was small, and they did not in any sense provide the flow of goods which the Confederacy so vitally needed.

In addition to depending on British naval might, the Confederacy made two important efforts to establish sea power of its own. To begin with, it fitted out the first large ironclad vessel ever to put to sea. A powerful steam frigate, the U.S.S. *Merrimac,* which the federals had scuttled in the Norfolk Navy Yard, was raised, renamed the *Virginia,* covered with armor plate, and sent out in March 1862—an iron giant against the wooden vessels of the Union navy. In its first day at sea it destroyed two large Union vessels with ease. The entire Union navy appeared to be in acute danger, and there was panic in Northern coastal cities. But the Union had been preparing a metal-clad vessel of its own—a small craft that lay low in the water, with a revolving gun turret. This *Monitor,* as it was called, challenged the *Virginia* on March 9, 1862. The battle ended in a draw, but with Monitor-type vessels the Union navy was again safe.

The Confederacy's second major endeavor at sea was to buy in England vessels and equipment which, under the technicalities of British law, could be combined on the high seas to produce fighting ships without violating Britain's neutrality. These vessels could then raid merchant vessels flying the Union flag. There were five such raiders, most famous of which was the *Alabama.* This great marauder, commanded by Admiral Raphael Semmes, roamed the seas for two years, from Newfoundland to Singapore, captured sixty-two merchant ships (most of which were burned, after careful attention to the safety of their crews and passengers), and sank the U.S.S. *Hatteras* in a major naval battle. It was at last cornered and sunk off Cherbourg, France, by the U.S.S. *Kearsarge,* but its career had made the American flag so unsafe on the high seas that prohibitive insurance costs caused more than seven hundred American vessels to transfer to British registry. The American merchant marine never again attained the place in the world's carrying trade it had held before the *Alabama* put to sea.

The Confederacy sought to have additional raiders built in British shipyards, and two immensely formidable vessels—the Laird rams—were actually constructed. But strenuous American diplomatic protests, coupled with British awareness that in spite of technicalities this was really a violation of neutrality, led the British government to stop their delivery in October 1863. After this the Confederate cause was lost at sea as well as on land, and the federal blockade tightened like a noose to strangle the Confederacy economically.

Economic Failures of the South. Meanwhile, on the home front, the Confederacy failed economically because it was caught between the need to stimulate production and the need to keep down prices and to control inflation. The Southern government began with almost no financial assets other than land and slaves, neither of which could be readily transformed into negotiable currency. It faced a dilemma: it could either encourage production by buying goods in the open market at an uncontrolled price, in which case inflation would mushroom; or it could control inflation by a system of requisitioning goods for its armies at arbitrarily fixed prices, in which case production would be discouraged rather than stimulated. Only a program of heavy taxation, by which the government would take back the inflationary dollars that had been spent, could have helped at all in reducing this problem, but the Confederacy was afraid to use its taxing power. It raised less than 1 percent of its revenue from taxes—a smaller proportion than any other nation in a modern war—and it procured funds by borrowing, which is the most inflationary method of all. Ultimately it failed either to stimulate production or to control inflation. Goods grew scarcer while money grew more plentiful: it was grimly said that at the beginning of the war people took their money to market in a purse and brought their goods home in a basket, but that by the end they took the money in a basket and brought their purchases home in a purse.

In short, the Confederacy died of economic starvation—an insufficiency of goods. Its government was too weak to cope with the nearly insoluble economic problems the war had caused. President Jefferson Davis was a bureaucrat who thought in legalistic rather than in dynamic terms; he was not an innovator but a conservative miscast as a revolutionist. The state governments competed against the Confederate government for the control of manpower and supplies; they insisted upon their sovereign status so strenuously that it has been said that the Confederacy was born of states' rights and died of states' rights. The only chance the Confederacy ever had, and it was perhaps a fairly good one, was to win a short war before the results of economic malnutrition set in. Once that failed, the cause was hopeless. A few Confederates, like Josiah Gorgas in the Ordnance Department, improvised brilliantly, and others did so desperately; but in a country where a vitally necessary rail line could be laid only be tearing up the rails somewhere else and re-laying them, a long war against a dynamic adversary could have but one ending.

Northern Industrialism and Republican Ascendancy. The problems and limitations of the Confederacy—problems of localism and decentralization, of an agricultural economy and of small-scale economic activities—were characteristic features of the kind of folk society the Confederacy was defending. But while the South was making a last stand against the forces of the modern mechanized world, the war was rushing the North along the path toward industrial domination. Before the Southern states withdrew from the Union, they had blocked some of the governmental measures most conducive to the new industrial economy. Southern secession, however, left the new Republican party in control; and though this party seemed what we call liberal in its opposition to slavery, it was from the outset Whiggish, or conservative, in its economic policies. It believed in using federal power to promote economic growth through the encouragement of various forms of private enterprise; and while this was believed to work to the advantage of everyone, it meant in direct terms the encouragement and sponsorship of measures favorable to industry and to private capital. Thus, in February 1861, while the empty seats of the departing Southern congressmen were still warm, and even before President Lincoln took office, Congress adopted the Morrill Tariff, which, though not very high, was higher than the existing tariff of 1857. This was the first of many tariff increases; there was not another perceptible reduction until 1913. Meanwhile Congress repeatedly strengthened the measures by which it gave American industrial producers more exclusive control in the American market, even if this forced American consumers to pay higher prices than they would have had to pay on the world market.

The Transcontinental Railroad. In 1862 Congress broke the long deadlock the sectional conflict had created over the building of a railroad to the Pacific. For a decade, advocates of a southern route and supporters of a northern route had blocked each other; but now, with the Southerners absent, Congress created the Union Pacific Railroad Company, incorporated with a federal charter, to build westward from Omaha and to meet another road, the Central Pacific, a California corporation, building eastward from Sacramento. To encourage this enterprise, Congress placed very large resources at the disposal of the railroads. It gave to the roads ten square miles of land, running back in alternate blocks from the tracks, for each mile of track built, and it granted loans (not gifts) of between $16,000 and $48,000 a mile—according to the difficulty of the terrain where construction took place. The value of the lands at that time was not great, and the munificence of this largesse has often been exaggerated. But the point is that the government was paying most of the costs of construction, and it might well have controlled or even owned the railroad. Instead, it placed these resources in the hands of private operators, who, if they succeeded, would become owners of the world's greatest railroad and, if they lost, would be losing the government's money rather than their own. It was "venture capitalism," as it is now called, but the government was doing most of the venturing and the private interests which constructed the road were getting most of the capital.

In 1869, four years after the war ended, the Union Pacific and the Central Pacific met at Promontory Point in Utah, and a golden spike was driven to mark the event. Travelers to California no longer were obliged to sail around Cape Horn, and the United States was a long step closer to being a transcontinental, two-ocean republic in an operative sense as well as in a purely geographical one.

The National Banking System. One other major economic measure resulting from Republican ascendancy was the creation of a new and far more centralized system of banking and money. Ever since Andrew Jackson's overthrow of the Bank of the United States in 1832, the country had had a decentralized, loose-jointed financial system—one which today it is difficult even to imagine. The United States, of course, issued coins and also bills; for each bill in circulation, a corresponding value of precious metal was held in the Treasury and could be claimed by the holder of the bill. The government handled all its own transactions in such currency and was thus on a "hard money" basis. Actually, this kind of money was not nearly sufficient to meet the economic needs of the country for a circulating medium. The principal circulating medium, therefore, had been provided by notes issued by banks operating under charters from the various states. State laws governing the incorporation of banks naturally varied, which meant that the financial soundness of the various banks also varied; this in turn meant that some of the notes circulated at face value, and others circulated at various degrees of discount from face value. Although the government was on a hard money basis, the economy of the country was not, and the federal government exercised no control whatever over the principal component in the monetary system of the country.

The National Bank Act of 1863, which changed all this, grew out of the government's need to raise the immense sums required for fighting a war. At times the government's need of funds was so acute that it resorted to the issue of "greenbacks"—bills which could not be redeemed in bullion. But primarily the Treasury relied upon borrowing—that is, upon selling bonds—and to borrow it had to make the bonds attractive as holdings for the banks. Accordingly, the National Banking Act provided that a bank which purchased government bonds to the amount of one third of its paid-in capital (not less than $30,000) might receive federally guaranteed notes, known as national bank notes, in an amount equal to 90 percent of its bond holdings. The bank would, of course, lend out the notes at interest, and thus would receive interest both on the bonds and on the notes it received for holding the bonds. At the same time, a tax was laid on the notes issued under state authority by state-chartered banks; the tax had the effect of making these notes unprofitable and thus driving them out of circulation. As a result of government borrowing policy, therefore, the United States acquired a new, uniform, federally sanctioned circulating medium of national bank notes.

These notes became the principal form of money for the next fifty years, but they had a great defect—they made the amount of money dependent upon the volume of federal debt rather than upon the economic needs of the country. They were inflexible, and in 1913 they were largely replaced by Federal Reserve notes as a result of the establishment of the Federal Reserve System. But the principles that the United States should have a uniform currency in use throughout the nation, and that the federal government should be responsible for this currency, had come to stay.

Women and the War. Although the Civil War brought suffering and loss to hundreds of thousands of American women, for women as a group the war meant progress toward independence and equality. It meant new opportunities for employment, broadened social and political interests, demonstrations of competence in activities previously reserved for men. Some women went to war, as nurses, spies, even as soldiers. But the vast majority who served at home—including those who stayed in the home—did most damage to the myth of the helpless female.

As in earlier wars, but in much greater numbers, women had to take their husbands' places as heads of households, running shops, managing farms and plantations, finding jobs to earn food for their families. In the South, many had to do housework—and field work—for the first time; some had to face armed, hostile blacks as well as enemy soldiers. In Minnesota and elsewhere on the frontier, women had to survive Indian uprisings.

Job opportunities for women multiplied as men went off to fight or quit old occupations for better paying ones. Schoolteaching paid so poorly that many men left it, and women—who were paid even less than the men they replaced—began their advance toward dominance of the profession. In both the Union and the Confederacy, women also went to work for the government. By the end of the war hundreds held government office jobs. Here, too, the change was permanent: Washington, D.C., would never again be without its corps of women workers. Many were employed, and some were killed, in government arsenals.

When the war began, women dominated the work force in the mills and factories of New England, while in the South women industrial workers were a small minority—another situation that favored the Union war effort. As men joined the service, women took their places in industry and helped produce military equipment and supplies. The demand for what was considered women's work also expanded: sewing women were hired by the thousands, and brutally exploited. In self-protection, the women organized, protested, and went out on strikes.

In addition to work for pay, there was a tremendous amount of unpaid activity by women in both South and North. Women volunteered to nurse and to teach; they joined aid societies; they organized activities to raise funds. They wrote and spoke for the causes they believed in. They were often brave, noble, self-sacrificing. They were also passionately partisan, pushing men and boys into enlisting and preaching hatred of the enemy to their children. In the South some turned food riots into excuses for looting; in the North some helped turn draft riots into murderous assaults on blacks.

The Civil War went a long way toward destroying the myth of the helpless female. It gave American women a chance to prove themselves quite as capable as men in many areas. They proved their smartness and their toughness. When the war ended, many lost their jobs to returning veterans. Some returned gratefully to domesticity. But there was no turning back the clock.

EMANCIPATION AND RECONSTRUCTION

The Road to Reunion.   Wars always bring results which are not intended by the men who fight them. The Civil War accelerated the growth of mass production and economic centralization in the North while it destroyed much of the economic plant in the South and convinced the rising generation of Southern leaders that future regional prosperity would depend upon industrialization. The war also caused an increase in federal power at the expense of the states, for no government could spend the funds, organize the forces, and wield the strength the federal government did, without increasing its power. But the main purpose of the war was to reunite a broken union of states, and there was a question whether the abolition of slavery was necessary to the objective of reunion. Some Republicans wanted to make emancipation one of the objects of the war, simply because they deplored slavery and did not believe that a Union which had slavery in it was worth saving. Others, who were relatively indifferent to the welfare of the blacks, believed that the slaveholding class, which they called the "slave power," was guilty of causing disunion, that to make the Union safe this power must be destroyed, and that the way to destroy it was to abolish slavery. Still others, including many of the "War Democrats" and the Unionists in the border states, regarded the war as one against secession, having nothing to do with slavery.

Emancipation.   For his part, Abraham Lincoln had stated his belief, long before he became President, that the Union could not endure permanently half-slave and half-free. He knew, however, that he could not free any slaves unless he won the war and that he could not win the war if he antagonized all the Unionists in the slave states of Delaware, Maryland, Kentucky (his own birthplace), and Missouri. As a result, he moved very slowly on the slavery question, and when two of his generals tried to move more quickly by emancipating slaves in the areas they had occupied, he counter-manded their orders. Few people realize it today, but the war had raged for seventeen months and was more than a third over before Lincoln moved to free the slaves in the Confederacy. In July 1862 he made up his mind to proclaim the freedom of slaves in the insurrectionary states, but he decided to wait for a victory before doing so. The Battle of Antietam (Sharpsburg) in September was not a great victory, but it sufficed; in that month Lincoln issued a proclamation that after January 1, 1863, all slaves in areas which were at that time in rebellion should be "forever free." This still did nothing about slaves in places like New Orleans, which was occupied by federal forces, nor in the border slave states, and it gave all the states of the Confederacy more than ninety days during which they could save slavery by coming back into the union. Strongly believing in persuasion rather than force, Lincoln in December 1862 proposed a constitutional amendment for the gradual emancipation of slaves in the border states by the year 1900, with compensation to the owners. But this was defeated in Congress by a combination of proslavery men who thought it went too far and antislavery men who thought it did not go far enough.

The caution with which Lincoln had proceeded with emancipation reflects his own scruples about the Constitution and the prudence of his own temperament, but it also reflects the fierceness of the divisions within the North and the dangers which these divisions held for the administration. On one flank, Lincoln was assailed by the Democrats. A minority of War Democrats gave him vigorous support, but a majority of "Copperheads" constantly called for peace, and especially assailed any move against slavery. Democratic propagandists helped convince white workingmen that they were being used in a war to free blacks who would take their jobs away; this conviction turned the "draft riots" in New York in July 1863 into mob assaults on blacks, in which hundreds were killed (most of them white rioters shot down by police).

On the other flank, the more militant antislavery men in the Republican party denounced Lincoln because he did not instantly take drastic action. These "radical

Republicans" hoped to dominate the administration by forcing all moderates on the slavery question out of the cabinet, and in 1864 some of them sought to prevent Lincoln's nomination for a second term. But by unrivaled political dexterity and skill Lincoln frustrated these attacks from both directions and maintained a broad base of support for the war.

As late as 1864 the House of Representatives defeated a constitutional amendment for the abolition of slavery. The Thirteenth Amendment was not finally voted by Congress for submission to the states until January 31, 1865. Maryland, Tennessee, and Missouri abolished slavery by state action at about this same time, but slavery was still legal in Kentucky and Delaware when the Civil War ended, and the amendment for the abolition of slavery was not ratified until eight months after Lincoln's death.

Lincoln as a War Leader. Long after these events, people who had grown up with an oversimplified image of Lincoln as a Great Emancipator became disillusioned by this record, and in the twentieth century some critics have sought to tear down his reputation. But in fact, he remains a figure of immense stature.

Born in 1809 in a log cabin in Kentucky, Lincoln grew up on the frontier in Indiana and Illinois, doing rough work as a rail splitter and a plowboy and receiving only a meager education. Later he became a self-taught lawyer with a successful practice in Springfield, served in the state legislature as a Whig, and rode the circuit on horseback to follow the sessions of the court. Except for one term in Congress, 1845–47, he virtually never went East and was unknown until the debates with Douglas gained him a reputation in 1858. In 1861, at a moment of crisis, this tall, gangling, plain-looking man, whose qualities of greatness were still unsuspected, became President.

Lincoln's relaxed and unpretentious manner masked remarkable powers of decision and qualities of leadership. Completely lacking in self-importance, he seemed humble to some observers. But in fact he acted with the patience and forbearance of a man who was very sure of what he was doing. Refusing to let the abolitionists push him into an antislavery war which would antagonize Union men who did not care about slavery, and refusing to let the Union men separate him from the antislavery contingent by restricting war aims too narrowly, he saw that the causes of Union and emancipation must support each other instead of opposing each other, or both would be defeated. Patiently he worked to fuse the idea of union with that of freedom and equality ("a new nation conceived in liberty and dedicated to the proposition that all men are created equal"). Thus he reaffirmed for American nationalism the idealism of freedom and gave to the ideal of freedom the strength of an undivided union. Knowing that in a democracy a man must win political success in order to gain a chance for statesmanship, he moved patiently and indirectly to his goals, and his opportunism greatly offended many abolitionists. But in the end he struck slavery a more deadly blow than any of them could ever strike.

Black Americans and the War. For black Americans, the Civil War years were a time of elation and rejoicing, frustration and despair. Many Northern blacks felt that, as a preliminary to emancipation and reconstruction, the separation of the slave states from the free states was long overdue. Men and women alike worked hard for the Union cause. Black intellectuals wrote and lectured, at home and abroad. Blacks organized their own aid and relief societies for the great numbers of freed slaves and went to them as teachers. Black women volunteered their services as nurses and hospital aids; black men by the hundreds of thousands went to war for the Union as sailors in the navy and as servants, cooks, and laborers with the army. When they were finally allowed to, they also went as soldiers.

But for a long time blacks were not allowed to serve in the army. Not until the summer of 1862 were blacks officially permitted to enlist, and it was another year before the bravery of black regiments in battle began to change the scornful attitude of whites, in and out of the service. Overall, black servicemen established an admirable record: twenty-one received the Congressional Medal of Honor. But they were denied commissions, and not until June 1864 were they given as much pay as their white counterparts.

Throughout the war, then, blacks continued to face injustice and discrimination, despite their major contribution to the Union cause. From the beginning, their most influential spokesman, Frederick Douglass, looked on Lincoln as much too conservative, and when the President took no decisive steps toward freeing the slaves, Douglass was outspoken in his criticism. Although Lincoln had his black supporters, including the beloved Harriet Tubman, he also gave offense by his continuing interest in some programs to move blacks out of the country to a colony in the tropics. There were some already so embittered that they welcomed the possibility of such separation. Martin R. Delany, who later joined with Douglass in working for black recruitment, favored the migration of American blacks to Haiti, a project that was tried unsuccessfully early in the war. After the rejection of black volunteers by the army, the subsequent mistreatment of black soldiers, and attacks on both black soldiers and black civilians in several Northern cities, there were blacks who agreed with white racists that the Civil War was indeed a white man's war—in a white man's country to which blacks owed no allegiance.

Nevertheless, there was progress. The Emancipation Proclamation was finally issued; the Thirteenth Amendment was adopted. The great slave population (which, as Douglass had repeatedly pointed out, enabled the Confederacy to put so large a proportion of its whites into uniform) was finally freed. Many blacks, Union soldiers as well as former slaves, were also freed from the bonds of illiteracy by dedicated teachers—both black and white—and through their own efforts. Blacks were recognized as full citizens by the federal government, and campaigns against discrimination in the law courts, the polling places, the schools, and public conveyances won victories in several states. In 1864 black representatives from eighteen states formed the National Equal Rights League. The long, agonizingly slow march toward equality was begun.

The Question of the Former Slave.   If the Union was slow to face the question of slavery, it was even slower to face the question of racism in America. From the perspective of the twentieth century we can now see the great misfortune of the Civil War: while it solved the problem of slavery, it did nothing whatever to solve the problem of racism, which was so closely linked with slavery. People recognized that slavery must end, but this was a negative decision, for it did not clarify what should be put in slavery's place. Was the former slave to occupy a subordinate status in American society, or was he to be put on the path toward equality? The answer was by no means clear, for although there were twenty-one free states, only a part of these permitted blacks to vote, and though Abraham Lincoln opposed slavery ("If slavery is not wrong, then nothing is wrong"), he did not accept the idea of racial equality ("I am not, nor ever have been, in favor of bringing about in any way the social and political equality of the white and black races"). In fact, to the end of his life he wanted to colonize the former slaves in Haiti or Central America, because he believed that whites and blacks could not live harmoniously together. (This belief, it should be noted, did not necessarily mean that he was discriminatory in his personal attitude; it might mean simply that he was pessimistic about biracial adjustments.)

Lincoln's Policy of Reconstruction. Along with this lack of conviction concerning racial equality, Lincoln and the Northern moderates were deeply impressed by a feeling that victory in war could not really restore the Union; it could only prevent secession. After that, if the Union were really restored, it would be because the Southern people again accepted the Union and gave their loyalty to it. To bring them back, Lincoln wanted a moderate and conciliatory policy. When in 1864 Congress adopted a measure known as the Wade-Davis Bill, imposing drastic terms for the restoration of the former Confederates, Lincoln vetoed it, and when people raised technical questions about the legal status of the Confederate states (Were they still states, or conquered territories? Had they committed "state suicide"?), he was impatient about such "pernicious abstractions." All that mattered was whether the states could be brought back into their proper relationship with the Union.

By 1864 the Union had regained enough control in Louisiana and Arkansas to start a process of restoring these states to the Union, and Lincoln laid down generous terms on which this could be done. He would grant amnesty to former Confederates who took an oath of allegiance, and when as many as one tenth of the number who had been citizens in 1860 did so, he would permit them to form a new state government. When this government accepted the abolition of slavery and repudiated the principle of secession, Lincoln would receive it back into the Union. It did not have to recognize the rights of blacks nor give a single one the vote. Louisiana was the first state reorganized on this basis, and despite its denial of black suffrage, Lincoln accepted it, though he did ask the governor "whether some of the colored people may not be let in, as for instance the very intelligent, and especially those who have fought gallantly in our ranks." In Virginia, Tennessee, and Arkansas, also, Lincoln recognized state governments which did not enfranchise the black American. But it was clear that Republicans in Congress were suspicious of these states—more because of their leniency toward the former Confederates than because of their treatment of the black—and that Congress might deny them recognition by refusing to seat their newly elected senators and representatives.

In 1864, when the time came for a new presidential election, the Democrats nominated General McClellan to run against Lincoln. Some of the so-called Radical Republicans, who were dissatisfied with Lincoln's leniency, tried to block his re-nomination and put up the Secretary of the Treasury, Salmon P. Chase, in his stead.

But this effort failed, and Lincoln was, of course, renominated. In an effort to put the ticket on a broad, bipartisan basis, the party dropped the name Republican, called itself the Union party and nominated for the vice-presidency a Southern Democrat and former slaveholder who had stood firmly for the Union, Andrew Johnson of Tennessee.

In November 1864 Lincoln and Johnson were elected, carrying all but three states (New Jersey, Delaware, and Kentucky). In the following March, the new term began, and Lincoln delivered his Second Inaugural Address, calling for "malice toward none and charity for all," in order "to bind up the nation's wounds." On April 9, Lee surrendered the Army of Northern Virginia; it was clear that the work of Reconstruction must now begin in earnest. On April 14, Lincoln attended a performance at Ford's Theater, where he was shot by an assassin, John Wilkes Booth. He died the next morning, without ever recovering consciousness, and Andrew Johnson became President of the United States.

Johnson's Policy of Reconstruction. Although a Southerner, Johnson was expected to be more severe in his Reconstruction policy than Lincoln. Johnson, a former tailor who had been illiterate until his wife taught him to write, and a man of strong emotions, hated both aristocrats and secessionists. But when his policy developed, Johnson proved even more lenient toward the Southern states than Lincoln had been.

On May 29, 1865, he issued a broad amnesty to all who would take an oath of allegiance, though men with property valued at more than $20,000 (in other words, planters) were required to ask special pardon, which was freely given. In the six weeks after May 29 he appointed provisional governors in each of the remaining Southern states to reorganize governments for these states. Only men who had been voters in 1860 and who had taken the oath of allegiance could participate in these reorganizations. This meant, of course, that blacks were excluded. When the new governments disavowed secession, accepted the abolition of slavery, and repudiated the Confederate debt, Johnson would accept them. As to what they were going to do about the blacks, no questions would be asked.

The Southern states moved swiftly under this easy formula. Before the end of the year, every state except Texas, which followed soon after, had set up a new government which met the President's terms. But two conspicuous features of these governments were deeply disturbing to many Republicans. First, these Southern states had adopted a series of laws known as "Black Codes," which denied to blacks many of the rights of citizenship—including the right to vote and to serve on juries—and which also excluded them from certain types of property ownership and certain occupations. Unemployed Negroes might be arrested as vagrants and bound out to labor in a new form of involuntary servitude. Second, the former Confederates were in complete control: the newly organized states, between them, elected to Congress the vice-president of the Confederacy, four Confederate generals, five Confederate colonels, six Confederate cabinet officers, and fifty-eight Confederate congressmen.

Congressional Radicals. When Congress met at the end of 1865, it was confronted by the fact that Reconstruction (on the President's terms) had been virtually completed without Congress having any voice in the matter. At this point, the Republicans were far from ready for the kind of all-out fight against Johnson which later developed, but they were not willing to accept the reorganized states, especially since they felt that these states would now claim a larger representation in Congress because of the free black population (only three fifths of the blacks had been counted when they were slaves), without actually allowing the blacks any voice in the government. It would be ironical indeed if the overthrow of slavery should increase the representation of the South in Congress and if the Rebels should come back into the Union stronger than when they went out.

For some months, the Republicans in Congress moved slowly, unwilling to face a break with a President of their own party, and far from ready to make a vigorous stand for the rights of blacks. But they would not seat the Southern congressmen-elect, and they set up a Joint Committee of the Senate and the House to assert their claim to a voice in the formulation of Reconstruction policy. They also passed a bill to extend the life and increase the activities of the Freedmen's Bureau—an agency created to aid blacks in their transition from slavery to freedom. When Johnson vetoed this measure and also vetoed a Civil Rights bill, tensions increased, and in June 1866, Congress voted a proposed Fourteenth Amendment. This amendment clearly asserted the citizenship of blacks; it also asserted that they were entitled to the "privileges and immunities of citizens," to the "equal protection of the laws," and to protection against being deprived of "life, liberty, and property without due process of law." The determination of exactly what these terms meant has kept lawyers busy for almost a century now, but one thing was clear: the amendment did not include a right of black suffrage. It did, however, provide that states which disfranchised a part of their adult male population would have their representation proportionately reduced. It almost seemed that Congress was offering the Southerners a choice: they might disfranchise the blacks if they were willing to pay the price of reduced representation, or they might have increased representation if they were willing to pay the price of black suffrage. This might not help the blacks, but it was certain to help the Republicans: it would either reduce the strength of Southern white Democrats or give the Republicans black political allies in the South.

The Fourteenth Amendment also excluded from federal office any person who had held any important public office before the Civil War and had then gone over to the Confederacy. This sweeping move to disqualify almost the entire leadership of the South led the Southern states to make the serious mistake of following President Johnson's advice to reject the amendment. During the latter half of 1866 and the first months of 1867, ten Southern states voted not to ratify.

Radical Reconstruction. Southern rejection of the Fourteenth Amendment precipitated the bitter fight which had been brewing for almost two years. Congress now moved to destroy the Johnson governments and to set up new governments of its own. Between March and July 1867, it adopted a series of Reconstruction Acts which divided ten Southern states into five military districts under five military governors. These governors were to hold elections for conventions to frame new state constitutions. In these elections adult males, including blacks, were to vote, but many whites, disqualified by their support of the Confederacy, were not to vote. The constitutions these conventions adopted must establish black suffrage, and the governments which they established must ratify the Fourteenth Amendment. Then and only then might they be readmitted to the Union. Thus, two years after the war was over, when the South supposed that the postwar adjustment had been completed, the process of Reconstruction actually began.

The period that followed has been the subject of more bitter feeling and more controversy than perhaps any other period in American history, and the intensity of the bitterness has made it hard to get at the realities. During 1867 the military governors conducted elections; in late 1867 and early 1868 the new constitutional conventions met in the Southern states. They complied with the terms Congress had laid down, including enfranchisement of the black, and within a year after the third Reconstruction Act (of July 1867), seven states had adopted new constitutions, organized new governments, ratified the Fourteenth Amendment, and been readmitted to the Union. In Virginia, Mississippi, and Texas the process was for one reason or another not completed until 1870.

All of these new governments, except the one in Virginia, began under Republican control, with more or less black representation in the legislatures. In one state after another, however, the Democrats, supporting a policy of white supremacy, gained the ascendancy. Military and "Radical" rule lasted for three years in North Carolina; four years in Tennessee (never under military government) and Georgia; six years in Texas; seven years in Alabama and Arkansas; eight years in Mississippi; and ten years in Florida, Louisiana, and South Carolina.

The experience of this so-called "carpetbag" rule has been interpreted in completely different terms by historians of the past and those of the present. The earlier interpretation reflected the feelings of the Southern whites who resented this regime bitterly as one of "military despotism" and "Negro rule." According to this version, later elaborated by a pro-Southern school of historians, the South was at the outset the victim of military occupation in which a brutal soldiery maintained bayonet rule. Then came the "carpetbaggers"—unscrupulous Northern adventurers whose only purpose was to enrich themselves by plundering the prostrate South. To maintain their ascendancy, the carpetbaggers incited the blacks, who were essentially well disposed, to assert themselves in swaggering insolence. Thereupon, majorities made up of illiterate blacks swarmed into the legislatures, where they were manipulated by the carpetbaggers. A carnival of riotous corruption and looting followed, until at last the outraged whites, excluded from all voice in public affairs, could endure these conditions no longer and arose to drive the vandals away and to redeem their dishonored states.

This picture of Reconstruction has a very real importance, for it has undoubtedly influenced Southern attitudes in the twentieth century, but it is an extreme distortion of the realities. Historical treatments since 1950 have presented quite a different version, stressing the brief nature of the military rule and constructive measures of the "carpetbag" governments. As for bayonet rule, the number of troops in the "Army of

Occupation" was absurdly small. In November 1869 there were 1000 federal soldiers scattered over the state of Virginia and 716 over Mississippi, with hardly more than a corporal's guard in any one place. As for the carpetbaggers, there were indeed looters among the newcomers who moved into the South, but there were also idealists: many Northern women came to teach the freed slaves; many men came to develop needed industry; many others worked with integrity and self-sacrifice to find a constructive solution for the problems of a society devastated by war and left with a huge population of former slaves to absorb and provide for. Many native Southerners, who joined with the "carpetbaggers" in their programs and who were therefore denounced as "scalawags," were equally public-spirited and high-minded.

As for "Negro rule," the fact is that the blacks were in a majority only in the convention and the first three legislatures of South Carolina. Elsewhere they were a minority, even in Mississippi and Louisiana, where they constituted a majority of the population. In view of their illiteracy and their political inexperience, the blacks handled their new responsibilities well. They tended to choose educated men for public office; many of the black legislators, congressmen, and state officials were well qualified. They were, on the whole, moderate and self-restrained in their demands, and they gave major support to certain policies of long-range value, including notably the establishment of public school systems, which the South had not had in any broad sense before the Civil War.

As for the "carnival of corruption," the post-Civil War era was marked by corruption throughout the country, and it is true that corruption presented especial hardships for the Southern states, already stripped of their resources by the war. Carpetbag governments in several states issued bonds pledging the state to pay one hundred cents on the dollar and then sold the bonds at immense discounts for whatever they would bring, pocketing the money as it came in. In South Carolina, corruptionists even stole a fund which was created to buy homesteads for blacks. But corruption was not confined to the South, and within the South it was not confined to the Republicans. Democrats also were among the guilty.

Finally, it should be noted that the Southern whites were never reduced to abject helplessness, as is sometimes imagined. From the outset they were present in all of the Reconstruction conventions and legislatures—always vocal, frequently aggressive, and sometimes dominating the proceedings.

The Fall of Radical Reconstruction.   For an average of six years the regimes of Radical Republican Reconstruction continued; then they gave way to the Democratic Redeemers—delaying further action on the question of the rights of blacks until the twentieth century. When one considers the fact that the South had just been badly defeated in war, that Radical Reconstruction was the policy of the dominant party in Washington, and that blacks constituted an actual majority of the potential electorate in several Southern states (with a certain proportion of the former Confederates disfranchised), it is difficult to understand why the Radical regimes were so promptly—almost easily—overthrown. Several contributing factors must be recognized.

First of all, of course, the former slaves were poorly fitted to assume political responsibility. Largely illiterate and conditioned for many decades to defer to the white man, they grasped their opportunity with uncertain hands. Very often they seemed to wish, quite realistically, for security of land tenure and for education more than for political rights. At the same time, however, a number of articulate and able black men, some of them former slaves, came to the fore and might have provided effective leadership for their race if Reconstruction had not been abandoned so soon. Second, and more important, one must recognize the importance of the grim resistance offered by the Southern whites. With their deep belief in the superiority of their own race, these Southerners were convinced that civilization itself was at stake, and they fought with proportionate desperation, not hesitating to resort to violence and terror. In 1867 a half-whimsical secret society formed in Tennessee and known as the Ku Klux Klan began to take on a more purposeful character and to spread across the South. Soon every Southern state had its organization of masked and robed riders, either as part of the Klan or under some other name, who, by use of threat, horsewhip, and even rope and gun, spread fear not only among blacks but perhaps even more among the Republican leaders. The states and even Congress passed laws to break up this activity, but the laws proved almost impossible to enforce, and the Klan ceased to operate only when its purposes had been accomplished.

The dramatic quality of the Klan has given it a prominent place in the public's mental picture of Reconstruction. But though the Klan played a prominent role, the white South had other, less spectacular weapons which were no less powerful. Southern whites owned virtually all of the land; they controlled virtually all employment; they dominated the small supply of money and credit that was to be found in the South; and they could, in unspectacular ways, make life very hard for individuals who did not comply with the system. This, perhaps more than the acts of night riders and violent men, made the pressure against Radical rule almost irresistible.

But still more important, perhaps, than either the limitations of the Southern blacks or the fierce determination of the Southern whites was the fact that, when all was said and done, neither the Republican party nor the Northern public was really committed to racial equality. Patterns of discrimination against the black, which still prevail today, had become well established in the Northern states long before the Civil War. Even antislavery men like the Free Soilers had taken the position they did because they wanted to keep blacks—whether slave or free—out of their bailiwicks. More than one free state had laws to prevent blacks from entering. Significantly, after emancipation all efforts to provide the former slaves with land ("forty acres and a mule") or to set up a federal program of education for blacks failed even in Congresses with large Radical majorities.

There were just not enough people who really cared about the freedmen. The decision to give the vote to the black was reached very reluctantly, as has been shown above, and it was really adopted not because of any belief that it was right in principle but because black participation in politics appeared to be the only alternative to Confederate rule—an unwelcome choice, but the only one. Later, Republicans found that the Northern voters did not support them in this choice; that the white South would not consent to a real reunion on this basis; and that the former Confederates had political objectives quite similar to the Republicans' objectives. As a result, the

Republicans let the existing forces in the South find their own resolution—which was one of white supremacy.

Yet Reconstruction was not a total failure. It established public schools in the South. It brought abolitionists and missionaries from the North to found such colleges as Howard, Fisk, Morehouse, and Talladega, which trained future generations of black leaders who in turn led the black protest movements of the twentieth century. Reconstruction also left as a permanent legacy the Fourteenth and Fifteenth Amendments, which formed the constitutional basis for the civil rights movements of the post-World War II generation.

Johnson versus the Radicals. The Radicals did not abandon their program all at once. Indeed, it faded out very gradually. While Johnson remained President, the Radicals remained militant, and in 1868 they tried to remove him by impeachment. Though he had denounced the Radicals in intemperate terms, he had done nothing to justify impeachment proceedings except to remove the Secretary of War, Edwin M. Stanton, from his post in the cabinet. In March 1867 Congress had passed a law, the Tenure of Office Act, which forbade such removals without senatorial consent and which has since been held by the courts to be unconstitutional. But when Johnson removed Stanton, who was reporting to the Radicals what went on in administration councils, there had been no judicial ruling, and the House of Representatives voted to impeach Johnson, which meant that he must be tried by the Senate on the articles of impeachment. The trial was conducted in a tense atmosphere and scarcely in a judicial way. Immense pressure was put on all Republican senators to vote for conviction. When a vote was finally taken on May 16, 1868, conviction failed by one vote of the two thirds required. Seven Republicans had stood out against the party; Johnson was permitted to serve out his term; and the balance between executive and legislative power in the American political system, which had almost been destroyed, was preserved.

The determination of the Republican leaders in Congress to beat down the opposition regardless of cost showed up in a parallel attack on the judiciary. When a Mississippi editor named McCardle appealed to the Supreme Court to rule on the constitutionality of one of the Reconstruction Acts, under which he had been arrested by the military, Congress in March 1868 passed an act changing the appellate jurisdiction of the Court so that it could not pass judgment on McCardle's case.

The Grant Administration. In 1868 the country faced another election, and the Republicans turned to General Grant as their nominee. He was elected over the Democratic candidate, Governor Horatio Seymour of New York, by a popular majority of only 300,000—a surprisingly close vote. Grant was not supported by a majority of the white voters: some 700,000 black votes helped to elect him. (The importance of the black vote in this election inspired Congress to propose the Fifteenth Amendment, forbidding any state from denying any citizen his right to vote "on account of race, color, or previous condition of servitude.")

President Grant supported the measures of the Radicals and in some ways gave his backing to their policies. Like the good military man he was, he believed that where violence broke out, it should be put down uncompromisingly. Accordingly, he favored the adoption of Enforcement Acts for the use of federal troops to break up the activities of the Ku Klux Klan. When these laws were adopted, he did not hesitate to invoke them, and troops were sent in on a number of occasions.

Fundamentally, however, Grant did not care much about politics or the rights of the black. He wanted to see tranquillity restored, and this meant reuniting North and South on any basis both would be willing to accept. Accordingly, he urged a broader extension of amnesty to all former Confederates, and he grew to resent the frequent appeals of Republican governments in the South for troops to uphold their authority. Though he realized that the tactics of the Redeemers were very bad—"bloodthirsty butchery," "scarcely a credit to savages"—he became convinced that constant federal military intervention was worse in the long run.

During the eight years of Grant's presidency, while the Radicals controlled the Congress and presumably the executive department, Radical governments were overthrown in eight of the Southern states. As Grant's second term neared its end, only three states—Louisiana, Florida, and South Carolina—remained under Radical rule.

The program of Radical Reconstruction still remained official policy in the Republican party, but it had lost its steam. The country was concerned about other things. In foreign affairs, Secretary of State Hamilton Fish was busy putting through an important settlement by which Great Britain and the United States adopted the principle of international arbitration as a means of settling American claims that had grown out of the raiding activities of the *Alabama,* which British shipyards had built for the Confederacy.

In financial circles there was a bitter contest over what to do about the greenback dollars issued during the war. Since greenbacks were not backed by gold, people had saved the more valuable gold dollars and spent the less valuable greenback dollars, thus driving gold out of circulation. The government was willing to give gold for greenbacks even though such a policy would tend to increase the value of the dollar. Debtor interests (such as farmers), who wanted a cheap dollar, fought hard against the policy of redemption, but the policy was adopted in 1875.

In politics, public confidence in the government was very much shaken by a series of disclosures concerning government corruption. In 1872 it was revealed that several congressmen had accepted gifts of stock in a construction company, the Crédit Mobilier, which was found to be diverting the funds of the Union Pacific Railroad—including the funds the government had granted to it—with the knowledge of the officers of the road. In 1875 Grant's private secretary was implicated in the operations of the "Whiskey Ring," which, by evading taxes, had systematically defrauded the government of millions of dollars. The following year, the Secretary of War was caught selling appointments to Indian posts. Meanwhile, in the New York City government, the Tweed Ring, headed by Tammany boss William Marcy Tweed, was exposed as guilty of graft and thefts which have seldom been equaled in size and never been surpassed in effrontery.

The epidemic of corruption inspired a revolt by reform Republicans, who bolted the party in 1872, organized the Liberal Republican party, and nominated Horace

Greeley, editor of the New York *Tribune,* for President. Although the Democrats also nominated Greeley and formed a coalition with the Liberal Republicans, Grant easily won reelection because most Northern voters were not yet prepared to trust the Democrats.

In the economic orbit, the country was trying to weather the financial depression that began with the panic of 1873. All in all, the problems posed by the South and the black seemed more and more distant, less and less important, to the people of the North.

The Hayes-Tilden Election of 1876. The election of 1876 brought to an end the program of Reconstruction, which probably would have ended soon in any case. In this election the Republicans, who were badly divided, turned to a Civil War veteran and governor of Ohio, Rutherford B. Hayes, as their nominee. Hayes was a conspicuously honest man, and so was his Democratic opponent, Samuel J. Tilden of New York, who owed his reputation to his part in breaking up the Tweed Ring.

When the votes were counted, Tilden clearly had a popular majority (obtained only by the suppression of black votes in several Southern states) and was within one vote of an electoral majority. But there were three states—Florida, Louisiana, and South Carolina—in which the result was contested, and two sets of returns were filed by rival officials. Congress had to count the votes, and the House of Representatives, with a Democratic majority, was in a position to prevent an election by refusing to go into joint session with the Senate, which the Constitution requires for the count. Congress agreed to appoint an Electoral Commission to provide an impartial judgment, but the commission divided along party lines, voting eight to seven for Hayes. As late as two days before the inauguration it was doubtful whether the Democrats in the House would allow the electoral count to proceed.

Many Northern Democrats were prepared to fight to a finish against what they regarded as a stolen election, but the Southern Democrats had found that one civil war

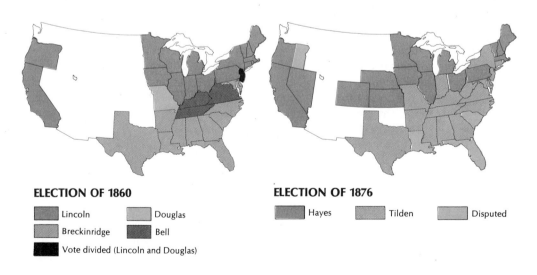

ELECTION OF 1860

Lincoln   Douglas

Breckinridge   Bell

Vote divided (Lincoln and Douglas)

ELECTION OF 1876

Hayes   Tilden   Disputed

was enough. Moreover, various negotiations had been in progress behind the scenes. Important groups of Southern Democrats who had been left out when the government largesse of the Union Pacific-Central Pacific was distributed now hoped for a Texas and Pacific Railroad which would provide bountiful federal grants for Southern interests. They received assurances from friends of Governor Hayes that he would look with favor upon such programs of internal improvement. Moreover, they were assured that he would withdraw the last remaining federal troops from Louisiana and South Carolina, which meant that their Republican governments would collapse and the score of states would be: redeemed, eleven; reconstructed, none.

With these understandings in mind, Southern congressmen voted to let the count proceed so that Hayes would be elected. Later, when they were explaining their conduct to their constituents, they thought it best to say quite a great deal about how they had ransomed South Carolina and Louisiana and very little about their hopes for the Texas and Pacific Railroad and other such enterprises. Thus a legend grew up that there had been a "compromise" by which Reconstruction was ended. What had really happened, however, was that Southern Democrats and Northern Republicans had discovered that there were many features of economic policy on which they were in close harmony. The slaves were emancipated; the Union was restored; bygones were bygones; and the harmony of their views made reconciliation natural and Reconstruction unnecessary. There was still the question of the blacks; but only a few whites had ever supported black suffrage or racial equality for its own sake. It had been an expedient, and now that the expedient was no longer needed, it could be laid aside. Such was the spirit of reconciliation.

Thus, the country ended a period of intense friction and entered upon a long era of sectional harmony and rapid economic growth. But this was done at the expense of leaving the question of racial relations still unattended to, even though slavery itself had, at immense cost, been removed.

CHAPTER 12

THE CHANGING NATION

THE ERA OF REFORM, 1830–60

Progress and Perfectibility.   In the world of today, which has experienced almost two centuries of industrialization, we have had time to see that the great changes of the industrial age brought with them many problems. We tend to think about industrialization very much in terms of these problems: the concentration of economic power; the deterioration of our cities; the congestion of our highway traffic; the waste of natural resources; the poisoning of our environment by smoke, water pollution, and the reckless use of chemicals; the population explosion; the serious gap between rich countries and poor ones; the destructive potentialities of atomic power; and, in general, the failure of social progress to keep pace with technical progress. We have been disillusioned by the fact that victory in two world wars has brought neither peace nor democracy to the world; and the highest living standards in history have not eliminated such social ills as alcoholism, drug addiction, delinquency, and crime.

It is difficult today, therefore, to understand what deep optimism and faith in progress permeated nineteenth-century thought. The experience of Americans confirmed their optimism, for they saw republics replacing monarchies; they saw equality spreading with the broadening of the suffrage and with frontier land selling at a price that would enable everyone to own a farm; they saw the wilderness brought under cultivation, the productivity of labor increased, the living standard rising, and opportunity broadened to reach an ever larger proportion of people.

The religion of nineteenth-century Americans contributed to their belief that man could become perfect and that society was making progress toward perfection. Most Americans believed in a Protestant version of Christianity which taught that man could achieve salvation—but that he must strive against the forces of evil in order to do so. This religious idea of personal salvation was easily extended to secular social thought, with the belief that society must practice right and must rid itself of evil, and that when all the evils were eliminated one by one, it would become a perfect society. Even though the old Puritan theology, with its intense concentration upon a future existence in heaven or hell, was breaking down, the spiritual drive that had been so strong a part of Puritanism was not lost. Instead, it was channeled into social thought, where it gave impetus to a crusade, on a broad front, for many kinds of reforms.

Emerson and the Reform Movement.   The spiritual drives and ideals underlying the reform movement of the pre-Civil War period are well illustrated in the career of

Ralph Waldo Emerson, whose belief in self-reliance has already been mentioned. Emerson was the descendant of a long line of Congregational ministers, and he began his career as a Unitarian minister. He had all the old Puritan concern with spiritual values, but instead of believing, as the Puritans did, in the depravity ("original sin") and unworthiness of man, he believed that man is inherently good and that, as he himself said, "God is in every man." Because of his belief in the direct relation of God and man, he rejected orthodox theology and soon gave up his ministry.

If man is inherently good, Emerson thought, it must follow that man has the potentiality of perfecting his own nature and perfecting his society. The steps that man made toward perfection would constitute progress, and in proportion as perfection was fulfilled, man would become truly free. Thus, in Emerson's thought, progress did not mean material gain ("success") as it has to many Americans. Rather it meant the fulfillment of man's spiritual potentialities and the progressively broader recognition of the worth of every man. Emerson took the eighteenth-century Enlightenment idea that men are equal and added to it the Romantic idea that every man has infinite capacity for goodness and greatness. His beliefs had an immense appeal, for they gave a spiritual dimension to the whole democratic principle that America was adopting at this time. But to fulfill their potentialities, according to Emerson, men must give up everything by which they degraded or exploited others. In personal terms, this meant that a man must be independent and must not follow the crowd—"Whoso would be a man," Emerson said, "must be a nonconformist." In social terms, it meant that there must be a constant drive to elevate the condition of man by means of various reforms.

The Reform Movement. The reform movement, of course, was immensely broader than Emerson, and he alone did not create the philosophy behind it. His importance lies in the fact that he expressed its basic attitude, better perhaps than anyone else. Sometimes he even spoke satirically of the excesses of some of the reformers ("What a fertility of projects for the salvation of the world!"). But he himself visited Brook Farm, where a group of transcendentalists were trying to create a perfect community. The reform impulse led to the launching of many such communitarian experiments, including the Mormon society.

The major way in which reform expressed itself, however, was not through a withdrawal from society but through efforts to improve society. Such efforts were a dominant feature of American activity from the age of Jackson to the Civil War and, indeed, down to the present. Reform expressed itself in a great variety of ways: in the abolition of imprisonment for debt; in prison reform and the abolition of flogging; in humane care for the mentally ill (previously treated like animals); in campaigns to limit labor to ten hours a day; in programs for the training of blind people. On a broader front, the temperance movement became an immense crusade. It began by appealing for voluntary abstinence and by campaigning against the bad influence of barrooms, where workingmen often squandered wages which were needed for the support of their families. By the 1850s, it had changed its character and become a drive for the adoption of prohibitory laws. Maine led the way with a prohibition law in 1851, and within ten years all the New England states, New York, and most of the Middle West except Illinois had followed. The laws were poorly enforced, especially in New

York, and most of them were soon repealed, but for a while nearly half of the country was legally "dry."

Women's Rights.   Another great crusade, but one which did not gain success so quickly, was the movement for women's rights. This was no mere matter of the ballot: women in mid-nineteenth-century America were denied full rights to own property, to be educated, or to enter many occupations. The first colleges were opened to women in the 1830s, but very few institutions followed their lead for many years. In 1839 Mississippi took the first steps toward correcting the common law rules which made even a wife's personal clothing the property of her husband, and between 1844 and 1850 about fifteen states changed their laws to abolish the more extreme legal disabilities of women. In 1848, at a convention at Seneca Falls, New York, feminists demanded general social and political equality. But the majority, even of women, did not actively support this demand, and it was to be another forty years before women gained the ballot in even a single state.[1] In the decade of the fifties, however, women began to hold most of the teaching positions in schools, and by their right to independent earnings they were undercutting the economic dependency which had been the basis of their traditional subordination.

Education.   Another major development of the mid-nineteenth century was the growth of public education. Although not usually counted in the list of reforms, the campaign for state-supported schools drew upon the same motives that sparked the reform movement and was led by reformers, the most notable of whom was Horace Mann. When Mann accepted the post of secretary of the Massachusetts state board of education 1837, he wrote, "So long as I hold this office I devote myself to the supremest welfare of mankind upon earth. . . . I have faith in the improvability of the race—in their accelerating improvability." Here, again, was the theme of the perfectibility of man.

At that time, education in the United States was not generally regarded as a matter of public responsibility. At the primary level, the New England towns did follow the old Puritan practice of maintaining schools so that no child need be unable to read the Bible. In other states, people paid for their children to learn reading and writing, just as one might pay for lessons in music or art today. Some states provided schools for the poor, but the very fact that these were for paupers caused people to shun them to avoid the embarrassing admission of poverty. Beyond the primary level, the work now done by high schools was then done by private "academies," of which there were more than six thousand (but with only twelve thousand teachers) in the United States by 1850.

At the college level there were a number of state universities, but most of these received paltry support from their states and were kept going mostly by tuition fees. The characteristic institution of "higher" learning was the small, church-supported denominational college, with a faculty of five or ten and a student body of anywhere from one hundred to three hundred. College was still the privilege of a limited few.

---

[1] Wyoming Territory adopted woman suffrage in 1869, and the territory became a state in 1890. Colorado followed in 1893, Utah and Idaho in 1896, but there were no others until the twentieth century.

More than five hundred such colleges were founded in the United States before the Civil War, and all were strictly teaching institutions, with little or no idea of actually increasing the body of knowledge.

Mid-century saw many developments in education. At the level of primary education, the pauper schools were largely eliminated during the 1830s, and taxation for at least partial support of the schools became widespread except in the South. But many states still required parents to pay part of the costs of schooling, and in some states these rates were not abolished until the 1860s. As late as 1827 more than half the children in Pennsylvania were not attending school at all (250,000 out of 400,000), and education was not compulsory anywhere until 1852, when Massachusetts passed the first compulsory attendance law. As late as 1870 the average American had received less than twenty-two months of schooling in his entire life, and until the 1860s girls fared far worse than boys in the amount of schooling they received.

High schools were still in their infancy. In 1860 half the high schools in America were in the three states of Massachusetts, New York, and Ohio, and the total number of public high schools (321) was less than the total number of colleges.

Colleges continued to increase in number—165 new institutions were founded between 1850 and 1870—but the total number was less significant than the development of truly advanced studies. Some of the old church-dominated colleges, where students had recited their classroom lessons almost like grammar school pupils, were turning into secular universities dedicated to free inquiry. In 1869 Harvard, for instance, inaugurated a chemist, Charles W. Eliot, to succeed a long line of clergymen in the presidency. In 1868 Andrew D. White launched another real university at Cornell, and in 1876 Daniel Coit Gilman started America's first true research university at Johns Hopkins. These institutions had broad curricula and a commitment to advance knowledge as well as to teach.

To many Americans who hailed the new schools with enthusiasm, public education meant vocational training—that is, better preparation for better-paying jobs. But to the leaders who fought the battle for free schools, universal education beyond the three R's, and teaching which emphasized understanding rather than mere memorization—to such leaders the new education, like other reforms, was important because it would help to make the ideal of equality a reality by giving all men a comparable opportunity to develop their talents. If man was perfectible, education would take him along the path toward perfection.

During the antebellum generation one other reform movement—the campaign against slavery—attracted much public attention and excited so much controversy that it eclipsed all the other reform movements. The antislavery movement has been discussed in Chapters 9 and 10, and some of its consequences appear in Chapter 11.

The Underlying Ideals of Freedom and Individualism. Looking at all the varied activities of the mid-nineteenth-century reformers, one must ask, what was the basic motivating drive? The question is perhaps too complex to answer in full, but clearly one important ideal that most of them shared was the ideal of the individual freed from all handicaps which interfered with the fulfillment of his potentialities as a human being. The public education movement was sparked by the belief that ignorance and illiteracy must not be allowed to retard the development of the abilities of poor persons. The movement for women's rights was based on a belief that the opportunities open to individuals ought not be restricted because of their sex. The antislavery movement aimed fundamentally at removing a harsh set of restrictions imposed upon individuals who happened to be blacks. Even the temperance and prohibition movements were designed to protect all individuals from a certain form of temptation.

This ideal of individual freedom was based upon the concept of a society in which power would be so widely diffused or atomized that no one individual or group could control other individuals or groups or do much injury to them. The ideal of freedom, then, would be fulfilled by the double condition of (1) removing inequalities and handicaps and (2) maintaining a dispersal of power such that no one could really control anyone else.

When nineteenth-century Americans thought of power, they pictured it in terms of privileged economic groups, and they believed that concentration of power could be avoided simply by devising a system to limit the action of government and by maintaining impartial rules for all elements in the economy. Accordingly, in politics they cherished the idea that the power of government should be restricted by a written constitution and that, where power was conferred, it should be divided between three branches of officials—legislative, executive, and judicial—which would restrain one another by a system of checks and balances.

In economics, they believed that a system of unrestricted buying and selling in a free market by unregulated producers and consumers (laissez faire) would prevent buyers from exercising power over sellers, or vice versa, and would leave all parties free to follow whatever occupations they preferred, to sell their products to anyone who would buy, and to buy what they needed from anyone who would sell. The rivalry (competition) among buyers would protect the seller from the power of any one buyer, and the rivalry among sellers would protect the buyer from the power of any one seller. The classic statement of this economic philosophy was made by the British political economist Adam Smith in *The Wealth of Nations* (1776). Americans tended to adopt Smith's views as basic doctrine, although they accepted deviations in practice, such as the protective tariff and the activities of state governments in building railroads, chartering banks, and regulating businesses.

Because of their confidence in what could be accomplished merely by freedom from controls in a system of diffused power, the idealists of the mid-nineteenth century sometimes fell unrealistically short of their purposes. In the case of slavery, for example, abolitionists underestimated the strength of racism in American society and the need for positive government action to force institutional change. When they did advocate strong federal programs for civil rights, land reform, and black education, the abolitionists received little support from a white population indifferent or hostile to racial equality. In the case of temperance, reformers assumed that alcoholism could be ended by destroying the power of the distillers and the saloons; they ignored the fact that alcoholism is usually a response by the individual to problems which are or which seem insoluble to him—so that laws against distillers cannot prevent some kind of pathological response as long as the problem remains.

Many critics today believe that the reformers also idealized the free individual too much. They wanted to free him so that he could fulfill his best potentialities of mind and spirit. But very often he used his freedom to take advantage of his fellowman more readily in the race for wealth. This disparity in purpose was particularly evident in educational reform: while the leaders of education advocated education for the purpose of giving men a better understanding and appreciation of life and the universe, the public supported it for vocational reasons, as a quicker means to better-paying jobs.

The believers in individualism especially emphasized the virtues of the frontiersman as the epitome of the independent, self-reliant man. But critics today argue that democratic reform came from the city more than from the frontier. They assert that the pioneer experience did more to brutalize the frontiersman than to ennoble him. He may have been truly self-reliant, they contend, but he was hardly individualistic in the sense of holding values different from those of his fellows. Instead, the rigors of frontier life forced him to adapt in a very specific way, leaving him little opportunity for individual self-development and self-expression. According to this negative verdict, he ended by killing the Indians, by exterminating the buffalo, by exploiting the natural resources, and by despoiling the beauty of primitive nature. At the end, he was impoverished rather than enriched in spirit—so isolated by his experience as an individual that he had become to some degree antisocial, distrustful of everything beyond his own limited horizon, and indifferent to the interests of the community and the possibilities of community life.

THE INDUSTRIAL SOCIETY EMERGENT

Competition versus Concentrated Power. At the midpoint of the nineteenth century, men were still thinking in terms of an agricultural age, with limited sources of energy and a relatively simple technology. But even while the ideas of an era of diffused power still flourished, a new technology of steam, of heavy machinery, and of mass production was beginning to revolutionize the society. The earlier society had believed in a competitive or free-market system of economics to keep power from being concentrated and had not recognized that it was really the earlier conditions of local markets, limited energy, and craftsmanship which had preserved the system of innumerable small economic units. Once these factors were gone, the competitive system tended to eliminate itself. In a new economy of national markets, large corporations, and mechanized production, concentration of power was possible. By the 1870s, some industrial and railroad enterprises were driving out rivals and creating monopolies affecting millions of individuals.

Reform had been directed toward correcting the flaws of an earlier model of society. But while it was being improved, the model itself was undergoing a great industrial transformation that tended to make some of the improvements obsolete even as they were being devised.

Urbanism. As Americans developed a more advance economic system for the country, they steadily shifted the normal basis of life from an economy of subsistence, where the average family produced most of its own needs ("making a living"), to an economy of exchange, where the average family produced one crop or did one job and sold its product or its labor for money with which to buy its needs from other specialized workers ("making an income"). As this shift took place, opportunities for nonagricultural work increased and the number of people who were drawn into the tasks of distribution (trade and commerce) or into the processing of goods (industry) multiplied far more rapidly than the total population.

This shift in economic occupations meant also a shift from country to city. Thus, even in the classic age of the American frontier, when the westward movement was still advancing across the plains and over the Rocky Mountains and when the migration west seemed the great American migration, it was already true that a reverse migration was setting in. This migration drew people from the farm to rapidly growing American cities—cities larger than colonial America had ever dreamed of. It also drew migrants from Europe in greater numbers than ever before. American urban growth was changing the population patterns of two continents.

In 1870 New York was the only city in the United States with a million population. But twenty-five cities were larger than any city had been in 1790, when Philadelphia had 42,000 and New York 33,000. Between 1830 and 1870, America's rural population increased about two and a half times, from 11 million to 28 million, but urban population increased no less than nine times, from 1.1 million to 9.9 million. The number of farms was increasing so much less rapidly than the population of cities that it would appear that the number of farm boys who moved to the city must have been several times more than the number of city boys who went to the frontier to occupy farms.

Another major source of recruits for the cities lay across the Atlantic in western Europe. In the first fifty years of the Republic, European immigrants did not come in large numbers, but in 1842, for the first time, their annual total surpassed 100,000. By 1855 it exceeded 200,000, and after declining during the Civil War, it reached 318,000 in 1866 and 459,000 in 1873. Immigration was still far below the peaks of a million or more which it was to attain six times between 1905 and 1914, but by 1850 the proportion of foreign-born in New England and the Middle Atlantic states was already 15 percent, rising to 20 percent by 1870. By the latter year the proportion of population that was either foreign-born or of foreign-born parentage was to rise to 33 percent in New England and to 42 percent in the Middle Atlantic states (54 percent and 50 percent respectively by 1900).

The Technological Effects of Urbanism. The growth of such metropolitan clusters of population and the heavy concentrations of immigrants in the cities required complex changes in American life. At the purely technical level, the sheer size of these urban concentrations presented many problems unknown to the small town. Since distances within the new cities were too great for walking, public transportation became a necessity—first horse-drawn cars and later steam-driven elevated railways and trolley cars. To control the dangers of fire—an immense hazard in nineteenth-century wooden cities—required more than the volunteer bucket brigade of rural districts, and fire engines were developed, though they continued to be operated by volunteer companies rather than by regular fire departments. Despite these facilities, the city of Chicago was virtually destroyed by fire in 1871, in what still remains America's worst urban conflagration.

Similarly, the old-fashioned county constable was inadequate to cope with crime in the cities, and full-scale police departments evolved. (The first policemen were put in uniform in New York in 1853.) But no police could make cities safe after dark as long as the only illumination came from dim and flickering oil lamps. Boston and New York met the need for better illumination by installing gas street lights in 1822 and 1823. The improved gas arc light replaced these in the 1870s, and electric lighting came to American cities in the 1880s.

Another serious problem was the protection of public health and the control of epidemics, for scourges of disease, the worst of which was yellow fever, killed one person in every twenty in Philadelphia in 1798, one in twelve in New Orleans in 1850, and one in eight in Memphis in 1878. The installation of public water supplies and sewage systems and the establishment of municipal health departments all were forms of response to this danger.

Community Relations. Essentially, these were technical problems—often very difficult ones—but problems on which everyone could agree and to which the technical solution could be sought. But at another level the cities presented a problem that could not be solved without deep social adjustments—namely, the problem of new kinds of relationships among new groupings of people. The city was too large and complex to form a natural community of people who were more or less acquainted with one another, as was the case in a village or small town. The city tended to separate its groups of people. The poor were situated in one district, the well-to-do in another. The community, therefore, could more easily forget about the condition of the poor, and landlords who thought only of maximum profits could build windowless, unheated tenement houses without adequate plumbing—tenements which soon became slums. Thus, as immigrant groups came in, they tended to be crowded into districts apart from the rest of the population.

The New Immigration. Students of American immigration have traditionally made a major distinction between what they call the "old immigration" and the "new immigration." The old—mostly before the Civil War—consisted largely of stock from northern and western Europe and especially from Germany, Ireland, and, to a lesser extent, Scandinavia. Predominantly, these immigrants were Protestant (except for the Irish); many of them had some education and some small savings. Culturally, it is said, they were similar to native Americans.

The new immigration, mostly since the Civil War, came heavily from eastern and southern Europe (and also from China and Japan until cut off in 1882 and 1908 respectively), especially from Italy, Poland, the Balkans, and Russia. To a great extent these were peasant folk, illiterate and poor; in religion they were mostly Catholic or Jewish, and culturally they contrasted sharply with the Yankees. A measure of validity endures in this contrast, for these differences were all real, but possibly this formula leaves out the most crucial factor: earlier immigrants, as farmers or agricultural laborers, came and adjusted to a country that was still basically rural and possessed rural values; beginning with the Irish, later immigrants, mostly unskilled industrial workers, arrived in an America that was rapidly becoming urban, and their adjustment was to the urban society. In concrete terms, they were forced to adjust to residential segregation, labor exploitation, and slums. As a result, they were not readily drawn into the mainstream of American life but remained overwhelmingly in a lower economic class and became the objects of prejudice.

It was in this variegated urban society, with its diversity of ethnic groups, cultural components, and religious faiths, that the traditional qualities of pioneer Americanism failed to fit adequately. Early Americanism had stressed individualism and self-reliance so much that it was not easily recognized that the problems of slums were in many respects social problems requiring action by society and not personal problems requiring action by the individual. Early American society had demanded the virtues that were needed on the frontier, and it was not cosmopolitan in recognizing the virtues of other cultures. American Protestantism, with its ancient memory of persecution at the hands of the Catholic Church and with its Old Testament scorn for faiths unlike its own, was not a tolerant religion; separation of church and state had been adopted more because of a fear of other religions than because of a respect for them.

The Know-Nothings. Thus it happened that, in spite of the tradition of the "melting pot" and in spite of the new opportunity which America gave to a great many immigrants, there grew up a kind of barrier between the native stock and the immigrant stock, with serious tensions between them. These tensions showed up very clearly for the first time in the 1850s with the development of what was called the Know-Nothing movement. The Know-Nothings—the secret, fraternal Supreme Order of the Star-Spangled Banner, organized in 1850—were opposed to foreigners and to Catholics; when questioned about their secrets, members would reply, "I know nothing." Between 1854 and 1856 the Know-Nothings moved into politics and won a number of smashing election victories in Massachusetts, Pennsylvania, New York, and Maryland. By 1858 the Know-Nothing movement had subsided as suddenly as it had flared up, but the social animosities of which it was symptomatic had survived and would appear again in the American Protective Association of the 1880s and 1890s, in the Ku Klux Klan of the 1920s, and in continuing patterns of prejudice and discrimination against foreigners, Catholics, and Jews.

"Americanization." For the immigrant, acceptance was possible, upon certain terms. These terms were that he become "Americanized." Americanization meant not only that he must substitute the American version of English for his native speech but, even more, that he must accept a whole range of American attitudes, values, and customs. He must accept the American goal of economic success and must reach this goal. He must dress, talk, and act like a native American; and he must sandpaper out of his personality any distinctive quality which made him "different." When Alexis de Toqueville came from France to visit America during the era of Andrew Jackson, he observed that in a country which repudiates aristocracy, as America did, the standards of the aristocrats cannot dominate; instead, the standards of the majority will become the standards of the society. The majority will insist that everyone conform to its standards, and the power of the majority will be so great that even in a land of liberty the principle of conformity will often be stronger than the principle of freedom. This is, in a sense, what happened to the immigrants, and it meant that even when the melting pot succeeded and the immigrant became Americanized, the success was gained at the expense of forcing him to renounce important parts of his cultural heritage, including portions that might have enriched American life had our society been tolerant and cosmopolitan enough to accept them.

The Black American. For the immigrant, Americanization was possible at a price. But there remained one group, forming one eighth of the population and consisting of native Americans of old colonial stock, for whom Americanization was not permitted on any terms, no matter how fully they adapted themselves to American standards. This was the black population, held mostly in slavery until 1865. Despite four years of war and a decade of strife over the status of the freedman, whites of the Civil War era saw the slavery question too narrowly as one involving the legality and morality of ownership of one man by another and did not see it as a problem of inequalities, based on race, in a democratic society. They did not grasp the fact that the slavery question was only a special aspect of the racial question.

During Reconstruction, as we have seen, the nation adopted three constitutional amendments, two civil rights acts, and Enforcement Acts to protect the rights of the freedmen. Many of the Radical Republicans recognized that, if the black was to have genuine freedom, his new status must be protected, but they did not fully agree on how this was to be done. One group advocated the distribution of land to the freedmen ("forty acres and a mule") so that the blacks could protect themselves economically; an overlapping group relied upon the guarantee of citizenship rights, especially the right to vote, so that freedmen could protect themselves politically.

But the distribution of land failed because the Republicans were not willing to do anything as drastic as confiscating the land of former Confederates or appropriating huge sums for the purchase of land to be distributed. Without land, the Negroes were economically at the mercy of Southern white landowners and could not assert themselves. The guarantee of citizenship rights failed essentially because the North, in the long run, did not believe in racial equality and would not fulfill the guarantee. The courts consistently construed the laws narrowly: for instance, in 1883 the Supreme Court voided the Civil Rights Act of 1875 on the ground that the Fourteenth Amendment forbade discrimination by the states but did not forbid discrimination by private persons. Between 1875 and 1957 Congress regularly turned down all proposals to enact further laws for civil rights or for the protection of voting rights.

The federal government was inactive essentially because the American public was indifferent. Most Northerners wanted reconciliation between North and South and resented the question of the rights of blacks as an impediment to intersectional harmony. Also, the public did not accept the idea of racial equality. Northern newspapers and magazines often presented a derogatory, stereotyped picture of the black as innately inferior, unattractive, and shiftless. Even educated and intelligent people throughout the nation accepted this stereotype.

In these circumstances, a whole series of institutions grew up to hold the black in subordination. Economically, the institution which did this was farm tenancy, or "share-cropping." Landowners, bankrupt after the war and without money to pay wages, needed labor to work their land; freedmen, with no economic assets except their agricultural skills, needed land on which to labor. The landowner furnished land; the freedman furnished labor; and each received an agreed portion, or "share," of the crop. But the cultivator needed food and supplies to remain alive until the crop was harvested, and he secured these things on credit, at a high rate of interest. Since the price of cotton was so low that one man could scarcely cultivate enough of it to make a living, even in the best of circumstances the cultivator who received only a part of the crop and had to pay for his advances out of this portion remained chronically impoverished and debt ridden. By the twentieth century many independent white farmers also fell into tenancy.

Socially, blacks were subjected to segregation, which grew increasingly rigid with the passage of time. During the first years after the Civil War, blacks and whites mingled to a limited extent in public places—trains, streetcars, theaters, restaurants. But racial intermarriage was strictly taboo, and separate schools for blacks and whites became the practice even while the Radicals were in power. Segregation received constitutional sanction in 1896, when the Supreme Court in the crucial decision of *Plessy* v. *Ferguson* held that laws requiring separation did not violate the Fourteenth Amendment if equal facilities were provided for both races. The "separate but equal" doctrine encouraged a flood of segregation laws, not confined entirely to the Southern states, and segregation continued to be sanctioned by law until 1954 (see page 530).

Politically, voting by blacks, apparently protected by the Fifteenth Amendment, persisted until the 1890s, though it was often a "captive" vote, used by machine politicians. But between 1890 and 1908 the Southern states, by constitutional amendment or by statute, instituted a series of devices to disfranchise blacks by indirect means, without explicit reference to their "race, color, or previous condition of servitude" (Fifteenth Amendment). The devices included: (1) a literacy or understanding test which gave great latitude to local registrars of voters, (2) a voluntary poll tax for voting, which blacks without money income could not easily pay, and (3) a direct exclusion of blacks from the Democratic party primary, which was equivalent to an election but was legally held to be a private selection of nominees, exempt from the laws which governed elections. These devices, of course, disfranchised many poor whites as well as virtually all blacks, even though the laws included escape clauses such as the "grandfather clause" which permitted nonqualifying whites to vote if their fathers or grandfathers had voted.

The forces of segregation and disfranchisement were so strong that Booker T. Washington, the dominant black leader of the period from 1885 to 1915, accepted them and concentrated his efforts instead upon economic improvement. His acquiescence encouraged the white community to regard the pattern of race relations as settled. Thus segregation became an accepted part of the social system, though not without protest from black activists and white liberals who dissented from Washington's approach. These reformers, heirs of the abolitionists, founded the Niagara Movement under the leadership of W. E. B. Du Bois in 1905, and broadened their base with the founding of the interracial National Association for the Advancement of Colored People in 1909. Although small in numbers at first, these forces of racial protest laid the groundwork for the later full-scale attack on segregation.

BIBLIOGRAPHY

On the entire period 1850–77, J. G. Randall and David Donald, *The Civil War and Reconstruction,* 2nd ed. (Boston: D. C. Heath, 1961) provides a masterful condensation of a vast amount of scholarly literature. For the prewar and war periods, the most comprehensive, detailed, and authoritative treatment is Allan Nevins, *Ordeal of the Union,* 2 vols. (1947); *The Emergence of Lincoln,* 2 vols. (1950); and *The War for the Union,* 4 vols. (New York: Charles Scribner's Sons, 1959–71).

On the background of the Civil War, the view that unrealistic emotionalism and blundering leadership played a large part is expressed in Avery O. Craven, *The Coming of the Civil War,* * 2nd rev. ed. (Chicago: University of Chicago Press, 1957) and in various writings of J. G. Randall, including *Lincoln the President,* 4 vols. (New York: Dodd Mead, 1945–55). Important essays by Arthur Schlesinger, Jr., and Pieter Geyl, controverting this view, are in Edwin C. Rozwenc, ed., *The Causes of the American Civil War** (Boston: D. C. Heath, 1961). This controversy is admirably reviewed in Thomas J. Pressly, *Americans Interpret Their Civil War** (New York: Free Press, 1965). A major account of the last four years preceding the war is Roy F. Nichols, *The Disruption of the American Democracy** (New York: Free Press, 1967). The best study of the rise of the Republican party is Eric Foner, *Free Soil, Free Labor, Free Men: The Ideology of the Republican Party Before the Civil War** (New York: Oxford University Press, 1971). On the compromise of 1850, see Holman Hamilton, *Prologue to Conflict** (New York: Norton, 1966). On the Fort Sumter crisis, see David M. Potter, *Lincoln and His Party in the Secession Crisis** (New Haven: Yale Press, 1962 ed.); Kenneth M. Stampp, *And the War Came; The North and the Secession Crisis* (Baton Rouge: Louisiana State University Press, 1950); Richard N. Current, *Lincoln and the First Shot** (Philadelphia: Lippincott, 1964).

On slavery, the best modern treatments are Kenneth Stampp, *The Peculiar Institution: Slavery in the Ante-Bellum South** (New York: Alfred A. Knopf, 1956), Stanley M. Elkins, *Slavery: A Problem in American Institutional and Intellectual Life** (Chicago: University of Chicago Press, 1968); Eugene D. Genovese, *The Political Economy of Slavery** (New York: Random House, 1965); and David B. Davis, *The Problem of Slavery in Western Culture** (first volume published; others to follow, Ithaca: Cornell University Press, 1969). See also Ann Lane, ed., *The Debate over Slavery: Stanley B. Elkins and His Critics** (Urbana, Ill.: University of Illinois Press, 1971). Older but still essential for economic aspects is Ulrich B. Phillips, *American Negro Slavery* (1918; reprint Baton Rouge: Louisiana State University Press, 1966). The best general account of the antislavery movement is Louis Filler, *The Crusade Against Slavery, 1830–1860** (New York: Harper & Row, 1960), but an important revision of previous adverse treatment of the abolitionists is Martin Duberman, ed., *The Antislavery Vanguard: New Essay on the Abolitionists** (Princeton: Princeton University Press, 1965). Benjamin Quarles, *Black Abolitionists** (New York: Oxford University Press, 1969) is the best treatment of its subject, and Herbert Aptheker, *American Negro Slave Revolts** (New York: International Publishing Company, 1969) chronicles every actual and rumored uprising. For the underground railroad, see Larry Gara, *The Liberty Line: The Legend of the Underground Railroad** (Lexington, Ky.: University of Kentucky Press, 1967).

Much of the most valuable history for this period is in the form of biography. Among leading items are lives of Henry Clay* by Glyndon G. Van Deusen (Boston: Little, Brown, 1937), of Daniel Webster by Claude M. Fuess, 2 vols. (New York: Plenum Publishing Corporation, 1968), and of John C. Calhoun by Charles M. Wiltse, 3 vols. (New York: Russell, 1970). There are also briefer, and perhaps more incisive biographies of Clay* by Clement Eaton (Boston: Little, Brown, 1964), of Webster* by Richard Current (Boston: Little, Brown, 1955), and of Calhoun* by Margaret Coit (Boston: Houghton Mifflin, 1950) and by Gerald M. Capers (Gainesville: University of Florida Press, 1960). On Thomas Hart Benton, see the biography by William N. Chambers (Boston: Little, Brown, 1956); on Stephen A. Douglas by Gerald M. Capers (Boston: Little, Brown, 1959); on Charles Sumner by David Donald, 2 vols. (New York: Alfred A. Knopf, 1960–70). On Lincoln, the best one-volume life is by Benjamin P. Thomas (New York: Alfred A. Knopf, 1952), but for the period before the presidency, see the brief but cogent Prelude to Greatness* by Don E. Fehrenbacher (Stanford: Stanford University Press, 1970); on Lincoln's presidency, Randall, cited above. On James Buchanan, see the life of Buchanan by Philip S. Klein (University Park, Pa.: Pennsylvania State University Press, 1962); on Salmon P. Chase and his family by Thomas G. and Marva R. Belden, entitled So Fell the Angels (Boston: Little, Brown, 1956), and on William H. Seward by Glyndon G. Van Deusen (New York: Oxford University Press, 1967). The most concise biography of Frederick Douglass is Benjamin Quarles, Frederick Douglass* (New York: Atheneum, 1968).

On the war itself, in addition to titles above, the military history has been treated with especial distinction by three writers: Douglas S. Freeman, R. E. Lee, 4 vols. (New York: Charles Scribner's Sons, 1935)—a classic—and Lee's Lieutenants, 3 vols. (New York: Charles Scribner's Sons, 1942–44); Kenneth P. Williams, who died before completing his account of the Union Armies, entitled Lincoln Finds a General, 5 vols. (New York: Macmillan, 1949); and Bruce Catton, many works, but especially his three-volume Centennial History of the Civil War (Garden City, N.Y.: Doubleday, 1961–65). For the Confederacy, the best brief account is Clement Eaton, A History of the Southern Confederacy (New York: Macmillan, 1954). The role of blacks in the war is treated in Benjamin Quarles, The Negro in the Civil War* (Boston: Little, Brown, 1969) and James M. McPherson, ed., The Negro's Civil War* (New York: Random House, 1965). For the role of women, see Mary Elizabeth Massey, Bonnet Brigades: American Women and the Civil War (New York: Alfred A. Knopf, 1966).

On Reconstruction, the traditional, anti-Radical interpretation by William A. Dunning, Reconstruction: Political and Economic, 1865–1877* (New York: Harper & Row, 1907), has been subjected to extensive revision. The two best, general revisionist treatments—both brief—are John Hope Franklin, Reconstruction After the Civil War* (Chicago: University of Chicago Press, 1961) and Kenneth M. Stampp, The Era of Reconstruction, 1865–1877 (New York: Alfred A. Knopf, 1965). Among more intensive studies, the following are especially important: C. Vann Woodward, Reunion and Reaction: The Compromise of 1877 and the End of Reconstruction* (Boston: Little, Brown, 1966); Eric L. McKitrick, Andrew Johnson and Reconstruction* (Chicago: University of Chicago Press, 1960); La Wanda Cox and John H. Cox, Politics, Principle, and Prejudice, 1865–1866* (New York: Free Press, 1969); W. R. Brock, An American Crisis: Congress and Reconstruction, 1865–1867 (New York: St. Martin's Press, 1963); Willie Lee Rose, Rehearsal for Reconstruction: The Port Royal Experiment* (New York: Random House, 1964); James M. McPherson, The Struggle for Equality: Abolitionists and the Negro in the Civil War and Reconstruction* (Princeton: Princeton University Press, 1964); Rembert W. Patrick, The Reconstruction of the Nation* (New York: Oxford University Press, 1967); W. E. B. Du Bois, Black Reconstruction in America* (New York: Atheneum, 1969); and Robert Cruden, The Negro in Reconstruction* (Englewood Cliffs, N.J.: Prentice-Hall, 1969).

For cultural and intellectual developments, see Ralph H. Gabriel, The Course of American Democratic Thought, 2nd ed. (New York: Ronald Press, 1956); Merle Curti, The Growth of American Thought, 3rd ed. (New York: Harper & Row, 1964); Carl Bode, Antebellum Culture* (Carbondale: Southern Illinois University Press, 1970); and Allan Nevins, The Emergence of Modern America, 1865–1878 (New York: Macmillan, 1927). For a broader view of industrial developments, see Thomas C. Cochran and William Miller, The Age of Enterprise* (New York: Harper & Row, 1968). On education see Edgar W. Knight, Education in the United States, 3rd ed. (Westport, Conn.: The Greenwood Press, 1951), and R. Freeman Butts and Lawrence A. Cremin, A History of Education in American Culture (New York: Holt, Rinehart, and Winston, 1953). On immigration consult Marcus Lee Hansen, The Atlantic Migration, 1607–1860* and The Immigrant in American History* (both New York:

Harper & Row, 1960), and Oscar Handlin, *The Uprooted** (Waltham, Mass.: Xerox College Publishing Co., 1957). On nativist reactions against the immigrant see Ray A. Billington, *The Protestant Crusade, 1800–1860** (Chicago: Quadrangle Books, 1964). On the American black see John Hope Franklin, *From Slavery to Freedom,** 3rd ed. (New York: Random House, 1969); C. Vann Woodward, *The Strange Career of Jim Crow,** 2nd rev. ed. (New York: Oxford University Press, 1966); and August Meier and Elliot M. Rudwick, *From Plantation to Ghetto,** 2nd rev. ed. (New York: Hill and Wang, 1970).

*Denotes a paperback.

AppenDices

THE DECLARATION OF INDEPENDENCE
In Congress, July 4, 1776.

*The unanimous Declaration
of the thirteen united States of America,*

When in the Course of human events, it becomes necessary for one people to dissolve the political bands which have connected them with another, and to assume among the Powers of the earth, the separate and equal station to which the Laws of Nature and of Nature's God entitle them, a decent respect to the opinions of mankind requires that they should declare the causes which impel them to the separation.

We hold these truths to be self-evident, that all men are created equal, that they are endowed by their Creator with certain unalienable Rights, that among these are Life, Liberty and the pursuit of Happiness. That to secure these rights, Governments are instituted among Men, deriving their just powers from the consent of the governed, That whenever any Form of Government becomes destructive of these ends, it is the Right of the People to alter or to abolish it, and to institute new Government, laying its foundation on such principles and organizing its powers in such form, as to them shall seem most likely to effect their Safety and Happiness. Prudence, indeed, will dictate that Governments long established should not be changed for light and transient causes; and accordingly all experience hath shown, that mankind are more disposed to suffer, while evils are sufferable, than to right themselves by abolishing the forms to which they are accustomed. But when a long train of abuses and usurpations, pursuing invariably the same Object evinces a design to reduce them under absolute Despotism, it is their right, it is their duty, to throw off such Government, and to provide new Guards for their future security.— Such has been the patient sufferance of these Colonies; and such is now the necessity which constrains them to alter their former Systems of Government. The history of the present King of Great Britain is a history of repeated injuries and usurpations, all having in direct object the establishment of an absolute Tyranny over these States. To prove this, let Facts be submitted to a candid world.

He has refused his Assent to Laws, the most wholesome and necessary for the public good.

He has forbidden his Governors to pass Laws of immediate and pressing importance, unless suspended in their operation till his Assent should be obtained; and when so suspended, he has utterly neglected to attend to them.

He has refused to pass other Laws for the accommodation of large districts of people, unless those people would relinquish the right of Representation in the Legislature, a right inestimable to them and formidable to tyrants only.

He has called together legislative bodies at places unusual, uncomfortable, and distant from the depository of their Public Records, for the sole purpose of fatiguing them into compliance with his measures.

He has dissolved Representative Houses repeatedly, for opposing with manly firmness his invasions on the rights of the people.

He has refused for a long time, after such dissolutions, to cause others to be elected; whereby the Legislative Powers, incapable of Annihilation, have returned to the People at large for their exercise; the State remaining in the mean time exposed to all the dangers of invasion from without, and convulsions within.

He has endeavoured to prevent the population of these States; for that purpose obstructing the Laws for Naturalization of Foreigners; refusing to pass others to encourage their migrations hither, and raising the conditions of new Appropriations of Lands.

He has obstructed the Administration of Justice, by refusing his Assent to Laws for establishing Judiciary Powers.

He has made Judges dependent on his Will alone, for the tenure of their offices, and the amount and payment of their salaries.

He has erected a multitude of New Offices, and sent hither swarms of Officers to harass our people, and eat out their substance.

He has kept among us, in times of peace, Standing Armies without the Consent of our legislatures.

He has affected to render the Military independent of and superior to the Civil Power.

He has combined with others to subject us to a jurisdiction foreign to our constitution, and unacknowledged by our laws; giving his Assent to their acts of pretended Legislation:

For quartering large bodies of armed troops among us:

For protecting them, by a mock Trial, from Punishment for any Murders which they should commit on the Inhabitants of these States:

For cutting off our Trade with all parts of the world:

For imposing taxes on us without our Consent:

For depriving us in many cases, of the benefits of Trial by Jury:

For transporting us beyond Seas to be tried for pretended offences:

For abolishing the free System of English Laws in a neighbouring Province, establishing therein an Arbitrary government, and enlarging its Boundaries so as to render it at once an example and fit instrument for introducing the same absolute rule into these Colonies:

For taking away our Charters, abolishing our most valuable Laws, and altering fundamentally the Forms of our Governments:

For suspending our own Legislatures, and declaring themselves invested with Power to legislate for us in all cases whatsoever.

He has abdicated Government here, by declaring us out of his Protection and waging War against us.

He has plundered our seas, ravaged our Coasts, burnt our towns, and destroyed the lives of our people.

He is at this time transporting large armies of foreign mercenaries to compleat the works of death, desolation and tyranny, already begun with circumstances of Cruelty & perfidy scarcely paralleled in the most barbarous ages, and totally unworthy the Head of a civilized nation.

He has constrained our fellow Citizens taken Captive on the high Seas to bear Arms against their Country, to become the executioners of their friends and Brethren, or to fall themselves by their Hands.

He has excited domestic insurrections amongst us, and has endeavoured to bring on the inhabitants of our frontiers, the merciless Indian Savages, whose known rule of warfare, is an undistinguished destruction of all ages, sexes and conditions.

In every stage of these Oppressions We have Petitioned for Redress in the most humble terms: Our repeated Petitions have been answered only by repeated injury. A Prince, whose character is thus marked by every act which may define a Tyrant, is unfit to be the ruler of a free people.

Nor have We been wanting in attentions to our British brethren. We have warned them from time to time of attempts by their legislature to extend an unwarrantable jurisdiction over us. We have reminded them of the circumstances of our emigration and settlement here. We have appealed to their native justice and magnanimity, and we have conjured them by the ties of our common kindred to disavow these usurpations which, would inevitably interrupt our connections and correspondence. They too have been deaf to the voice of justice and of consanguinity. We must, therefore, acquiesce in the necessity, which denounces our Separation, and hold them, as we hold the rest of mankind, Enemies in War, in Peace Friends.

We, therefore, the Representatives of the united States of America, in General Congress, Assembled, appealing to the Supreme Judge of the world for the rectitude of our intentions, do, in the Name, and by authority of the good People of these Colonies, solemnly publish and declare, That these United Colonies are, and of Right ought to be Free and Independent States; that they are Absolved from all Allegiance to the British Crown, and that all political connection between them and the State of Great Britain, is and ought to be totally dissolved; and that as Free and Independent States, they have full power to levy War, conclude Peace, contract Alliances, establish Commerce, and to do all other Acts and Things which Independent States may of right do. And for the support of this Declaration, with a firm reliance on the Protection of Divine Providence, we mutually pledge to each other our Lives, our Fortunes and our sacred Honor.

JOHN HANCOCK	GEO. TAYLOR
BUTTON GWINNETT	JAMES WILSON
LYMAN HALL	GEO. ROSS
GEO. WALTON	CAESAR RODNEY
WM. HOOPER	GEO. READ
JOSEPH HEWES	THO. M'KEAN
JOHN PENN	WM. FLOYD
EDWARD RUTLEDGE	PHIL. LIVINGSTON
THOS. HEYWARD, Junr.	FRANS. LEWIS
THOMAS LYNCH, Junr.	LEWIS MORRIS
ARTHUR MIDDLETON	RICHD. STOCKTON
SAMUEL CHASE	JNO. WITHERSPOON
WM. PACA	FRAS. HOPKINSON
THOS. STONE	JOHN HART
CHARLES CARROLL	ABRA. CLARK
OF CARROLLTON	JOSIAH BARTLETT
GEORGE WYTHE	WM. WHIPPLE
RICHARD HENRY LEE	SAML. ADAMS
TH. JEFFERSON	JOHN ADAMS
BENJ. HARRISON	ROBT. TREAT PAINE
THOS. NELSON, JR.	ELBRIDGE GERRY
FRANCIS LIGHTFOOT LEE	STEP. HOPKINS
CARTER BRAXTON	WILLIAM ELLERY
ROBT. MORRIS	ROGER SHERMAN
BENJAMIN RUSH	SAM'EL. HUNTINGTON
BENJA. FRANKLIN	WM. WILLIAMS
JOHN MORTON	OLIVER WOLCOTT
GEO. CLYMER	MATTHEW THORNTON
JAS. SMITH	

THE CONSTITUTION OF
THE UNITED STATES OF AMERICA

We the People of the United States, in Order to form a more perfect Union, establish Justice, insure domestic Tranquility, provide for the common defence, promote the general Welfare, and secure the Blessings of Liberty to ourselves and our Posterity, do ordain and establish this Constitution for the United States of America.

ARTICLE I.

Section 1.

All legislative Powers herein granted shall be vested in a Congress of the United States, which shall consist of a Senate and House of Representatives.

Section 2.

The House of Representatives shall be composed of Members chosen every second Year by the People of the several States, and the Electors in each State shall have the Qualifications requisite for Electors of the most numerous Branch of the State Legislature.

No Person shall be a Representative who shall not have attained to the Age of twenty five Years, and been seven Years a Citizen of the United States, and who shall not, when elected, be an Inhabitant of that State in which he shall be chosen.

Representatives and direct Taxes shall be apportioned among the several States which may be included within this Union, according to their respective Numbers, which shall be determined by adding to the whole Number of free Persons, including those bound to Service for a Term of Years, and excluding Indians not taxed, three fifths of all other Persons.[1] The actual Enumeration shall be made within three Years after the first Meeting of the Congress of the United States, and within every subsequent Term of ten Years, in such Manner as they shall by Law direct. The Number of Representatives shall not exceed one for every thirty Thousand, but each State shall have at Least one Representative; and until such enumeration shall be made, the State of New Hampshire shall be entitled to chuse three, Massachusetts eight, Rhode-Island and Providence Plantations one, Connecticut five, New-York six, New Jersey four, Pennsylvania eight, Delaware one, Maryland six, Virginia ten, North Carolina five, South Carolina five, and Georgia three.

When vacancies happen in the Representation from any State, the Executive Authority thereof shall issue Writs of Election to fill such Vacancies.

The House of Representatives shall chuse their Speaker and other Officers; and shall have the sole Power of Impeachment.

Section 3.

The Senate of the United States shall be composed of two Senators from each State, chosen by the Legislature thereof, for six Years; and each Senator shall have one Vote.

Immediately after they shall be assembled in Consequence of the first Election, they shall be divided as equally as may be into three Classes. The Seats of the Senators of the first Class shall be vacated at the Expiration of the second Year, of the second Class at the Expiration of the fourth Year, and of the third Class at the Expiration of the sixth Year, so that one third may be chosen every second Year; and if Vacancies happen by Resignation, or otherwise, during the Recess of the Legislature of any State, the Executive thereof may make temporary Appointments until the next Meeting of the Legislature, which shall then fill such Vacancies.[2]

No Person shall be a Senator who shall not have attained to the Age of thirty Years, and been nine Years a Citizen of the United States, and who shall not, when elected, be an Inhabitant of that State for which he shall be chosen.

The Vice President of the United States shall be President of the Senate, but shall have no Vote, unless they be equally divided.

The Senate shall chuse their other Officers, and also a President pro tempore, in the Absence of the Vice President, or when he shall exercise the Office of President of the United States.

The Senate shall have the sole Power to try all Impeachments. When sitting for that Purpose, they shall be on Oath or Affirmation. When the President of the United States is tried the Chief Justice shall preside: And no Person shall be convicted without the Concurrence of two thirds of the Members present.

Judgment in Cases of Impeachment shall not extend further than to removal from Office, and disqualification to hold and enjoy any Office of honor, Trust or Profit under the United States: but the Party convicted shall nevertheless be liable and subject to Indictment, Trial, Judgment and Punishment, according to Law.

Section 4.

The Times, Places and Manner of holding Elections for Senators and Representatives, shall be prescribed in each State by the Legislature thereof; but the Congress may at

---

[1]"Other Persons" being black slaves. Modified by Amendment XIV, Section 2.

[2]Provisions changed by Amendment XVII.

any time by Law make or alter such Regulations, except as to the Places of chusing Senators.

The Congress shall assemble at least once in every Year, and such Meeting shall be on the first Monday in December, unless they shall by Law appoint a different Day.[3]

Section 5.

Each House shall be the Judge of the Elections, Returns and Qualifications of its own Members, and a Majority of each shall constitute a Quorum to do Business; but a smaller Number may adjourn from day to day, and may be authorized to compel the Attendance of absent Members, in such Manner, and under such Penalties as each House may provide.

Each House may determine the Rules of its Proceedings, punish its Members for disorderly Behaviour, and, with the Concurrence of two thirds, expel a Member.

Each House shall keep a Journal of its Proceedings, and from time to time publish the same, excepting such Parts as may in their Judgment require Secrecy; and the Yeas and Nays of the Members of either House on any question shall, at the Desire of one fifth of those Present, be entered on the Journal.

Neither House, during the Session of Congress, shall, without the Consent of the other, adjourn for more than three days, nor to any other Place than that in which the two Houses shall be sitting.

Section 6.

The Senators and Representatives shall receive a Compensation for their Services, to be ascertained by Law, and paid out of the Treasury of the United States. They shall in all Cases, except Treason, Felony and Breach of the Peace, be privileged from Arrest during their Attendance at the Session of their respective Houses, and in going to and returning from the same; and for any Speech or Debate in either House, they shall not be questioned in any other Place.

No Senator or Representative shall, during the Time for which he was elected, be appointed to any civil Office under the Authority of the United States, which shall have been created, or the Emoluments whereof shall have been encreased during such time; and no Person holding any Office under the United States, shall be a Member of either House during his Continuance in Office.

Section 7.

All Bills for raising Revenue shall originate in the House of Representatives; but the Senate may propose or concur with Amendments as on other Bills.

Every Bill which shall have passed the House of Representatives and the Senate, shall, before it become a Law,

---

[3]Provision changed by Amendment XX, Section 2.

be presented to the President of the United States; If he approve he shall sign it, but if not he shall return it, with his Objections to that House in which it shall have originated, who shall enter the Objections at large on their Journal, and proceed to reconsider it. If after such Reconsideration two thirds of that House shall agree to pass the Bill, it shall be sent, together with the Objections, to the other House, by which it shall likewise be reconsidered, and if approved by two thirds of that House, it shall become a Law. But in all such Cases the Votes of both Houses shall be determined by yeas and Nays, and the Names of the Persons voting for and against the Bill shall be entered on the Journal of each House respectively. If any Bill shall not be returned by the President within ten Days (Sundays excepted) after it shall have been presented to him, the Same shall be a Law, in like Manner as if he had signed it, unless the Congress by their Adjournment prevent its Return, in which Case it shall not be a Law.

Every Order, Resolution, or Vote to which the Concurrence of the Senate and House of Representatives may be necessary (except on a question of Adjournment) shall be presented to the President of the United States; and before the Same shall take Effect, shall be approved by him, or being disapproved by him, shall be repassed by two thirds of the Senate and House of Representatives, according to the Rules and Limitations prescribed in the Case of a Bill.

Section 8.

The Congress shall have Power To lay and collect Taxes, Duties, Imposts and Excises, to pay the Debts and provide for the common Defence and general Welfare of the United States; but all Duties, Imposts and Excises shall be uniform throughout the United States;

To borrow Money on the credit of the United States;

To regulate Commerce with foreign Nations, and among the several States, and with the Indian Tribes;

To establish an uniform Rule of Naturalization, and uniform Laws on the subject of Bankruptcies throughout the United States;

To coin Money, regulate the Value thereof, and of foreign Coin, and fix the Standard of Weights and Measures;

To provide for the Punishment of counterfeiting the Securities and current Coin of the United States;

To establish Post Offices and post Roads;

To promote the Progress of Science and useful Arts, by securing for limited Times to Authors and Inventors the exclusive Right to their respective Writings and Discoveries;

To constitute Tribunals inferior to the supreme Court;

To define and punish Piracies and Felonies committed on the high Seas, and Offences against the Law of Nations;

To declare War, grant Letters of Marque and Reprisal, and make Rules concerning Captures on Land and Water;

To raise and support Armies, but no Appropriation of

Money to that Use shall be for a longer Term than two Years;

To provide and maintain a Navy;

To make Rules for the Government and Regulation of the land and naval Forces;

To provide for calling forth the Militia to execute the Laws of the Union, suppress Insurrections and repel Invasions;

To provide for organizing, arming, and disciplining, the Militia, and for governing such Part of them as may be employed in the Service of the United States, reserving to the States respectively, the Appointment of the Officers, and the Authority of training the Militia according to the discipline prescribed by Congress;

To exercise exclusive Legislation in all Cases whatsoever, over such District (not exceeding ten Miles square) as may, by Cession of particular States, and the Acceptance of Congress, become the Seat of the Government of the United States, and to exercise like Authority over all Places purchased by the Consent of the Legislature of the State in which the Same shall be, for the Erection of Forts, Magazines, Arsenals, dock-Yards, and other needful Buildings;—And

To make all Laws which shall be necessary and proper for carrying into Execution the foregoing Powers, and all other Powers vested by this Constitution in the Government of the United States, or in any Department or Officer thereof.

Section 9.

The Migration or Importation of such Persons as any of the States now existing shall think proper to admit, shall not be prohibited by the Congress prior to the Year one thousand eight hundred and eight, but a Tax or duty may be imposed on such Importation, not exceeding ten dollars for each Person.

The Privilege of the Writ of Habeas Corpus shall not be suspended, unless when in Cases of Rebellion or Invasion the public Safety may require it.

No Bill of Attainder or ex post facto Law shall be passed.

No Capitation, or other direct, Tax shall be laid, unless in Proportion to the Census or Enumeration herein before directed to be taken.

No Tax or Duty shall be laid on Articles exported from any State.

No Preference shall be given by any Regulation of Commerce or Revenue to the Ports of one State over those of another: nor shall Vessels bound to, or from, one State, be obliged to enter, clear, or pay Duties in another.

No Money shall be drawn from the Treasury, but in Consequence of Appropriations made by Law; and a regular Statement and Account of the Receipts and Expenditures of all public Money shall be published from time to time.

No Title of Nobility shall be granted by the United States: And no Person holding any Office of Profit or Trust under them, shall, without the Consent of the Congress, accept of any present, Emolument, Office, or Title, of any kind whatever, from any King, Prince, or foreign State.

Section 10.

No State shall enter into any Treaty, Alliance, or Confederation; grant Letters of Marque and Reprisal; coin Money; emit Bills of Credit; make any Thing but gold and silver Coin a Tender in Payment of Debts; pass any Bill of Attainder, ex post facto Law, or Law impairing the Obligation of Contracts, or grant any Title of Nobility.

No State shall, without the Consent of the Congress, lay any Imposts or Duties on Imports or Exports, except what may be absolutely necessary for executing its inspection Laws: and the net Produce of all Duties and Imposts, laid by any State on Imports or Exports, shall be for the Use of the Treasury of the United States; and all such Laws shall be subject to the Revision and Controul of the Congress.

No State shall, without the Consent of Congress, lay any Duty of Tonnage, keep Troops, or Ships of War in time of Peace, enter into any Agreement or Compact with another State, or with a foreign Power, or engage in War, unless actually invaded, or in such imminent Danger as will not admit of delay.

ARTICLE II.

Section 1.

The executive Power shall be vested in a President of the United States of America. He shall hold his Office during the Term of four Years, and, together with the Vice President, chosen for the same Term, be elected, as follows:

Each State shall appoint, in such Manner as the Legislature thereof may direct, a Number of Electors, equal to the whole Number of Senators and Representatives to which the State may be entitled in the Congress: but no Senator or Representative, or Person holding an Office of Trust or Profit under the United States, shall be appointed an Elector.

The Electors shall meet in their respective States, and vote by Ballot for two Persons, of whom one at least shall not be an Inhabitant of the same State with themselves. And they shall make a List of all the Persons voted for, and of the Number of Votes for each; which List they shall sign and certify, and transmit sealed to the Seat of the Government of the United States, directed to the President of the Senate. The President of the Senate shall, in the Presence of the Senate and House of Representatives, open all the Certificates, and the Votes shall then be counted. The Person having the greatest Number of Votes shall be the President, if such Number be a Majority of the whole Number of Electors appointed; and if there be more than one who have such Majority, and have an equal Number of Votes, then the House of

Representatives shall immediately chuse by Ballot one of them for President; and if no Person have a Majority, then from the five highest on the List the said House shall in like Manner chuse the President. But in chusing the President, the Votes shall be taken by States, the Representation from each State having one Vote; A quorum for this Purpose shall consist of a Member or Members from two thirds of the States, and a Majority of all the States shall be necessary to a Choice. In every Case, after the Choice of the President, the Person having the greatest Number of Votes of the Electors shall be the Vice President. But if there should remain two or more who have equal Votes, the Senate shall chuse from them by Ballot the Vice President.[4]

The Congress may determine the Time of chusing the Electors, and the Day on which they shall give their Votes; which Day shall be the same throughout the United States.

No Person except a natural born Citizen, or a Citizen of the United States, at the time of the Adoption of this Constitution, shall be eligible to the Office of President; neither shall any Person be eligible to that Office who shall not have attained to the Age of thirty five Years, and been fourteen Years a Resident within the United States.

In Case of the Removal of the President from Office, or of his Death, Resignation, or Inability to discharge the Powers and Duties of the said Office, the Same shall devolve on the Vice President, and the Congress may by Law provide for the Case of Removal, Death, Resignation or Inability, both of the President and Vice President, declaring what Officer shall then act as President, and such Officer shall act accordingly, until the Disability be removed, or a President shall be elected.

The President shall, at stated Times, receive for his Services, a Compensation, which shall neither be encreased nor diminished during the Period for which he shall have been elected, and he shall not receive within that Period any other Emolument from the United States, or any of them.

Before he enter on the Execution of his Office, he shall take the following Oath or Affirmation:—"I do solemnly swear (or affirm) that I will faithfully execute the Office of President of the United States, and will to the best of my Ability, preserve, protect and defend the Constitution of the United States."

Section 2.

The President shall be Commander in Chief of the Army and Navy of the United States, and of the Militia of the several States, when called into the actual Service of the United States; he may require the Opinion, in writing, of the principal Officer in each of the executive Departments, upon any Subject relating to the Duties of their respective Offices, and he shall have Power to grant Reprieves and Pardons for Offences against the United States, except in Cases of Impeachment.

He shall have Power, by and with the Advice and Consent of the Senate, to make Treaties, provided two thirds of the Senators present concur; and he shall nominate, and by and with the Advice and Consent of the Senate, shall appoint Ambassadors, other public Ministers and Consuls, Judges of the supreme Court, and all other Officers of the United States, whose Appointments are not herein otherwise provided for, and which shall be established by Law: but the Congress may by Law vest the Appointment of such inferior Officers, as they think proper, in the President alone, in the Courts of Law, or in the Heads of Departments.

The President shall have Power to fill up all Vacancies that may happen during the Recess of the Senate, by granting Commissions which shall expire at the End of their next Session.

Section 3.

He shall from time to time give to the Congress Information of the State of the Union, and recommend to their Consideration such Measures as he shall judge necessary and expedient; he may, on extraordinary Occasions, convene both Houses, or either of them, and in Case of Disagreement between them, with Respect to the Time of Adjournment, he may adjourn them to such Time as he shall think proper; he shall receive Ambassadors and other public Ministers; he shall take Care that the Laws be faithfully executed, and shall Commission all the Officers of the United States.

Section 4.

The President, Vice President and all civil Officers of the United States, shall be removed from Office on Impeachment for, and Conviction of, Treason, Bribery, or other high Crimes and Misdemeanors.

ARTICLE III.

Section 1.

The judicial Power of the United States, shall be vested in one supreme Court, and in such inferior Courts as the Congress may from time to time ordain and establish. The Judges, both of the supreme and inferior Courts, shall hold their Offices during good Behaviour, and shall, at stated Times, receive for their Services, a Compensation, which shall not be diminished during their Continuance in Office.

Section 2.

The judicial Power shall extend to all Cases, in Law and Equity, arising under this Constitution, the Laws of the United States, and Treaties made, or which shall be made, under their Authority;—to all Cases affecting

---

[4]Provisions superseded by Amendment XII.

Ambassadors, other public Ministers and Consuls;—to all Cases of admiralty and maritime Jurisdiction;—to Controversies to which the United States shall be a Party;—to Controversies between two or more States;—between a State and Citizens of another State;—between Citizens of different States,—between Citizens of the same State claiming Lands under Grants of different States, and between a State, or the Citizens thereof, and foreign States, Citizens or Subjects.[5]

In all Cases affecting Ambassadors, other public Ministers and Consuls, and those in which a State shall be Party, the supreme Court shall have original Jurisdiction. In all the other Cases before mentioned, the supreme Court shall have appellate Jurisdiction, both as to Law and Fact, with such Exceptions, and under such Regulations as the Congress shall make.

The Trial of all Crimes, except in Cases of Impeachment, shall be by Jury; and such Trial shall be held in the State where the said Crimes shall have been committed, but when not committed within any State, the Trial shall be at such Place or Places as the Congress may by Law have directed.

Section 3.

Treason against the United States, shall consist only in levying War against them, or in adhering to their Enemies, giving them Aid and Comfort. No person shall be convicted of Treason unless on the Testimony of two Witnesses to the same overt Act, or on Confession in open Court.

The Congress shall have Power to declare the Punishment of Treason, but no Attainder of Treason shall work Corruption of Blood, or Forfeiture except during the Life of the Person attainted.

ARTICLE IV.

Section 1.

Full Faith and Credit shall be given in each State to the public Acts, Records, and judicial Proceedings of every other State. And the Congress may by general Laws prescribe the Manner in which such Acts, Records and Proceedings shall be proved, and the Effect thereof.

Section 2.

The Citizens of each State shall be entitled to all Privileges and Immunities of Citizens in the several States.

A Person charged in any State with Treason, Felony, or other Crime, who shall flee from Justice, and be found in another State, shall on Demand of the executive Authority of the State from which he fled, be delivered up, to be removed to the State having Jurisdiction of the Crime.

---

[5]Clause changed by Amendment XI.

No Person held to Service or Labour in one State, under the Laws thereof, escaping into another, shall, in Consequence of any Law or Regulation therein, be discharged from such Service or Labour, but shall be delivered up on Claim of the Party to whom such Service or Labour may be due.

Section 3.

New States may be admitted by the Congress into this Union; but no new State shall be formed or erected within the Jurisdiction of any other State; nor any State be formed by the Junction of two or more States, or Parts of States, without the Consent of the Legislatures of the States concerned as well as of the Congress.

The Congress shall have Power to dispose of and make all needful Rules and Regulations respecting the Territory or other Property belonging to the United States; and nothing in this Constitution shall be so construed as to Prejudice any Claims of the United States, or of any particular State.

Section 4.

The United States shall guarantee to every State in this Union a Republican Form of Government, and shall protect each of them against Invasion; and on Application of the Legislature, or of the Executive (when the Legislature cannot be convened) against domestic Violence.

ARTICLE V.

The Congress, whenever two thirds of both Houses shall deem it necessary, shall propose Amendments to this Constitution, or, on the Application of the Legislatures of two thirds of the several States, shall call a Convention for proposing Amendments, which, in either Case, shall be valid to all Intents and Purposes, as Part of this Constitution, when ratified by the Legislatures of three fourths of the several States, or by Conventions in three fourths thereof, as the one or the other Mode of Ratification may be proposed by the Congress; Provided that no Amendment which may be made prior to the Year One thousand eight hundred and eight shall in any Manner affect the first and fourth Clauses in the Ninth Section of the first Article; and that no State, without its Consent, shall be deprived of its equal Suffrage in the Senate.

ARTICLE VI.

All Debts contracted and Engagements entered into, before the Adoption of this Constitution, shall be as valid against the United States under this Constitution, as under the Confederation.

This Constitution, and the Laws of the United States which shall be made in Pursuance thereof; and all Treaties made, or which shall be made, under the Authority of the United States, shall be the supreme Law of the Land; and the Judges in every State shall be bound thereby, any Thing in the Constitution or Laws of any State to the Contrary notwithstanding.

The Senators and Representatives before mentioned, and the Members of the several State Legislatures, and all executive and judicial Officers, both of the United States and of the several States, shall be bound by Oath or Affirmation, to support this Constitution; but no religious Test shall ever be required as a Qualification to any Office or public Trust under the United States.

---

[6]The Constitution was submitted on September 17, 1787, by the Constitutional Convention, was ratified by the conventions of several states at various dates up to May 29, 1790, and became effective on March 4, 1789.

ARTICLE VII.

The Ratification of the Conventions of nine States, shall be sufficient for the Establishment of this Constitution between the States so ratifying the Same.

done in Convention by the Unanimous Consent of the States present the Seventeenth Day of September in the Year of our Lord one thousand seven hundred and Eighty seven and of the Independence of the United States of America the Twelfth[6] IN WITNESS whereof We have hereunto subscribed our Names,

GEORGE WASHINGTON,
President and Deputy
from Virginia

New Hampshire
JOHN LANGDON
NICHOLAS GILMAN
Massachusetts
NATHANIEL GORHAM
RUFUS KING
Connecticut
WILLIAM S. JOHNSON
ROGER SHERMAN
New York
ALEXANDER HAMILTON
New Jersey
WILLIAM LIVINGSTON
DAVID BREARLEY
WILLIAM PATERSON
JONATHAN DAYTON
Pennsylvania
BENJAMIN FRANKLIN
THOMAS MIFFLIN
ROBERT MORRIS
GEORGE CLYMER
THOMAS FITZSIMONS
JARED INGERSOLL
JAMES WILSON
GOUVERNEUR MORRIS

Delaware
GEORGE READ
GUNNING BEDFORD, JR.
JOHN DICKINSON
RICHARD BASSETT
JACOB BROOM
Maryland
JAMES MCHENRY
DANIEL OF ST. THOMAS
JENIFER
DANIEL CARROLL
Virginia
JOHN BLAIR
JAMES MADISON, JR.
North Carolina
WILLIAM BLOUNT
RICHARD DOBBS
SPRAIGHT
HU WILLIAMSON
South Carolina
J. RUTLEDGE
CHARLES C. PINCKNEY
PIERCE BUTLER
Georgia
WILLIAM FEW
ABRAHAM BALDWIN

AMENDMENTS TO THE CONSTITUTION

[AMENDMENT I]

Congress shall make no law respecting an establishment of religion, or prohibiting the free exercise thereof; or abridging the freedom of speech, or of the press; or the right of the people peaceably to assemble, and to petition the Government for a redress of grievances.

[AMENDMENT II]

A well regulated Militia being necessary to the security of a free State, the right of the people to keep and bear Arms, shall not be infringed.

[AMENDMENT III]

No Soldier shall, in time of peace be quartered in any house, without the consent of the Owner, nor in time of war, but in a manner to be prescribed by law.

[AMENDMENT IV]

The right of the people to be secure in their persons, houses, papers, and effects, against unreasonable searches and seizures, shall not be violated, and no Warrants shall issue, but upon probable cause, supported by Oath or affirmation, and particularly describing the place to be searched, and the persons or things to be seized.

[AMENDMENT V]

No person shall be held to answer for a capital, or otherwise infamous crime, unless on a presentment or indictment of a Grand Jury, except in cases arising in the land or naval forces, or in the Militia, when in actual service in time of War or public danger; nor shall any person be subject for the same offense to be twice put in jeopardy of life or limb; nor shall be compelled in any criminal case to be a witness against himself, nor be deprived of life, liberty, or property, without due process of law; nor shall private property be taken for public use, without just compensation.

[AMENDMENT VI]

In all criminal prosecutions, the accused shall enjoy the right to a speedy and public trial, by an impartial jury of the State and district wherein the crime shall have been committed, which district shall have been previously ascertained by law, and to be informed of the nature and cause of the accusation; to be confronted with the witnesses against him; to have compulsory process for obtaining witnesses in his favor, and to have the Assistance of Counsel for his defence.

[AMENDMENT VII]

In Suits at common law, where the value in controversy shall exceed twenty dollars, the right of trial by jury shall be preserved, and no fact tried by a jury, shall be otherwise re-examined in any Court of the United States, than according to the rules of the common law.

[AMENDMENT VIII]

Excessive bail shall not be required, nor excessive fines imposed, nor cruel and unusual punishments inflicted.

[AMENDMENT IX]

The enumeration in the Constitution, of certain rights, shall not be construed to deny or disparage others retained by the people.

[AMENDMENT X]

The powers not delegated to the United States by the Constitution, nor prohibited by it to the States, are reserved to the States respectively, or to the people.[7]

[AMENDMENT XI]

The Judicial power of the United States shall not be construed to extend to any suit in law or equity, commenced or prosecuted against one of the United States by Citizens of another State, or by Citizens or Subjects of any Foreign State.[8]

[AMENDMENT XII]

The Electors shall meet in their respective states, and vote by ballot for President and Vice-President, one of

---

[7]The first ten amendments were all proposed by Congress on September 25, 1789, and were ratified and adoption certified on December 15, 1791.

[8]Proposed by Congress on March 4, 1794, and declared ratified on January 8, 1798.

whom, at least, shall not be an inhabitant of the same state with themselves; they shall name in their ballots the person voted for as President, and in distinct ballots the person voted for as Vice-President, and they shall make distinct lists of all persons voted for as President, and of all persons voted for as Vice-President, and of the number of votes for each, which lists they shall sign and certify, and transmit sealed to the seat of the government of the United States, directed to the President of the Senate;— The President of the Senate shall, in the presence of the Senate and House of Representatives, open all the certificates and the votes shall then be counted;—The person having the greatest number of votes for President, shall be the President, if such number be a majority of the whole number of Electors appointed; and if no person have such majority, then from the persons having the highest numbers not exceeding three on the list of those voted for as President, the House of Representatives shall choose immediately, by ballot, the President. But in choosing the President, the votes shall be taken by states, the representation from each state having one vote; a quorum for this purpose shall consist of a member or members from two-thirds of the states, and a majority of all the states shall be necessary to a choice. And if the House of Representatives shall not choose a President whenever the right of choice shall devolve upon them, before the fourth day of March next following, then the Vice-President shall act as President, as in the case of the death or other constitutional disability of the President.—The person having the greatest number of votes as Vice-President, shall be the Vice-President, if such number be a majority of the whole number of Electors appointed, and if no person have a majority, then from the two highest numbers on the list, the Senate shall choose the Vice-President; a quorum for the purpose shall consist of two-thirds of the whole number of Senators, and a majority of the whole number shall be necessary to a choice. But no person constitutionally ineligible to the office of President shall be eligible to that of Vice-President of the United States.[9]

[AMENDMENT XIII]

Section 1.

Neither slavery nor involuntary servitude, except as a punishment for crime whereof the party shall have been duly convicted, shall exist within the United States, or any place subject to their jurisdiction.

Section 2.

Congress shall have power to enforce this article by appropriate legislation.[10]

---

[9]Proposed by Congress on December 9, 1803; declared ratified on September 25, 1804; supplemented by Amendments XX and XXIII.

[10]Proposed by Congress on January 31, 1865; declared ratified on December 18, 1865.

[AMENDMENT XIV]

Section 1.

All persons born or naturalized in the United States, and subject to the jurisdiction thereof, are citizens of the United States and of the State wherein they reside. No State shall make or enforce any law which shall abridge the privileges or immunities of citizens of the United States; nor shall any State deprive any person of life, liberty, or property, without due process of law; nor deny to any person within its jurisdiction the equal protection of the laws.

Section 2.

Representatives shall be apportioned among the several States according to their respective numbers, counting the whole number of persons in each State, excluding Indians not taxed. But when the right to vote at any election for the choice of electors for President and Vice-President of the United States, Representatives in Congress, the Executive and Judicial officers of a State, or the members of the Legislature thereof, is denied to any of the male inhabitants of such State, being twenty-one years of age, and citizens of the United States, or in any way abridged, except for participation in rebellion, or other crime, the basis of representation therein shall be reduced in the proportion which the number of such male citizens shall bear to the whole number of male citizens twenty-one years of age in such State.

Section 3.

No person shall be a Senator or Representative in Congress, or elector of President and Vice President, or hold any office, civil or military, under the United States, or under any State, who, having previously taken an oath, as a member of Congress, or as an officer of the United States, or as a member of any State legislature, or as an executive or judicial officer of any State, to support the Constitution of the United States, shall have engaged in insurrection or rebellion against the same, or given aid or comfort to the enemies thereof. But Congress may by a vote of two-thirds of each House, remove such disability.

Section 4.

The validity of the public debt of the United States, authorized by law, including debts incurred for payment of pensions and bounties for services in suppressing insurrection or rebellion, shall not be questioned. But neither the United States nor any State shall assume or pay any debt or obligation incurred in aid of insurrection or rebellion against the United States, or any claim for the loss or emancipation of any slave; but all such debts, obligations and claims shall be held illegal and void.

Section 5.

The Congress shall have power to enforce, by appropriate legislation, the provisions of this article.[11]

[AMENDMENT XV]

Section 1.

The right of citizens of the United States to vote shall not be denied or abridged by the United States or by any State on account of race, color, or previous condition of servitude.

Section.

The Congress shall have power to enforce this article by appropriate legislation.[12]

[AMENDMENT XVI]

The Congress shall have power to lay and collect taxes on incomes, from whatever source derived, without apportionment among the several States, and without regard to any census or enumeration.[13]

[AMENDMENT XVII]

The Senate of the United States shall be composed of two Senators from each State, elected by the people thereof, for six years; and each Senator shall have one vote. The electors in each State shall have the qualifications requisite for electors of the most numerous branch of the State legislatures.

When vacancies happen in the representation of any State in the Senate, the executive authority of such State shall issue writs of election to fill such vacancies: *Provided,* That the legislature of any State may empower the executive thereof to make temporary appointments until the people fill the vacancies by election as the legislature may direct.

This amendment shall not be so construed as to affect the election or term of any Senator chosen before it becomes valid as part of the Constitution.[14]

---

[11]Proposed by Congress on June 13, 1866; declared ratified on July 28, 1868.

[12]Proposed by Congress on February 26, 1869; declared ratified on March 30, 1870.

[13]Proposed by Congress on July 12, 1909; declared ratified on February 25, 1913.

[14]Proposed by Congress on May 13, 1912; declared ratified on May 31, 1913.

[AMENDMENT XVIII]

Section 1.

After one year from the ratification of this article the manufacture, sale, or transportation of intoxicating liquors within, the importation thereof into, or the exportation thereof from the United States and all territory subject to the jurisdiction thereof for beverage purposes is hereby prohibited.

Section 2.

The Congress and the several States shall have concurrent power to enforce this article by appropriate legislation.

Section 3.

This article shall be inoperative unless it shall have been ratified as an amendment to the Constitution by the legislatures of the several States, as provided in the Constitution, within seven years from the date of the submission hereof to the States by the Congress.[15]

[AMENDMENT XIX]

The right of citizens of the United States to vote shall not be denied or abridged by the United States or by any State on account of sex.

Congress shall have power to enforce this article by appropriate legislation.[16]

[AMENDMENT XX]

Section 1.

The terms of the President and Vice President shall end at noon on the 20th day of January, and the terms of Senators and Representatives at noon on the 3d day of January, of the years in which such terms would have ended if this article had not been ratified; and the terms of their successors shall then begin.

Section 2.

The Congress shall assemble at least once in every year, and such meeting shall begin at noon on the 3d day of January, unless they shall by law appoint a different day.

---

[15]Proposed by Congress on December 18, 1917; declared ratified on January 29, 1919; repealed by Amendment XXI.

[16]Proposed by Congress on June 4, 1919; declared ratified on August 26, 1920.

Section 3.

If, at the time fixed for the beginning of the term of the President, the President elect shall have died, the Vice President elect shall become President. If a President shall not have been chosen before the time fixed for the beginning of his term, or if the President elect shall have failed to qualify, then the Vice President elect shall act as President until a President shall have qualified; and the Congress may by law provide for the case wherein neither a President elect nor a Vice President elect shall have qualified, declaring who shall then act as President, or the manner in which one who is to act shall be selected, and such person shall act accordingly until a President or Vice President shall have qualified.

Section 4.

The Congress may by law provide for the case of the death of any of the persons from whom the House of Representatives may choose a President whenever the right of choice shall have devolved upon them, and for the case of the death of any of the persons from whom the Senate may choose a Vice President whenever the right of choice shall have devolved upon them.

Section 5.

Sections 1 and 2 shall take effect on the 15th day of October following the ratification of this article.

Section 6.

This article shall be inoperative unless it shall have been ratified as an amendment to the Constitution by the legislatures of three-fourths of the several States within seven years from the date of its submission.[17]

[AMENDMENT XXI]

Section 1.

The eighteenth article of amendment to the Constitution of the United States is hereby repealed.

Section 2.

The transportation or importation into any States, Territory, or possession of the United States for delivery or use therein of intoxicating liquors, in violation of the laws thereof, is hereby prohibited.

Section 3.

This article shall be inoperative unless it shall have been ratified as an amendment to the Constitution by

conventions in the several States, as provided in the Constitution, within seven years from the date of the submission hereof to the States by the Congress.[18]

[AMENDMENT XXII]

Section 1.

No person shall be elected to the office of the President more than twice, and no person who has held the office of President, or acted as President, for more than two years of a term to which some other person was elected President shall be elected to the office of the President more than once. But this Article shall not apply to any person holding the office of President when this Article was proposed by the Congress, and shall not prevent any person who may be holding the office of President, or acting as President, during the term within which this Article becomes operative from holding the office of President or acting as President during the remainder of such term.

Section 2.

This article shall be inoperative unless it shall have been ratified as an amendment to the Constitution by the legislatures of three-fourths of the several States within seven years from the date of its submission to the States by the Congress.[19]

[AMENDMENT XXIII]

Section 1.

The District constituting the seat of Government of the United States shall appoint in such manner as the Congress shall direct:

A number of electors of President and Vice President equal to the whole number of Senators and Representatives in Congress to which the District would be entitled if it were a State, but in no event more than the least populous State; they shall be in addition to those appointed by the States, but they shall be considered, for the purposes of the election of President and Vice President, to be electors appointed by a State; and they shall meet in the District and perform such duties as provided by the twelfth article of amendment.

Section 2.

The Congress shall have power to enforce this article by appropriate legislation.[20]

---

[18]Proposed by Congress on February 20, 1933; declared ratified on December 5, 1933.

[19]Proposed by Congress on March 24, 1947; declared ratified on March 1, 1951.

[20]Proposed by Congress on June 16, 1960; declared ratified on April 3, 1961.

---

[17]Proposed by Congress on March 2, 1932; declared ratified on February 6, 1933.

[AMENDMENT XXIV]

Section 1.

The right of citizens of the United States to vote in any primary or other election for President or Vice President, for electors for President or Vice President, or for Senator or Representative in Congress, shall not be denied or abridged by the United States or any state by reason of failure to pay any poll tax or other tax.

Section 2.

The Congress shall have the power to enforce this article by appropriate legislation.[21]

[AMENDMENT XXV]

Section 1.

In case of the removal of the President from office or his death or resignation, the Vice President shall become President.

Section 2.

Whenever there is a vacancy in the office of the Vice President, the President shall nominate a Vice President who shall take the office upon confirmation by a majority vote of both houses of Congress.

Section 3.

Whenever the President transmits to the President pro tempore of the Senate and the Speaker of the House of Representatives his written declaration that he is unable to discharge the powers and duties of his office, and until he transmits to them a written declaration to the contrary, such powers and duties shall be discharged by the Vice President as Acting President.

Section 4.

Whenever the Vice President and a majority of either the principal officers of the executive departments or of such other body as Congress may by law provide, trans-

mit to the President pro tempore of the Senate and the Speaker of the House of Representatives their written declaration that the President is unable to discharge the powers and duties of his office, the Vice President shall immediately assume the powers and duties of the office as Acting President.

Thereafter, when the President transmits to the President pro tempore of the Senate and the Speaker of the House of Representatives his written declaration that no inability exists, he shall resume the powers and duties of his office unless the Vice President and a majority of either the principal officers of the executive department or of such other body as Congress may by law provide, transmit within four days to the President pro tempore of the Senate and the Speaker of the House of Representatives their written declaration that the President is unable to discharge the powers and duties of his office. Thereupon Congress shall decide the issue, assembling within 48 hours for that purpose if not in session. If the Congress, within 21 days after receipt of the latter written declaration, or, if Congress is not in session, within 21 days after Congress is required to assemble, determines by two-thirds vote of both houses that the President is unable to discharge the powers and duties of his office, the Vice President shall continue to discharge the same as Acting President; otherwise, the President shall resume the powers and duties of his office.[22]

[AMENDMENT XXVI]

Section 1.

The right of citizens of the United States, who are 18 years of age or older, to vote shall not be denied or abridged by the United States or any state on account of age.

Section 2.

The Congress shall have the power to enforce this article by appropriate legislation.[23]

---

[21]Proposed by Congress on August 27, 1962; declared ratified on January 23, 1963.

[22]Proposed by Congress on July 6, 1965; declared ratified on February 10, 1967.

[23]Proposed by Congress on March 23, 1971; declared ratified on June 30, 1971.

JUSTICES OF THE UNITED STATES SUPREME COURT

NAME *Chief Justices in Capital Letters*	Terms of Service[1]	Appointed By	NAME *Chief Justices in Capital Letters*	Terms of Service[1]	Appointed By
JOHN JAY, N.Y.	1789–1795	Washington	Henry B. Brown, Mich.	1891–1906	B. Harrison
James Wilson, Pa.	1789–1798	Washington	George Shiras, Jr., Pa.	1892–1903	B. Harrison
John Rutledge, S.C.	1790–1791	Washington	Howell E. Jackson, Tenn.	1893–1895	B. Harrison
William Cushing, Mass.	1790–1810	Washington	Edward D. White, La.	1894–1910	Cleveland
John Blair, Va.	1790–1796	Washington	Rufus W. Peckham, N.Y.	1896–1909	Cleveland
James Iredell, N.C.	1790–1799	Washington	Joseph McKenna, Cal.	1898–1925	McKinley
Thomas Johnson, Md.	1792–1793	Washington	Oliver W. Holmes, Mass.	1902–1932	T. Roosevelt
William Paterson, N.J.	1793–1806	Washington	William R. Day, Ohio	1903–1922	T. Roosevelt
JOHN RUTLEDGE, S.C.[2]	1795	Washington	William H. Moody, Mass.	1906–1910	T. Roosevelt
Samuel Chase, Md.	1796–1811	Washington	Horace H. Lurton, Tenn.	1910–1914	Taft
OLIVER ELLSWORTH, Conn.	1796–1800	Washington	Charles E. Hughes, N.Y.	1910–1916	Taft
Bushrod Washington, Va.	1799–1829	J. Adams	Willis Van Devanter, Wy.	1911–1937	Taft
Alfred Moore, N.C.	1800–1804	J. Adams	Joseph R. Lamar, Ga.	1911–1916	Taft
JOHN MARSHALL, Va.	1801–1835	J. Adams	EDWARD D. WHITE, La.	1910–1921	Taft
William Johnson, S.C.	1804–1834	Jefferson	Mahlon Pitney, N.J.	1912–1922	Taft
Brockholst Livingston, N.Y.	1807–1823	Jefferson	James C. McReynolds, Tenn.	1914–1941	Wilson
Thomas Todd, Ky.	1807–1826	Jefferson	Louis D. Brandeis, Mass.	1916–1939	Wilson
Gabriel Duvall, Md.	1811–1835	Madison	John H. Clarke, Ohio	1916–1922	Wilson
Joseph Story, Mass.	1812–1845	Madison	WILLIAM H. TAFT, Conn.	1921–1930	Harding
Smith Thompson, N.Y.	1823–1843	Monroe	George Sutherland, Utah	1922–1938	Harding
Robert Trimble, Ky.	1826–1828	J. Q. Adams	Pierce Butler, Minn.	1923–1939	Harding
John McLean, Ohio	1830–1861	Jackson	Edward T. Sanford, Tenn.	1923–1930	Harding
Henry Baldwin, Pa.	1830–1844	Jackson	Harlan F. Stone, N.Y.	1925–1941	Coolidge
James M. Wayne, Ga.	1835–1867	Jackson	CHARLES E. HUGHES, N.Y.	1930–1941	Hoover
ROGER B. TANEY, Md.	1836–1864	Jackson	Owen J. Roberts, Penn.	1930–1945	Hoover
Philip P. Barbour, Va.	1836–1841	Jackson	Benjamin N. Cardozo, N.Y.	1932–1938	Hoover
John Catron, Tenn.	1837–1865	Van Buren	Hugo L. Black, Ala.	1937–1971	F. Roosevelt
John McKinley, Ala.	1838–1852	Van Buren	Stanley F. Reed, Ky.	1938–1957	F. Roosevelt
Peter V. Daniel, Va.	1842–1860	Van Buren	Felix Frankfurter, Mass.	1939–1962	F. Roosevelt
Samuel Nelson, N.Y.	1845–1872	Tyler	William O. Douglas, Conn.	1939–	F. Roosevelt
Levi Woodbury, N.H.	1845–1851	Polk	Frank Murphy, Mich.	1940–1949	F. Roosevelt
Robert C. Grier, Pa.	1846–1870	Polk	HARLAN F. STONE, N.Y.	1941–1946	F. Roosevelt
Benjamin R. Curtis, Mass.	1851–1857	Fillmore	James F. Byrnes, S.C.	1941–1942	F. Roosevelt
John A. Campbell, Ala.	1853–1861	Pierce	Robert H. Jackson, N.Y.	1941–1954	F. Roosevelt
Nathan Clifford, Me.	1858–1881	Buchanan	Wiley B. Rutledge, Iowa	1943–1949	F. Roosevelt
Noah H. Swayne, Ohio	1862–1881	Lincoln	Harold H. Burton, Ohio	1945–1958	Truman
Samuel F. Miller, Iowa	1862–1890	Lincoln	FREDERICK M. VINSON, Ky.	1946–1953	Truman
David Davis, Ill.	1862–1877	Lincoln	Tom C. Clark, Texas	1949–1967	Truman
Stephen J. Field, Cal.	1863–1897	Lincoln	Sherman Minton, Ind.	1949–1956	Truman
SALMON P. CHASE, Ohio	1864–1873	Lincoln	EARL WARREN, Cal.	1953–1969	Eisenhower
William Strong, Pa.	1870–1880	Grant	John Marshall Harlan, N.Y.	1955–1971	Eisenhower
Joseph P. Bradley, N.J.	1870–1892	Grant	William J. Brennan, Jr., N.J.	1956–	Eisenhower
Ward Hunt, N.Y.	1873–1882	Grant	Charles E. Whittaker, Mo.	1957–1962	Eisenhower
MORRISON R. WAITE, Ohio	1874–1888	Grant	Potter Stewart, Ohio	1958–	Eisenhower
John M. Harlan, Ky.	1877–1911	Hayes	Byron R. White, Colo.	1962–	Kennedy
William B. Woods, Ga.	1881–1887	Hayes	Arthur J. Goldberg, Ill.	1962–1965	Kennedy
Stanley Matthews, Ohio	1881–1889	Garfield	Abe Fortas, Tenn.	1965–1970	Johnson
Horace Gray, Mass.	1882–1902	Arthur	Thurgood Marshall, Md.	1967–	Johnson
Samuel Blatchford, N.Y.	1882–1893	Arthur	WARREN E. BURGER, Va.	1969–	Nixon
Lucius Q. C. Lamar, Miss.	1888–1893	Cleveland	Harry A. Blackmun, Minn.	1970–	Nixon
MELVILLE W. FULLER, Ill.	1888–1910	Cleveland	Lewis F. Powell, Jr., Va.	1971–	Nixon
David J. Brewer, Kan.	1890–1910	B. Harrison	William H. Rehnquist, Ariz.	1971–	Nixon

[1]The date on which the justice took his judicial oath is here used as the date of the beginning of his service, for until that oath is taken he is not vested with the prerogatives of his office. Justices, however, receive their commissions ("letters patent") before taking their oath—in some instances, in the preceding year.

[2]Acting Chief Justice; Senate refused to confirm appointment.

PRESIDENTS, VICE-PRESIDENTS, AND CABINET MEMBERS

President and Vice-President	Secretary of State	Secretary of the Treasury	Secretary of War
George Washington (F) .... 1789 J. Adams .... '89	T. Jefferson .... '89 E. Randolph .... '94 T. Pickering.......... '95	A. Hamilton .... '89 O. Wolcott........... '89	H. Knox............. '89 T. Pickering.......... '95 J. McHenry .... '96
John Adams (F)..................... 1797 T. Jefferson (R^J)................... '97	T. Pickering.......... '97 J. Marshall .... '00	O. Wolcott........... '97 S. Dexter .... '01	J. McHenry .... '97 J. Marshall .... '00 S. Dexter .... '00 R. Griswold.......... '01
Thomas Jefferson (R^J) .... 1801 A. Burr (R^J) .... '01 G. Clinton (R^J).................... '05	J. Madison........... '01	S. Dexter .... '01 A. Gallatin........... '01	H. Dearborn .... '01
James Madison (R^J) .... 1809 G. Clinton (R^J)................... '09 E. Gerry (R^J)...................... '13	R. Smith............. '09 J. Monroe............ '11	A. Gallatin........... '09 G. Campbell .... '14 A. Dallas .... '14 W. Crawford......... '16	W. Eustis .... '09 J. Armstrong......... '13 J. Monroe .... '14 W. Crawford........ '15
James Monroe (R^J) .... 1817 D. Tompkins (R^J) .... '17	J. Q. Adams.......... '17	W. Crawford......... '17	I. Shelby............. '17 G. Graham............ '17 J. Calhoun .... '17
John Quincy Adams (NR)............. 1825 J. Calhoun (R^J).................... '25	H. Clay.............. '25	R. Rush.............. '25	J. Barbour........... '25 P. Porter............. '28
Andrew Jackson (D)................ 1829 J. Calhoun (D)...................... '29 M. Van Buren (D)................... '33	M. Van Buren........ '29 E. Livingston .... '31 L. McLane .... '33 J. Forsyth .... '34	S. Ingham .... '29 L. McLane .... '31 W. Duane............ '33 R. Taney............. '33 L. Woodbury........ '34	J. Eaton.............. '29 L. Cass .... '31 B. Butler............. '37
Martin Van Buren (D) .... 1837 R. Johnson (D).................... '37	J. Forsyth .... '37	L. Woodbury........ '37	J. Poinsett .... '37
William H. Harrison (W)............. 1841 J. Tyler (W)........................ '41	D. Webster .... '41	T. Ewing .... '41	J. Bell............... '41
John Tyler (W and D)................ 1841	D. Webster .... '41 H. Legare............ '43 A. Upshur .... '43 J. Calhoun .... '44	T. Ewing .... '41 W. Forward.......... '41 J. Spencer............ '43 G. Bibb.............. '44	J. Bell............... '41 J. McLean............ '41 J. Spencer............ '41 J. Porter .... '43 W. Wilkins .... '44
James K. Polk (D) .... 1845 G. Dallas (D)....................... '45	J. Buchanan.......... '45	R. Walker............ '45	W. Marcy............ '45
Zachary Taylor (W)................. 1849 M. Fillmore (W).................... '49	J. Clayton............ '49	W. Meredith .... '49	G. Crawford .... '49
Millard Fillmore (W)................ 1850	D. Webster .... '50 E. Everett............ '52	T. Corwin .... '50	C. Conrad .... '50
Franklin Pierce (D) .... 1853 W. King (D) .... '53	W. Marcy............ '53	J. Guthrie............ '53	J. Davis.............. '53
James Buchanan (D)................ 1857 J. Breckinridge (D) .... '57	L. Cass .... '57 J. Black .... '60	H. Cobb............. '57 P. Thomas .... '60 J. Dix................ '61	J. Floyd............. '57 J. Holt............... '61
Abraham Lincoln (R) .... 1861 H. Hamlin (R) .... '61 A. Johnson (U)..................... '65	W. Seward........... '61	S. Chase............. '61 W. Fessenden .... '64 H. McCulloch .... '65	S. Cameron .... '61 E. Stanton .... '62
Andrew Johnson (U) 1865	W. Seward........... '65	H. McCulloch .... '65	E. Stanton .... '65 U. Grant............. '67 L. Thomas .... '68 J. Schofield .... '68

Party affiliations: D, Democratic; F, Federalist; NR, National Republican; R, Republican; R^J, Republican (Jeffersonian); U, Unionist; W, Whig.

Secretary of the Navy	Attorney General	Postmaster General	Secretary of the Interior
Established April 30, 1798 B. Stoddert .... '98	E. Randolph .... '89 W. Bradford .... '94 C. Lee .... '95 C. Lee .... '97 T. Parsons .... '01		
B. Stoddert .... '01 R. Smith .... '01 J. Crowninshield .... '05	L. Lincoln .... '01 R. Smith .... '05 J. Breckinridge .... '05 C. Rodney .... '07		
P. Hamilton .... '09 W. Jones .... '13 B. Crowninshield .... '14	C. Rodney .... '09 W. Pinkney .... '11 R. Rush .... '14		
B. Crowninshield .... '17 S. Thompson .... '18 S. Southard .... '23	R. Rush .... ↑17 W. Wirt .... '17	*Cabinet status since March 9, 1829*	
S. Southard .... '25	W. Wirt .... '25		
J. Branch .... '29 L. Woodbury .... '31 M. Dickerson .... '34	J. Berrien .... '29 R. Taney .... '31 B. Butler .... '33	W. Barry .... '29 A. Kendall .... '35	
M. Dickerson .... '37 J. Paulding .... '38	B. Butler .... '37 F. Grundy .... '38 H. Gilpin .... '40	A. Kendall .... '37 J. Niles .... '40	
G. Badger .... '41	J. Crittenden .... '41	F. Granger .... '41	
G. Badger .... '41 A. Upshur .... '41 D. Henshaw .... '43 T. Gilmer .... '44 J. Mason .... '44	J. Crittenden .... '41 H. Legare .... '41 J. Nelson .... '43	F. Granger .... '41 C. Wickliffe .... '41	
G. Bancroft .... '45 J. Mason .... '46	J. Mason .... '45 N. Clifford .... '46 I. Toucey .... '48	C. Johnson .... '45	*Established March 3, 1849*
W. Preston .... '49	R. Johnson .... '49	J. Collamer .... '49	Thomas Ewing .... '49
W. Graham .... '50 J. Kennedy .... '52	J. Crittenden .... '50	N. Hall .... '50 S. Hubbard .... '52	A. Stuart .... '50
J. Dobbin .... '53	C. Cushing .... '53	J. Campbell .... '53	R. McClelland .... '53
I. Toucey .... '57	J. Black .... '57 E. Stanton .... '60	A. Brown .... '57 J. Holt .... '59	J. Thompson .... '57
G. Welles .... '61	E. Bates .... '61 T. Coffey .... '63 J. Speed .... '64	H. King .... '61 M. Blair .... '61 W. Dennison .... '64	C. Smith .... '61 J. Usher .... '63
G. Welles .... '65	J. Speed .... '65 H. Stanbery .... '66 W. Evarts .... '68	W. Dennison .... '65 A. Randall .... '66	J. Usher .... '65 J. Harlan .... '65 O. Browning .... '66

PRESIDENTS, VICE-PRESIDENTS, AND CABINET MEMBERS

President and Vice-President	Secretary of State	Secretary of the Treasury	Secretary of War	Secretary of the Navy
Ulysses S. Grant (R) . . . . . . 1869 S. Colfax (R) . . . . '69 H. Wilson (R) . . . . '73	E. Washburne. . '69 H. Fish . . . . '69	G. Boutwell . . . . '69 W. Richardson . . '73 B. Bristow . . . . . '74 L. Morrill . . . . . . '76	J. Rawlins. . . . . '69 W. Sherman . . '69 W. Belknap . . '69 A. Taft . . . . '76 J. Cameron. . . . '76	A. Borie . . . . . . '69 G. Robeson . . . '69
Rutherford B. Hayes (R) . . 1877 W. Wheeler (R) . . . . '77	W. Evarts . . . . . . '77	J. Sherman . . . . . '77	G. McCrary . . . '77 A. Ramsey . . . . '79	R. Thompson. . '77 N. Goff . . . . '81
James A. Garfield (R) . . . . . 1881 C. Arthur (R) . . . . '81	J. Blaine. . . . . . . '81	W. Windom . . . '81	R. Lincoln . . . . . '81	W. Hunt . . . . . . '81
Chester A. Arthur (R) 1881	F. Freling- huysen. . . . . . '81	C. Folger . . . . . . '81 W. Gresham . . . '84 H. McCulloch . . '84	R. Lincoln . . . . . '81	W. Chandler. . . '81
Grover Cleveland (D). . . . . 1885 T. Hendricks (D) . . . . '85	T. Bayard. . . . . . '85	D. Manning . . . '85 C. Fairchild. . . . '87	W. Endicott. . . . '85	W. Whitney . . . '85
Benjamin Harrison (R). . . . . 1889 L. Morton (R) . . . . '89	J. Blaine. . . . . . . '89 J. Foster . . . . '92	W. Windom . . . '89 C. Foster . . . . . . '91	R. Proctor . . . . . '89 S. Elkins . . . . . . '91	B. Tracy . . . . . . '89
Grover Cleveland (D). . . . . 1893 A. Stevenson (D). . . . . . . '93	W. Gresham . . . '93 R. Olney . . . . . . '95	J. Carlisle. . . . . . '93	D. Lamont. . . . . '93	H. Herbert . . . . '93
William McKinley (R) . . . . . 1897 G. Hobart (R). . . . . '97 T. Roosevelt (R). . . . . '01	J. Sherman . . . . '97 W. Day . . . . '97 J. Hay. . . . . '98	L. Gage . . . . '97	R. Alger. . . . . . . '97 E. Root. . . . . '99	J. Long. . . . . '97
Theodore Roosevelt (R). . . . 1901 C. Fairbanks (R) . . . . '05	J. Hay. . . . . '01 E. Root. . . . . '05 R. Bacon . . . . . . '09	L. Gage . . . . '01 L. Shaw . . . . '02 G. Cortelyou. . . '07	E. Root. . . . . '01 W. Taft. . . . . '04 L. Wright. . . . . . '08	J. Long. . . . . '01 W. Moody. . . . . '02 P. Morton . . . . . '04 C. Bonaparte. . . '05 V. Metcalf . . . . '07 T. Newberry. . . '08
William Howard Taft (R) . . 1909 J. Sherman (R) . . . . '09	P. Knox . . . . '09	F. MacVeagh . . '09	J. Dickinson . . . '09 H. Stimson . . . . '11	G. Meyer . . . . . . '09
Woodrow Wilson (D). . . . . 1913 T. Marshall (D) . . . . '13	W. Bryan. . . . . . '13 R. Lansing . . . . '15 B. Colby . . . . . . '20	W. McAdoo . . . '13 C. Glass. . . . . . . '18 D. Houston. . . . '20	L. Garrison . . . . '13 N. Baker . . . . . . '16	J. Daniels. . . . . . '13
Warren G. Harding (R) . . . . 1921 C. Coolidge (R) . . . . '21	C. Hughes. . . . . '21	A. Mellon . . . . . '21	J. Weeks. . . . . . . '21	E. Denby . . . . . . '21
Calvin Coolidge (R) . . . . 1923 C. Dawes (R) . . . . '25	C. Hughes. . . . . '23 F. Kellogg . . . . . '25	A. Mellon . . . . . '23	J. Weeks. . . . . . . '23 D. Davis . . . . '25	E. Denby . . . . . . '23 C. Wilbur . . . . . '24
Herbert Hoover (R) . . . . 1929 C. Curtis (R). . . . . '29	H. Stimson . . . . '29	A. Mellon . . . . . '29 O. Mills. . . . . . . '32	J. Good. . . . . '29 P. Hurley. . . . . . '29	C. Adams . . . . . '29
Franklin D. Roosevelt (D). . 1933 J. Garner (D). . . . . '33 H. Wallace (D). . . . . '41 H. Truman (D). . . . . '45	C. Hull. . . . . '33 E. Stettinius . . . '44	W. Woodin. . . '33 H. Morgen- thau . . . . '34	G. Dern . . . . . . '33 H. Woodring . . '36 H. Stimson . . . . '40	C. Swanson. . . . '33 C. Edison . . . . . '40 F. Knox . . . . '40 J. Forrestal. . . . . '44
Harry S. Truman (D) . . . . . . 1945 A. Barkley (D) . . . . '49	J. Byrnes . . . . . . '45 G. Marshall. . . . '47 D. Acheson. . . . '49	F. Vinson . . . . . '45 J. Snyder . . . . . . '46	R. Patterson . . . '45 K. Royall . . . . . . '47	J. Forrestal. . . . . '45

Party affiliations: D, Democratic; R, Republican.

Attorney General	Postmaster General	Secretary of the Interior	Secretary of Agriculture	Secretary of Commerce and Labor	
E. Hoar........'69 A. Ackerman...'70 G. Williams....'71 E. Pierrepont...'75 A. Taft.........'76	J. Creswell....'69 J. Marshall....'74 M. Jewell.....'74 J. Tyner.......'76	J. Cox........'69 C. Delano.....'70 Z. Chandler...'75			
C. Devens......'77	D. Key........'77 H. Maynard...'80	C. Schurz.....'77			
W. Mac- Veagh.....'81	T. James.......'81	S. Kirkwood...'81			
B. Brewster....'81	T. Howe ......'81 W. Gresham...'83 F. Hatton......'84	H. Teller ......'81	*Cabinet status since Feb. 9, 1889*		
A. Garland ....'85	W. Vilas......'85 D. Dickinson ..'88	L. Lamar.....'85 W. Vilas.......'88	N. Colman ....'89		
W. Miller.....'89	J. Wanamaker..'89	J. Noble.......'89	J. Rusk........'89		
R. Olney ......'93 J. Harmon....'95	W. Bissell .....'93 W. Wilson.....'95	H. Smith......'93 D. Francis.....'96	J. Morton......'93		
J. McKenna....'97 J. Griggs ......'97 P. Knox ....'01	J. Gary........'97 C. Smith ......'98	C. Bliss ....'97 E. Hitchcock...'99	J. Wilson ......'97	*Established Feb. 14, 1903*	
P. Knox .....'01 W. Moody.....'04 C. Bonaparte...'07	C. Smith ......'01 H. Payne......'02 R. Wynne .....'04 G. Cortelyou...'05 G. Meyer......'07	E. Hitchcock...'01 J. Garfield.....'07	J. Wilson ......'01	G. Cortelyou...'03 V. Metcalf .....'04 O. Straus......'07	
G. Wicker- sham........'09	F. Hitchcock...'09	R. Ballinger....'09 W. Fisher .....'11	J. Wilson ......'09	C. Nagel ......'09	
J. McReynolds .'13 T. Gregory...'14 A. Palmer .....'19	A. Burleson....'13	F. Lane........'13 J. Payne.......'20	D. Houston....'13 E. Meredith....'20	**Secretary of Commerce** *Established March 4, 1913* W. Redfield....'13 J. Alexander ...'19	**Secretary of Labor** *Established March 4, 1913* Wm. Wilson ...'13
H. Daugherty..'21	W. Hays ......'21 H. Work ......'22 H. New ....'23	A. Fall ....'21 H. Work ......'23	H. C. Wallace ..'21	H. Hoover.....'21	J. Davis ....'21
H. Daugherty..'23 H. Stone ......'24 J. Sargent......'25	H. New ....'23	H. Work ......'23 R. West ......'28	H. C. Wallace ..'23 H. Gore ....'24 W. Jardine.....'25	H. Hoover.....'23 W. Whiting....'28	J. Davis ....'23
W. Mitchell....'29	W. Brown .....'29	R. Wilbur .....'29	A. Hyde.......'29	R. Lamont.....'29 R. Chapin .....'32	J. Davis ....'29 W. Doak ......'30
H. Cummings .'33 F. Murphy.....'39 R. Jackson .....'40 F. Biddle.....'41	J. Farley ......'33 F. Walker......'40	H. Ickes.......'33	H. A. Wallace ..'33 C. Wickard ....'40	D. Roper ......'33 H. Hopkins....'39 J. Jones.........'40 H. A. Wallace ..'45	F. Perkins.....'33
T. Clark ......'45 J. McGrath.....'49 J. McGranery ..'52	R. Hannegan ..'45 J. Donaldson...'47	H. Ickes.......'45 J. Krug.......'46 O. Chapman...'49	C. Anderson...'45 C. Brannan ....'48	H. A. Wallace ..'45 W. A. Harri- man ....'46 C. Sawyer .....'48	L. Schwellen- bach ....'45 M. Tobin......'48

PRESIDENTS, VICE-PRESIDENTS, AND CABINET MEMBERS

President and Vice-President	Secretary of State	Secretary of the Treasury	Secretary of Defense[1]	Attorney General	Postmaster General
			Established July 26, 1947 J. Forrestal[2] .... '47 L. Johnson[2] .... '49 G. Marshall[2] ... '50 R. Lovett[2] ..... '51		
Dwight D. Eisenhower (R)................. 1953 R. Nixon (R)........... '53	J. Dulles....... '53 C. Herter...... '59	G. Humphrey.. '53 R. Anderson... '57	C. Wilson ..... '53 N. McElroy .... '57	H. Brownell ... '53 W. Rogers ..... '57	A. Summer- field .... '53
John F. Kennedy (D) ...... 1961 L. Johnson (D).......... '61	D. Rusk....... '61	D. Dillon...... '61	R. McNamara.. '61	R. Kennedy.... '61	J. Day......... '61 J. Gronouski... '63
Lyndon B. Johnson (D) .... 1963 H. Humphrey (D)....... '65	D. Rusk....... '63	D. Dillon...... '63 H. Fowler ..... '65 J. Barr......... '68	R. McNamara.. '63 C. Clifford..... '68	R. Kennedy.... '63 N. Katzenbach. '65 R. Clark....... '67	J. Gronouski... '63 L. O'Brien..... '65 W. Watson .... '68
Richard M. Nixon (R) ..... 1969 S. Agnew (R) .... '69	W. Rogers..... '69	D. Kennedy ... '69 J. Connally .... '70 G. Schultz..... '72	M. Laird ...... '69	J. Mitchell ..... '69 R. Kleindienst . '72	W. Blount ..... '69 *Abolished Aug. 8, 1970*

Party affiliations: D, Democratic; R, Republican.

[1]The Department of Defense, established during the Truman Administration, was a combination of the Departments of War and the Navy.

[2]Appointed during the Truman Administration.

Secretary of the Interior	Secretary of Agriculture	Secretary of Commerce	Secretary of Labor	Secretary of Health, Education, and Welfare	Secretary of Housing and Urban Development	Secretary of Trans- portation
				Established April 1, 1953		
D. McKay .... '53 F. Seaton ..... '56	E. Benson ..... '53	S. Weeks ..... '53 L. Strauss .... '58 F. Mueller .... '59	M. Durkin.... '53 J. Mitchell .... '53	O. Hobby .... '53 M. Folsom.... '55 A. Flemming . '58		
S. Udall ...... '61	O. Freeman... '61	L. Hodges.... '61	A. Goldberg .. '61 W. Wirtz ..... '62	A. Ribicoff ... '61 A. Celebrezze. '62		
S. Udall ...... '63	O. Freeman... '63	L. Hodges.... '63 J. Connor..... '65 A. Trow- bridge ..... '67 C. Smith ..... '68	W. Wirtz ..... '63	A. Celebrezze. '63 J. Gardner.... '65 W. Cohen .... '68	*Established Sept. 9, 1965*	
					R. Weaver .... '66 R. Wood ..... '68	*Established Oct. 15, 1966*
						A. Boyd...... '66
W. Hickel .... '69 R. Morton .... '71	C. Hardin .... '69 E. Butz....... '71	M. Stans ..... '69 P. Peterson ... '71	J. Hodgson ... '69	R. Finch...... '69 E. Richardson. '71	G. Romney ... '69	J. Volpe ...... '69

PARTY DISTRIBUTION IN CONGRESS

CONGRESS	YEAR	PRESIDENT	SENATE			HOUSE		
			Majority Party	Minority Party	Others	Majority Party	Minority Party	Others
1	1789–91	F (Washington)	Ad 17	Op 9	0	Ad 38	Op 26	0
2	1791–93	F (Washington)	F 16	R^J 13	0	F 37	R^J 33	0
3	1793–95	F (Washington)	F 17	R^J 13	0	R^J 57	F 48	0
4	1795–97	F (Washington)	F 19	R^J 13	0	F 54	R^J 52	0
5	1797–99	F (J. Adams)	F 20	R^J 12	0	F 58	R^J 48	0
6	1799–01	F (J. Adams)	F 19	R^J 13	0	F 64	R^J 42	0
7	1801–03	R^J (Jefferson)	R^J 18	F 14	0	R^J 69	F 36	0
8	1803–05	R^J (Jefferson)	R^J 25	F 9	0	R^J 102	F 39	0
9	1805–07	R^J (Jefferson)	R^J 27	F 7	0	R^J 116	F 25	0
10	1807–09	R^J (Jefferson)	R^J 28	F 6	0	R^J 118	F 24	0
11	1809–11	R^J (Madison)	R^J 28	F 6	0	R^J 94	F 48	0
12	1811–13	R^J (Madison)	R^J 30	F 6	0	R^J 108	F 36	0
13	1813–15	R^J (Madison)	R^J 27	F 9	0	R^J 112	F 68	0
14	1815–17	R^J (Madison)	R^J 25	F 11	0	R^J 117	F 65	0
15	1817–19	R^J (Monroe)	R^J 34	F 10	0	R^J 141	F 42	0
16	1819–21	R^J (Monroe)	R^J 35	F 7	0	R^J 156	F 27	0
17	1821–23	R^J (Monroe)	R^J 44	F 4	0	R^J 158	F 25	0
18	1823–25	R^J (Monroe)	R^J 44	F 4	0	R^J 187	F 26	0
19	1825–27	C (J. Q. Adams)	Ad 26	J 20	0	Ad 105	J 97	0
20	1827–29	C (J. Q. Adams)	J 28	Ad 20	0	J 119	Ad 94	0
21	1829–31	D (Jackson)	D 26	NR 22	0	D 139	NR 74	0
22	1831–33	D (Jackson)	D 25	NR 21	2	D 141	NR 58	14
23	1833–35	D (Jackson)	D 20	NR 20	8	D 147	AM 53	60
24	1835–37	D (Jackson)	D 27	W 25	0	D 145	W 98	0
25	1837–39	D (Van Buren)	D 30	W 18	4	D 108	W 107	24
26	1839–41	D (Van Buren)	D 28	W 22	0	D 124	W 118	0
27	1841–43	W (W. Harrison)						
		W (Tyler)	W 28	D 22	2	W 133	D 102	6
28	1843–45	W (Tyler)	W 28	D 25	1	D 142	W 79	1
29	1845–47	D (Polk)	D 31	W 25	0	D 143	W 77	6
30	1847–49	D (Polk)	D 36	W 21	1	W 115	D 108	4
31	1849–51	W (Taylor)						
		W (Fillmore)	D 35	W 25	2	D 112	W 109	9
32	1851–53	W (Fillmore)	D 35	W 24	3	D 140	W 88	5
33	1853–55	D (Pierce)	D 38	W 22	2	D 159	W 71	4
34	1855–57	D (Pierce)	D 40	R 15	5	R 108	D 83	43
35	1857–59	D (Buchanan)	D 36	R 20	8	D 118	R 92	26
36	1859–61	D (Buchanan)	D 36	R 26	4	R 114	D 92	31
37	1861–63	R (Lincoln)	R 31	D 10	8	R 105	D 43	30
38	1863–65	R (Lincoln)	R 36	D 9	5	R 102	D 75	9
39	1865–67	R (Lincoln)						
		R (Johnson)	U 42	D 10	0	U 149	D 42	0
40	1867–69	R (Johnson)	R 42	D 11	0	R 143	D 49	0
41	1869–71	R (Grant)	R 56	D 11	0	R 149	D 63	0
42	1871–73	R (Grant)	R 52	D 17	5	D 134	R 104	5
43	1873–75	R (Grant)	R 49	D 19	5	R 194	D 92	14
44	1875–77	R (Grant)	R 45	D 29	2	D 169	R 109	14
45	1877–79	R (Hayes)	R 39	D 36	1	D 153	R 140	0
46	1879–81	R (Hayes)	D 42	R 33	1	D 149	R 130	14
47	1881–83	R (Garfield)						
		R (Arthur)	R 37	D 37	1	R 147	D 135	11
48	1883–85	R (Arthur)	R 38	D 36	2	D 197	R 118	10
49	1885–87	D (Cleveland)	R 43	D 34	0	D 183	R 140	2
50	1887–89	D (Cleveland)	R 39	D 37	0	D 169	R 152	4
51	1889–91	R (B. Harrison)	R 39	D 37	0	R 166	D 159	0
52	1891–93	R (B. Harrison)	R 47	D 39	2	D 235	R 88	9

CONGRESS	YEAR	PRESIDENT	SENATE			HOUSE		
			Majority Party	Minority Party	Others	Majority Party	Minority Party	Others
53	1893–95	D (Cleveland)	D 44	R 38	3	D 218	R 127	11
54	1895–97	D (Cleveland)	R 43	D 39	6	R 244	D 105	7
55	1897–99	R (McKinley)	R 47	D 34	7	R 204	D 113	40
56	1899–01	R (McKinley)	R 53	D 26	8	R 185	D 163	9
57	1901–03	R (McKinley)						
		R (T. Roosevelt)	R 55	D 31	4	R 197	D 151	9
58	1903–05	R (T. Roosevelt)	R 57	D 33	0	R 208	D 178	0
59	1905–07	R (T. Roosevelt)	R 57	D 33	0	R 250	D 136	0
60	1907–09	R (T. Roosevelt)	R 61	D 31	0	R 222	D 164	0
61	1909–11	R (Taft)	R 61	D 32	0	R 219	D 172	0
62	1911–13	R (Taft)	R 51	D 41	0	D 228	R 161	1
63	1913–15	D (Wilson)	D 51	R 44	1	D 291	R 127	17
64	1915–17	D (Wilson)	D 56	R 40	0	D 230	R 196	9
65	1917–19	D (Wilson)	D 53	R 42	0	D 216	R 210	6
66	1919–21	D (Wilson)	R 49	D 47	0	R 240	D 190	3
67	1921–23	R (Harding)	R 59	D 37	0	R 303	D 131	1
68	1923–25	R (Coolidge)	R 51	D 43	2	R 225	D 205	5
69	1925–27	R (Coolidge)	R 56	D 39	1	R 247	D 183	4
70	1927–29	R (Coolidge)	R 49	D 46	1	R 237	D 195	3
71	1929–31	R (Hoover)	R 56	D 39	1	R 267	D 167	1
72	1931–33	R (Hoover)	R 48	D 47	1	D 220	R 214	1
73	1933–35	D (F. Roosevelt)	D 60	R 35	1	D 310	R 117	5
74	1935–37	D (F. Roosevelt)	D 69	R 25	2	D 319	R 103	10
75	1937–39	D (F. Roosevelt)	D 76	D 16	4	D 331	R 89	13
76	1939–41	D (F. Roosevelt)	D 69	R 23	4	D 261	R 164	4
77	1941–43	D (F. Roosevelt)	D 66	R 28	2	D 268	R 162	5
78	1943–45	D (F. Roosevelt)	D 58	R 37	1	D 218	R 208	4
79	1945–47	D (F. Roosevelt)						
		D (Truman)	D 56	R 38	1	D 242	R 190	2
80	1947–49	D (Truman)	R 51	D 45	0	R 246	D 188	1
81	1949–51	D (Truman)	D 54	R 42	0	D 263	R 171	1
82	1951–53	D (Truman)	D 49	R 47	0	D 235	R 199	1
83	1953–55	R (Eisenhower)	R 48	D 47	1	R 221	D 212	1
84	1955–57	R (Eisenhower)	D 48	R 47	1	D 232	R 203	0
85	1957–59	R (Eisenhower)	D 49	R 47	0	D 232	R 199	0
86	1959–61	R (Eisenhower)	D 62	R 34	0	D 280	R 152	0
87	1961–63	D (Kennedy)	D 65	R 35	0	D 261	R 176	0
88	1963–65	D (Kennedy)						
		D (Johnson)	D 68	R 32	0	D 258	R 177	0
89	1965–67	D (Johnson)	D 68	R 32	0	D 295	R 140	0
90	1967–69	D (Johnson)	D 64	R 36	0	D 248	R 187	0
91	1969–71	R (Nixon)	D 57	R 43	0	D 243	R 192	0
92	1971–72	R (Nixon)	D 54	R 44	2	D 254	R 180	0

Ad: Administration; AM: Anti-Masonic; C: Coalition; D: Democratic; F: Federalist; J: Jacksonian; NR: National Republican; Op: Opposition; R: Republican; R^J: Republican (Jeffersonian); U: Unionist; W: Whig.

PRESIDENTIAL ELECTIONS*: ELECTORAL AND POPULAR VOTE

Presidential Candidate[1]	Electoral Vote	Popular Vote
1789[2]: 11 States		
GEORGE WASHINGTON	69	
John Adams	34	
John Jay	9	
R. H. Harrison	6	
John Rutledge	6	
John Hancock	4	
George Clinton	3	
Samuel Huntington	2	
John Milton	2	
James Armstrong	1	
Benjamin Lincoln	1	
Edward Telfair	1	
(Not voted)	12	
1792[2]: 15 States		
GEORGE WASHINGTON	132	
Federalist		
John Adams	77	
Federalist		
George Clinton	50	
Republican		
Thomas Jefferson	4	
Aaron Burr	1	
1796[2]: 16 States		
JOHN ADAMS	71	
Federalist		
Thomas Jefferson	68	
Republican		
Thomas Pinckney	59	
Federalist		
Aaron Burr	30	
Anti-Federalist		
Samuel Adams	15	
Republican		
Oliver Ellsworth	11	
Federalist		
George Clinton	7	
Republican		
John Jay	5	
Independent-Federalist		
James Iredell	3	
Federalist		
George Washington	2	
Federalist		
John Henry	2	
Independent		

Presidential Candidate[1]	Electoral Vote	Popular Vote
S. Johnston	2	
Independent-Federalist		
C. C. Pinckney	1	
Independent-Federalist		
1800[2]: 16 States		
THOMAS JEFFERSON	73	
Republican		
Aaron Burr	73	
Republican		
John Adams	65	
Federalist		
C. C. Pinckney	64	
Federalist		
John Jay	1	
Federalist		
1804: 17 States		
THOMAS JEFFERSON	162	
Republican		
C. C. Pinckney	14	
Federalist		
1808: 17 States		
JAMES MADISON	122	
Republican		
C. C. Pinckney	47	
Federalist		
George Clinton	6	
Independent-Republican		
(Not voted)	1	
1812: 18 States		
JAMES MADISON	128	
Republican		
DeWitt Clinton	89	
Fusion		
(Not voted)	1	
1816: 19 States		
JAMES MONROE	183	
Republican		
Rufus King	34	
Federalist		
(Not voted)	4	

*Source: U.S. Bureau of the Census, *Historical Statistics of the United States, Colonial Times to 1957* (Washington, D.C., 1960).

[1]Excludes unpledged tickets and minor candidates polling under 10,000 votes; various party labels may have been used by a candidate in different states; the more important of these are listed.

[2]Prior to the election of 1804, each elector voted for two candidates for President; the one receiving the highest number of votes, if a majority, was declared elected President, the next highest, Vice-President. This provision was modified by adoption of the Twelfth Amendment which was proposed by the Eighth Congress, December 12, 1803, and declared ratified by the legislatures of three fourths of the states in a proclamation of the Secretary of State, September 25, 1804.

[3]No candidate having a majority in the electoral college, the election was decided in the House of Representatives.

Presidential Candidate[1]	Electoral Vote	Popular Vote
1820: 24 States		
JAMES MONROE	231	
Republican		
John Quincy Adams	1	
Independent-Republican		
(Not voted)	3	
1824: 24 States		
JOHN QUINCY ADAMS	84[3]	108,740
Andrew Jackson	99[3]	153,544
Henry Clay	37	47,136
W. H. Crawford	41	46,618
1828: 24 States		
ANDREW JACKSON	178	647,286
Democratic		
John Quincy Adams	83	508,064
National Republican		
1832: 24 States		
ANDREW JACKSON	219	687,502
Democratic		
Henry Clay	49	530,189
National Republican		
William Wirt	7	
Anti-Masonic		
John Floyd	11	
Nullifiers		
(Not voted)	2	
1836: 26 States		
MARTIN VAN BUREN	170	765,483
Democratic		
William Henry Harrison	73	
Whig		
Hugh L. White	26	739,795[4]
Whig		
Daniel Webster	14	
Whig		
W. P. Mangum	11	
Anti-Jackson		
1840: 26 States		
WILLIAM HENRY HARRISON	234	1,274,624
Whig		
Martin Van Buren	60	1,127,781
Democratic		
1844: 26 States		
JAMES K. POLK	170	1,338,464
Democratic		
Henry Clay	105	1,300,097
Whig		
James G. Birney		62,300
Liberty		

Presidential Candidate[1]	Electoral Vote	Popular Vote
1848: 30 States		
ZACHARY TAYLOR	163	1,360,967
Whig		
Lewis Cass	127	1,222,342
Democratic		
Martin Van Buren		291,263
Free Soil		
1852: 31 States		
FRANKLIN PIERCE	254	1,601,117
Democratic		
Winfield Scott	42	1,385,453
Whig		
John P. Hale		155,825
Free Soil		
1856: 31 States		
JAMES BUCHANAN	174	1,832,955
Democratic		
John C. Frémont	114	1,339,932
Republican		
Millard Fillmore	8	871,731
American		
1860: 33 States		
ABRAHAM LINCOLN	180	1,865,593
Republican		
John C. Breckinridge	72	848,356
Democratic (South)		
Stephen A. Douglas	12	1,382,713
Democratic		
John Bell	39	592,906
Constitutional Union		
1864: 36 States		
ABRAHAM LINCOLN	212	2,206,938
Republican		
George B. McClellan	21	1,803,787
Democratic		
(Not voted)	81	
1868: 37 States		
ULYSSES S. GRANT	214	3,013,421
Republican		
Horatio Seymour	80	2,706,829
Democratic		
(Not voted)	23	
1872: 37 States		
ULYSSES S. GRANT	286	3,596,745
Republican		
Horace Greeley	[5]	2,843,446
Democratic		
Charles O'Conor		29,489
Straight Democratic		
Thomas A. Hendricks	42	
Independent-Democratic		

[4]Whig tickets were pledged to various candidates in various states.

[5]Greeley died shortly after the election and presidential electors supporting him cast their votes as indicated, including three for Greeley, which were not counted.

PRESIDENTIAL ELECTIONS: ELECTORAL AND POPULAR VOTE

Presidential Candidate[1]	Electoral Vote	Popular Vote	Presidential Candidate[1]	Electoral Vote	Popular Vote
B. Gratz Brown	18		**1896: 45 States**		
Democratic			WILLIAM McKINLEY	271	7,102,246
Charles J. Jenkins	2		*Republican*		
Democratic			William Jennings Bryan	176	6,492,559
David Davis	1		*Democratic[6]*		
Democratic			John M. Palmer		133,148
(Not voted)	17		*National Democratic*		
			Joshua Levering		132,007
			Prohibition		
1876: 38 States			Charles M. Matchett		36,274
RUTHERFORD B. HAYES	185	4,036,572	*Socialist Labor*		
Republican			Charles E. Bentley		13,969
Samuel J. Tilden	184	4,284,020	*Nationalist*		
Democratic					
Peter Cooper		81,737			
Greenback			**1900: 45 States**		
			WILLIAM McKINLEY	292	7,218,491
			Republican		
1880: 38 States			William Jennings Bryan	155	6,356,734
JAMES A. GARFIELD	214	4,453,295	*Democratic[6]*		
Republican			John C. Wooley		208,914
Winfield S. Hancock	155	4,414,082	*Prohibition*		
Democratic			Eugene V. Debs		87,814
James B. Weaver		308,578	*Socialist*		
Greenback-Labor			Wharton Barker		50,373
Neal Dow		10,305	*People's*		
Prohibition			Joseph F. Malloney		39,739
			Socialist Labor		
1884: 38 States					
GROVER CLEVELAND	219	4,879,507			
Democratic			**1904: 45 States**		
James G. Blaine	182	4,850,293	THEODORE ROOSEVELT	336	7,628,461
Republican			*Republican*		
Benjamin F. Butler		175,370	Alton B. Parker	140	5,084,223
Greenback-Labor			*Democratic*		
John P. St. John		150,369	Eugene V. Debs		402,283
Prohibition			*Socialist*		
			Silas C. Swallow		258,536
			Prohibition		
1888: 38 States			Thomas E. Watson		117,183
BENJAMIN HARRISON	233	5,447,129	*People's*		
Republican			Charles H. Corregan		31,249
Grover Cleveland	168	5,537,857	*Socialist Labor*		
Democratic					
Clinton B. Fisk		249,506			
Prohibition					
Anson J. Streeter		146,935	**1908: 46 States**		
Union Labor			WILLIAM HOWARD TAFT	321	7,675,320
			Republican		
1892: 44 States			William Jennings Bryan	162	6,412,294
GROVER CLEVELAND	277	5,555,426	*Democratic*		
Democratic			Eugene V. Debs		420,793
Benjamin Harrison	145	5,182,690	*Socialist*		
Republican			Eugene W. Chafin		253,840
James B. Weaver	22	1,029,846	*Prohibition*		
People's			Thomas L. Hisgen		82,872
John Bidwell		264,133	*Independence*		
Prohibition			Thomas E. Watson		29,100
Simon Wing		21,164	*People's*		
Socialist Labor			August Gillhaus		14,021
			Socialist Labor		

[6]Includes a variety of joint tickets with People's party electors commited to Bryan.

Presidential Candidate[1]	Electoral Vote	Popular Vote
1912: 48 States		
WOODROW WILSON *Democratic*	435	6,296,547
Theodore Roosevelt *Progressive*	88	4,118,571
William Howard Taft *Republican*	8	3,486,720
Eugene V. Debs *Socialist*		900,672
Eugene W. Chafin *Prohibition*		206,275
Arthur E. Reimer *Socialist Labor*		28,750
1916: 48 States		
WOODROW WILSON *Democratic*	277	9,127,695
Charles Evans Hughes *Republican*	254	8,533,507
A. L. Benson *Socialist*		585,113
J. Frank Hanly *Prohibition*		220,506
Arthur E. Reimer *Socialist Labor*		13,403
1920: 48 States		
WARREN G. HARDING *Republican*	404	16,143,407
James M. Cox *Democratic*	127	9,130,328
Eugene V. Debs *Socialist*		919,799
P. P. Christensen *Farmer-Labor*		265,411
Aaron S. Watkins *Prohibition*		189,408
James E. Ferguson *American*		48,000
W. W. Cox *Socialist Labor*		31,715
1924: 48 States		
CALVIN COOLIDGE *Republican*	382	15,718,211
John W. Davis *Democratic*	136	8,385,283
Robert M. La Follette *Progressive*	13	4,831,289
Herman P. Faris *Prohibition*		57,520
Frank T. Johns *Socialist Labor*		36,428
William Z. Foster *Workers*		36,386
Gilbert O. Nations *American*		23,967
1928: 48 States		
HERBERT HOOVER *Republican*	444	21,391,993
Alfred E. Smith *Democratic*	87	15,016,196
Norman Thomas *Socialist*		267,835
Verne L. Reynolds *Socialist Labor*		21,603
William Z. Foster *Workers*		21,181
William F. Varney *Prohibition*		20,106
1932: 48 States		
FRANKLIN D. ROOSEVELT *Democratic*	472	22,809,638
Herbert Hoover *Republican*	59	15,758,901
Norman Thomas *Socialist*		881,951
William Z. Foster *Communist*		102,785
William D. Upshaw *Prohibition*		81,869
William H. Harvey *Liberty*		53,425
Verne L. Reynolds *Socialist Labor*		33,276
1936: 48 States		
FRANKLIN D. ROOSEVELT *Democratic*	523	27,752,869
Alfred M. Landon *Republican*	8	16,674,665
William Lemke *Union*		882,479
Norman Thomas *Socialist*		187,720
Earl Browder *Communist*		80,159
D. Leigh Colvin *Prohibition*		37,847
John W. Aiken *Socialist Labor*		12,777
1940: 48 States *		
FRANKLIN D. ROOSEVELT *Democratic*	449	27,307,819
Wendell L. Willkie *Republican*	82	22,321,018
Norman Thomas *Socialist*		99,557
Roger Q. Babson *Prohibition*		57,812
Earl Browder *Communist*		46,251
John W. Aiken *Socialist Labor*		14,892
1944: 48 States		
FRANKLIN D. ROOSEVELT *Democratic*	432	25,606,585
Thomas E. Dewey *Republican*	99	22,014,745
Norman Thomas *Socialist*		80,518

PRESIDENTIAL ELECTIONS: ELECTORAL AND POPULAR VOTE

Presidential Candidate[1]	Electoral Vote	Popular Vote
Claude A. Watson *Prohibition*		74,758
Edward A. Teichert *Socialist Labor*		45,336
1948: 48 States		
HARRY S. TRUMAN *Democratic*	303	24,105,812
Thomas E. Dewey *Republican*	189	21,970,065
J. Strom Thurmond *States' Rights*	39	1,169,063
Henry Wallace *Progressive*		1,157,172
Norman Thomas *Socialist*		139,414
Claude A. Watson *Prohibition*		103,224
Edward A. Teichert *Socialist Labor*		29,244
Farrell Dobbs *Socialist Workers*		13,613
1952: 48 States		
DWIGHT D. EISENHOWER *Republican*	442	33,936,234
Adlai E. Stevenson *Democratic*	89	27,314,992
Vincent Hallinan *Progressive*		140,023
Stuart Hamblen *Prohibition*		72,949
Eric Haas *Socialist Labor*		30,267
Darlington Hoopes *Socialist*		20,203
Douglas A. MacArthur *Constitution*		17,205
Farrell Dobbs *Socialist Workers*		10,312
1956: 48 States		
DWIGHT D. EISENHOWER *Republican*	457	35,590,472
Adlai E. Stevenson *Democratic*	73[7]	26,022,752
T. Coleman Andrews *States' Rights*		107,929
Eric Haas *Socialist Labor*		44,300
Enoch A. Holtwick *Prohibition*		41,937
1960: 50 States		
JOHN F. KENNEDY *Democratic; Liberal*	303	34,227,096

Presidential Candidate	Electoral Vote	Popular Vote
Richard M. Nixon *Republican*	219	34,108,546
Harry F. Byrd *Independent*	15*	116,248
Orville Faubus *States' Rights*		214,549
Eric Haas *Socialist Labor*		46,560
Rutherford B. Decker *Prohibition*		46,203
Farrell Dobbs *Socialist Workers*		39,541
Charles L. Sullivan *Constitution*		19,570
J. Bracken Lee *Conservative*		12,912
1964: 50 States and D.C.		
LYNDON B. JOHNSON *Democratic*	486	43,126,506
Barry Goldwater *Republican*	52	27,176,799
Eric Haas *Socialist Labor*		45,186
Clifton DeBerry *Socialist Workers*		32,705
Earle H. Munn *Prohibition*		23,267
John Kasper *States' Rights*		6,953
Joseph B. Lightburn *Constitution*		5,060
1968: 50 States and D.C.		
RICHARD NIXON *Republican*	301	31,770,237
Hubert Humphrey *Democratic*	191	31,270,533
George Wallace *American Independent*	46	9,906,141
Hennings Blomen *Socialist Labor*		52,588
Dick Gregory *Freedom and Peace*		47,097
Fred Halstead *Socialist Worker*		41,300
Eldridge Cleaver *Peace and Freedom*		36,385
Eugene McCarthy *New Party*		25,858
Earle H. Munn *Prohibition*		14,519
Charlene Mitchell *Communist*		1,075

[7]One Democratic elector voted for Walter Jones.

*Byrd's electoral count includes the votes of fourteen unpledged electors from Mississippi and Alabama, in addition to one vote pledged to Nixon but cast for Byrd by an Oklahoma elector.

POPULATION OF THE UNITED STATES: 1800-1880

Division and State	1800	1810	1820	1830	1840	1850	1860	1870	1880
UNITED STATES	5,308,483	7,239,881	9,638,453	12,866,020	17,069,453	23,191,876	31,443,321	39,818,449	50,189,209
New England	1,233,011	1,471,973	1,660,071	1,954,717	2,234,822	2,728,116	3,135,283	3,487,924	4,010,529
Maine	151,719	228,705	298,335	399,455	501,793	583,169	628,279	626,915	648,936
New Hampshire	183,858	214,160	244,161	269,328	284,574	317,976	326,073	318,300	346,991
Vermont	154,465	217,895	235,981	280,652	291,948	314,120	315,098	330,551	332,286
Massachusetts	422,845	472,040	523,287	610,408	737,699	994,514	1,231,066	1,457,351	1,783,085
Rhode Island	69,122	76,931	83,059	97,199	108,830	147,545	174,620	217,353	276,531
Connecticut	251,002	261,942	275,248	297,675	309,978	370,792	460,147	537,454	622,700
Middle Atlantic	1,402,565	2,014,702	2,669,845	3,587,664	4,526,260	5,898,735	7,458,985	8,810,806	10,496,878
New York	589,051	959,049	1,372,812	1,918,608	2,428,921	3,097,394	3,880,735	4,382,759	5,082,871
New Jersey	211,149	245,562	277,575	320,823	373,306	489,555	672,035	906,096	1,131,116
Pennsylvania	602,365	810,091	1,049,458	1,348,233	1,724,033	2,311,786	2,906,215	3,521,951	4,282,891
South Atlantic	2,286,494	2,674,891	3,061,063	3,645,752	3,925,299	4,679,090	5,364,703	5,835,610	7,597,197
Delaware	64,273	72,674	72,749	76,748	78,085	91,532	112,216	125,015	146,608
Maryland	341,548	380,546	407,350	447,040	470,019	583,034	687,049	780,894	934,943
Dist. of Columbia	8,144	15,471	23,336	30,261	33,745	51,687	75,080	131,700	177,624
Virginia	886,149	983,152	1,075,069	1,220,978	1,249,764	1,421,661	1,596,318	1,225,163	1,512,565
West Virginia	....	....	....	....	....	....	....	442,014	618,457
North Carolina	478,103	555,500	638,829	737,987	753,419	869,039	992,622	1,071,361	1,399,750
South Carolina	345,591	415,115	502,741	581,185	594,398	668,507	703,708	705,606	995,577
Georgia	162,686	252,433	340,989	516,823	691,392	906,185	1,057,286	1,184,109	1,542,180
Florida	....	....	....	34,730	54,477	87,445	140,424	187,748	269,493
East South Central	335,407	708,590	1,190,489	1,815,969	2,575,445	3,363,271	4,020,991	4,404,445	5,585,151
Kentucky	220,955	406,511	564,317	687,917	779,828	982,405	1,155,684	1,321,011	1,648,690
Tennessee	105,602	261,727	422,823	681,904	829,210	1,002,717	1,109,801	1,258,520	1,542,359
Alabama	1,250	9,046	127,901	309,527	590,756	771,623	964,201	996,992	1,262,505
Mississippi	7,600	31,306	75,448	136,621	375,651	606,526	791,305	827,922	1,131,597
West South Central	....	77,618	167,680	246,127	449,985	940,251	1,747,667	2,029,965	3,334,220
Arkansas	....	1,062	14,273	30,388	97,574	209,897	435,450	484,471	802,525
Louisiana	....	76,556	153,407	215,739	352,411	517,762	708,002	726,915	939,946
Oklahoma	....	....	....	....	....	....	....	....	....
Texas	....	....	....	....	....	212,592	604,215	818,579	1,591,749
East North Central	51,006	272,324	792,719	1,470,018	2,924,728	4,523,260	6,926,884	9,124,517	11,206,668
Ohio	41,365	230,760	581,434	937,903	1,519,467	1,980,329	2,339,511	2,665,260	3,198,062
Indiana	5,641	24,520	147,178	343,031	685,866	988,416	1,350,428	1,680,637	1,978,301
Illinois	....	12,282	55,211	157,445	476,183	851,470	1,711,951	2,539,891	3,077,871
Michigan	....	4,762	8,896	31,639	212,267	397,654	749,113	1,184,059	1,636,937
Wisconsin	....	....	....	....	30,945	305,391	775,881	1,054,670	1,315,497
West North Central	....	19,783	66,586	140,455	426,814	880,335	2,169,832	3,856,594	6,157,443
Minnesota	....	....	....	....	....	6,077	172,023	439,706	780,773
Iowa	....	....	....	....	43,112	192,214	674,913	1,194,020	1,624,615
Missouri	....	19,783	66,586	140,455	383,702	682,044	1,182,012	1,721,295	2,168,380
North Dakota	....	....	....	....	....	....	4,837	2,405	36,909
South Dakota	....	....	....	....	....	....	....	11,776	98,268
Nebraska	....	....	....	....	....	....	28,841	122,993	452,402
Kansas	....	....	....	....	....	....	107,206	364,399	996,096
Mountain	....	....	....	....	....	72,927	174,923	315,385	653,119
Montana	....	....	....	....	....	....	....	20,595	39,159
Idaho	....	....	....	....	....	....	....	14,999	32,610
Wyoming	....	....	....	....	....	....	....	9,118	20,789
Colorado	....	....	....	....	....	....	34,277	39,864	194,327
New Mexico	....	....	....	....	....	61,547	93,516	91,874	119,565
Arizona	....	....	....	....	....	....	....	9,658	40,440
Utah	....	....	....	....	....	11,380	40,273	76,786	143,963
Nevada	....	....	....	....	....	....	6,857	42,491	62,266
Pacific	....	....	....	....	....	105,871	444,053	675,125	1,148,004
Washington	....	....	....	....	....	1,201	11,594	23,955	75,116
Oregon	....	....	....	....	....	12,093	52,465	90,923	174,768
California	....	....	....	....	....	92,597	379,994	560,247	864,694
Alaska	....	....	....	....	....	....	....	....	33,426
Hawaii	....	....	....	....	....	....	....	....	....

POPULATION OF THE UNITED STATES: 1890-1970

Division and State	1890	1900	1910	1920	1930	1940	1950	1960	1970
UNITED STATES	62,979,766	76,212,168	92,228,622	106,021,568	123,202,660	132,165,129	151,325,798	179,323,175	203,184,772
New England	4,700,749	5,592,017	6,552,681	7,400,909	8,166,341	8,437,290	9,314,453	10,509,367	11,847,186
Maine	661,086	694,466	742,371	768,014	797,423	847,226	913,774	969,265	993,663
New Hampshire	376,530	411,588	430,572	443,083	465,293	491,524	533,242	606,921	737,681
Vermont	332,422	343,641	355,956	352,428	359,611	359,231	377,747	389,881	444,732
Massachusetts	2,238,947	2,805,346	3,366,416	3,852,356	4,249,614	4,316,721	4,690,514	5,148,578	5,689,170
Rhode Island	345,506	428,556	542,610	604,397	687,497	713,346	791,896	859,488	949,723
Connecticut	746,258	908,420	1,114,756	1,380,631	1,606,903	1,709,242	2,007,280	2,535,234	3,032,217
Middle Atlantic	12,706,220	15,454,678	19,315,892	22,261,144	26,260,750	27,539,487	30,163,533	34,168,452	37,152,813
New York	6,003,174	7,268,894	9,113,614	10,385,227	12,588,066	13,479,142	14,830,192	16,782,304	18,190,740
New Jersey	1,444,933	1,883,669	2,537,167	3,155,900	4,041,334	4,160,165	4,835,329	6,066,782	7,168,164
Pennsylvania	5,258,113	6,302,115	7,665,111	8,720,017	9,631,350	9,900,180	10,498,012	11,319,366	11,793,909
South Atlantic	8,857,922	10,443,480	12,194,895	13,990,272	15,793,589	17,823,151	21,182,335	25,971,732	30,671,337
Delaware	168,493	184,735	202,322	223,003	238,380	266,505	318,085	446,292	548,104
Maryland	1,042,390	1,188,044	1,295,346	1,449,661	1,631,526	1,821,244	2,343,001	3,100,689	3,922,399
Dist. of Columbia	230,392	278,718	331,069	437,571	486,869	663,091	802,178	763,956	756,510
Virginia	1,655,980	1,854,184	2,061,612	2,309,187	2,421,851	2,677,773	3,318,680	3,966,949	4,648,494
West Virginia	762,794	958,800	1,221,119	1,463,701	1,729,205	1,901,974	2,005,552	1,860,421	1,744,237
North Carolina	1,617,949	1,893,810	2,206,287	2,559,123	3,170,276	3,571,623	4,061,929	4,556,155	5,082,059
South Carolina	1,151,149	1,340,316	1,515,400	1,683,724	1,738,765	1,899,804	2,117,027	2,382,594	2,590,516
Georgia	1,837,353	2,216,331	2,609,121	2,895,832	2,908,506	3,123,723	3,444,578	3,943,116	4,589,575
Florida	391,422	528,542	752,619	968,470	1,468,211	1,897,414	2,771,305	4,951,560	6,789,443
East South Central	6,429,154	7,547,757	8,409,901	8,893,307	9,887,214	10,778,225	11,477,181	12,050,126	12,804,552
Kentucky	1,858,635	2,147,174	2,289,905	2,416,630	2,614,589	2,845,627	2,944,806	3,038,156	3,219,311
Tennessee	1,767,518	2,020,616	2,184,789	2,337,885	2,616,556	2,915,841	3,291,718	3,567,089	3,924,164
Alabama	1,513,401	1,828,697	2,138,093	2,348,174	2,646,248	2,832,961	3,061,743	3,266,740	3,444,165
Mississippi	1,289,600	1,551,270	1,797,114	1,790,618	2,009,821	2,183,796	2,178,914	2,178,141	2,216,912
West South Central	4,740,983	6,532,290	8,784,534	10,242,224	12,176,830	13,064,525	14,537,572	16,951,255	19,322,458
Arkansas	1,128,211	1,311,564	1,574,449	1,752,204	1,854,482	1,949,387	1,909,511	1,786,272	1,923,295
Louisiana	1,118,588	1,381,625	1,656,388	1,798,509	2,101,593	2,363,880	2,683,516	3,257,022	3,643,180
Oklahoma	258,657	790,391	1,657,155	2,028,283	2,396,040	2,336,434	2,233,351	2,328,284	2,559,253
Texas	2,235,527	3,048,710	3,896,542	4,663,228	5,824,715	6,414,824	7,711,194	9,579,677	11,196,730
East North Central	13,478,305	15,985,581	18,250,621	21,475,543	25,297,185	26,626,342	30,309,368	36,225,024	40,252,678
Ohio	3,672,329	4,157,545	4,767,121	5,759,394	6,646,697	6,907,612	7,946,627	9,706,397	10,652,017
Indiana	2,192,404	2,516,462	2,700,876	2,930,390	3,238,503	3,427,796	3,934,224	4,662,498	5,193,669
Illinois	3,826,352	4,821,550	5,638,591	6,485,280	7,630,654	7,897,241	8,712,176	10,081,158	11,113,976
Michigan	2,093,890	2,420,982	2,810,173	3,668,412	4,842,325	5,256,106	6,371,766	7,823,194	8,875,083
Wisconsin	1,693,330	2,069,042	2,333,860	2,632,067	2,939,006	3,137,587	3,434,575	3,951,777	4,417,933
West North Central	8,932,112	10,347,423	11,637,921	12,544,249	13,296,915	13,516,990	14,061,394	15,394,115	16,324,389
Minnesota	1,310,283	1,751,394	2,075,708	2,387,125	2,563,953	2,792,300	2,982,483	3,413,864	3,805,069
Iowa	1,912,297	2,231,853	2,224,771	2,404,021	2,470,939	2,538,268	2,621,073	2,757,537	2,825,041
Missouri	2,679,185	3,106,665	3,293,335	3,404,055	3,629,367	3,784,664	3,954,653	4,319,813	4,677,399
North Dakota	190,983	319,146	577,056	646,872	680,845	641,935	619,636	632,446	617,761
South Dakota	348,600	401,570	583,888	636,547	692,849	642,961	652,740	680,514	666,257
Nebraska	1,062,656	1,066,300	1,192,214	1,296,372	1,377,963	1,315,834	1,325,510	1,411,330	1,483,791
Kansas	1,428,108	1,470,495	1,690,949	1,769,257	1,880,999	1,801,028	1,905,299	2,178,611	2,249,071
Mountain	1,213,935	1,674,657	2,633,517	3,336,101	3,701,789	4,150,003	5,074,998	6,855,060	8,283,585
Montana	142,924	243,329	376,053	548,889	537,606	559,456	591,024	674,767	694,409
Idaho	88,548	161,772	325,594	431,866	445,032	524,873	588,637	667,191	713,008
Wyoming	62,555	92,531	145,965	194,402	225,565	250,742	290,529	330,066	332,416
Colorado	413,249	539,700	799,024	939,629	1,035,791	1,123,296	1,325,089	1,753,947	2,207,259
New Mexico	160,282	195,310	327,301	360,350	423,317	531,818	681,187	951,023	1,016,000
Arizona	88,243	122,931	204,354	334,162	435,573	499,261	749,587	1,302,161	1,772,482
Utah	210,779	276,749	373,351	449,396	507,847	550,310	688,862	890,627	1,059,273
Nevada	47,355	42,335	81,875	77,407	91,058	110,247	160,083	285,278	488,738
Pacific	1,920,386	2,634,285	4,448,660	5,877,819	8,622,047	10,229,116	15,114,964	21,198,044	26,525,774
Washington	357,232	518,103	1,141,990	1,356,621	1,563,396	1,736,191	2,378,963	2,853,214	3,409,169
Oregon	317,704	413,536	672,765	783,389	953,786	1,089,684	1,521,341	1,768,687	2,091,385
California	1,213,398	1,485,053	2,377,549	3,426,861	5,677,251	6,907,387	10,586,223	15,717,204	19,953,134
Alaska	32,052	63,592	64,356	55,036	59,278	72,524	128,643	226,167	302,173
Hawaii	....	154,001	192,000	255,912	368,336	423,330	499,794	632,772	769,913

Key, Francis Scott, 107
King, Rufus, 84, 101, 111
King George's War, 26
"King Mob," 101, 150–151
King's Mountain, Battle of, 44
"Kitchen Cabinet," 163
Know-Nothing movement, 272
Knox, Henry, 79, 84, 87
Ku Klux Klan, 259, 261, 272
Kyle, Alexander, 184

Labor: 1824–48, 185–186
Lafayette, Marquis, 44, 45
Laissez-faire, 268
Lake Champlain, 107
Lake Erie, Battle of, 106
Land: public, sale of, 156–157
Land Ordinance of 1785, 75–76
Latrobe, Benjamin, 136
Laurens, Henry, 45
Law, 124–125
Laws of nature, 38
Lecompton Constitution, 228
Lee, Richard Henry, 37, 72
Lee, Robert E., 135, 238, 240, 241, 243, 244, 255
Levant Company, 9
Lewis, Meriwether, 100
Lexington, Mass., Battle of, 37
Liberal Republican party, 251–262
Liberator, The, 200
Lincoln, Abraham, 231–232; debates, 229–230; as President, 233, 234–235, 251–252, 253, 254–255
Literature: in colonies, 56–57, 59; 1783–1830, 133–135; 1824–48, 194–195, 196; Boston Brahmins, 193
Loan Office Certificates, 39
Locke, John, 18, 38, 121, 122, 129
London, Treaty of, 91
Longfellow, Henry Wadsworth, 133, 193, 201
Lords of Trade, 18–19
Louisiana, 101, 102, 232
Louisiana Purchase, 97–98, 116, 117
Louisiana Territory, 100
Lowell, James Russell, 193, 201
Loyalists, 38
Lundy, Benjamin, 200
Luther, Martin, 4
Lutherans, 127

McCarthy, Joseph R., 141
McClellan, George Brinton, 238–239, 240–241
McCulloch v. *Maryland,* 100
McDowell, Irvin, 238
McGovern, George S., 141
McLeod, Alexander, 160
Macon's Bill No. 2, 104
Madison, Dolley, 200
Madison, James: on Articles of Confederation, 78–79; and Constitution, 81, 82, 84; as President, 104–111; as Secretary of State, 98, 99
Magellan, Ferdinand, 9
Maine, 14, 46, 116

Manassas Junction, Battle of, 238, 241
Mangum, Willie P., 159
Manifest Destiny, 165–166
Mann, Horace, 266
Marbury v. *Madison,* 99
Marcy, William L., 163
Marshall, John, 68; and Constitution, 84; as Chief Justice, 98–99, 99–100; XYZ Affair, 94
Martin, Luther, 84
Martineau, Harriet, 132
Martin v. *Hunter's Lessee,* 100
Maryland: colonial period, 12, 13–15, 22–23, 50–51; Confederation, 75; and Constitution, 85; slavery, 42, 252
Maryland Toleration Act, 15, 61
Mason, George, 33, 84
Mason, James, 246
Massachusetts: colonial period, 18–19, 48–49, 52; Constitution, 73, 85; education, 267; slavery, 41
Massachusetts Bay Colony, 9–10, 13–14, 15, 18, 58
Massachusetts Bay Company, 13
Massachusetts Government Act, 35
Materialism, 191
Mather, Cotton, 63, 121
Mayflower, 13
Maysville Road, 153
Meade, George Gordon, 241, 243
Melville, Herman, 194, 201
Mercantilism, 10
Merrimac, 246
Methodists, 127, 128, 230
Mexican War, 176–178
Mexico: and Andrew Jackson, 258; and Texas, 173–174, 176
"Midnight Judges," 98
Miller, Alfred Jacob, 198
Miller, Perry, 57, 191
Miller, Samuel, 133, 136
Miller, William, 67
Minutemen, 36–37
Mississippi, 232
Mississippi River, 46, 216
Missouri, 116, 167, 252
Missouri Compromise, 115–116, 176, 225, 226
Mitchell, Elisha, 198
Mitchell, John (of Virginia, 18th Century), 63
Molasses Act, 25
Monitor, 246
Monmouth, Battle of, 132
Monroe, James: on Articles of Confederation, 78; Louisiana Purchase, 97–98; Monroe Doctrine, 117–118; as President, 111, 114, 146; as Secretary of State, 108
Monroe Doctrine, 117–118
Montcalm, Marquis de, 27
Montesquieu, 80, 121, 122
Monticello, 136
Morgan, Daniel, 44
Morison, Samuel Eliot, 58
Mormons, 179, 191, 192, 265
Morrill Tariff, 248

Morris, Gouverneur, 79
Morris, Robert, 40, 79
Morris Notes, 40
Morse, Samuel F. B., 198
Mott, Lucretia, 200
Mount, William Sidney, 198
Murray, Judith Sargent, 132
Muscovy Company, 9
Music, 136, 214

Napoleon Bonaparte, 95, 97–98, 102, 105, 106–107, 109
Nashville, Tenn., 243
National Association for the Advancement of Colored People (NAACP), 275
National Bank Act (of 1863), 249
National Equal Rights League, 253
Nationalism, 120–121, 188
National Road, 148
National Trades Union, 185
National Typographical Union, 186
Navigation Acts: (1651), 24; (1660), 24–25; (1663), 25; (1673), 25; (1696), 15
Navy, Department of the, 94–95
Neutrality Acts: (1794), 91
New Amsterdam, 15
New England: Anglican Church, 58; colonial period, 13–14, 52; economic development, 21–22; industrialism in, 182; literature, 59
New France, 26, 29
New Hampshire, 14, 18–19
New Harmony, 191
New Haven, Conn., 14
New Jersey: colonial period, 15, 16, 18–19, 23, 24; and Constitution, 85; slavery, 41; suffrage, 74
New Jersey Plan, 81
New Netherland, 15
New Orleans, 243
New Orleans, Battle of, 107
Newspapers, eighteenth century, 61
Newton, Isaac, 59, 121, 122, 123
New York: colonial period, 15, 18–19, 23, 24, 52; confederation, 48–49; and Constitution, 85; education in, 267; population, 270; slavery, 41, 53
New York and New Haven Railroad, 184
Niagara Movement, 274–275
Non-Conforming Congregationalists, 54–55
Non-Conforming Congregational Separatists, 55
Non-Intercourse Act, 104
North American Phalanx, 191
North Carolina, 12, 23
Northern Confederacy, 101
Northwest Ordinance, 76, 114
Northwest Territory, 116
Nullification Controversy, 153, 155, 216

Of Plymouth Plantation, 57
Ohio, 101, 267
Ohio Company, 26

1 2 3 4 5 6 7 8 9 10 11 12 13 14 15 16 17 18 19 20 21 22 23 24 25   82 81 80 79 78 77 76 75 74 73